Religion and the Individual: Belief, Practice, and Identity

Special Issue Editors

Douglas J. Davies
Michael J. Thate

MDPI • Basel • Beijing • Wuhan • Barcelona • Belgrade

MDPI

Special Issue Editors

Douglas J. Davies
Durham University,
UK

Michael J. Thate
Princeton University
USA

Editorial Office
MDPI AG
St. Alban-Anlage 66
Basel, Switzerland

This edition is a reprint of the Special Issue published online in the open access journal *Religions* (ISSN 2077-1444) from 2016–2017 (available at: http://www.mdpi.com/journal/religions/special_issues/religion_individual).

For citation purposes, cite each article independently as indicated on the article page online and as indicated below:

Author 1; Author 2. Article title. *Journal Name* **Year**, *Article number*, page range.

First Edition 2017

ISBN 978-3-03842-466-6 (Pbk)
ISBN 978-3-03842-467-3 (PDF)

Photo courtesy of Jeremy Bishop

Table of Contents

About the Special Issue Editors

Douglas J. Davies is both an anthropologist and theologian with theoretical and practical interests. After an initial degree in Anthropology at Durham he engaged in his first research on Mormonism at the Oxford Institute of Social Anthropology under the supervision of the sociologist Bryan Wilson. He then read a theology degree at Durham and shortly afterwards became Lecturer at Nottingham University where he became Professor of Religious Studies before leaving for Durham in 1997. During that period he engaged in further work on Mormonism, as well as in Sikhism and Anglicanism, and in death rites. He also completed his first doctorate there on the issue of meaning and salvation. In Durham, as Professor in the Study of Religion, he helps teach undergraduate modules on the Introduction to the Study of Religion, and Death, Ritual and Belief, and a module for postgraduates on Ritual, Symbolism and Belief in the Anthropology of Religion. Academically speaking, he also holds the degree of D.Litt. from Oxford as well as an Honorary Dr. Theol. from the University of Uppsala in Sweden. In 2009 he was made an Academician of the Academy of Social Sciences, and in 2017 was elected as a Fellow of The British Academy. A great deal of his general work has sought to relate issues in theology and social (Anthropology and Theology, Berg 2002). He then has several other areas of research interest. Special research in Mormonism has resulted in An Introduction to Mormonism, (CUP 2003) and The Mormon Culture of Salvation, (Ashgate 2000) along with other books, chapters and encyclopaedia entries. He has also been a visiting professor at Brigham Young University in Utah. In terms of death Studies He has edited the Encyclopedia of Cremation, (with Lewis Mates: Ashgate 2005), and also written A Brief History of Death, (Blackwell, 2004), Death, Ritual and Belief, (Revised and expanded edition, Continuum 2002). Extensive empirical research for Reusing Old Graves. (With A. Shaw 1995) has been influential in relation to issues of burial reform in the UK. In terms of Christian church life he has, for example, joint edited (with Helen Cameron, Philip Richter and Frances Ward) Studying Local Churches: A Handbook, (SCM Press 2005). My Private Passions, (Canterbury Press 2000) was the Archbishop of Wales's Lent Book for that year. Church and Religion in Rural England. (With C. Watkins and M. Winter 1991) involved a major study of the Church of England. Many other papers and book chapters reflect on numerous aspects of religious life including, for example, some biblical interests in, 'Purity, Spirit and Reciprocity in the Acts of the Apostles', in Anthropology and Biblical Studies, (eds) L.J.Lawrence and M.I. Aguilar, Leiden: Deo Publishing. 2004), and 'Rebounding Vitality: Resurrection and Spirit in Luke -Acts'. The Bible in Human Society. eds. M.D.Carroll, D.Clines and P. Davies. Sheffield Academic Press, 1995.

Michael J. Thate is a post-doctoral Research Associate at Princeton University, Fellow at Faith and Work Initiative; Visiting Fellow at the Center for the Study of Religion. Prior to coming to Princeton and Tübingen, Thate was a Lecturer of New Testament Interpretation at Yale Divinity School as well as a Post-Doctoral Visiting Research Fellow at Yale where he worked on a kind of comparative sea mythology within Jewish, Greek, and Roman texts along with early Christian configurations of identity with respect to the sea. This research will be published in a forthcoming monograph, "The Godman and the Sea." His research interests revolve around the formation and reception of discourses, particularly the ways in which the religious, the secular, and the scientific inscribe themselves. His first book, "Remembrance of Things Past?" (Mohr Siebeck), is a social history of Leben-Jesu-Forschung during the 19th and 20th centuries. He is the editor of two projects: one on participation themes in antiquity and Paul (Mohr Siebeck 2015); the other on the philosophical ethics of Albert Schweitzer (Syracuse University Press 2016). His current research is on conceptions of labor and status in antiquity and current post-Marxist theory. Specifically, he will be working on second- through the sixth-century labor manuals in early Christian monasteries, translating them into current political and theoretical discussions relating to Capitalism and labor policy. He received his PhD in Religious Studies and History of New Testament Interpretation from the University of Durham (UK).

religions   MDPI

Editorial

Monstrosities: Religion, Identity and Belief

Douglas J. Davies [1] and Michael J. Thate [2],*

[1] Department of Theology and Religion, Durham University, Stockton Rd, Durham, County Durham DH1, UK; douglas.davies@durham.ac.uk
[2] Center for the Study of Religion, Princeton University, Princeton, NJ 08544, USA
* Correspondence: Mthate@princeton.edu; Tel.: +1-507-848-5863

Received: 17 May 2017; Accepted: 22 May 2017; Published: 23 May 2017

In the summer of 1816, a young woman of nineteen eloped with the poet Percy Bysshe Shelley to Geneva, Switzerland. There they passed the rainy summer evenings with Lord Byron, discussing philosophy and poetry, and experimenting with the telling of ghost stories. The young woman was Mary Shelley. And the "ghost story" she shared with the small Swiss Salon, finished in 1817 though published in 1818, would become the macabre classic, *Frankenstein*.

In her Introduction to the third edition, written on 15 October 1831, she reflected of her struggle to compose an original idea for the imposing Salon.

> Life appeared to me too common-place an affair as regarded myself. I could not figure to myself that romantic woes or wonderful events would ever be my lot; but I was not confined to my own identity, and I could people the hours with creations far more interesting to me at that age, than my own sensations (1, p. 6).

After long hours spent peering into the "blank incapability of invention," that "dull Nothing" which terrifies any author (1, p. 8), she turned her thinking along "the mysterious fears of our nature," in order to "awaken [a] thrilling horror—one to make the reader dread to look round, to curdle the blood, and quicken the beatings of the heart" (1, p. 8).

The relevance of Shelley's *Meisterwerk* for this special edition reaches beyond the serendipity of its bicentenary. Its provenance and plot raise fundamental questions and problems for each of the topics which organize this special issue: religion, identity, belief and the practices of each. Shelley's narration of her ghost-story's origins reflects an *instability within rigidity*—a form-of-life too snug for the constellation of sentiments brewing in and all about her. This instability within the rigidities of form-of-life exemplified fundamental fissures in a nineteenth-century western imaginary along the axes of subject location: religion, identity, belief, and their practices.

In her Introduction, the instability and the rigidity receive similes of attribution: "myself," "my own identity," "I," "own," "Life." It was within this form-of-life which both produced the point of self-reflection and the desire to escape from it. The affective quality of an "awakening thrilling horror" was necessary in order to shock the latent instability from within the inherited rigid formations, loosing itself into fresh possibilities of being. And yet, as Victor Frankenstein would painfully discover,

> Nothing is so painful to the human mind as a great and sudden change. The sun might shine, or the clouds might lower: but nothing could appear to me as it had done the day before (2, p. 197).

The loosing of instability from rigidity recalibrates settled postures of belief and points of view, out of which emerge a thousand little monsters all seeking revenge on their creator.

This special issue attempts to conjure the spirit of Shelley by placing the well-worn descriptors of "belief," "practice," and "identity" in conversation across a broad range of disciplinary approaches in order to re-think the monstrosity of the "individual" within the laboratories of the study of religion. Though each author inhabits a specific disciplinary field, the special issue appropriates these disciplinary idioms into a wider problematic of these most fundamental constellations. In this respect, the special issue is experimental and comparative. The issue attempts to place scholars from anthropology, sociology, African-American history, Asian religions, philosophy, religious studies, critical theory, and ancient history alongside one another. It does so unashamedly in order to demonstrate the remarkable diversity enacted by the signifier, "religious;" as well as bring into conversation a series of interesting people working on remarkably engaging topics.

The special issue begins with the intriguing proposal of Bosco Bae, "Believing Selves and Cognitive Dissonance: Connecting Individual and Society via 'Belief'." Bae highlights how "belief" as an analytical tool and critical category of investigation for the study of religion has been a resurging topic of interest. After raising critical questions regarding the language and practice of "belief," specifically as they relate to assumed logics of "consistency," Bae argues for the utility and value of a "believing selves" framework, in conjunction with revisionist theories of cognitive dissonance, to advance the claim that beliefs are representations, as well as functions, of cultural history which bind individual and society.

Vaughn Booker, in a fascinating engagement with archival materials from prominent African American jazz musicians, comes next in his "Performing, Representing, and Archiving Belief: Religious Expressions among Jazz Musicians" These archives, Booker suggests, demonstrate rich sites for studying expressions of religious belief and daily religious practice in public and private arenas, in professional and personal capacities. Booker's focus is on print material from the archives of Edward Kennedy "Duke" Ellington (1899–1974) and Mary Lou Williams (1910–1981), and examines the articulations of beliefs in print and meaning-making practices of their routines. Ellington and Williams left records of their aspirations for a non-clerical religious authority and leadership, new formulations of religious community, and conceptions of quotidian writing tasks as practices with devotional value in the middle decades of the twentieth century. Booker has produced an important study of the making of a religious subjectivity of African and the complex political bricolage of religious interiority.

Josh Furnall, follows with his "Abraham Joshua Heschel and *Nostra Aetate*: shaping the Catholic reconsideration of Judaism during Vatican II." Although *Nostra Aetate* is only comprised of five short paragraphs, this document represents for Furnall a turning point not just for Catholic-Jewish relations, but also sketches the fundamental aims of embodying the Christian faith in a pluralistic age. Furnall re-examines crucial details in the back-story of the provenance of *Nostra Aetate*, arguing that recent events and scholarship within Catholic studies suffer from neglecting to attend to the role that Jewish people have played in the development of Catholic learning. In particular, Furnall considers how Rabbi Abraham Joshua Heschel played an important role during the Second Vatican Council, and provides an instructive example for contemporary Catholic-Jewish dialogue.

In "'It's not the money but the love of money that is the root of all evil': social subjection, machinic enslavement and the limits of Christian social teaching," Marika Rose participates within contemporary theory's considerations of capitalism and its subject formation. Following Maurizio Lazzarato, who argues that contemporary capitalism functions through the central apparatuses of social subjection and machinic enslavement, Rose states that social subjection equips individuals with a subjectivity (identities, sexes, bodies, professions, etc.), with a sense of their own freedom. This machinic enslavement, as she refers to it, arises out of processes of production that function increasingly independently of human awareness or intention. Drawing on this analysis of the contemporary functioning of capitalism, her paper explores the concepts of individuals and society at work in recent Anglican social theology—particularly those of Eve Poole and Malcolm Brown—suggesting that, within the contemporary Church of England, mainstream attempts to reckon with political questions tend to understand the role of individual agency and ethical behaviour in ways which actually support existing social, political and economic structures rather than disrupting them.

Erin Johnston, draws on her fieldwork with an Integral Yoga studio and a Catholic prayer house in her "Spirituality as an Aspirational Identity." Johnston, sees within existing research on religious identity, especially from a narrative perspective, a tendency to focus primarily on accounts of the past (especially on religious change) or on conceptions of religious identity in the present. The religious communities she surveys, however, provide not only a sense of identity and belonging in the present, they also promote a particular vision of the religious ideal: a way of being-in-the-world that adherents are (or ought to be) striving to achieve. From her fieldwork and interviews, Johnston finds that both communities defined themselves by three key characteristics: a sacred gaze, a simultaneous sense of presence and detachment, and a holistic style of identity management. In constructing and transmitting a shared vision of the "enlightened self," she argues, these organizations offer practitioners a highly desirable but elusive *possible identity*, which shapes practitioners' actions and self-understandings in the present. Johnston's original study calls attention to religious organizations as important suppliers of possible identities, and reveals the situated and contextual nature religious aspirations.

In another impressive study originating out of original field work, Sitna Quiroz considers "The Dilemmas of Monogamy: pleasure, discipline and the Pentecostal moral self in the Republic of Benin." Quiroz explores how Pentecostal teachings on marriage and the management of sexual pleasure contribute to shaping converts' moral selves. For Pentecostals, argues Quiroz, fidelity towards God, when single, and fidelity between partners, once married, is presented as the ideal model of partnership to which everyone should aspire. In a context where polygamous unions are socially accepted, a satisfactory sexual life restricted to the context of marriage is presented as the means to building successful monogamous unions. Sexual satisfaction might not always guarantee success, especially when people face problems of infertility. Quiroz suggests that the disciplinary regimes that these teachings promote, contribute to shaping new modes of intimacy, which are often at odds with extant social norms and ideals. The moral dilemmas which arise from this tension are key to understanding how Pentecostal Christianity shapes the moral self. Quiroz surveys how Pentecostals in Benin navigate and negotiate cultural continuities and discontinuities in relation to church authority and family life.

In "The Apparatus of Belief: Prayer, Technology, and Ritual Gesture," Anderson Blanton describes what he calls "the apparatus of belief," or the specific ways in which individual religious belief has become intimately related to tele-technologies such as the radio through a focus on the early history of a mass mediated ritual practice. More specifically, Blanton examines the performance of prayers during the *Healing Waters Broadcast* by the famous charismatic faith healer, Oral Roberts. Blanton's analysis of these healing prayers reveals the ways in which the old charismatic Christian gesture of manual imposition, or laying on of hands, took on new somatic registers and sensorial attunements when mediated, or *transduced*, through technologies such as the radio loudspeaker. Emerging from these mid-twentieth-century radio broadcasts, this technique of healing prayer popularized by Roberts has now become a key ritual practice and theological motif within the global charismatic Christian healing movement. Critiquing established conceptions of prayer in the disciplines of anthropology and religious studies, Blanton's fascinating essay repositions "belief" as a particular structure of intimacy between sensory capacity, media technology, and pious gesture.

George Gonzalez in his important, "Towards an Existential Archeology of Capitalist Spirituality," examines contemporary networked Capitalism, the discourse of "workplace spirituality," and the life history of one management reformer as case studies in an effort both to historicize experiences of neoliberal "spirituality," as an archaeology of knowledge might, while also attempting to account for intentionality and biography, as existential approaches would. Turning to work in contemporary critical theory which associates strident anti-humanism in social theory with the rise of neoliberal discourse, Gonzalez wager is that sustained attention to the ways in which personal and social history always entail one another and are mutually arising makes not only for better phenomenology but makes for better critical scholarship as well.

The peculiar evangelical work of Marilla Baker Ingalls, an American Baptist missionary to Burma from 1851–1902, is the subject of study by Alex Koloyanides in, "Show Us Your God:" The Power of Religious Objects in Nineteenth-Century Burma." By the time of her death in Burma at the age of seventy-five, Ingalls was known as one of the most successful Baptist evangelists among Burmese Buddhists. In an attempt to explicate the extraordinary dynamic within Ingalls' expanding Christian community, Koloyanides focuses on two prominent objects at the Baptist mission: a life-sized dog statue that Ingalls kept chained at the edge of her property and a massive banyan tree covered with biblical illustrations and revered by locals as the abode of divine beings. Koloyanides argues that these objects transformed Ingalls' American Baptist Christianity into a kind of Burmese religion that revolved around revered objects. Through an examination of the particular shrine practices that pulled people into the Baptist mission, this fascinating essay places these particular happenings into the larger context of religious encounter, conflict, and representation in colonizing Burma.

In "Women and Spirits," Candi Cann examines the intersection of women and alcohol in funerals and death memorialization through a comparative analysis in European and Chinese culture. Two central religious texts regarding the roles of women and alcohol in Christianity and Chinese religious thought are examined. Cann then contextualizes her ethnographic work by turning to the historical and textual background of current death rituals in Mexican Catholicism, Chinese religions, and American Southern Baptist funerals. In this impressive mixed-methods essay, Cann argues that both alcohol and temperance are used as a way to forge, cement, and create gender identity and construct alternate discourses of inclusivity in afterlife conceptions.

Michael J. Thate, in "Messianic Time and Monetary Value," turns to recent materialist messianic readings, and brings them into conversation with Walter Benjamin's notion of messianic time as outlined particularly in his *Theses on the Philosophy of History*. Messianic time is read stylistically with Benjamin's *Sonnets* as subject divestment from historical time. Thate places the trope of messianic time as the divestment of the subject from historical time into a brief consideration on monetary value's relationship market time. In this essay, Thate pushes for a rereading of Benjamin's notion of messianic time as divestment from historical time, thus breaking the uneven distribution of time, accumulation, and monetary value of market time.

Devin Singh, in his provocative, "Speculating the Monetary Subject: Georg Simmel on Human Value," initiates an inquiry into the sources and frameworks of value used to denote human subjects within modernity. In particular, Singh considers the conflation of monetary, legal, and theological registers employed to demarcate human worth. Singh, in a careful reading of Simmel, draws from his speculative genealogy of the money equivalent of human values, in order to establish a spectrum of ascriptions from specifically quantified to infinite human value. Predications of infinite human value, Singh argues, require and imply quantified—and specifically monetary-economic—human value. As such, cost and worth, economically and legally defined, provide a foundation for subsequent eternal projections in a theological imaginary. The interventionist potential of claims to infinite or unquantifiable human value in attempts to resist the contemporary financialization of human life and society in Singh's analysis are thus called into question.

Recalling Mary Shelley's "thrilling horror," itself not far removed from Rudolph Otto's century-later *mysterium fascinans*, we ponder the echoing resonances between *Frankenstein's* protest against masterly creativity, and, perhaps, Luther's longing for the freedom of the Christian amidst institutional constraints. Such emotional waves bring their own pressure to bear upon Religion, Identity, and Belief, and whether tectonic or merely mildly intrusive, they rise from the dissonances sensed by any reflective self-pervaded by music, strangely familiar Jewish narratives, or visionary gazing after perfection. The diverse worldviews that kaleidoscope through these essays call for seeking our own enchanted garden where, sexuality, holy hands, alongside symbolic animals, plants, and alcohol's mystification, all lurk to surprise. Less nuanced are those other forces of gender and money that sustain or subvert our identities in life's possibilities, all cusped by mortality. Just as the biblical Acts, energized by its own Holy Ghost engagement, set money as the soteriological medium of community authenticity, martyrdom or betrayal, so do our essays, in their own small way, post a challenge for collaborative ponderings over the monstrosities of religion, identity, and belief.

Conflicts of Interest: The authors declare no conflict of interest.

References

1. Shelley, Mary. 1998a. Introduction. In *Frankenstein*. Oxford: Oxford University Press, pp. 5–11, First published 1817.
2. Shelley, Mary. 1998b. *Frankenstein*. Oxford: Oxford University Press, First published 1817.

religions

MDPI

Article

Believing Selves and Cognitive Dissonance: Connecting Individual and Society via "Belief"

Bosco B. Bae

Human Economy Programme, Centre for the Advancement of Scholarship, University of Pretoria, Old College House, Pretoria 0002, South Africa; bosco.bae@up.ac.za; Tel.: +27-012-420-6792

Academic Editors: Douglas James Davies and Michael J. Thate
Received: 12 April 2016; Accepted: 13 June 2016; Published: 28 June 2016

Abstract: "Belief" as an analytical tool and critical category of investigation for the study of religion has been a resurging topic of interest. This article discusses the problems of language and practice in the discussion of "belief" and proceeds to map a few of the emergent frameworks, proposed within the past decade, for investigating "belief". The issue of inconsistency, however, continues to remain a perennial issue that has not been adequately explained. This article argues for the utility and value of the "believing selves" framework, in conjunction with revisionist theories of cognitive dissonance, to advance the claim that beliefs are representations, as well as functions, of cultural history which bind individual and society.

Keywords: study of religion; belief; believing selves; cognitive dissonance; individual; society

1. Introduction

"Truth cannot be out there—cannot exist independent of the human mind—because sentences cannot so exist, or be out there. The world is out there, but descriptions of the world are not. Only descriptions of the world can be true or false. The world on its own—unaided by the describing activities of human beings cannot."

—Richard Rorty, *Contingency, Irony and Solidarity* [1]

"Words do not express thoughts very well. They always become a little different immediately after they are expressed, a little distorted, a little foolish. And yet it also pleases me and seems right that what is of value and wisdom to one man seems nonsense to another."

—Herman Hesse, *Siddhartha* [2]

The two quotes note the mediating function of language in translating and expressing our thoughts. This places a fundamental dilemma with the study of beliefs in religious contexts. Given linguistic differences, cultural and subcultural nuances, the translation from cognition to language and the observer's subsequent inference from language to cognition leads us to wonder the extent to which we can truly understand one another. Not only do misunderstandings and misinterpretations happen between persons of the same neighborhood but the issue is accentuated when we aim to understand persons of another language and culture. In *Belief, Language and Experience* [3], anthropologist Rodney Needham began his inquiry by raising the question whether a non-English speaking person, from a culture without a concept of "belief," can say: "I believe in God." Within this proposition, the concepts of "belief" and 'God' are put into question. What does it mean to "believe" and what does this person mean by "God"? Moreover, we can beg the question of that singular pronoun: "I," which evokes notions of self, identity, and the individual. While each of these concepts can be discussed and their respective meanings excavated, this article will focus only on "belief."

The article will first discuss the problems of language and practice that have complicated the discussion of belief as an analytic tool and critical category for the study of religion. It then proceeds to sketch a few emerging frameworks for the investigation of belief followed by some critical thoughts on their respective proposals. Taking up the framework of "believing selves," and its emphasis on commitment, the issue of inconsistency is addressed through the theory of cognitive dissonance and its four emergent revisionist theories. This combination situates religion's meaning-making capacities in relation to identity and the individual as a reflective index of social structures. This is not to say that persons are one-to-one reflections of society but are rather embodied beings possessing particular trajectories and experiences along individualized space-time continuums. Beliefs are not only reflections of our being but they facilitate our orientations to our respective realities. In this regard, the concept of belief is taken out of its "religious" context and considered in terms of its quotidian features through the field of social psychology before being re-applied to religion. The article argues that beliefs are embodied representations, a function of cultural histories, that bind individual and society together.

2. The Problem of Language and Practice

Within anthropological literature, the concept of belief—as represented in the English language—has been thoroughly discussed with respect to its etymological history [3,4], syntax and semantics [5], and the influence of Christian history including the dynamics of power that have influenced the meaning of belief [4,6]. In this regard, critical analysis of the concept has declared belief a Christian concept [7] and its employment creates translational and cultural concerns in the description and analysis of non-Christian religious traditions. Quite famously, Needham [3] called for the abandonment of belief by arguing the concept's analytic inadequacy and indeterminacy for any meaningful study of religion. However, this is a dramatic and hasty conclusion. Instead, his analysis illustrates the inadequacy of the English language and the constraints of Christian history. This critical stance towards Christianity's influence on the study of religion has prompted a reflexive turn towards the religious background of social scientists [8,9], their implicit influences, contextual relationships in the field, and even the consideration of their emotions as a source of data [10]. Despite such efforts, the concerns of the English language persist in the depiction and investigation of belief.

As a major source of empirical data, language is an intuitive starting point when thinking about belief. Ludwig Wittgenstein, at the end of his critique of Fraser's *Golden Bough*, claimed that in order to understand belief—and go beyond the levels of description and explanation—we must take a holistic approach to language [11]. And indeed, much research has taken this approach by focusing on language as a vehicle of thought and, therefore, a window into belief. What emerged from ethnographic investigations, however, is not what people *believe* but rather what they *think* about belief and the various methods of verification and justification of their beliefs being true [12,13].

Anthropologist, Charles Lindholm notes that the justification and maintenance of belief can be discussed along a Durkheim-Weber continuum. At one end, we have the Durkheimian camp which discusses belief in terms of an "affirmation of identity, emotional commitment, belonging and authenticity within a sacred community." At the other, the Weberian camp discusses the effort and appeal of "constructed types of legitimated meaning systems that confirm belief" ([13], p. 348). Lindholm acknowledges that the two camps for "inculcating belief" are limited and that a focus on one camp is necessarily supplemented by the other ([13], p. 353). In other words, the two camps are neither mutually exclusive nor independent of each other but complementary and necessarily dependent without lending primacy to any one. Constructed types of legitimated meaning systems (examples include sacred texts or systems of thought, which confirm a belief as true) require recipients who affirm and commit to those meaning systems for their efficacy and function as legitimizing and confirming systems. Conversely, the formation of identity and the embodiment of meaning presupposes social structures that support various constructed systems of meaning which inform the development of identity and embodiment; "thought can live only on grounds which we adopt in the service of a reality to which we submit" ([14], p. 19). This dynamic is further illustrated by "moral-somatic processes" presented by Douglas Davies. He discusses how Weberian forms of belief become associated with Durkheimian forms through embodied feelings that are experienced through "powerful but quickly passing emotions or influentially enduring moods" ([15], p. 2187). Scott Atran and Ara Norenzayan [16] argue for the importance of ritual in affirming, supplementing, and sustaining emotions and moods pervading religious postulates. While Roy Rappaport sees rituals as enabling the performative quality of such postulates with the persistence of their "validity as a social fact" being "contingent upon its continual enunciation" ([17], p. 281) and informing one's identity and beliefs.

Although the methods of justification and verification assist in convincing persons of the veracity of their beliefs, the methods themselves are not beliefs and we should not presume that utilizing such methods entails a belief in the advocated proposition. In other words, there are degrees of belief and levels of commitment to the truth-value of a proposition. Appealing to a particular system of meaning, or an emotional experience, does not necessarily entail that one holds a corresponding belief. Moreover, the degrees of belief and varying levels of commitment include the possibility of discrepant, situational, and inconsistent beliefs [3,7,18–20] that can be contradictory, seemingly "syncretic," and vague [21]. The field of anthropology has well-documented the observation that "religious behavior and language are not explained by systems of well thought out belief" ([21], p. 451). For example, David Hicks notes that, in the 1960s, "none of his Timorese informants—not even professed members of the [Catholic] Church—expressed any doubts" regarding the "existence" of ancestral spirits. Even avowed Catholics would consult their village shamans (*matan do'ok*) and while they might attend Mass, they may still "give ritual offerings to 'lords of the earth'—nature spirits linked with specific localities in their countryside—without apparently feeling the least concern about intellectual contradiction or about how priests might interpret their conduct" ([22], pp. 172–73). Similarly, Thomas Kirsch [23] described the negotiation of beliefs among the Gwembe Tonga of southern Zambia who move between various Christian denominations in search of the Holy Spirit's healing power. The emphasis is not on dogma or creed but rather practical and experiential efficacy of practice. This draws parallels with Alice Street's ethnographic work with hospital residents in Papua New Guinea [24]. Street argues for belief as a form of "relational action." She notes the shift from "belief," *bilip*, that emphasizes kinship relations and witchcraft to a notion of belief that was exclusively a relationship with a Christian God and "forgetting" the context of discordant kin relations. However, this shift was due primarily with a concern for social and medicinal efficacy rather than a notion of truth ([24], p. 272). In this regard, the variability of belief is not sufficiently determined by publicly declared methods of justification and verification especially in cases of behavior that seemingly contradict such statements.

The investigation of belief for the study of religion therefore lies within a set of issues concerning the relationship between cognition, language, and behavior. In religious contexts, inconsistency and skepticism are ubiquitous. If we are to take persons seriously as culturally informed cognitive agents, it is necessary to delineate what is meant by "belief" and how we can think about it without being constrained by the influences of Christianity. Is there a model for thinking about belief that can exist independently of Christian constructions while still remaining applicable to Christian and non-Christian traditions alike?

3. Emergent Frameworks of "Belief"

Over the past decade, several frameworks have emerged with the resurgent interest in the topic of "belief." In 2008, *Social Analysis* produced a journal issue discussing the merits of writing "against belief." While it is near impossible to abandon the term, Galina Lindquist and Simon Coleman [25] argue that we can be skeptical and draw on the ongoing discussion, as well as the criticisms, of "belief" to present a different notion of "culture." For example, Lindquist draws on the discussion of belief to present a view of "social styles" not in terms of fixed cognitive stances but in terms of modes of "being in the world" as well as "practices that are not merely repeated, but are forms of *poesis* whereby cultural perception and practice mutually constitute each other" ([25], p. 15). Jon and Hildi Mitchell draw on criticisms of "belief" to present a performative rather than a propositional stance toward culture in their discussion of embodiment among Mormons and Catholics [26]. Hicks wrote "against belief" by investigating belief as an index of attitudes to sacred artefacts. Based on his fieldwork in East Timor, he noted that the differing attitudes to sacred objects and engagement in rituals reflected a range of commitment and attitudes persons had regarding religious propositions, i.e., belief in ancestral ghosts [22].[1] In this regard, "belief" can be utilized as a concept and critical category to contrast ethnographic investigations against what has typically been considered to be "belief." This retains the concept as a problematic category with its own set of criticisms in the study of religion but utilized as a methodological platform of analysis to present a different notion of culture.

Tanya Luhrmann in building upon her notion of "interpretive drift"—which notes the gradual transition from the suspension of disbelief to a period of ambiguity and ultimately a submersion into a framework of thought, interpretation, and commitment [27]—develops the role of the imagination, or training the imagination. In this, God becomes/is a real entity in a U.S. evangelical Christian community that taught people to talk to God through prayer, with whom they could laugh and get angry, have conversations, and even "go on dates" with God [28]. She further explains:

"None of these subjects had those experiences willfully. They did not intentionally decide to hear God say, 'Excuse me.' They did not intentionally decide to have an angel wake them up. They entered the project with a broad, generic desire to hear God speak or perhaps just to get their prayer life moving again; they spent thirty minutes a day imaginatively immersed in the scriptures; and then they had unplanned, idiosyncratic experiences that they saw with their eyes and heard with their ears" ([28], p. 216).

For Luhrmann, the imagination plays a pivotal role that enables a transition from voluntary engagement to involuntary visual and auditory experiences. The focus on imagination, and "interpretive drift," emphasizes the meaning-making process via practice, which then serves as a method of justification and verification. By describing the psychological and social contexts, Luhrmann engages with a "culture of belief." Jonathan Mair has explicitly advocated that the study of belief should engage in a comparative approach of different, historically specific modes, and styles or "cultures of belief." In his discussion of Inner Mongolian Buddhists, he argues that rather than the particular content of belief the emphasis is placed on *style* which is associated with a set of attitudes, modes of experience, practice, and the relationships that stipulate cognitive and non-cognitive associations to propositional content ([21], p. 450).

In 2013, the *Journal of Contemporary Religion* produced an issue focusing on the performative dimensions of belief. This view builds upon Talal Asad's criticism of Clifford Geertz's definition of religion, which emphasized meaning over practice [6]. He states, "it is a modern idea that a practitioner cannot know how to live religiously without being able to articulate that knowledge" ([6], p. 120). Abby Day and Gordon Lynch state that, over the past decade, studies utilizing "qualitative methods to establish patterns of belief in Britain and North America have found that respondents struggle to articulate beliefs that are consistent or have a high degree of salience in their lives" ([20], p. 200). They further observe three common, "default yet not universal," assumptions in the sociology of religion ([20], p. 200):

---

[1] Hicks' approach to "belief" and material religion is applicable to instances of uproar and anger when the "sacred" is violated. Not only does this pertain to caricatures of the prophet Muhammad, notably Denmark in 2005 and France in 2015, and the crucifix or images of Jesus (examples include: the practice of *fumi-e*, stepping on an image of Jesus or Mary, in Japan during the 17th century as a method of discerning and persecuting Christians; Andres Serrano's 1987 photograph, *Piss Christ* of a crucifix submerged in a glass of his own urine, which created a stir in New York at the time of its exhibition and again in Paris in 2011; a teenager facing jail time for mimicking fellatio with a Jesus statue in Pennsylvania in 2014; and another case of two teenagers in Utah, 2015, for vandalizing a Mormon meetinghouse) but it also engages with discussions of the sacred in secular contexts (e.g., *Charlie Hebdo* in Paris, 2015; and debates regarding the violation of human rights).

(1) "all people all have some form of religious or existential belief system which forms a central reference point for their lives and belief can be universally found in all human cultures.

(2) Religious beliefs exist as cognitive, creedal propositions, in relation to which people orient their identities and practices in a direct and generally consistent way.

(3) A person's religious beliefs, or spirituality, can be explicitly stated as a set of propositions and are therefore open to the gaze of the researcher through methods such as surveys (which measure degrees of assent to creedal propositions) and the research interview (which allows for a more open-ended explication of an individual's "beliefs")."

The noted studies of inarticulacy and inconsistency of beliefs question these assumptions. Day and Lynch go on to argue for a "three modes" model of belief that emerged from their research among "young people." The first notes "belief as a *marker of cultural identity*" ([20], p. 201). That is, belief is a mode by which "they" could distinguish themselves from "other" cultural groups. This mode was particularly significant for "those who identified as being part of a minority group within a wider dominant religious/non-religious milieu or who wished to distinguish themselves from another minority group" (which minority groups are not specified). Moreover, this mode of belief is "learned and cultivated as a visible marker of difference in the context of establishing a distinct cultural identity." The second mode is "*an expression of significant social relationships and networks of belonging.*" They reflect a "sense of belonging" and "express a sense of bond with others who are taken to be important sources of guidance, and affiliation." The third mode is stated as "*an organizing centre for an individual's or a group's life*" and involves a "sustained attempt to shape thought, emotion, body, and practice in accordance with an explicitly stated set of beliefs derived from experiential, textual or institutional sources of religious and spiritual authority" ([20], p. 202). In this regard, Day and Lynch focus on the function of belief and its expression as, what Erving Goffman called, a "presentation of self" [29]. In this sense, they agree with Coleman and Lindquist that it would be premature to abandon belief despite its limited utility. Instead, the sociology of religion, they state, needs to "conceptualize belief in more diverse and complex ways" ([20], p. 200; [19]).

4. A Few Critical Thoughts

At this juncture, it is worth briefly noting Emile Durkheim's theory of *homo duplex*: "On the one hand is our individuality—and, more particularly, our body in which it is based; on the other is everything in us that expresses something other than ourselves" ([30], p. 152). Each of us have been molded by our own "modes of existence"—thoughts, emotions, and experiences—navigating our "awareness of reality" as bodily agents: "My experience of life within the floating time structure of past, present, and future cannot be experienced by anyone else." And yet, we are "a member of a species, a social being" functioning within society according to the "rules and patterns of society" ([31], p. 13). Our sense of becoming and social belonging is thus a "mixture of [social] enforcement and personal freedom" ([32], p. 182) by which our seemingly free actions become acts of reproducing and perpetuating a particular culture. With this duality in mind, Durkheim fashions the social and human sciences:

> "Although sociology is defined as the science of societies, it cannot, in reality, deal with the human groups that are the immediate object of its investigation without eventually touching on the individual who is the basic element of which these groups are composed. For society can exist only if it penetrates the consciousness of individuals and fashions it in 'its image and resemblance.' We can say, therefore, with assurance and without being excessively dogmatic, that a great number of our mental states, including some of the most important ones, are of social origin" ([30], p. 149).

In this regard, the individual is a necessary subject of inquiry for belief as a reflection of broader social structures. As Claude Lèvi-Strauss notes, "The proof as to what is social can only be a mental one [. . .] we can never be sure we have fathomed the meaning and function of an institution if we are not capable of reliving its impact upon the individual consciousness" ([33], p. 14; [34,35]). The study of belief is then a study, among many, of the diverse relationships between individual and society.

However, between individuals and society lies the problem of language, the interpretation of propositional statements and performativity, and the complexities in that discussion for the investigation of belief. As noted above, many studies "reveal *how* believers convince themselves that their beliefs are true," which prompted Lindholm to discuss the two camps of justification and verification ([13], p. 341). In part, the observed methods of justification and verification, as well as the varieties of discourse, present a range of ways by which social institutions and structures influence individual thought, value, and meaning-making processes. Tanya Luhrmann's work on "interpretive drift" (in the case of modern witchcraft in England) and the "imagination" (among evangelical Christians in the U.S.) contributes to the discussion about this process. Jonathan Mair's proposal of "cultures of belief" also configures within this dynamic by which persons, as historically-situated beings, develop and justify their beliefs and propositional attitudes as true through practice.

The three modes of belief, by contrast, are not modes of justification—although they can contribute to them—but instead they note the function of beliefs in relation to identity and community. For Day and Lynch, identity is conveyed and represented by belief. However, this framework lacks a working definition, set of characteristics, or discussion that delineates belief and how it functions as a mode denoting a "marker of cultural identity," an "expression of significant social relationships," or an "organizing center." Categorizing such functional modes of belief does not distinguish beliefs from other propositional statements nor is it clear how these modes are different enough from each other to warrant a distinct category. How is the expression of belief as a marker of cultural identity different from belief as an expression of one's social relations or an organizing center? A cultural identity implies social relations and should not be considered as something particular for "minority groups" (this is evident in Day's *Believing in Belonging* [36] of the white Britons in North Yorkshire). Contingent upon life style, belief as a marker of cultural identity can also be an organizing center for either the individual or a community—religious (e.g., Southern Baptist Convention) or non-religious (e.g., English Defense League), both of which represent a particular "culture." Nonetheless, the view that belief is performative and functions as three modes of cultural identity provides a significant contribution to the discussion regarding the relationship between individual and society.

The framework of writing "against belief" suggests that we anchor our discussions and remain beholden to the critiques of Christian conceptions of belief and present contrasting evidence that give rise to alternative accounts of cognition and culture. While this can be useful for comparative purposes and is capable of yielding considerable insight into conceptualizations of belief in non-Christian religions it places the English language and Christian forms of belief as the antagonized measure by which non-Christian religions are compared. By negation, the framework unintentionally affirms a form of Christian exceptionalism. Rodney Needham [3] makes a similar move when he conducts a cross-cultural survey of the term belief in non-English languages. In comparative fashion, Needham draws on the work by Evans-Pritchard on the Nuer and looks to comparative terms for belief among the Navajo in the U.S., Hindi in India, the Kikchi in Guatemala, the Cuicatec, Tzeltal, and Huichol in Mexico, various dialects in the Philippines, the Uduk of Ethiopia, the Shipibo and the Piro of Peru, and terms in Indonesia, as well as China. This is certainly an impressive range of cultures and terms that *could* be, and *have* been translated into belief or the act of believing. According to Needham, many of the terms vary and express concepts like trust, commitment, obedience, faithfulness, integrity, or singularity. Needham speculates that "it is as though the faculty of belief, and perhaps even the necessity to believe were thought to be given in human experience and to be adequately recognized in Greek, Latin, and modern European languages" ([3], p. 38). So why is it that some languages lack or vary in their verbal equivalents to belief and other "psychological vocabularies"? Needham posits that "the concept of belief is not simple but covers a very wide range of meanings. The definitions indicate no central or essential meaning, and it is obvious why the English word must be hard to translate into other languages" ([3], p. 40). This motivates Needham to turn and investigate the etymology of the English word for belief instead of considering the dynamic social and historical contexts of non-English languages and their various uses of the term. While this investigation has been useful for many subsequent scholars, it reinforces a particular exceptionalism about the English language and excludes a more dynamic anthropology of thinking through a more sophisticated analysis of language.

In this sense, it is not necessary to write "against belief" but we can give each comparable term its due justice and equal treatment by considering the etymological history and the linguistic nuances contained in each of them. Furthermore, just as Talal Asad [6] and Malcolm Ruel [4] considered the relationship between language, power, and history enabling them to further problematize belief by noting its saturation with Christian history, non-English languages may also be laden with their respective histories of religious or philosophical thought. In other words, it is possible to retain the methods of etymological inquiry and historical critiques of power without taking a stance "against belief." Not only does this enable a richer consideration of non-English languages but it also contributes to a more nuanced approach to cognition and thought across various historical and cultural contexts. However, this is not the task of this article.

Asad's critique of Clifford Geertz's definition of religion was not intended to get away from meaning and focus solely on performative dimensions but rather to emphasize the meaning-making processes by which practice is critical in its contribution to the construction of meaning. In writing "against belief," many have noted the performative dimensions of practice that contribute to the meaning-making process (e.g., [26,37]). Moreover, this view further accentuates the inconsistencies between propositional statements of belief and its performative dimensions, which were illustrated by Hicks [22] and Kirsch [23]. This latter point also directs us to proceed with caution. If we conjoin propositional and performative dimensions of lived religion under a singular category of belief, without considering the relationship between thought, emotion, language, and behavior and their subsequent variations, textures, and nuances, we flatten the category to include all linguistic and behavioral dimensions of religion as if they hold the same degree of commitment and meaning. This is less than helpful and simplifies the complexities involved with belief; not only is it misleading to ascribe a religious belief when there is none but it obfuscates the ontic dimensions of what belief is with the epistemic dimensions of how we study whether a person has a belief. That is, the methodology for investigating belief—by observing propositional statements and behaviors—supersedes whether there is indeed a belief which effectively conflates "how we know" and "what it is." This is not necessarily to argue that there are non-religious elements in religious beliefs nor is it to argue that there are not propositional and performative dimensions to religious belief (language and behavior are certainly germane). Rather, it notes the simple observation that not all things said or done within a religious context entail a religious belief.

The frameworks of writing "against belief," the role of imagination, investigating "cultures of belief," and the three modes of belief, all suggest inter-linking relations between cognition, self, and identity engaged with meaning-making processes and their expressions. However, these frameworks lack a sufficient consideration of language and the implications of inarticulacy and inconsistencies that suggest varied commitments, degrees and textures, of belief.

5. Believing Selves and (In)consistency

As social animals, it is a truism that any individual is, what Marilyn Strathern [38] has called, a dividual. That is, an individual must be situated within the parameters of one's non-individualist dimensions of personhood highlighting the "social," "relational," or "intersubjective" perspective. Additionally, despite our relational and situational embeddedness that invariably connects individual to society, we are still—individually—at the center of our perceptions and experiences. In other words, persons are not only socially, culturally, and historically situated beings but also actively thinking beings informed by our orientations to the world and our embodied engagement with it.

In this sense, Carlise and Simon define belief "as subjective commitments to truth, by which we mean subjective commitments to those truths as being true" ([12], p. 222). Beliefs are then socially and culturally informed attitudes and dispositions which enable us to discern what is and is not, to what extent something is or is not, true, as well as what should and ought to be true. They are embodied methods of discernment by virtue of our being and becoming[2] within the world. There is a diversity and range of epistemologies intimately tied to our respective cultural histories and personal experiences. This acknowledges that different operational epistemologies are functioning at various levels, intersections, and experiences of realities enough to present the claim of multiple worlds and multiple realities. In this regard, not only do beliefs orient ourselves to the world but they inform how our agency navigates the world within the parameters by which we understand ourselves, as "believing selves," in relation to it. Through various practices, discourses, and meditations, persons will "find ways to believe particular truths amid many possible truths" and determine what it means to believe such particular truths, what that entails in practice, and how it contributes in "understanding the nature and moral status of human beings" ([12], p. 222). Attention is thus given to the negotiation and "the interaction between individuals as centers of experience and agency, and the sociocultural structures within which those individuals live" ([12], p. 223; [39–42]). In this regard, commitments to truth are not constrained by epistemology as it has been conceived within the Western paradigm of philosophy and its normative claims on truth nor are they constrained by Christian forms of belief. Instead, the framework of "believing selves" emphasizes the relational dimensions of persons within their respective socio-cultural and historical contexts, varieties of discourse, and their subjective commitments and attitudes to truth and to what is real (textured commitments of what is and ought to be the case). This opens up the epistemological realm by which meaning can be obtained and value derived from an open-ended range of possible truths and a variety of forms.

Even within this framework, however, the inarticulacy and "inconsistency" of beliefs (noted above) continues to remain an issue. According to David Graeber, the word "fetish" has often been invoked "when people seem to talk one way and act another. The surprising thing is that this can happen in entirely contrary ways" ([43], p. 11). As discussed by Asad [6], and recently by Graeber [43][3], we can certainly acknowledge that a systematic and coherent understanding of one's religious tradition or worldview is not a necessary condition to be a religious practitioner. However, the descriptive observations of inconsistency do present a concern with respect to how persons may depend on contradictory positions or premises in practice and how persons navigate and negotiate them ([44], p. 245). A greater appreciation of this can be seen with respect to the development of ethics and morals within a religious tradition by contrast to the development of moral and ethical positions in society-at-large instantiated by law. Emile Durkheim stated that it seems that "human malaise continues to increase. The great religions of modern man are those which insist the most on the existence of the contradictions in the midst of which we struggle" ([30], p. 156). The issue of "inconsistency" and skepticism is thus relevant for the investigation of religion and its intersections—among other things, with gender, sexuality, race, as well as institutions such as law and economics—each of which contain a diverse range of concerns and contradictions as they pertain to religion. This presents methodological concerns regarding how persons embody, negotiate, and navigate contradictions, inconsistencies and various forms of bias in religious contexts [46–53]. Moreover, additional challenges are presented with the issue of how to

---

2   Kirsch [23], based on fieldwork that emphasized practicality and efficacy, suggested that we substitute belief (conceived as a stable interior state) for *believing* to denote a state of becoming in the internalization process.

3   "I went to Madagascar expecting to encounter something much like a different ontology, a set of fundamentally different ideas about how the world worked; what I encountered instead were people who admitted they did not really understand what was going on with *fanafody*, who said wildly different, and often contradictory, things about it, but who were all in agreement that most practitioners were liars, cheats, or frauds. Coming back from the field, I consulted with colleagues who had been in similar situations (in the Andes, Andaman Islands, Papua New Guinea . . .) and discovered that such sentiments are actually quite commonplace. They also confessed they never knew quite what to do with them. And in fact, this is precisely the aspect of magical practice that is most often dismissed as unimportant, or simply left out of ethnographic accounts" ([43], p. 11). Graeber [44] also notes that Evans-Pritchard encountered a similar dynamic among the Azande and that "in the case of any particular witchdoctor they are never quite certain whether reliance can be placed on his statements or not" ([45], p. 276).

make sense of discrepancies among propositional statements of belief, as well as their discrepancies with behavior and action.

6. The Theory of Cognitive Dissonance

In social psychology, one of the areas of research devoted specifically to this phenomenon of discrepancy is the theory of cognitive dissonance (or "dissonance theory"). Since Leon Festinger first proposed the theory in the early 1950s—writing about it in *When Prophecy Fails* [54] and explicating the theory in a book by the same name [55]—decades of research has yielded four emergent revisionist theories. Notably: Self-consistency, Self-affirmation, New Look, and Action-based (each of which is discussed further in the following section). These models all frame the theory of cognitive dissonance in relation to the self. When Festinger first proposed the theory, he began with the assumption that we, as persons, strive toward consistency ([55], p. 1); an ideal of cognitive integrity and subsequently congruent behavior. He further posited that when persons are made aware of two discrepant or inconsistent cognitions, "psychological discomfort" (that is, dissonance) would result thereby motivating one to reduce the discomfort by finding some form of consistency. By "cognition," Festinger referred to "any knowledge, opinion, or belief about the environment, about oneself, or about one's behavior" ([55], pp. 2–3). Joel Cooper further adds that, within the theory of cognitive dissonance, cognition can "refer to many different types of psychological concepts. An action is different from an attitude which, in turn, is different from an observation of reality. However, each of these has a psychological representation—and that is what is meant by cognition" ([56], p. 6). In this sense, cognition is navigational and relational to the world in which one is living and becomes critical in meaning-making processes.

Festinger suggests that holding any two discrepant cognitions will result in the affective experience of dissonance. This is further qualified by noting that the "magnitude of dissonance" will be in direct relation to the importance of the cognitions involved. In other words, the experience of dissonance is related to the degree of commitment one has to one or more of the cognitions. Rodney Needham, while dismissing a distinctive emotional or affective characteristic of belief, noted that "there *is* a feeling associated with (actually, provoked by) a challenge to belief" ([3], p. 96) which becomes much more apparent when a significant belief—with a stronger commitment than others—is challenged ([3], p. 97). Needham's observation and the significance of the "magnitude of dissonance" both highlight the relationship between emotions and embodiment and "the way human bodies respond to social values and the actions of other people" ([15], p. 186). This is the affinity between the theory of cognitive dissonance and the "believing selves" framework by which the former develops the affective dimensions of commitment in the latter. That is, the focus on dissonance and its affective elements of discomfort contributes to the various emotional dimensions involved with subjective commitments to truth and meaning-making processes in "believing selves."

7. Revisionist Theories of Cognitive Dissonance

The four emergent revisionist theories delve into this area of research and illustrate a consensus that dissonance is most salient with regard to cognitions relevant to the self but diverge on the particulars. The first revisionist theory argues that cognitive dissonance was most apparent with cognitions involved with one's self-concept [57]. This view presupposes that persons possess a particular view about one's self (i.e., what kind of person I think I am) and maintain expectations of competent and moral behavior in accordance with "conventional morals and prevailing values of society" ([57], p. 592). Dissonance thereby occurs when behavior is discrepant with one's self-concept, which itself incorporates personal standards as well as expectations of competence and morality one has about one's self. The reduction of dissonance, in this theory, is thereby aimed at maintaining one's self-concept by justifying discrepant behavior ([58], p. 229). Furthermore, as the self-concept is intimately tied with one's self-esteem in terms of self-expectations, self-consistency theory proposes that dissonance will occur with behaviors or actions that are incongruent with one's self-esteem. That is, if one has low self-esteem (low expectations for competent or moral behavior) dissonance will occur after a moral and competent act, but *not* after an immoral or incompetent act because those actions are expected of him/her self [59,60]. This has been the case of those with negative expectancies [61] and those with mild depression [62]. By contrast, "people with higher expectations of competent and moral character (i.e., high self-esteem) would perceive a discrepancy [with the immoral or incompetent act] and be motivated to seek justification" ([58], p. 230). This has also been observed with perceptions of extroversion or introversion regarding one's self-concept [63].

In a similar, yet different manner, self-affirmation theory argued that dissonance occurs primarily due to behaviors that "threaten one's sense of moral and adaptive integrity" ([64], p. 14). The presumption here is that "a motive high on people's priority list is the protection of the integrity of their self-system" ([56], p. 90). Unlike Festinger's original proposal and self-consistency theory above, self-affirmation theory argued that the particular inconsistencies did not matter so much as the holistic integrity of the self. In other words, one could "do almost *anything* to make it right. The problem is not one of rectifying the specific wrong, but [of] finding some way to affirm the global integrity of the self" ([56], p. 92). In this way, it is possible to focus on other positive aspects of one's self and reduce dissonance without directly addressing the discrepant cognitions in question ([58], p. 230).

The New Look theory places an indirect emphasis on the self by arguing that dissonance occurs from "feeling personally responsible for producing aversive consequences" ([64], p. 14). That is, the effects of dissonance are greatest when persons feel "personally responsible for their actions" and when "their actions have serious consequences [...] the greater the consequence and the greater our responsibility for it, the greater the dissonance" and thereby "the greater our own attitude change" ([65], p. 216).

The action-based model of cognitive dissonance argues that "dissonance between cognitions evokes an aversive state because it has the potential to interfere with effective and unconflicted action" ([66], p. 1524). This model further proposes two modes of motivation for the reduction of dissonance: proximal and distal. The former is the motivation to reduce or eliminate the negative affect of cognitive dissonance. The latter is the motivation for effective and unconflicted action ([67], p. 138).

In this regard, all four revisionist models engage with the self in terms of preserving a sense of self and the consequences of one's actions. However, the theory of cognitive dissonance raises questions about the degree of cross-cultural variability: the construction of self is subject to cultural and subcultural nuance. In the original theory, Festinger noted that dissonance was subject to cultural variance: "Dissonance could arise because of cultural mores [...] because the culture defines what is consonant and what is not. In some other culture [...] two cognitions might not be [discrepant and evoke dissonance] at all" ([55], p. 14). One of the ways in which cultural variance is apparent is in the different logical implications certain propositions have for the perception of consistency: "the *subjective* nature of personal beliefs supplements the *objective* nature of logical implication, such that (in)consistency within an individual's system of beliefs is determined by the application of logical principles to what this individual believes to be true or false" ([68], p. 229). Moreover, what is proper or improper, correct or incorrect, right or wrong, in both behavior and ethics contributes to, and can conflate, what is considered to be "objective." Cultural frameworks of courtesy, etiquette, value, and respect do not *necessarily* involve a truth value and yet they can influence the application of logical principles with regard to what is "rational" and "irrational." Not only does this entail variance across cultures and conceptions of the self [56,68–72], which play out in the dynamics of multiple social identities [18,73], but variability within cultures [74–76] in the assignment of what is value as well.

8. Summary and Conclusions

Both the frameworks of believing selves and the revisionist theories of dissonance not only emphasize the subjective commitments that integrate "experience and socially learned doctrines and discourses—including those concerning what it means to believe—into truths to live through" but they also "show that the work of believing is motivated by efforts to achieve an internally consistent and emotionally satisfying sense of the self's relationship to particular truths" ([12], p. 223).

Dissonance theory illustrates that this can take different forms and points of emphasis; whether it is on one's self-concept and self-esteem, one's sense of integrity, the consequences of one's actions, or active engagement and efficacy of one's actions, all of which can vary from context to context, culture to culture, and even subcultures within a culture. In other words, the self is conceived in culturally-relative ways and subsequently influences what is meant to be self-interested. Moreover, subjective commitments "may be made to the truth of something's existence, the truth of some proposition about the world or the nature of the self, the truth of someone's or something's abilities or the quality of relationship to oneself (and, thus, "trust" in those abilities or that relationship), or the moral truth of an orientation for living one's life." They are that which we hold dear [77]. These commitments do not necessarily require articulation as propositions and "may not even be consciously recognized as beliefs, but they nonetheless form part of an individual's subjective engagement with the world" ([12], p. 223).

After discussing the problems of language and practice, as well as their limitations, for the investigation of belief in the study of religion, the article presented a few emergent frameworks for belief and commentary on them. However, despite their insights, these frameworks do not adequately address or explain the issue of inconsistency. This article aimed to converge the framework of "believing selves" with its emphasis on belief as a subjective commitment to truth with the emergent revisionist theories of cognitive dissonance. Both implicate the role of the "self" within their respective disciplinary developments that address discrepancies between language and practice as well as the various ways of thinking that reduce dissonance and the perception of inconsistency. Cross-cultural studies in psychology and ethnographic studies in anthropology have shown that inconsistencies and the experience of dissonance are managed in culturally-specific ways according to the variability by which the self is conceived and the social identities involved in the situation at hand. Moreover, this variance also entails a variance in concepts of "truth" as well as the forms of evidence that provide verification and justification to the instantiation of those "truths." This creates additional variance on how persons from various cultures determine what is of "self-interest." By opening up the epistemology by which belief is conceived, a focused convergence emerges on the self and the individual in relation to society.

The individual is necessarily unique. No two persons occupy the same space-time continuum nor will they have the same set of experiences within that continuum. This is much different from considering "individualism" as a cultivated value [78,79]. Belief is a culturally embodied cognitive phenomenon that turns the focus on the individual self and his/her beliefs that ground, situate, and relate one's personhood to one's social contexts and "dividual" relationality. In other words, our beliefs are reflections of an embodied cultural history and ethos that enable our relational connectivity. Whether they are correct/incorrect, right/wrong, proper/improper is beside the point, what is significant is that they function as "true" within the broader parameters of "meaning" [80] in orientation to one's respective reality. Religious beliefs, in all their shapes and forms, are no different and continue to provide a source of meaning and promote our meaning-making capabilities.

Religion is, thus, one among many avenues that connects the individual and the social, the personal and the impersonal. Within the context of Durkheim's notion of *homo duplex*, the individual is necessarily a reflection of on-going history [81] at its many levels and intersections: "the collective is not entirely outside us, and does not act upon us wholly from without; but rather, since society cannot exist except in and through individual consciousness, this force must also penetrate us and organize itself within us. It thus becomes an integral part of our being" ([82], p. 230). Belief is one function of this relationship that enables our individual and collective agency.

Acknowledgments: Many thanks to Douglas J. Davies and Michael Thate, Chris Insole, Mathew Guest, Martin Stringer, and the Human Economy Programme at the University of Pretoria.

Conflicts of Interest: The author declares no conflict of interest.

References

1. Rorty, Richard. *Contingency, Irony and Solidarity*. Cambridge: Cambridge University Press, 1989.
2. Hesse, Herman. *Siddhartha*. Translated by Hilda Rosner. New York: New Directions, 1951.
3. Needham, Rodney. *Belief, Language, and Experience*. Oxford: Basil Blackwell, 1972.
4. Ruel, Malcolm. "Christians as believers." In *A Reader in the Anthropology of Religion*, 1st ed. Edited by Michael Lambek. Oxford: Blackwell, 2002, pp. 99–113.
5. Pouillon, Jean. "Remarks on the verb 'to believe'." In *Between Belief and Transgression: Structuralist Essays in Religion, History and Myth*. Edited by Michel Izard and Pierre Smith. Translated by John Leavitt. Chicago: Chicago University Press, 1982.
6. Asad, Talal. "The construction of religion as an anthropological category." In *A Reader in the Anthropology of Religion*, 1st ed. Edited by Michael Lambek. Oxford: Blackwell, 2002, pp. 114–32.
7. Stringer, Martin D. "Towards a situational theory of belief." *Journal of the Anthropological Society of Oxford* 27 (1996): 217–34.
8. Engelke, Matthew. "The problem of belief." *Anthropology Today* 18 (2002): 3–8. [CrossRef]
9. Larsen, Timothy. *The Slain God: Anthropologists and the Christian Faith*. Oxford: Oxford University Press, 2014.
10. Davies, James, and Dimitrina Spencer, eds. *Emotions in the Field: The Psychology and Anthropology of Fieldwork Experience*. Stanford: Stanford University Press, 2010.
11. Wittgenstein, Ludwig. "Remarks on Frazer's golden bough." In *A Reader in the Anthropology of Religion*, 1st ed. Edited by Michael Lambek. Oxford: Blackwell, 2002, pp. 85–89.
12. Carlisle, Steven, and Gregory M. Simon. "Believing selves: Negotiating social and psychological experiences of belief." *Ethos* 40 (2012): 221–36. [CrossRef]
13. Lindholm, Charles. "'What is bread?' The anthropology of belief." *Ethos* 40 (2012): 341–57. [CrossRef]
14. Polanyi, Michael. *Tacit Dimension*. Chicago: University of Chicago Press, 2009.
15. Davies, Douglas J. *Emotion, Identity, and Religion: Hope, Reciprocity, and Otherness*. Oxford: Oxford University Press, 2011.
16. Atran, Scott, and Ara Norenzayan. "Religion's evolutionary landscape: Counterintuition, commitment, compassion, communion." *Behavioral and Brain Sciences* 27 (2004): 713–70. [CrossRef] [PubMed]
17. Rappaport, Roy. A. *Ritual and Religion in the Making of Humanity*. Cambridge: Cambridge University Press, 1999.
18. Rudiak-Gould, Peter. "Being Marshallese and Christian: A case of multiple identities and contradictory beliefs." *Culture and Religion* 11 (2010): 69–87. [CrossRef]
19. Day, Abby, and Simon Coleman. "Introduction: Broadening boundaries: Creating inter-disciplinary dialogue on belief." *Culture and Religion* 11 (2010): 1–8. [CrossRef]
20. Day, Abby, and Gordon Lynch. "Introduction: Belief as cultural performance." *Journal of Contemporary Religion* 28 (2013): 199–206. [CrossRef]
21. Mair, Jonathan. "Cultures of belief." *Anthropological Theory* 12 (2012): 448–66. [CrossRef]
22. Hicks, David. "Glimpses of alternatives—The *Uma Lulik* of East Timor." *Social Analysis* 52 (2008): 166–80. [CrossRef]
23. Kirsch, Thomas. "Restaging the will to believe: Religious pluralism, anti-syncretism, and the problem of belief." *American Anthropologist* 106 (2004): 699–709. [CrossRef]
24. Street, Alice. "Belief as relational action: Christianity and cultural change in Papua New Guinea." *Journal of the Royal Anthropological Institute* 16 (2010): 260–78. [CrossRef]
25. Lindquist, Galina, and Simon Coleman. "Introduction: Against Belief? " *Social Analysis* 52 (2008): 1–18. [CrossRef]
26. Mitchell, Jon P., and Hildi J. Mitchell. "For belief: Embodiment and immanence in Catholicism and Mormonism." *Social Analysis* 52 (2008): 79–94. [CrossRef]
27. Luhrmann, Tanya. *Persuasions of the Witch's Craft: Ritual Magic and Witchcraft in Present-Day England*. Oxford: Blackwell, 1989.
28. Luhrmann, Tanya. *When God Talks Back: Understanding the American Evangelical Relationship with God*. New York: Vintage Books, 2012.
29. Goffman, Erving. *The Presentation of Self in Everyday Life*. London: Penguin, 1959.
30. Durkheim, Emile. *On Morality and Society*. Edited by Robert Bellah. Chicago: University of Chicago Press, 1973.
31. Zijderveld, Anton C. *The Abstract Society: A Cultural Analysis of Our Time*. Middlesex: Penguin, 1970.

32. Simmel, Georg. "Religion." In *Essays on Religion*. Edited and translated by Horst Jürgen Helle in collaboration with Ludwig Nieder. London: Yale University Press, 1997, pp. 137–214.
33. Moscovici, Serge. *The Invention of Society: Psychological Explanations for Social Phenomena*. Translated by Wilfred D. Halls. Cambridge: Polity Press, 1993.
34. Lévi-Strauss, Claude. "Introduction to M. Mauss." In *Sociologie et Anthropologie*. Paris: Presses Universitaires de France, 1960.
35. Bloch, Maurice. *Anthropology and the Cognitive Challenge*. Cambridge: Cambridge University Press, 2012.
36. Day, Abby. *Believing in Belonging*. Oxford: Oxford University Press, 2011.
37. Lindquist, Galina. "Loyalty and command: Shamans, lamas, and spirits in a Siberian ritual." *Social Analysis* 52 (2008): 111–26. [CrossRef]
38. Strathern, Marilyn. *The Gender of the Gift: Problems with Women and Problems with Society in Melanesia*. Berkeley: University of California Press, 1988.
39. Simon, Gregory M. "The soul freed of cares? Islamic prayer, subjectivity, and the contradictions of moral selfhood in Minanghabam, Indonesia." *American Ethnologist* 36 (2009): 258–75. [CrossRef]
40. Biehl, João G., Byron Good, and Arthur Kleinman. "Introduction: Rethinking subjectivity." In *Subjectivity: Ethnographic Investigations*. Edited by João G. Biehl, Byron Good and Arthur Kleinman. Berkeley: University of California Press, 2007, pp. 1–23.
41. Luhrmann, Tanya. "Subjectivity." *Anthropological Theory* 6 (2006): 345–61. [CrossRef]
42. Ortner, Sherry B. "Subjectivity and cultural critique." *Anthropological Theory* 5 (2005): 31–52. [CrossRef]
43. Graeber, David. "Radical alterity is just another way of saying 'reality'." *HAU: Journal of Ethnographic Theory* 5 (2015): 1–41. [CrossRef]
44. Graeber, David. *Toward an Anthropological Theory of Value: The False Coin of Our Dreams*. New York: Palgrave, 2001.
45. Evans-Pritchard, Evans E. *Witchcraft, Oracles, and Magic among the Azande*. Oxford: Clarendon Press, 1937.
46. Wright, Bradley R. E., Michael E. Wallace, Annie S. Wisnesky, Christopher M. Donnelly, Stacy Missari, and Christine Zozula. "Religion, race, and discrimination: A field experiment of how American churches welcome newcomers." *Journal for the Scientific Study of Religion* 54 (2015): 185–204. [CrossRef]
47. Brandt, Mark J., and Daryl R. Van Tongeren. "People both high and low on religious fundamentalism are prejudiced toward dissimilar groups." *Journal of Personality and Social Psychology*, 2015. [CrossRef] [PubMed]
48. Perry, Samuel L. "Hoping for a godly (white) family: How desire for religious heritage affects whites' attitudes toward interracial marriage." *Journal for the Scientific Study of Religion* 53 (2014): 202–18. [CrossRef]
49. Gurrentz, Benjamin T. "God is 'color-blind': The problem of race in a diverse Christian fraternity." *Critical Research on Religion* 2 (2014): 246–64. [CrossRef]
50. Boellstorff, Tom. "Between religion and desire: Being Muslim and gay in Indonesia." *American Anthropologist* 107 (2005): 575–85. [CrossRef]
51. Hunt, Matthew O. "Religion, race/ethnicity, and beliefs about poverty." *Social Science Quarterly* 83 (2002): 810–31. [CrossRef]
52. Emerson, Michael O., and Christian Smith. *Divided by Faith: Evangelical Religion and the Problem of Race in America*. New York: Oxford University Press, 2000.
53. Bonilla-Silva, Eduardo. "Rethinking racism: Toward a structural interpretation." *American Sociological Review* 62 (1997): 465–80. [CrossRef]
54. Festinger, Leon, Henry W. Riecken, and Stanley Schachter. *When Prophecy Fails*. Foreword by Elliot Aronson; London: Pinter & Martin, 2008.
55. Festinger, Leon. *A Theory of Cognitive Dissonance*. Stanford: Stanford University Press, 1957.
56. Cooper, Joel. *Cognitive Dissonance: Fifty Years of a Classic Theory*. London: Sage, 2007.
57. Thibodeau, Ruth, and Elliot Aronson. "Taking a closer look: Reasserting the role of the self-concept in dissonance theory." *Personality and Social Psychology Bulletin* 18 (1992): 591–602. [CrossRef]
58. Stone, Jeff, and Joel Cooper. "A self-standards model of cognitive dissonance." *Journal of Experimental Social Psychology* 37 (2001): 228–43. [CrossRef]
59. Glass, David C. "Changes in liking as a means of reducing cognitive discrepancies between self-esteem and aggression." *Journal of Personality* 32 (1964): 531–49. [CrossRef] [PubMed]
60. Maracek, Jeanne, and David R. Mettee. "Avoidance of continued success as a function of self-esteem, level of esteem certainty, and responsibility for success." *Journal of Personality and Social Psychology* 22 (1972): 98–107. [CrossRef]

61. Aronson, Elliot, and J. Merill Carlsmith. "Performance expectancy as a determinant of actual performance." *Journal of Abnormal and Social Psychology* 65 (1962): 178–82. [CrossRef] [PubMed]
62. Rhodewalt, Frederick, and Sjöfn Agustsdottir. "Effects of self-presentation on the phenomenal self." *Journal of Personality and Social Psychology* 50 (1986): 47–55. [CrossRef]
63. Cooper, Joel, and Charles J. Scalise. "Dissonance produced by deviations from lifestyles: The interaction of Jungian typology and conformity." *Journal of Personality and Social Psychology* 29 (1974): 566–71. [CrossRef] [PubMed]
64. Harmon-Jones, Eddie, and Judson Mills. "An introduction to cognitive dissonance theory and an overview of current perspectives on the theory." In *Cognitive Dissonance: Progress on a Pivotal Theory in Social Psychology*. Edited by Eddie Harmon-Jones and Judson Mills. Washington: American Psychological Association, 1999, pp. 3–21.
65. Aronson, Elliiot. *The Social Animal*, 10th ed. New York: Worth Publishers, 2008.
66. Harmon-Jones, Eddie, and Cindy Harmon-Jones. "Action-based model of dissonance: A review of behavioral, anterior cingulate, and prefrontal cortical mechanisms." *Social and Personality Psychology Compass* 2 (2008): 1518–38. [CrossRef]
67. Harmon-Jones, Eddie. "An update on cognitive dissonance theory, with a focus on the self." In *Psychological Perspectives on Self and Identity*. Edited by Abraham Tesser, Richard B. Felson and Jerry M. Suls. Washington: American Psychological Association, 2000.
68. Gawronski, Betram, Kurt R. Peters, and Fritz Stack. "Cross-Cultural differences versus universality in cognitive dissonance: A conceptual analysis." In *Handbook of Motivation and Cognition across Cultures*. Edited by Richard M. Sorrentino and Susumu Yamaguchi. New York: Elsevier, 2008, pp. 297–314.
69. Hoshino-Browne, Etsuko, Adam S. Zanna, Steven J. Spencer, Mark P. Zanna, Shinobu Kitayama, and Sandra Lackenbauer. "On the cultural guises of cognitive dissonance: The case of Easterners and Westerners." *Journal of Personality and Social Psychology* 89 (2005): 294–310. [CrossRef] [PubMed]
70. Heine, Steven J., and Darrin R. Lehman. "Culture, dissonance, and self-affirmation." *Personality and Social Psychology Bulletin* 23 (1997): 389–400. [CrossRef]
71. Markus, Hazel R., and Shinobu Kitayama. "Culture and the self: Implications for cognition, emotion, and motivation." *Psychological Review* 98 (1991): 224–53. [CrossRef]
72. Miller, Joan G. "Culture and the development of everyday social explanation." *Journal of Personality and Social Psychology* 46 (1984): 961–78. [CrossRef] [PubMed]
73. Sökefeld, Martin. "Debating self, identity, and culture in anthropology." *Current Anthropology* 40 (1999): 417–47. [CrossRef]
74. Snibbe, Alana C., and Hazel R. Markus. "You can't always get what you want: Educational attainment, agency, and choice." *Journal of Personality and Social Psychology* 88 (2005): 703–20. [CrossRef] [PubMed]
75. Hill, Diana M. "Race and Cognitive Dissonance: The Role of Double-Consciousness in the Experience of Dissonance." Master's Thesis, Princeton University, Princeton, NJ, USA, 2005.
76. Mackie, Diane M., Leila T. Worth, and Arlene G. Asuncion. "Processing of persuasive in-group messages." *Journal of Personality and Social Psychology* 58 (1990): 812–22. [CrossRef] [PubMed]
77. Hart, Keith. "Kinship, contract, and trust: The economic organization of migrants in an African city slum." In *Trust: Making and Breaking Cooperative Relations*. Edited by Diego Gambetta. Oxford: University of Oxford Press, 2000, pp. 176–93.
78. Robbins, Joel. "Dumont's hierarchical dynamism: Christianity and individualism revisited." *HAU: Journal of Ethnographic Theory* 5 (2015): 173–95. [CrossRef]
79. Robbins, Joel. *Becoming Sinners: Christianity and Moral Torment in a Papua New Guinea Society*. Berkeley: University of California Press, 2004.
80. Bae, Bosco B. "Belief and acceptance for the study of religion." *Method and Theory in the Study of Religion*, 2016. [CrossRef]
81. Bourdieu, Pierre. *The Logic of Practice*. Stanford: Stanford University Press, 1990.
82. Durkheim, Emile. *Selected Writings*. Edited by Anthony Giddens. Cambridge: Cambridge University Press, 1972.

![religions logo] religions   MDPI

Article

Performing, Representing, and Archiving Belief: Religious Expressions among Jazz Musicians

Vaughn A. Booker

Department of Religion, Princeton University, 1879 Hall, Princeton, NJ 08544, USA; vbooker@princeton.edu

Academic Editors: Douglas James Davies and Michael J. Thate
Received: 30 March 2016; Accepted: 12 August 2016; Published: 19 August 2016

Abstract: The archives of African American jazz musicians demonstrate rich sites for studying expressions of religious belief and daily religious practice in public and private arenas, in professional and personal capacities. Highlighting print material from the archives of Edward Kennedy "Duke" Ellington (1899–1974) and Mary Lou Williams (1910–1981), this article examines the ways that these musicians worked to articulate their beliefs in print and to make meaning of their routine practices. Ellington and Williams produced written records of their aspirations for non-clerical religious authority and leadership, novel notions of religious community, and conceptions of quotidian writing tasks as practices with devotional value in the middle decades of the twentieth century. In preparation for his Sacred Concert tours of American and Western European religious congregations, Ellington theologized about the nature of God and the proper language to address God through private hotel stationery. Following her conversion to Roman Catholicism, Williams managed a Harlem thrift shop and worked to create the Bel Canto Foundation for musicians struggling with substance abuse and unemployment. This study of the religious subjectivity of African Americans with status as race representatives employs archival historical methods in the effort to vividly approximate complex religious interiority.

Keywords: African American religious history; Religion in America; jazz; Duke Ellington; Mary Lou Williams

---

1. Introduction: Records of Religious Rigor

This article focuses on two African American pianists and composers in the jazz tradition, Edward Kennedy "Duke" Ellington and Mary Lou Williams, who fashioned public personae as race representatives and who had significant religious statements to say—or express—in the late 1950s and 1960s. These musicians operated within a jazz profession that underwent a decades-long transition in social perception from its association with a vicious urban nightlife that corrupted black youth to its treatment as a virtuosic art form conducive to progressive race representation [1]. Key to these famous musicians' self-awareness as race representatives is the preservation of their documents in national and university archives, with Ellington's materials at the Smithsonian and Williams's records at Rutgers University's Institute of Jazz Studies [2]. Both Ellington and Williams produced sacred jazz music through album recordings and religious concerts, and their archives often reflected the detailed thought processes and business organization to manage and produce these professional endeavors. This article locates religious practice and the articulation of belief in these musicians' archives.

This work originates from a broader project that explores religious practice at the intersection of public racial identity (race representation) and personal articulations of religious identity (expressions of belief) in twentieth-century African American religious history.[1] The contemplative private practices of Ellington and Williams shaped and refined the linguistic and performative choices these individuals made to present their religious identities to various publics. However, the presentation of such choices became public via historical bodies situated within cultural and national contexts and affiliations. Raced, gendered, classed, and aged religious subjects employ choices of language and expression in their presentations of self, and these choices also inherently constitute representations of other subjects with whom they claim association or with whom other publics identify them. For African Americans in the mid-twentieth century, public religious expression always entailed race representation [3].

Duke Ellington's archive of undated hotel stationery expressed his belief in God, his frustrations with language to refer to God, and his appeal to the very act of believing. This hotel stationery, in conversation with his religious literature and ministerial friends, serves as an unexamined arena of his personal religious exploration, reflection, and contention in the process of crafting music to make public expressions of belief. Ellington's ultimate aspiration was to use his preferred language of music to express wordlessly the proper reverence for God; in the process, however, he wrote lyrics attempting to accurately convey his assessment that existing language was inadequate to capture what it meant to believe in and to speak of God. Ultimately, the concepts of God and of love became synonymous for Ellington, articulated most vocally in his final Sacred Concert. The primary context for examining Ellington's expressions of belief and conceptions of God is the composition of specific songs for performance in his Three Sacred Concerts, premiering in 1965, 1968, and 1973—which also served to revitalize Ellington's career as he entered his seventies.

Additionally, my study of Mary Lou Williams through her Bel Canto Foundation archive articulates personal and communal meaning in what appeared to be her professional failure. To render Williams's rigorous daily activity visible through an exploration of her business archive is to contest the portrait of her work from 1958 to about 1966 as insufficient, amateurish folly and an eccentric preoccupation which distracted Williams from her more laudable musical pursuits. Williams's daily labor was a manifestation of her personal conception of a divine call, and with this material, I also reveal how Williams practiced and articulated her personal beliefs—making one African American/Catholic convert/jazzwoman's meticulous labor visible while also making her business records legible as a form of print culture which documented her religious work. Through an attempt to restructure a community of African American jazz artists and their supporters, Williams pursued charitable social work as the institutionalization of personal accountability. She attempted to institutionalize personal habits of supporting others in order to aid musicians who experienced many of the frustrations with their profession that she knew well. This was a translation of personal practices, prior to her Catholic conversion, into the language of charitable organizations, following her Catholic conversion, as recognized by the governmental bureaucracy. Such a charitable strategy was not unfamiliar to many Christian denominations in the United States, and in Williams's personal case, the production of "good sounds" was her ultimate goal for rehabilitated, creative African American jazz musicians.

---

[1] With this larger project, I claim that black jazz musicians emerged as "race professionals" because of an African American middle-class Protestantism in the first half of the twentieth century that modeled religious and racial representations of African Americans as professional duties. The emergence of jazz presented a leisure culture that religious African American middle-class professional men and women decried, while black Protestant middle-class youth who enjoyed this culture emerged from it as the black jazz professionals and aficionados in the black press who shaped the music they loved into an art form they deemed an appropriate, alternative vehicle for race representation. Accompanying that race representation in (un)intentional forms were various expressions of prominent African American religious belief and practices in the early twentieth century, evident through three major themes: irreverent performances of African American religious leadership and expressive acts of worship; a sacralization of "Africa" in narratives of African American history; and with celebrated jazz musicians who committed to black Protestants' social and political activism against Jim Crow through the desegregation of performing venues, financial support of civil rights activism, and intentional crossover racial appeal.

2. "An Eligible light of Semantics that's Right for the One God Divine"

Duke Ellington grew up in Washington, D.C.'s black middle class at the turn of the twentieth century, and his mother took him to at least two churches every Sunday (Nineteenth Street Baptist and John Wesley A. M. E. Zion, his father's family church) ([4], pp. 12–15). The young Ellington was educated in an environment that saw the staging of historical plays and pageants by civic groups, schools, and churches to instill race pride for Africa's descendants. Ellington the composer "musicalized" African American history, and the first two decades of his career saw conscious attempts to assert an appreciation for blackness in songs like "Black and Tan Fantasy" (1927), "Symphony in Black" (1934), "Black Butterfly" (1936), "Black Beauty" (1938), and in *Black, Brown and Beige* (1943), Ellington's extended symphonic "tone parallel to the history of the Negro in America" [5]. As he prepared his musical compositions for his first Sacred Concert in 1965, Ellington wrote in a rough copy of his program text, "In the beginning, we only existed in the mind of GOD, and so GOD, very graciously, shared with us a life of our own" [6]. These hotel stationery notes reveal that while traveling, Ellington made constant attempts to characterize God in his own language, and he debated the precise language others employed to capture the nature of God for his songs. In one private hotel moment, Ellington expressed a definition of God through personal experience with the natural world: "I Can Hear GOD Anytime/I Can Feel GOD in the Sun Rise/the Smell & the Taste/of the Wind & the Sea/MAKES ME See GOD When I Close My Eyes" [7]. At other times, Ellington turned to religious literature to encounter other conceptions of God within Christian traditions. Some of this literature he acquired from his fans and friends in positions of religious leadership, and he sustained an engagement with it in the process of composing his three Sacred Concerts.

Ellington read *Destined for Greatness*, a booklet by Life Messengers, "an evangelical non-profit organization" based in Seattle, Washington. Life Messengers was a publishing ministry founded in 1944 by Ray W. Johnson and his wife, Vera. Johnson, a graduate of the Moody Bible Institute, was also the publisher of *The Last Days Bible*, which focused on premillennial evangelical concepts of the impending apocalypse [8]. *Destined for Greatness* is an apologetic narrative tract, with "Dr. Fronkby" at the center of the encounter over proof of God's existence and the literal reliability of the Bible. Dr. Fronkby is a scientist who is convinced of God's existence and biblical infallibility, and he engages a group of students who challenge his rationale behind evangelical Christian commitment versus modern science's presumed opposition to it. Dr. Fronkby fielded students' various questions: John asked, "...[I]f there is a God and He created everything, who made God?" followed by "'But **why** didn't God reveal something about how He came to be?' John persisted. 'If He does exist why hasn't He explained His existence? Maybe I could believe if He would explain His own beginning'" [bold in original]. In his booklet, Ellington drew a question mark and circled it next to this passage. In response to Steve, who asked Dr. Fronkby, "But **why** is God so secretive about His beginnings?" Ellington wrote "HOW DARE WE" at the page bottom, and at the top of the next page he wrote "WE DON'T UNDERSTAND ALL THINGS ON EARTH—TANGIBLE." In his response to this series of questioning, Dr. Fronkby speaks of God's beginning, "What He has chosen **not** to reveal is none of our business." Here, Ellington bracketed this sentence and wrote "GOD" on top of "He," placing this sentence, which he considered a compelling response, in his preferred theological language ([9], pp. 12–14). Similarly, Susan's question to Dr. Fronkby about the concept of the Trinity and God permitting Jesus Christ's substitutionary atonement ("[W]hy didn't He show His great love for us by coming Himself instead of sending His Son to suffer? Why didn't **He** suffer for us instead?") irked Ellington, as evidenced by the addition of a question mark to the paragraph and the writing of "STUPID" after Susan's question ([9], p. 22).

Precise language to address directly (and speak about) God was a paramount concern for Ellington, as expressed in his hotel stationery. An Ellington stationery writing at the Hilton in Jacksonville, Florida adds texture to his expressed frustrations with the exchange between the fictional Dr. Fronkby and the students:

What Made You Think ^ (That) You Can Use the Word HIM
Why Do You Refer to the Almighty as HE
When You Pray ^ (First Person) How Dare You Address the LORD as YOU
Him, You & He
Are Correct When Addressing Me [10].

Addressing an unspecified believing subject, Ellington adopted privately a tone of frustration with the commonplace usage of masculine pronouns and titles to refer to God. Ellington even attempted to craft lyrics for a tune, titled "There is No Pronoun Good Enough for GOD," which expressed his belief that regal addresses like "His or Her Majesty" and "Your Highness" for royals or "Your Honor" for a judge fall short of adequacy when speaking to the divine [11]. A Washington, D.C. reflection expressed his lament over the absence of sufficiently exclusive language: "With So Many ^ (Educated[,] Brilliant) People (Scholars) With Such Highly Developed Vocabularies—In So Many, Many ^(Sophisticated) Languages & Not One, Who Think[?] of a Worthy Pronoun." When referring to God, the archaic "thou" and capitalized masculine pronouns were apparently insufficient for Ellington. And he ended this note by declaring, "GOD is Beyond Gender" [12].

To consider the supreme deity "Beyond Gender" was, at base, a clear statement relegating gendered language to the created, material world. However, this particular phrasing is likely significant in Ellington's language, given his history of considering others "beyond" standard classification. For other artists, to be "Beyond Category" in the jazz world was to bear Ellington's highest praise. Fellow musicians Mary Lou Williams and Ella Fitzgerald received this veneration, with the latter artist receiving a musical tribute when Ellington and Billy Strayhorn composed "Portrait of Ella Fitzgerald" with a third movement titled, "Beyond Category." It is likely, therefore, that this assertion of a genderless deity is simultaneously Ellington's assertion of God's superiority to gendered descriptions and an expression of high religious praise.

The evidence of this descriptive theological assertiveness would not appear as a direct message in any of the songs from Ellington's three Sacred Concerts. However, Ellington created a symphonic composition, titled "New World A-Comin'," inspired by Roi Ottley's Peabody award-winning 1943 book on African American society, *New World A-Coming: Inside Black America.* Ellington's "New World A-Comin'," with the composer's spoken-word introduction in the 1970 orchestral album recording, envisioned a future where "there will be no war, no greed, no categorization, no nonbelievers, where love is unconditional, and there is no pronoun good enough for God" [13]. Ellington included his solo piano performance of "New World A-Comin'" in his First Sacred Concert tour.

The composer pursued the use of terminology to address and describe God that could not apply to any other subject or concept. This must have been a constant thought process for Ellington while traveling, for his poetic reflection in San Antonio, Texas describes his pursuit of such elusive language:

My Dear GOD I've Been Searching
Searching For the Word or the Phrase
that Cannot Be Use[d] [for?] any Purpose
& Has Not Been Used Through All the Universal Days

My Dear GOD I've Been looking,
Listening, looking & Trying to Find
An Eligible light of Semantics
that's Right For the One God Divine

When Speaking to or Of My Dear GOD
There's Not One Pronoun
that Hasn't Been Used for Others
& Not One That Hasn't Been Used I've Found No Not One I've Found [14].

With music, Ellington was able to find or create a particular phrase, theme, or melody to express a particular concept, mood, person, or group of people. However, he appeared unsatisfied with an inability to do likewise with existing language about the divine. Additional hotel stationery reflections in Greensboro, North Carolina and Baltimore, Maryland indicate that Ellington momentarily considered the exclusive use of the first person pronoun by God—and God alone—acceptable. He declared "The Only Pronoun Good Enough for God is 'I' When used in the FIRST PERSON" at one moment, and he also wrote, "There is only ^(the) ONE Pronoun/good Enough For GOD/& It Can only Be Use[d] By the ONE/GOD—I AM" [15]. Relegating the address of God to God's self may have served to convey the essential ineffability Ellington felt in his reverence for the divine. The practice of generating such written statements about God may have even served as acts of private worship for Ellington. However, this work would not suffice for Ellington's attempt to capture the worshipful rhetoric of believers in the God of the Hebrew Bible for the songs he was composing. The Baltimore reflection in which Ellington refers to God as "the ONE" reveals an attempt to employ a numerical pronoun to address the Almighty, and a reflection in Honolulu, Hawaii reveals Ellington's seemingly meditative attempts to spell out this form of reverence through repetition of the title "the One" [16].

Ellington had used "the One" to refer to God in a composition predating his three Sacred Concerts. In 1963, he composed a stage play, *My People*, what he deemed a "social significance" work intended for a children's audience during the height of the Civil Rights Movement—reminiscent of the pageants from Ellington's childhood like W. E. B. Du Bois's *The Star of Ethiopia*. This play was broadcast so that black children, the larger white American viewership, and a wider European audience would know that "there are Negro doctors, lawyers, businessmen, nurses, teachers, telephone operators, policemen, and housewives," and that they are worthy of admiration ([17], pp. 393, 395). One of the particularly religious compositions for this broadcast was titled, "Ain't But the One," performed by Ellington's orchestra and featuring the lead vocals of Jimmy McPhail and the backing vocals of the Irving Bunton Singers. Employing the familiar "call and response" singing method of black gospel music, "Ain't But The One" reflected Ellington's strident monotheism through a recording of God's activity as chronicled primarily in the Hebrew Bible, invoking events that would have been familiar to any African Americans attached to the tradition of music derived from African American spirituals. But the lyrics for "Ain't But the One" made use of implied pronouns (and interrogative pronouns) when describing God, effectively serving Ellington's linguistic contention by evading their usage altogether. McPhail and the Irving Bunton Singers alternated choruses of "Ain't but the One (just One)" when describing the "one good Lord above" or the "one great God of love." McPhail spoke of a God who "made a serpent wiggle from a walking stick/made a snake out of a cane," and he asked "who set the stars (sun and the moon)?" and "who knows the judgment (just who)?" without the use of "He" [18]. Ellington later incorporated "Ain't But the One" into his first Sacred Concert, thereby conveying to religious audiences nationwide his appraisal of the African American Christian musical tradition while subtly omitting the use of the masculine pronoun most Christians associated with God.[2]

---

[2] For the televised *We Love You Madly Tribute* to an ailing Duke Ellington in 1973, Ray Charles and Aretha Franklin re-imagined Ellington's "Ain't But the One" by setting his lyrics to the basic structure of their song, "Spirit in the Dark." The song includes not only an organ, electric guitar, and a mass gospel choir behind Charles and Franklin, intimately familiar with the idioms of modern gospel music, but it also contains a "praise break" showcasing these two musicians' improvisational spirit. In a sense, this reworking of the song affirms the theological content of Ellington's lyrics as sufficiently representative of African American Christianity. However, the Franklin and Charles version uses the pronoun "He" when referring to God. Coupled with their musical arrangement, which supplants Ellington's as a more authentic representation of modern gospel music that is conducive to Pentecostal worship practices, Charles and Franklin translate Ellington's message into the words and sounds most familiar to the black Christian communities with which they were well acquainted. These changes also simply signal generational and religious differences between musicians—Ellington had not been a church-attending religious person, and his Washington, DC black Baptist and Methodist upbringing in the black middle class bore mainly the strong influence of African American spirituals, not gospel music.

Besides use of "the One," Ellington composed "Supreme Being" for his Second Sacred Concert, an epic song similar to the first Sacred Concert's "In the Beginning, God" in its focus on the Hebrew Bible's Genesis creation narrative, but relying primarily on the choir and soloists' spoken word following an arranged instrumental opening:

> Supreme Being!
> Supreme Being
> There is a Supreme Being
> There is one, only one, one Supreme Being
> Out of lightning, thunder, chaos and confusion
> The Supreme Being organized and created
> Created and organized heaven and earth
> [...]
> Supreme Being.
> The immortal creator and ruler of the universe, eternal and all-powerful
> Supreme Being
> Called God! [19].

To speak repeatedly of one "Supreme Being" allowed Ellington to marshal many familiar religious descriptors for this divine concept, contemplating this being and its attributes for over four minutes, before the chorus reveals (by building to an exclamation) that it is also "called God!" But this prose also allowed Ellington to signify that the capitalized word "God" that many English-speaking monotheists use to refer to this "Supreme Being" inevitably fell short of fully capturing the divine object of reverence. In this instance, more words rather than fewer were necessary for Ellington to represent to the listener the particular, epic biography of this entity of utmost existence.

Why wasn't "Jesus" a sufficient noun? Language about Jehovah, Yahweh, the Holy Ghost (or Spirit) is absent from Ellington's hotel stationery reflections. Similarly, Jesus's name appears once in this collection.[3] According to Ellington biographer Harvey Cohen, a 1958 interview revealed that Ellington regularly wore a gold cross under his shirt but also that he "almost never spoke about Jesus Christ directly, either in conversation or in the lyrics for his sacred compositions" ([17], p. 448). In Ellington's first Sacred Concert, the gospel singer Esther Marrow stated in "The Lord's Prayer" that she was "beggin you, Jesus, to give me more grace/I need your power to help me to run this race" before improvising on the New Testament "Our Father"/model prayer. It is possible that Ellington granted Marrow the improvisational freedom to use her preferred divine language; nevertheless, the almost total absence of the name Jesus or the title Christ from Ellington's compositions is significant. Two exceptions are possible allusions to Jesus in "Ain't But the One" and "Tell Me It's the Truth." In "Ain't But the One," Jimmy McPhail's line "Made the cripple walk and the blind man see" refers to two acts of Jesus that the New Testament gospels provide, although this lyrical presentation also allows for attribution of the healings to the power of God. "Tell Me It's the Truth" references "the Gospel truth," because "the truth is the light and the light is right"—and to Marrow's "right?" Ellington answered, "right" [20]. However, Marrow appears to sing "Tell me it's *a* truth" in the Grace Cathedral premiere and on the album version, despite the album version's song title and versions by other Sacred Concert singers since.[4] Through the song, the singer appears in need of assurance that something is

---

[3] One undated piece of hotel stationery (without a location) reveals Ellington similarly thought about how to properly address Jesus Christ as God's son: "People Who Have the Honor to Be Presented to a prince or Princess—[the] Son or Daughter—of a King is addressed ˆ(or referred to) as your ˆ (or His) Highness—Not He or She/But Not Jesus Christ—& Jesus is the Son of GOD/Why is Proper Protocol ˆ NOT Provided [to?] the Son of GOD—Jesus Christ—" Although Ellington's desire for exclusive language to appropriately address the "Son of GOD" may reveal a significant place for Jesus in Ellington's theology, it does not indicate conclusively that he held God and Jesus (alongside the Holy Spirit) as equal deities, or that the "Son of GOD" was also "God the Son."

[4] This appears to also be the case for Duke Ellington's recorded concert at Fountain Street Church in Grand Rapids, Michigan on 17 April 1966.

either true or "the truth," and the allusion to Jesus as either the biblical "truth" or "light" is possible but unclear with this song. In both cases, Ellington elected to avoid direct mentions of Jesus or Christ.

A rhyming reflection that Ellington wrote on hotel stationery in Houston, Texas serves as his attempt at a proverb, imitating a Shakespearean line from *The Merchant of Venice*: "It's a Wise Man Who Knows His Father/It's a Wise Man Who Knows His Son/It's a Wise Man Who Knows that GOD/& that GOD is the One and Only One" [21]. A *Christianity Today* profile of Ellington possibly shed light on these theological absences:

> His Washington, D.C. boyhood was filled with sermons and Sunday school, but Ellington has rarely attended services during his career and never joined a church. At 23, with a jazz career beginning to bloom, "I began to read the Bible for myself, to see what there was. I have my own idea, and I think it makes sense." This idea strays from the orthodox belief on the Trinity, but he is conservative about the Bible itself. "I believe the whole story," he said. "I am always in a position to have it out with people who say the Bible contradicts itself. I'm not a formal Bible student, but I can correct people on things like that." [22].

While the profile offered no specific stances Ellington many have had regarding the idea of God existing simultaneously in three persons, it conveyed the musician's confidence in his own ability to comprehend, interpret, and defend Hebrew and Christian scriptures without conventional clerical guidance. The article glossed the prospect of Ellington's unitarian personal theology (perhaps this explains his frustration with the fictional student questioning Dr. Fronkby about God suffering in Jesus's crucifixion?) in order to focus on his affirmation of the existence of God. *Christianity Today*'s mission was to promote a more conservative evangelical Christian voice in print magazine culture than the mainline Protestant magazine, *The Christian Century*.

Ellington's sacred music represented an attempt to craft new religious sounds, and his presence in various churches and synagogues indicated the prospect of interracial fellowship and the creativity it was able to produce if more Americans committed to integration and welcomed African Americans into their religious spaces. His Sacred Concerts proclaimed belief, albeit a general belief in a supreme deity, and the defense of believing was sufficient for those religious participants like Ellington who elected to operate within an interfaith world. However, the lyrics of his compositions never expressed the particular belief in Jesus's resurrection, atonement, or divinity.

As a public representative of receptivity to religious belief, Ellington became a repository or vessel for other religious leaders' more pronounced and firm religious commitments, and they sent him religious materials as gifts in order to persuade him to join their religious communities. For Ellington to express divine belief without adhering to any particular Christian denomination meant that others were willing to send him scriptures and religious literature to compel him in particular theological directions. Ellington's apparent openness left him vulnerable to accusations by his critics of insincere piety and superficial belief. But such openness also made him likely to forge new religious relationships that became friendly correspondences, some of which fed into the Sacred Concerts. Ellington's collection of religious literature reveals that a profession of religious commitment in twentieth-century America did not seal the individual off from the reality of competing religious commitments, which may even have appeared as the well-intentioned proselytizing of others who admired the popular jazz musician and sought to welcome him into their particular fellowships. Nevertheless, Ellington received these gifts as clergy encouraging him to create sacred music "not as a matter of career, but in response to a growing understanding of my own vocation" [23]. In general, for Ellington to proclaim divine ineffability in public songs and private writings was both a product and practice of his personal religious wrestling, contemplation, and devotion.

Endowed with the trust of many ministers and religious institutions to present a statement of faith, Ellington made use of these public settings to serve as an African American representative of religious fidelity who was privately in the constant process of working out the nature of that belief. Although granted a unique opportunity, Ellington's wrestling reflects the individual lives of many religious adherents and troubles the assumption that an individual's commitment to religious institutions, assent to doctrinal statements, or participation in religious rituals implies a shared, uncomplicated understanding of those spaces, languages, actions, or objects of reverence. The following section on Mary Lou Williams explores another jazz musician's sense of personal religious calling that resulted in her diligent, detailed, daily work to forge a position of unconventional religious leadership and race representation.

3. Personal Mission, Professional Accountability

Mary Lou Williams was born with a "veil" and had visions as a child, and she likely had a family of religious people around her who encouraged a notion of her wielding spiritual gifts. But Williams did not explore "conventional" religious traditions until after the death of jazz saxophonist and composer Charlie Parker from years of hard substance abuse. Williams engaged in prayer and "ascetic" practices like fasting and abstaining from purchasing luxuries. This followed an intense period of continued visions and accompanied close friendships with jazz trumpeter John Birks "Dizzy" Gillespie and his wife Lorraine, a Catholic convert. Lorraine encouraged Williams's exploration of Catholicism, while Gillespie encouraged her to return to performing music. She viewed her music, and the music industry itself, as antithetical to her religious mission before meeting a black Catholic friar, Mario Hancock, who encouraged her to compose religious reflections as part of her calling.

The 1960s and 1970s saw Williams composing many religious works. The Roman Catholic reforms of Vatican II afforded her a vehicle to promote the concept of "sacred jazz" by providing music "for the disturbed soul." Her music for Catholic liturgy contained gospel influences, and Williams, as a champion of jazz education, sought to make clear to others the roots of authentic American music in spirituals and the blues. *Black Christ of the Andes* celebrated the seventeenth-century Afro-Peruvian Catholic Saint Martin de Porres, "Dirge Blues" was a memorial to President Kennedy (the first Catholic U.S. president), and concerts like *Praise the Lord in Many Voices*, *Mass for Lenten Season*, and *Mass for Peace* saw Williams and her music circulating throughout Catholic churches in an attempt to get a male-dominated and formerly segregated religious institution to take seriously her musical talents, religious sincerity, and the general presence of black Catholics. In the early 1970s, Williams articulated the sacred origins of jazz through a particular African American heritage:

> Through our suffering God took pity on us and created the world's greatest true art: the "Negro Spirituals" and from the Spirituals: Jazz was born in all its creative and progressive forms...Jazz is also a healer of the mind and soul. God reaches others through it to bring peace and happiness to those who know how to listen to it. [24]

Williams reiterated her belief about jazz music's divine origins in a 1978 interview, adding the notion that performing and listening to the music had spiritually therapeutic benefits: "God did blacks a favor by creating jazz especially for them. God helps people through jazz; people have been healed through it. It has happened to me" ([25], p. 36).

Williams articulated her new religious calling following the death Charlie Parker, her friend whose musical creativity in forging "bebop" (along with trumpeter Dizzy Gillespie and pianist Earl Rudolph "Bud" Powell) she encouraged. Having returned to the United States from Europe in 1954, and familiar with Parker's heroin addiction, Williams received word in 1955 about Parker's declining state from her brother, Jerry, who spotted him leaving Harlem Hospital. Since she often cared for musicians in her Hamilton Terrace apartment, Williams relayed to Parker through Jerry that he should "come by the house" ([26], p. 144; [27], p. 67). Unfortunately, Parker died a few days later. According to Williams biographer Tammy Kernodle, this loss made her despondent about the state of the jazz community and its music, given its demonstrated inability to provide care and safety nets for others:

> [Charlie Parker's] death symbolized for Mary everything she thought had gone wrong with the jazz scene and the larger black community. Personal accountability and responsibility to the community had been replaced by an attitude focused on the individual and on

personal advancement. Apparently no one had considered intervening with Parker; those around him simply distanced themselves when his behavior became too much to bear. Some fed his chemical demons in order to anesthetize or control him. ([28], pp. 167–77)

Unrealized creativity for jazz musicians, and the material insecurities it produced, became Williams's chief concerns, which she sought to remedy through religious care. Following Charlie Parker's death, Williams served as a co-chairperson of the Charlie Parker Foundation, established to support the late musician's children. A memorial concert for Parker, featuring Williams, Gillespie, and others, raised $10,000. This success inspired in Williams a desire to establish an organization for struggling musicians and children, which she named the Bel Canto Foundation ([28], p. 177, and [29], p. 245).

To raise funds for the foundation, Williams opened a thrift shop to sell second-hand goods (including luxury items) to New York City's low-income patrons. As she reflected, the thrift shop came to occupy a place in Williams's daily routine, at first alongside nursing musicians in her home and attending Catholic worship services:

> I'd meet the musicians and like if anybody was hung up I'd take them into church and I'd teach them to pray, how to do the rosary beads. I used to sit in the Lady of Lourdes. I'd go to the mass in the morning, 7 o'clock mass, and sit through all the masses. I'd get out about 9 or 10. I'd come home and fix lunch for all the poor people I had in the house I was feeding. I'd go right back and meditate a couple hours and then I'd come home. I was from the house to the store to the church. ([26], p. 156)

Eventually, Williams ceased housing musicians in her apartment to focus her efforts more fully on fundraising for her foundation and managing the store (although she continued to provide their convalescence elsewhere) ([26], p. 160; [27], pp. 78–80).[5] In part, this Bel Canto Foundation story illuminates an African American woman managing a business, attentive to her income and influence. But the Bel Canto Foundation story has also been about failure, born of Williams's insufficient income and experience. Criticisms of Williams's efforts to establish the Bel Canto Foundation regarded the thrift shop she managed as "more a place to socialize than to do business." Williams biographer Linda Dahl even quoted the jazz musician's friend and later manager, Father Peter O'Brien, who stated, "She was not tough enough to run a business" ([29], p. 294). Dahl characterizes her donation standards and practices as unfeasible and unwise: "All an applicant had to do was give his name and address to receive a small check from Mary. This of course could not, and did not, last long" ([29], p. 265). Ultimately, this critical voice stemmed from the negative reflections of Williams's friends and fellow jazz musicians, who watched Williams care for other musicians with extreme devotion but found her religious exhortations off-putting ([29], p. 255). The value of revisiting Williams's Bel Canto Foundation archive is to reassess her management, fundraising, and store operation as daily religious labor that ensured her care—and creation of community—for many struggling jazz musicians.

With the legal assistance of Herbert Bliss, Williams incorporated the Bel Canto Foundation ([28], p. 190). The Bel Canto Foundation, Inc.'s charter stated the following primary purpose: "To voluntarily assist in relief of every kind and nature to those persons suffering from or exposed to alcohol or drugs in any degree, but primarily to musicians whose health or work is affected by alcohol or drugs" [30]. As of 8 August 1958, Mary Lou Williams had established a Bel Canto bank account. The total deposits to the account were $851.75 by 28 August. She counted personal

---

5   In 1964, Williams revealed, "I put the worst cases in a room down the hall from my place I rent cheap from a neighbor. They stay a couple of weeks, and I talk to them and pray with them and help them get a job. But I can be very hard in my charity, and sometimes I tell them, 'You've got to be a man. Stand up and go downtown and get a job. No use lying around Harlem and feeling sorry for yourself.' Sometimes they come back in worse shape and ask for money, and sometimes they get on their feet. One boy I've been helping has a job at Gimbels, and he's doing just fine. I've also sent musicians to the Graymoor Monastery, near Garrison. Brother Mario [Hancock] there has been a lot of help to me."

withdrawals from this account as loans to herself [31]. A 23 September 1958 bank deposit statement recorded that the Carnegie concert raised $2,922.75, excluding sizable and minor donations totaling $690.00 from jazz pianist Erroll Garner, Dave Brubeck (who could not attend but contributed $10) [32], the noted jazz patroness Baronness Pannonica de Koenigswarter, Evie Ellington, and various judges and doctors whom Williams knew [33]. This total existed against a cost to Williams of $3,211.42 for promoting and holding the concert, a sign for several of her invested friends that the foundation effort was a wash and should not proceed further ([28], p. 266). Williams intended to record a live album of the Carnegie Hall concert, with all proceeds benefiting her foundation. At her request, Bliss contacted the American Federation of Musicians for permission to record the volunteer musicians. However, Bliss received the response that "unless the performing musicians are paid recording wage scales," the union could not grant recording permission [34]. The unintended consequence of the musicians' charitable gesture, in foregoing payment for the concert, was that the profession's established labor practices prevented a potentially lucrative source of revenue (and avenue for broader publicity) for Williams's foundation. Nevertheless, Williams continued to navigate America's charitable landscape through publicity and fundraising letters [35].

Over the next few years, Williams sent fundraising letters as she devised new efforts to foster a sense of accountability between musicians and audiences. She organized rummage sales, offering "New Items from Saks Fifth Ave" including "children's clothes, shoes, dresses, books, house ware, dishes, antiques, men's clothes, original paintings, [and] lamps." She advertised the location of her rummage sales at 310 and 318 East 29th street in New York City, with weekly operational hours from "10[a.m.]-till" [36]. Advertisements for the rummage sales appear to be hand-drawn leaflets Williams likely distributed throughout her neighborhood. Despite the Carnegie concert's publicity, Williams was perhaps the only person truly convinced of her ability to establish the foundation. But the rummage sales served as a charitable concept that Williams maintained into the 1960s. Successful folks, musicians and otherwise, enjoyed an excess of material goods with which they could easily part. And even though all of these items were perishable in the long run, wealthier individuals had the means to buy sturdier, more durable goods that would be of great use, even through second-hand ownership. Williams and her successful friends donated their own luxury clothes, household items, and antiques in the ongoing effort to raise money for the Bel Canto Foundation. The rummage sale fostered the (re)circulation of material goods—within a local community, between two financially disparate socioeconomic classes, and for cheaper than original costs. This stood as an alternative to the conventional circulation of economic resources between these two classes, such as money dispensed through an hourly wage employment system. For her ultimate goal of benefiting jazz musicians on the social margins, Williams came to rely on a charitable commercial practice that linked the most marginalized of New York City's working class with its successful elites whose friendship, favor, and admiration she had earned over several years.

In 1959, Williams chose 308 East 29th Street as the location of a thrift shop to continue her practice of selling donated goods from musicians, socialites, and others, to fundraise for her foundation. In the long effort to realize her dream—to support musicians by holding others accountable for their care, Williams encountered the reality that in American society, the institutionalization of care required its own measures of accountability with which Williams had to become familiar. There were three related aspects of Williams's accountability: her personal bookkeeping, the maintenance of federal and state licenses to operate as a tax-free charity in the city, and establishing and maintaining her professional trustworthiness to (re)negotiate contracts and terms with her creditors. Official legal forms, bureaucratic liaisons, and constant personal correspondences served as the modes to institutionalize trust and credibility through accountability and transparency. To maintain her thrift shop in its more unprofitable moments, Williams also became responsible for drafting requests to revise payment terms and explaining insufficient funds for overdue bills, justifying her store's viability in order to renew licenses. Additionally, alongside continued appeals for funds and advertisements, she was responsible for diligent accounting of daily expenses.

On Williams's individual part, her detailed expense books recorded the donations, sales, and personal finances she put into the thrift shop. Regular expenses in 1959 and 1960 included travel (train cost, cab and bus fare, tolls, parking tickets), transportation of materials (shipping, car rental), meals (for herself, relatives, and others), repairs (for the shop, the shop's car), shop maintenance (hardware, personal care products, cleaning supplies, office furniture and supplies), care for donated clothes (hangers, dry-cleaning), publicity (stamps, paint, posters, cardboard, printing), the shop's bills (telephone and gas), rental payments for the shop, and Williams's personal loans to the shop, for which she also recorded the shop's repayments to her. However, these expense books were also essential for holding her accountable about her own daily expenses, serving at times to remind her of the degree to which her time and income went toward personal errands and spending. Williams consistently recorded payments for her sister, Grace Mickles (who struggled with alcoholism), and for Grace's children [37]. Other expenses included her performance trips to other cities, the one-time services of an accountant, and the annual cost of a post office box. Total receipts for the shop, from 1 September through 31 December 1960 amounted to $1,035.32. Against $357.38 in expenses for that quarter, the total gain amounted to $677.94 [38].

Naturally, accounting was central to participating in any institutionalized system of accountability. For the year ending 31 May 1960, Williams filed the New York State Department of Social Welfare's Annual Report for Charitable Organizations, declaring an income of $3,260.63 ($727.30 from the rummage sale and $2,533.33 in donations) and $1,952.50 in expenses ($973.74 for the rummage sale, and $978.76, possibly related to fundraising donations), for a total net income of $1,308.13 (although because of a miscalculation, she reported $100 less than the actual total) [39]. Williams filed a financial report on 15 February 1961, a required submission to New York's Department of Welfare, Division of Public Solicitation. She declared $3,322.19 in receipts ($1,531.77 from the thrift shop sales and $1,790.42 in donor contributions) and $1,599.64 in total expenses, for a net income of $1,722.55 (although Williams again mistakenly calculated the total as $10 less than the actual amount). On the reverse page of the form, she indicated that the foundation's bank account contained $1,806.20 for the purpose of "helping needy and deserving musicians." She also needed to explain two other expenses she titled "Loan repaid to M. L. Williams" and "Aid $62.38" in writing on the reverse page:

> Aid: Check in the amount of 47.38 was given to Diane Coles to pay back room rent and to rehabilitate herself.

> Aid: George Gordon, Musician, had heart attack on job. Took care of him by letting him watch thrift shop. Gave George Gordon 1 check for $10.00 and 1 for $5.00.

> $100.00 of $165.00 loan made to fund by Mary Lou Williams. [40]

With this financial form and others, there were obvious descriptive limitations on what Williams could classify as her "care" for particular musicians, given her professional traveling schedule and other financial obligations in addition to managing the shop. Fifteen dollars for George Gordon was certainly not enough to cover his healthcare costs, but perhaps the relatively insubstantial amount obscures the degree of Williams's actual involvement when she "took care of him" in her shop—constant communication with Gordon over his period of recuperation, errands she may have run for him, recruiting others to check in on his progress, preparing meals for him, and even regular conversations with him about life, music, and future goals beyond his immediate illness. The checks may have even represented the official amount that she provided Gordon once he was well enough to leave the shop, concealing Williams's true religious labor—her investment of time and finances—to ensure his recovery. Such matters of personal care are not as easy to quantify on federal forms, particularly when time was constantly a precious and limited resource for the busy Williams. Additionally, the George Gordon Singers performed for one of Williams's albums of religious jazz in 1964, so her personal and financial relationship with this musician extended well beyond what one individual form could capture.

In the 1960s, several musicians appeared in Williams's checkbooks as the recipients of payments for performances with her (in addition to personal loans): bassist George Tucker (1927–1965), who performed for Williams's trio; Andrew Cyrille (b. 1939), eventually an avant-garde drummer for jazz pianist Cecil Taylor, whose musical style represented a comical foe for Williams in her normative articulation of jazz as music ([28], pp. 259–62); drummer Berisford "Shep" Shepherd (b. 1917); drummer, arranger, and singer James "Osie" Johnson (1923–1966); double bassist and photographer Milton John "Milt" Hinton (1910–2000); and drummer Percy Brice (b. 1923) [41]. These musicians likely had stable enough employment to maintain bank accounts, whereas the thrift shop employees and struggling musicians Williams encountered most likely received "out-of-pocket" compensation or charity, respectively. In her 1965 income tax files, Williams indicated a total of $227.76 in personal payments to several African American musicians: bassist Eustis Guillemet (b. 1934), drummer Granville William "Mickey" Roker (b. 1932), bassist Melbourne R. "Bob" Cranshaw (b. 1932), and a donation to pianist and composer Tadley Ewing Peake "Tadd" Dameron (1917–1965) [42]. It is plausible that Williams enlisted these musicians, and others, as her sidemen for various concert performances in order to afford them steady income and to allow them to continue exercising their musical gifts. But Williams also maintained lasting correspondences with some musicians, who shared with her their progress in (and frustrations with) the music industry, the details of their daily prayer habits, and their reflections on social unrest [43].

The irony of Williams never succeeding in raising the profile (and resources) of this foundation was that the constant care for her immediate family diverted her income, which she could have otherwise put towards the Bel Canto mission. As reflected in her checkbook, Williams's sister, Grace Mickles, and her children were the perpetual recipients of funds for essentials like food, overdue rent, clothing, and bus fare. Williams even paid Mickles's life insurance policy. Beyond the care of relatives, included in Williams's regular expenses were items essential to her embrace of Catholicism: she wrote checks regularly to Our Lady of Lourdes church for $20 worth of prayer candles, $4 for a Catholic pamphlet, $5 for prayers from the Mother Mary Missions, $30 for the Franciscan Missionary, a $25 donation to the poor, and a $400 donation to the Catholic Youth Organization. She recorded her donations to other congregations, like the Holy Rosary Church, St. Leo's Church, St. Mary's Catholic Church, and St. Patrick's Church. In addition to substantial (but infrequent) personal expenses, like $300 gowns for her concerts, $124 to cover recording session costs, $75 expenses for hair care, the circulation of Williams's personal income for charitable and business purposes siphoned off potential resources for the foundation [41]. Sizable deposits of her own money into the thrift shop's account—such as personal checks totaling $864, $2,000 in concert revenues, her regular salary of $512.71 for performing at the Hickory House nightclub in New York city, and a bank loan for $2,000, all in 1965—never became enough to offset the store's preexisting rental debt, overdue utility bills, and her perpetual aid to others [44]. These expenses accompanied Williams's support for her mother, by this point ailing from cancer. In part, Williams's immediate charitable generosity and substantial family obligations counteracted the long-term religious mission she envisioned for a specific musical population.

4. Conclusions: Alternative Modes of Religious Community and Discourse, Novel Practices of Devotional Labor and Leadership

Duke Ellington sympathized with any effort to affirm God and to affirm believing in God. While on the road in the mid-1960s, in preparation for his Sacred Concerts, he used hotel stationery to make notes to himself concerning potential lyrics for his sacred music. In this process, he was transcribing his efforts to verbalize what it meant to express belief in God. A reflection at the Detroit Hilton hotel became a driving assertion of his sacred concerts: "Every Man Prays in His Own Language & there is No Language GOD Does Not Understand." With the opposite side of the paper, Ellington explained that music was "My Language," that it "Got Me into Church," and that it was "Possibly My Most Eligible Form of Semantics—if I am to Speak to GOD" [45]. The constantly touring Ellington made sense of God on the road without a regular church home, theologizing as he read the Christian Bible and engaged mostly liberal religious literature [46]. When he finally attended houses of worship, it was without adhering to their specific doctrinal commitments—it was as a celebrated musician, similar to an honored guest preacher, but bearing a primarily musical and nondenominational message. In these moments, the famous composer could bypass lay status within any denomination and enjoy a relatively exalted status in white religious spaces (and in the black religious spaces where ministers and congregants respected his jazz career) as a professional African American artist who enjoyed more than forty years of career success.

Ellington was a prominent African American race representative and served such a role in white religious spaces, although the religious literature he enjoyed did not emerge from African American Christian denominations or thinkers. The home of Ellington's Sacred Concert music was not the mainline African American Protestantism of Washington, D.C. in which his parents raised him. Rather, Ellington engaged an explicitly ecumenical religious project that brought him into the world of white mainline liberal Protestantism in the United States and of Western Europe. Additionally, the theological reflections that Ellington produced with his sacred musical compositions represented his responses to the discourses and concerns of liberal Christianity, particularly in his manner of wrestling with appropriate language to address and characterize the nature of God, and with the noteworthy absence of Jesus Christ and the Holy Spirit from the language of a composer moving primarily throughout mainline Christian religious spaces.

Moreover, while Ellington bore implicitly the task of representing African American Christianity in his new music, his primary familiarity with African American religious life was relegated to his childhood, where he spent Sundays between his father's African Methodist Episcopal Zion church and his mother's National Baptist Convention, USA church. Engagement with the evolving expressions and theologies of Afro-Protestantism in the first half of the twentieth century was absent in Ellington's adulthood, and he gravitated more toward white mainline Protestant leaders, thinkers, and religious spaces. His sister, Ruth, a significant champion of Ellington's religious legacy, a congregant at St. Peter's Lutheran Church in Manhattan, and his family member most responsible for creating his archive, was similarly situated between white mainline and evangelical religious worlds [47]. Gospel developed as an African American music form and industry in the years between Ellington's religious youth and his Sacred Concerts in the mid-1960s, and its popularity spread throughout African American Christianity (from Holiness-Pentecostal churches to the Baptist and Methodist mainline). Consequently, a significant temporal and theological gulf existed between Ellington's religious life and that of many African American Christians, despite Ellington's de facto identity as an African American racial and religious representative to predominantly white mainline Protestant audiences. In this light, the greater posthumous popularity of Ellington's sacred music in white American mainline and European Protestant churches is not an ironic outcome, and these are the congregations that continue to perform his compositions annually.

Undeniably, Mary Lou Williams's Bel Canto Thrift Shop failed as a sustainable business. However, the overwhelmingly negative assessments of her work on this project from the late 1950s through the 1960s deals insufficiently with the worth of her daily labor to run her shop, to manage her finances, and to aspire to realize a support system for musicians in need and, thereby, forge a new sense of community between jazz artists and broader societies. Biographer Dahl's sources for analysis of the foundation effort and management of the thrift shop did not include the musicians who were recipients of Williams's charity. The primary voices are those who financed Williams's initial mission efforts (ultimately at a loss) and those who sought to refocus her attention on composing and performing new jazz music. Williams, ever the meticulous record-keeper, maintained many of the documents related to her foundation efforts that reveal moments of promise, setback, progress, and failure. These documents also provide a record of several musicians who experienced Williams's charity, regardless of the foundation's ultimate fate.

To probe the worth of establishing and maintaining the Bel Canto Foundation for Williams, the professional jazz musician, convert, and African American woman, is to explore the persistent diligence of an entrepreneurial (and Catholic) newcomer whose primary musical profession likely prevented established social service organizations, prospective financiers, and Catholic authorities from taking her efforts seriously enough to robustly support her mission. This effort to establish the Bel Canto Foundation represented tensions for Williams the musician. There was the fundamental tension in managing her professional output (traveling to perform and produce new music) versus managing her Bel Canto Foundation's daily affairs (the local operation of her thrift shop and maintaining correspondences with potential donors). However, there was another tension for Williams the *successful* African American jazz artist. While she was a newcomer to the Roman Catholic faith, having been baptized and confirmed on 9 May 1957 following several years of religious exploration, she was anything but a novice in her musical profession. Williams was an adult who charted a path to prominence within one jazz community, confident in her ability to manage a substantial project like this foundation because she had secured revenue for herself through the ongoing retrieval and management of her composition copyrights. Consequently, she strived to become more than a regular parishioner in her new Catholic community. She attracted the friendship of many Catholic priests and enjoyed retreats with religious Catholic women, like the Cenacle Sisters Convent in Lancaster, Massachusetts [48]. These were relationships where Williams sought conversation and prayer partners about matters mundane, grave, and lighthearted; yet she also actively sought the Catholic hierarchy's legitimization of the moral work she began prior to her formal conversion, partially through the Church's financial investment in her entrepreneurial efforts. The Catholic authorities she befriended, however, were fans of Williams the prominent jazz artist, not necessarily Williams the charitable organization executive. They encouraged her to put her full energies into developing her music (in particular, developing her concept of "sacred jazz") rather than treading into unfamiliar professional territory.

By 1966, Mary Lou Williams was no longer involved in the daily management of her Bel Canto Thrift Shop. Williams strived to provide musicians their own contemplative, creative space through her daily labor to realize her foundation by managing her thrift shop and seeking various fundraising strategies. And some of those musicians made daily journeys into her Catholic community through mass attendance, priestly consultations, and correspondences with Williams herself. For Williams, the labor of her thrift shop activity served an interstitial purpose—between a sense of divine calling without a specific religious home, and her explicitly Catholic practices and production of sacred jazz.

Duke Ellington embraced the authority to speak about God that listening audiences afforded him, and he sought to do so publicly so that Protestants, Jews, and Catholics would accept his musical messages. However, Ellington's private reflections in hotels reveal that the composer never used specifically Protestant, Jewish, or Catholic language to speak of his God. For many other jazz musicians in need, Mary Lou Williams served as the financial and communal intermediary between personal (and emotional) destitution and professional stability. She sought to create a new social institution with a new understanding of her divine calling. However, Williams's pursuit of reviving jazz creativity to forge "good" jazz music did not require making new Catholics. For scholars of American religion, engaging the archives of these two African American jazz musicians reveals complex individual religious identities, expressions, and practices that allow us to view women and men attempting to define precisely their religious roles and affiliations as well as articulating belief in their personal and professional lives.

Acknowledgments: I am grateful to Judith Weisenfeld, Wallace Best, Jessica Delgado, Clifton Granby, Kijan Bloomfield, Irene Elizabeth Stroud, and the Religion in the Americas and Religion and Culture workshops at Princeton University for their feedback on earlier papers that became this publication. Additionally, I am grateful to Tad Hershorn and Joe Peterson of the Institute of Jazz Studies, and to Wendy Shay and Joe Hursey of the National Museum of American History Archives Center at the Smithsonian, for their research assistance in locating archival materials for this publication.

Conflicts of Interest: The author declares no conflict of interest.

References

1. While concerns about the cultural and moral worth of jazz lingered for black Christian clergy over the next few decades, the music came to represent an idealized set of democratic and expressive possibilities in the Cold War era and functioned as a reflection on the progressive strides of civil rights activism. This evolution in perception accompanied innovations and developments in music and performance, where jazz enjoyed a smaller audience no longer interested in big band dance music and more invested in the music as a listening, intellectual artistic experience that small instrumental combos created. Fans and professional critics signified jazz musicians as artistic virtuosos, America's international cultural ambassadors, and representatives of an elite African American culture capable of capturing, through music, the sounds, moods, and political desires of a people. For more, see Penny M. Von Eschen. *Satchmo Blows Up the World: Jazz Ambassadors Play the Cold War*. Cambridge: Harvard University Press, 2004.

2. For jazz scholar Holly Farrington, racial representation is evident in the jazz profession because of the production of more than forty jazz autobiographies between 1936 and 1996. Duke Ellington's 1973 autobiography, *Music Is My Mistress*, revealed that the musician was "always on stage" when performing, and "his racial identity forced him to become a representative, linking public perception of African Americans irretrievably to the individual achievement of celebrities and artists such as himself." See Holly E. Farrington. "Narrating the Jazz Life: Three Approaches to Jazz Autobiography." *Popular Music and Society* 29 (2006): 375–86. [CrossRef]

3. In the history of civil rights legal activism, according to historian Kenneth Mack, race representation refers to "those who claimed to speak for, stand in for, and advocate for the interests of the larger group." Since the nineteenth century, for African Americans to call for a "representative colored man" or "representative Negro" has involved a tension between an atypical member of the race in terms of her or his accomplishments and an "authentic" member of the race who was "as much like the masses of black people as possible." The representative colored men, "...the lucky few who had attained enough education and training to become doctors, dentists, schoolteachers, ministers, and lawyers," were to serve as the best cases for full and equal African American citizenship. See Kenneth W. Mack. *Representing the Race: The Creation of the Civil Rights Lawyer*. Cambridge: Harvard University Press, 2012, pp. 4, 5, 20. Popular black jazz professionals became de facto race representatives because of their coverage in the black and white press, due to their inter/national travel and publicity, and because of the emergence of music criticism.

4. Edward Kennedy Ellington, and Mercer Ellington. *Music Is My Mistress*. Garden City: Doubleday, 1973.

5. For further analysis of Ellington's racial and religious themes in his popular compositions, see Vaughn Booker. "'An Authentic Record of My Race': Exploring the Popular Narratives of African American Religion in the Music of Duke Ellington." *Religion and American Culture: A Journal of Interpretation* 25 (2015): 1–36. [CrossRef]

6. "Rough Copy," p. 2, Series 5: Performances and Programs, 1963–1989, Box 5, Folder 4 (Duke Ellington's Festival of Religion and the Arts, 1966), Ruth Ellington Collection, Archives Center, National Museum of American History.

7. "The Baltimore Hilton, Baltimore, MD," Series 5: Personal Correspondence and Notes, 1941–1974, Box 6, Folder 1 (Notes, undated), Duke Ellington Collection, Archives Center, National Museum of American History.

8. "Obituary—Raymond Walter Johnson." *The Seattle Times*, 2010. Available online: http://www.legacy.com/obituaries/seattletimes/obituary.aspx?pid=146007696 (accessed on 10 October 2014).

9. "Destined For Greatness," (Seattle, WA: Life Messengers, date unknown), Series 14: Religious Material, 1928–1974, Box 2, Folder 2, Duke Ellington Collection, Archives Center, National Museum of American History.

10. "Jacksonville Hilton, Jacksonville, FL," Series 5: Personal Correspondence and Notes, 1941–1974, Box 6, Folder 1 (Notes, undated), Duke Ellington Collection, Archives Center, National Museum of American History.

11. "Downtowner/Rowntowner Motor Inns, location unknown," Series 5: Personal Correspondence and Notes, 1941–1974, Box 6, Folder 1 (Notes, undated), Duke Ellington Collection, Archives Center, National Museum of American History.

12. "Hotel Washington, Washington, DC," Series 5: Personal Correspondence and Notes, 1941–1974, Box 6, Folder 1 (Notes, undated), Duke Ellington Collection, Archives Center, National Museum of American History.

13. Duke Ellington with Erich Kunzel and the Cincinnati Symphony Orchestra. "Poetic Commentary 'A'," *Orchestral Works,* © 1989, 1970 by MCA Records, Inc., MCAD-42318, Compact disc.

14. "Ramada Inn Roadside Hotel, San Antonio, TX," Series 5: Personal Correspondence and Notes, 1941–1974, Box 6, Folder 1 (Notes, undated), Duke Ellington Collection, Archives Center, National Museum of American History.

15. "Ramada Inn Roadside Hotel, Greensboro, NC," and "The Baltimore Hilton, Baltimore, M.D.," Series 5: Personal Correspondence and Notes, 1941–1974, Box 6, Folder 1 (Notes, undated), Duke Ellington Collection, Archives Center, National Museum of American History.

16. "Ilikai Wakiki, Honolulu, HI," Series 5: Personal Correspondence and Notes, 1941–1974, Box 6, Folder 1 (Notes, undated), Duke Ellington Collection, Archives Center, National Museum of American History.

17. Harvey G. Cohen. *Duke Ellington's America.* Chicago: University of Chicago Press, 2010.

18. Edward Kennedy Ellington. *Duke Ellington's My People.* © 1992, 1963 by Legacy Recordings, AK-52759, Compact disc. The line "Snatched Jonah, yes He did, from the belly of the whale" contains the masculine pronoun to refer to God. However, Ellington's manuscript lyrics for this song do not include "yes He did," appearing instead as "Snatched Jona/From the belly of the whale." This indicates McPhail's original improvisation of the line. Nevertheless, this inclusion of exclamatory speech acknowledges the importance of this way of testifying about God in African American Protestantism. This composition existed prior to his composition of the Sacred Concerts, and it is the only instance of the use of "He" in Ellington's original Sacred Concert lyrics. See "My People by Duke Ellington—Ain't But The One," p. 5, Series 5: Handwritten Notes, Etc., Queenie Pie, Box 8, Folder 12, Duke Ellington Collection, Archives Center, National Museum of American History.

19. Edward Kennedy Ellington. "Supreme Being," *Second Sacred Concert,* © 1990, 1968 by Prestige Records, PCD 24045-2, Compact disc.

20. Wilbert Hill writes that "Tell Me It's the Truth" is an example of Ellington incorporating characteristics of 1950s and 1960s gospel music in his First Sacred Concert, namely, "...use of the tambourine, triple meter, a simple harmonic progression, call and response, and idiomatic orchestration of the gospel style accompaniment part supporting the melody sung by a contralto." See Wilbert Weldon Hill. "The Sacred Concerts of Edward Kennedy 'Duke' Ellington." Ph.D. Dissertation, The Catholic University of America, 1995. p. 76.

21. "The Shamrock Hilton, Houston, TX," Series 5: Personal Correspondence and Notes, 1941–1974, Box 6, Folder 1 (Notes, undated), Duke Ellington Collection, Archives Center, National Museum of American History.

22. "Jazz Goes to Fifth Avenue Church." *Christianity Today* 10 (1966): 42.

23. "A Statement from Duke Ellington," Series 5: Performances and Programs, 1963–1989, Box 5, Folder 4 (Duke Ellington's Festival of Religion and the Arts, 1966), Ruth Ellington Collection, Archives Center, National Museum of American History.

24. "Has the Black American Musician Lost His Creativeness and Heritage in Jazz?" p. 1, 4, Series 5: Personal Papers, ca. 1970–1971, Box 2, Folder 25, Mary Lou Williams Collection, Institute of Jazz Studies, Rutgers University.

25. Lowell D. Holmes, and John W. Thomson. *Jazz Greats: Getting Better with Age.* New York: Holmes & Meier Publishers, Inc., 1986.

26. Smithsonian Institution Interviews with Jazz Musicians: Williams, Mary Lou, Jazz Oral History Project 117.5.5, Transcript, Institute of Jazz Studies, Rutgers University. After she stopped performing at Café Society, Williams regarded her apartment as "...a headquarters for young musicians." She stated, "I'd even leave the door open for them if I was out. Tadd Dameron would come to write, when he was out of inspiration, and Monk did several of his pieces there. Bud Powell's brother, Richie, who also played piano, learned how to improvise at my house. And everybody came or called for advice. Charlie Parker would ask what did I think about him putting a group with strings together, or Miles Davis would ask about his group with the tuba—the one that had John Lewis and Gerry Mulligan and Max Roach and J. J. Johnson in it. It was still like the thirties—musicians helped each other, and didn't just think of themselves."

27. Whitney Balliett. "Profiles: Out Here Again." *The New Yorker*, 2 May 1964.
28. Tammy L. Kernodle. *Soul on Soul: The Life and Music of Mary Lou Williams*. Boston: Northeastern University Press, 2004.
29. Linda Dahl. *Morning Glory: A Biography of Mary Lou Williams*. New York: Pantheon Books, 1999.
30. "Certificate of Incorporation of Bel Canto Foundation, Inc., Pursuant to the Membership Corporation Law," p. 1, Series 4: Business Papers, Subseries 4L: Bel Canto, ca. 1950–1971, 1977, undated, Box 67, Folder "Bel Canto, Certificate of Incorporation, New York, New York, 1958," Mary Lou Williams Collection, Institute of Jazz Studies, Rutgers University.
31. "Bel Canto Account—Disbursement and Receipts," Series 4: Business Papers, Subseries 4L: Bel Canto, ca. 1950–1971, 1977, undated, Box 47, Folder 6 (Benefit Activities [Concert, Rummage Sale, etc.]), Mary Lou Williams Collection, Institute of Jazz Studies, Rutgers University.
32. "Letter to Mary Lou Williams from Dave Brubeck, September 23, 1958," Series 4: Business Papers, Subseries 4L: Bel Canto, ca. 1950–1971, 1977, undated, Box 47, Folder 6 (Benefit Activities [Concert, Rummage Sale, etc.]), Mary Lou Williams Collection, Institute of Jazz Studies, Rutgers University.
33. "Bell Telephone Company—Deposits," Series 4: Business Papers, Subseries 4L: Bel Canto, ca. 1950–1971, 1977, undated, Box 47, Folder 6 (Benefit Activities [Concert, Rummage Sale, etc.]), Mary Lou Williams Collection, Institute of Jazz Studies, Rutgers University.
34. "Letter from Herbert J. Bliss to Mr. Henry Zaccardi, American Federation of Musicians, September 10, 1958," and "Letter from Henry Zaccardi to Herbert J. Bliss, September 16, 1958," Series 4: Business Correspondence, Subseries 4I: Legal Affairs, 1941–1980, undated, Box 41, Folder 2 (Bliss, Herbert J., 1958), Mary Lou Williams Collection, Institute of Jazz Studies, Rutgers University.
35. "Bell Telephone Company—'Loot to Boot' Paid Out," Series 4: Business Papers, Subseries 4L: Bel Canto, ca. 1950–1971, 1977, undated, Box 47, Folder 6 (Benefit Activities [Concert, Rummage Sale, etc.]), Mary Lou Williams Collection, Institute of Jazz Studies, Rutgers University. Williams wrote checks for advertisements in the New York Times, the New York Amsterdam News, and for poster and banner advertisements. The Carnegie Hall booking cost $1,740.38, while other miscellaneous costs like parking tickets, supplies, and car rental added to her total. Additionally, Williams' bank statement lists the total cost as $3,210.42, $1 lower than the accurate total.
36. "Rummage Sale—at 318 East 29 St" and "Rummage Sale! 310 East 29th Street," Series 4: Business Papers, Subseries 4L: Bel Canto, ca. 1950–1971, 1977, undated, Box 47, Folder 6 (Benefit Activities [Concert, Rummage Sale, etc.]), Mary Lou Williams Collection, Institute of Jazz Studies, Rutgers University.
37. "Bel Canto Expenses," Series 4: Business Papers, Subseries 4L: Bel Canto, ca. 1950–1971, 1977, undated, Box 47, Folder 8 (Bound Notebook, New York, New York, 1959–1960), Mary Lou Williams Collection, Institute of Jazz Studies, Rutgers University.
38. "Bel Canto Foundation Expenses...1960," pp. 1, 2, and "Summary," Series 4: Business Papers, Subseries 4L: Bel Canto, ca. 1950–1971, 1977, undated, Box 48, Folder 5–8 (Financial Records—Expenditures, Inventory, Transactions, New York, 1958–1971, undated), Mary Lou Williams Collection, Institute of Jazz Studies, Rutgers University.
39. "Form CR-131, 'Annual Report—Charitable Organizations,'" Series 4: Business Papers, Subseries 4L: Bel Canto, ca. 1950–1971, 1977, undated, Box 49, Folder 4 (Licenses, Leases, Insurance, State and Local Documents, 1959–1961), Mary Lou Williams Collection, Institute of Jazz Studies, Rutgers University.
40. "Form M-537g, 'Financial Report'," Series 4: Business Papers, Subseries 4L: Bel Canto, ca. 1950–1971, 1977, undated, Box 48, Folder 5–8 (Financial Records—Expenditures, Inventory, Transactions, New York, 1958–1971, undated), Mary Lou Williams Collection, Institute of Jazz Studies, Rutgers University.
41. "Checkbooks and Balance Registers, 1962–1964," Series 4: Business Papers, Subseries 4M: Banking, Box 50, Mary Lou Williams Collection, Institute of Jazz Studies, Rutgers University.
42. "Mary Lou Williams (Income Tax)," p. 1, Series 4: Business Papers, Box 62, Folder "Taxes-Federal Income Taxes, 1965," Mary Lou Williams Collection, Institute of Jazz Studies, Rutgers University.
43. Between 1965 and 1966, Eustis Guillemet updated Williams on his decision to leave New York City, in addition to his occasional requests for financial support for music equipment and rent. While staying at a YMCA in Atlantic City, NJ, Guillemet informed Williams of the changing social climate: "...[T]here might be more marches and sit ins this summer. The whites live on one side[,] the colored on the other. Most of the youngsters are participating in either marches or sit ins. So say some extra prayers that God will show His

justice and graces in bettering conditions of both people if it be His Holy Will and salvation of the Souls involved." On his regular Catholic practices, Guillemet conveyed to Williams his dedication in moments of personal frustration: "Good talking to you and very good reading from ya. I was uptight at the time and at a very low point. Not that I didn't know what to do, I just couldn't get together but I did as I talked to a priest and he told [me] that sometimes God permits stress and strain to show us how weak we are and upon asking His Graces, He lets us know that we are still dependent on Him...One day I got a good look at the people I've been around and it frightened me. I hope I wasn't looking at myself. If I was I have a long way to go and a lot of work to do. Anyway I went to New York and sat with the Blessed Sacrament and a day later I got myself together. I guess I was away too long. The Sacrament isn't exposed too often here and there aren't too many Catholics, active that is. But like you said[,] pray and keep your mind on the music. That I will do with all determination because every time I look the other way I start getting in trouble." See "Letter from Eustis Guillemet to Mary Lou Williams, February 5, 1965," "Letter from Eustis Guillemet to Mary Lou Williams, May 30, 1966," and "Letter from Eustis Guillemet to Mary Lou Williams, 22 June 1966," Series 3: Personal Correspondence, Subseries 3B: Correspondence with Friends, ca. 1925–1952, 1958–1981, Box 8, Folder 11 (Eustis Guillemet, 1965–1973, undated), Mary Lou Williams Collection, Institute of Jazz Studies, Rutgers University.

44. "Mary Lou Williams (Income Tax)," p. 3, Series 4: Business Papers, Box 62: Folder Taxes-Federal Income Taxes, 1965, Mary Lou Williams Collection, Institute of Jazz Studies, Rutgers University.
45. "The Detroit Hilton, Detroit, MI," Series 5: Personal Correspondence and Notes, 1941–1974, Box 6, Folder 1 (Notes, undated), Duke Ellington Collection, Archives Center, National Museum of American History.
46. Ellington received much of his religious literature as gifts from clerical fans. His collection of religious literature reveals that a profession of religious commitment in twentieth-century America does not seal the individual off from the reality of competing religious commitments, which may even appear as the well-intentioned proselytizing of others who admire a popular jazz musician and wished for him to join their particular fellowship. Nevertheless, Ellington received these gifts as clergy encouraging him to create sacred music "not as a matter of career, but in response to a growing understanding of my own vocation." See "A Statement from Duke Ellington," Series 5: Performances and Programs, 1963–1989, Box 5, Folder 4 (Duke Ellington's Festival of Religion and the Arts, 1966), Ruth Ellington Collection, Archives Center, National Museum of American History.
47. Douglas Martin. "Ruth Ellington Boatwright, 88, the Sister of Duke Ellington." *The New York Times*, 11 March 2004. Available online: http://www.nytimes.com/2004/03/11/arts/ruth-ellington-boatwright-88-the-sister-of-duke-ellington.html (accessed on 31 October 2014).
48. See Series 3: Personal Correspondence, Subseries 3D: Correspondence with Religious, Box 20, Folder 14 (Sister Martha Morris: Correspondence, 1967), Mary Lou Williams Collection, Institute of Jazz Studies, Rutgers University.

religions

MDPI

Article

Abraham Joshua Heschel and *Nostra Aetate*: Shaping the Catholic Reconsideration of Judaism during Vatican II

Joshua Furnal

Faculty of Philosophy, Theology, and Religious Studies, Radboud University,
Erasmusplein 1, 6525 HT Nijmegen, The Netherlands; j.furnal@ftr.ru.nl

Academic Editors: Douglas James Davies and Michael J. Thate
Received: 6 March 2016; Accepted: 30 May 2016; Published: 8 June 2016

Abstract: Although *Nostra Aetate* is only comprised of five short paragraphs, this document represents a turning point, not just for Catholic-Jewish relations, but also sketches the fundamental aims of embodying the Christian faith in a pluralistic age. There is a complex but important narrative that needs to be revisited so that we do not forget the ways in which Catholic learning has developed, and how this development has often been prompted by non-Catholics. In this article, I will re-examine some crucial details in the back-story of the formulation of *Nostra Aetate* and offer some observations about the potential consequences of omitting these details. My argument is that some recent events and scholarship suffer from a form of amnesia about the role that Jewish people have played in the development of Catholic learning—a form of amnesia that manifests in explicit proselytizing tendencies. In particular, I want to highlight the role that Rabbi Abraham Joshua Heschel played during the Second Vatican Council as an instructive example for Catholic-Jewish dialogue today.

Keywords: Abraham Joshua Heshel; *Nostra Aetate*; Vatican II; Judaism; Pope Francis; inter-faith dialogue

On the 50th anniversary of the Second Vatican Council, it is important not to forget about one of the Council's shortest but most significant declarations about the Church's relationship to other faiths. In the recent past, one could think that the shared spiritual patrimony of Christians and Jews highlighted in *Nostra Aetate* (1965) has been forgotten entirely.[1] In 2008, Pope Emeritus Benedict XVI reintroduced the Tridentine prayer for Good Friday, which says "illumine [Jewish] hearts, so that they will recognize Jesus Christ, the Savior of all men".[2] In 2009, the US Bishops issued a statement saying that "the whole people of Israel" will be included into the Church. In the same year, Benedict XVI brought Richard Williamson (a Holocaust denying bishop) back into fold, who was later excommunicated this year by Pope Francis. It would seem that despite all the recent Catholic-Jewish engagement, the legacy and teaching of *Nostra Aetate* is still haunted by forgetfulness.

Although *Nostra Aetate* is only comprised of five short paragraphs, this document represents a turning point not just for Catholic-Jewish relations, but also sketches new ways of articulating the relationship between Christians and non-Christians. There is a complex but important story that needs to be revisited so that we do not forget the ways in which Catholic learning has developed, and how this development has often been prompted by non-Catholics. In this short essay, I will re-examine

---

[1] "Nostra Aetate." Available online: http://www.vatican.va/archive/hist_councils/ii_vatican_council/documents/vat-ii_decl_19651028_nostra-aetate_en.html (accessed on 3 June 2016) [1].

[2] Pope Benedict XVI rewrote this prayer and inserted it into the pre-Vatican II Tridentine Mass text. It was placed under the heading "pro conversio iudaeorum", which is still very problematic. For more, see [2] John T. Pawlikowski. "Defining Catholic Identity against the Jews: Pope Benedict XVI and the Question of Mission to the Jewish People." In *Trialogue and Terror: Judaism, Christianity, and Islam after 9/11*. Edited by Alan L. Berger. Eugene: Cascade Books, 2012, chap. 7.

some crucial details in the back-story of the formulation of *Nostra Aetate* and offer some observations about the potential consequences of omitting these details. My argument is that some recent events and scholarship suffer from a form of amnesia about the role that Jewish people have played in the development of Catholic learning—a form of amnesia that manifests in explicit proselytizing tendencies. In particular, I want to highlight the role that Rabbi Abraham Joshua Heschel played during the Second Vatican Council as an instructive example for Jewish-Catholic dialogue today. Prior to the Second Vatican Council, Abraham Heschel had a long history of collaboration between Jews and Catholics and other Christians in France, Central Europe, Great Britain and the United States. It was not something that Heschel decided to begin once the Council was underway. Therefore, the inter-continental and inter-faith story behind the formation of its sentences is dramatic and, for Catholics especially, worth remembering—especially in light of recent reforms by Pope Francis.[3]

1. The Contested Legacy of *Nostra Aetate*

Indirectly set in motion by Pope John XXIII, *Nostra Aetate* was the first official document that recognized the search for meaning, holiness, and truth among the various religions of the world.[4] From a Jewish perspective, *Nostra Aetate* was seen as revolutionary because it repudiated the centuries-long oppression of Jewish people by Church Councils.[5] In fact, this document was the first time that anti-Semitism was condemned by a Council, and the Jewish people were acknowledged uniquely as God's chosen people. Today, this may seem like an uncontroversial declaration. Yet, as John Connelly has shown, a re-examination of the history of the Roman Catholic Church during this era reveals that this position was hardly uncontroversial.[6] After establishing the "Kingdom of Christ" heralded in *Quas Primas* (1925) by signing the Lateran Treaty with Mussolini in 1929, no mention is made of the Jews or a disavowal of anti-Semitism in Pope Pius XI's encyclical *Non abbiamo bisogno* (1931) [9]:

> In everything that We have said up to the present, We have not said that We wished to condemn the [Fascist] party as such. Our aim has been to point out and to condemn all those things in the programme and in the activities of the party which have been found to be contrary to Catholic doctrine and Catholic practice, and therefore irreconcilable with the Catholic name and profession. And in doing this We have fulfilled a precise duty of Our episcopal ministry towards Our dear sons who are members of the party, so that their conscience may be at peace ([1931], n. 62).[7]

Yet after signing the concordat with Hitler, Pius XI says in *Mit brennender Sorge* (1937) [10] that:

> Whoever exalts race, or the people, or the State, or a particular form of State, or the depositories of power, or any other fundamental value of the human community—however

3   For more on Heschel's interfaith relations after World War II and his influence on Pope Francis, see [3–5]. Harold Kasimow. *Interfaith Activism: Abraham Joshua Heschel and Religious Diversity*. Eugene: Wipf and Stock, 2015, esp. chap. 8. See also, Harold Kasimow, and Byron L. Sherwin, eds. *No Religion Is an Island: Abraham Joshua Heschel and Interreligious Dialogue*. Maryknoll: Orbis, 1991. Also see, Michael Signer's essay "Body and Soul: Interreligious Dialogue" in *Abraham Joshua Heschel: Philosophy, Theology and Interreligious Dialogue*. Edited by Stanislaw Krajewski and Adam Lipszyc. Wiesbaden: Harrassowitz, 2009, pp. 181–87.

4   Although Pope John XXIII did not request that a document be created, he did establish the Secretariat for Promoting Christian Unity and appointed Cardinal Augustin Bea to be president a few days before the meeting with Jules Isaac. The pope asked Isaac to discuss his memorandum with Bea. Only later was it decided that Bea would facilitate reflection on the relations between the Church and the Jewish people in the Council. It was out of this process that a document would be developed. For more on the relation between the AJC, Bea, and Heschel, see [6] Reuven Kimelman. "Rabbis Joseph B. Soloveitchik and Abraham Joshua Heschel on Jewish-Christian Relations." *Modern Judaism* 24 (2004): 251–71.

5   Consider the anti-Jewish legislation in the Councils of Vannes, Epaone, Orleans, Lateran IV, and Florence discussed and defended at length in [7] Gavin D'Costa. *Vatican II: Catholic Doctrines on Jews and Muslims*. Oxford: Oxford University Press, 2014, chap. 3.

6   For more see [8] John Connelly. *From Enemy to Brother: The Revolution in Catholic Teaching on the Jews (1933–1965)*. Cambridge: Harvard University Press, 2012.

7   "Non abbiamo bisogno." Available online: http://w2.vatican.va/content/pius-xi/en/encyclicals/documents/hf_p-xi_enc_29061931_non-abbiamo-bisogno.html (accessed on 3 June 2016) [9].

necessary and honorable be their function in worldly things—whoever raises these notions above their standard value and divinizes them to an idolatrous level, distorts and perverts an order of the world planned and created by God; he is far from the true faith in God and from the concept of life which that faith upholds ([1937], n. 8).[8]

Nevertheless, prior to *Nostra Aetate*, a rejection of anti-Semitism had not been made official teaching of the Church by a Council. The extensive commentary on the formulation of *Nostra Aetate* was written by Johannes Oesterreicher (who was himself a Jewish convert to Catholicism).[9] The story that Oesterreicher tells can give the false impression that this document had always been motivated *solely* by Catholic concerns and the heroes in this story were nearly *all* eventually members of sub-committees in the Roman Curia.[10] To a certain extent, there are some Catholics that deserve honorable mention despite the effects of the tumultuous history of Catholicism during the 1930s. For instance, it is heartening to learn that when he was the Vatican diplomat to Istanbul, Giuseppe Roncalli forged baptismal documents for Jews in Turkey to escape Nazi extermination camps.[11] After the War in 1959, as Pope John XXIII, he removed the anti-Jewish language from the Good Friday liturgy (*perfidia Iudaica*). One year later, John XXIII set up the possibility for an official document on Catholic-Jewish relations to be formulated, appointing Cardinal Augustin Bea to oversee the Secretariat for Christian Unity and charging him to draft the document. Bea was a renowned Hebrew Bible scholar, the rector of the *Biblicum*, and the confessor of Pope Pius XII. However, we need to attend to Bea's efforts during this time period to break out of the Curia's insular mindset because it often involved relying upon Jewish scholars, and especially Rabbi Heschel.

By 1960, Jewish concerns had already been brought to the attention of the Pope regarding false statements about Israel, the collective guilt of the Jews, and the punishment of Jews for the crucifixion of Jesus.[12] For instance, the French historian Jules Isaac gave the Pope an extract of The Tridentine Catechism (1566) which emphasized the guilt of *all sinners* as the cause of the crucifixion of Jesus—indicating that this is the view that needs to be recovered in public discourse because the charge of *deicide* (God-killers) has been used as justification for the murder of the Jewish people.

In response to Jewish efforts, there was a consensus emerging in Rome that "the Jews" were *not* responsible for the death of Jesus, yet there was still the assertion that Christians were the true heirs of Abraham (Gal 6:16), and there remained the eschatological hope of a Jewish conversion to Christianity (Rom 11:15, 25).[13] This proselytizing position gets threaded through Oesterreicher's commentary on how the Council itself treated such issues even though there were others that altered this position in slightly different ways.[14] The competing positions emerged through four drafts of the document and a comparison of them reveals how the Council Fathers went back-and-forth on this issue. The explicit proselytizing tendencies of the early draft of *Nostra Aetate* is often overlooked, especially since

---

8 "Mit brennender Sorge." Available online: http://w2.vatican.va/content/pius-xi/en/encyclicals/documents/hf_p-xi_enc_14031937_mit-brennender-sorge.html (accessed on 3 June 2016) [10].

9 [11] John Oesterreicher. "Declaration on the Relationship of the Church to Non-Christian Religions." *Commentary on the Documents of Vatican II* 3 (1967): 1–136.

10 Although Oesterreicher focuses on the hierarchy and other Roman Catholic clergy members in his *Commentary*, he does briefly mention the contribution of Jews and Protestants. However, he does not give them the proper attention that they deserve.

11 [12] Massimo Faggioli. *John XXIII: Medicine of Mercy*. Collegeville: Liturgical Press, 2014, chap. 4.

12 (Oesterreicher 1967: 2).

13 This is the position presented on 24 April 1960 in a petition signed by the Jesuit professors at the *Biblicum* to urge the Council to address "the problem of the people of Israel" when the Council addresses ecumenical matters (Oesterreicher 1967: 8–9) [11].

14 For instance in 1961, Gregory Baum presents a revision at a meeting in Ariccia Italy on 6–9 February. Baum inserts a rejection of anti-Semitism and the view that sees Jews as an accursed race (Oesterreicher 1967: 18) [11].

it contradicts the final draft of *Nostra Aetate*.[15] What can account for this shift away from an emphasis upon proselytizing Jewish people in an attempt convert them to Christianity?

In his recent book on Vatican II, Gavin D'Costa neglects this shift altogether and claims that *Nostra Aetate* "implicitly taught that mission to the Jewish people was appropriate".[16] Much of what D'Costa reads as the summation of "Council teaching" on the destiny of world religions is a privileged reading of *Lumen Gentium* 16 and *Ad Gentes* 7, and a subordination of the canonical status of *Nostra Aetate* as a second-class Council document. For instance, D'Costa defends his claim by drawing a distinction between ethnicity and religion: according to D'Costa, the Church repudiates anti-Semitism, but promotes non-coercive mission toward Jewish people despite the fact that many subsequent post-conciliar documents firmly reject this position.[17] So this raises an important question: is this what *Nostra Aetate* explicitly teaches? *Nostra Aetate* does not even use the word "mission" in the text, instead, it encourages "mutual understanding and respect".[18] *Nostra Aetate* explicitly teaches that Jewish people are not guilty of Christ's death nor are they "rejected or accursed by God", and re-emphasizes "the spiritual patrimony" that is shared across the covenants. Then why are some Catholics theologians still encouraging the continuation of proselytizing efforts? Reading D'Costa's remarks, one might recall a fierce debate from over a decade ago about a document from the US Catholic Bishops entitled *Reflections on Covenant and Mission* and the responses to Cardinal Avery Dulles.[19] However, the question that still lingers is whether or not this entails a revocation of what *Nostra Aetate* teaches? The hope of "one accord" expressed in n. 4 leaves this task up to God, not the Church. By emphasizing the "ultimate inexpressible mystery" shared across covenants ([1965], n. 1), a different interpretation of Romans 9–11 is affirmed regarding the salvation of Israel without evoking the certainty of knowing *how* Israel will be saved.[20] It must continue to be repeated: after *Nostra Aetate*, Catholics learned that proselytism is no longer necessary or desirable for their Jewish older brothers. This is why St John Paul II said that proselytism is "an attempt to do away with one's own brother".[21] In order to provide an alternative account from D'Costa, I would like to examine briefly the back story of this shift away from proselytism in the formulation of *Nostra Aetate* and the role Rabbi Heschel had during this process.

---

[15] This tendency is discouraged in a statement issued in 2009 by the US Catholic Bishops: "Jewish covenantal life endures till the present day as a vital witness to God's saving will for His people Israel and for all of humanity" and that Catholic-Jewish dialogue "has never been and never will be used by the Catholic Church as a means of proselytism", nor is it "a disguised invitation to baptism" [13] USCCB. Statement of Principles for Catholic-Jewish Dialogue. Available online: http://www.usccb.org/beliefs-and-teachings/ecumenical-and-interreligious/jewish/upload/Statement-of-Catholic-Principles-for-Catholic-Jewish-Dialogue-2009.pdf (accessed on 17 March 2016). For more, see [14] *Never Revoked: Nostra Aetate as Ongoing Challenge for Jewish-Christian Dialogue.* Edited by Marianne Moyaert and Didier Polleyfeyt. Grand Rapids: Eerdmans, 2010.

[16] D'Costa 2014: 135. [7]

[17] *Ibid.* D'Costa himself admits that the use of the 'shoulder to shoulder" phrase from Zephaniah 3:9 "avoids any sense of proselytizing and it avoids making any decision on exegetically disputed aspects of Romans 11:25, especially the means of the Jewish [sic] coming in" (D'Costa 2014: 137) ([7], p. 137). For a response from a Jewish perspective, see [15] Edward Kessler's reply to D'Costa in *Theological Studies* 73: 3 (2012) 614–29.

[18] For more on the historical development and the different conceptions and usages of "mission", see [16] David J. Bosch. *Transforming Mission: Paradigm Shifts in Theology of Mission, American Society of Missiology Series No. 16.* Maryknoll: Orbis Books, 1991, chap. 12. See also [17] Andrew F. Walls. *The Missionary Movement in Christian History: Studies in the Transmission of Faith.* Maryknoll: Orbis Books, 1996.

[19] For more, see [18] Avery Dulles. "Covenant and Mission." *America* (21 October 2002), pp. 8–11. The article includes responses by Mary Boys, Philip Cunningham, and John T. Pawlikowski. Available online: http://americamagazine.org/issue/408/article/covenant-and-mission (accessed on 2 May 2016). For more about this debate, see the relevant essays in [19] Berger, ed. *Trialogue and Terror: Judaism, Christianity, and Islam after 9/11.*

[20] For more, see [20] Joseph Fitzmeyer's Anchor Bible commentary on *Romans.* New York: Doubleday, 1993, p. 862.

[21] Cited in Connelly 2012: 287. [8] In 1977, Tommaso Federici prepared a paper that explicitly rejected proselytism for the Committee for Catholic-Jewish relations, but this document was not adopted as official policy [21] Tommaso Federici. "Study Outline on the Mission and Witness of the Church." Available online: https://www.bc.edu/content/dam/files/research_sites/cjl/texts/cjrelations/resources/articles/Federici.htm(accessed on 17 March 2016).

2. Bringing Rabbi Heschel Back into the Story

One detail that is suppressed in D'Costa's account of the formulation of *Nostra Aetate* is the important role played by the philosopher and theologian, Rabbi Abraham Joshua Heschel (1907–1972).[22] It is necessary to appreciate the role of Rabbi Heschel, especially since some scholars, like D'Costa, have reduced the contribution that Heschel made during this time merely to providing Catholics with feedback about how Jewish people felt.[23] Yet, without Rabbi Heschel it is doubtful that *Nostra Aetate* would have taken the shape that it did. After Heschel's rightful protest, the final version of *Nostra Aetate* did not include the earlier proselytizing remarks regarding the conversion of the Jewish people as the Christian hope.

In August 1961, Cardinal Bea set up his first commission to identify the relevant dogmatic, moral, and liturgical principles to make concrete proposals toward the formulation of *Nostra Aetate*. By November, Bea was already in conversation with Rabbi Heschel because Heschel had supplied Bea with a draft of what should be involved regarding any Catholic declaration on Jewish people—namely, a condemnation of any accusation of Jews killing God (*deicide*), and to drop all references to Jewish people joining the Church. For Heschel, the problem was not that Judaism was incompatible with Christianity, but rather that the proselytizing claims of the Church were at odds with the integrity of the shared spiritual heritage of Judaism and Christianity. This fact in the timeline is often neglected. For instance, in his commentary on *Nostra Aetate*, Oesterreicher explicitly says that the American Jewish Committee and Abraham Joshua Heschel in particular, "deserve mention, even though [political initiatives] took place at a later stage, and had no influence to speak of on the discussion of the Council Declaration or the form of its text".[24]

Oesterreicher's report is misleading because as a representative of the American Jewish Committee, Heschel was already in conversation with Bea since 1961.[25] Indeed, Rabbi Heschel was a close friend of Cardinal Bea and Willebrands, and scholars have documented Heschel's influence leading up to the final form of *Nostra Aetate*.[26] This took shape in May 1962, when Rabbi Heschel sent a Memorandum to Cardinal Bea outlining the proposed agenda for a meeting with specific proposals for improving the cause for reconciliation between Jews and Catholics:

(1)   a full condemnation of anti-Semitism, and any teachings that hold Jews responsible for *deicide* as sinful.

(2)   a full recognition of holiness and faithfulness to the Torah be accorded to Judaism as a distinct feature of Jewish identity that should be preserved and celebrated today.

(3)   to maximize efforts to mutually enhance religious literacy among Christians and Jews, through public discussions, research projects, and publications.

(4)   that a high-level commission be put together at the Vatican regarding Christian-Jewish relations.

In his official commentary, Oesterreicher reproduces Heschel's "demands" from the May 1962 memo in a footnote, but provides no comment on the contribution of this external, "secular", and

---

[22]   D'Costa 2014: 88–89, 132, 135. [7] I am indebted to several conversations with Susannah Heschel for this observation. Abraham Heschel also played a significant role in the anti-war and Civil Rights movements. Martin Luther King, Jr. referred to Heschel as "my rabbi" and there are iconic photos of them marching "shoulder to shoulder" on Selma.

[23]   D'Costa 2014: 89. [7]

[24]   Oesterreicher 1967: 16. [11]

[25]   Oesterreicher 1967: 16 n. 20. [11] Oesterreicher refers to the AJC memo on the image of the Jew in Catholic teaching (June 1961), the memo on anti-Jewish elements in Catholic liturgy (November 1961), and "the memorandum of the rabbi and seminary professor Abraham Joshua Heschel" (May 1962). These documents have been made available online in the [22] American Jewish Committee Archives: http://ajcarchives.org/ajcarchive/DigitalArchive.aspx (accessed on 2 May 2016).

[26]   For more, see the detailed account in [23] Edward Kaplan. *Spiritual Radical*. New Haven: Yale, 2007, chaps. 13–14. Kaplan's account follows closely that of [24] Marc Tanenbaum. "Jewish-Christian Relations: Heschel and Vatican Council II." 21 February 1983. Available online: http://www.ajcarchives.org/AJC_DATA/Files/Z582.CV01.pdf (accessed on 17 March 2016). See also, [25] Gary Spruch. *Wide Horizons: Abraham Joshua Heschel, AJC, and the Spirit of Nostra Aetate*. New York: American Jewish Committee, 2008.

Jewish element in the formulation of *Nostra Aetate*.[27] Heschel's influence is reflected implicitly in the way Oesterreicher reports that despite Cardinal Bea's attempts to keep this wording in the council document, it was eventually dropped in the final draft.[28]

Between 28–31 August 1960, a group of scholars gathered in Apeldoorn that was comprised of Anton Ramselaar (*Katholieke Raad voor Israel*), Karl Thieme (*Freiburger Rundbrief*), Paul Demann (*Cahiers Sioniens*), Jean Roger (*Oeuvre de St. Jacques*), and Oesterreicher (*The Bridge*). For Oesterreicher's narrative, it was this group that "formed the prophetic element that over the years prepared a place in the Church, intellectually and spiritually, emotionally and theologically, for the Council Declaration of which they too as yet knew nothing" ([10], p. 12). Later, Oesterreicher presents himself as offering an important position paper in Ariccia on 6–21 April 1961 that refocuses the discussion upon the exegetical insights of Romans 9–11. It is at this point in the story that Oesterreicher begins to insert himself into the plot as an implicit representative of the Church's eschatological aims.[29]

The buffered Vatican mindset during this time is repeated in Oesterreicher's commentary, which creates a narrative that stresses the *theological* nature of Council deliberations so as to downplay any *political* maneuvers behind the scenes. The stated reason for this apolitical strategy was to deflect any negative interpretations by Arab governments of a perceived Vatican endorsement of the State of Israel and its political agenda.[30] However, Cardinal Bea was in conversation with important Jewish voices during this time. For instance, Bea flew to New York to meet privately with Rabbi Heschel at the American Jewish Committee on 31 March 1963 to discuss with Heschel and some others "the basic issues of Jewish concern" regarding Vatican II. In advance of the meeting on 7 March, Heschel had sent to Bea a revised version of his memo from the year before. One notable difference in this version was how Heschel drew to the Cardinal's attention the need to condemn 'sins against charity"—that is, "attributing the worst possible motive" to the intentions of any human being based upon 'superficial evidence [and] generalizations".[31] The timing of this private meeting between Bea and Heschel was crucial because the issues needed to be addressed before 8 September 1963 when the council reconvened. The meeting was meant to last 90 minutes. It was reported to have lasted three hours.

Bea returned to Rome with a new draft of the Council document—significantly influenced by the issues that Heschel brought to his attention. But by 1964, Heschel's memo had been heavily redacted and the penultimate draft had removed the condemnation of proselytism, which was leaked to the New York Times and Herald Tribune (12 June 1964). Because of the controversy surrounding this document, all things looked like this document would be thrown out of the Council process altogether. So Heschel went to the press and he made headlines in *Time Magazine* (11 September 1964) where he is quoted as saying "As I have repeatedly stated to leading personalities of the Vatican, I am ready to go to Auschwitz any time, if faced with the alternative of conversion or death". It has been said that after Heschel met with Pope Paul VI, the Pope crossed out the line of text with his own pen.[32]

---

[27] Oesterreicher 1967: 17 n. 20. [9]
[28] See [26] John M. Oesterreicher. *The New Encounter: Between Christians and Jews*. New York: Philosophical Library, 1986, pp. 188–92.
[29] Oesterreicher 1967: 20–21. [9]
[30] Oesterreicher 1967: 18–19. D'Costa repeats Oesterreicher's narrative in this regard, see, D'Costa 2014: 88–89; chap. 3. For Arab responses to the "apolitical" stance of the Council, see [27] Meir Litvak, and Esther Webman. *From Empathy to Denial: Arab Responses to the Holocaust*. New York: Columbia University Press, 2009, chap. 4. Also see, [28] James L. Fredericks, and Tracy Sayuki Tiemeier, eds. *Interreligious Friendship after Nostra Aetate, Interreligious Studies in Theory and Practice*. New York: Palgrave Macmillan, 2015.
[31] Page 2 of the proposed agenda attached to Rabbi Heschel's private correspondence dated 25 March 1963 to Rabbi Albert Minda.
[32] [29] Doris Donnelly. "Lovingly Observant: an interview with Susannah Heschel." Available online: http://americamagazine.org/issue/618/article/lovingly-observant (accessed on 17 March 2016).

3. Fifty Years on with Pope Francis

This essay began with the problem of forgetting the legacy and teaching of *Nostra Aetate* and the undesirable consequence of proselytism toward Judaism as evidenced by the perspective that continues to resurface with some Catholic theologians like D'Costa. I briefly reviewed the back-story of the document's formulation to reveal how Jewish thinkers like Rabbi Heschel played a key role in the development of Catholic teaching. For St Paul it is to the Jewish people that "belong the adoption, the glory, the covenants, the giving of the Law, the worship, and the promises" (Rom 9:4). After Heschel's contribution, Oesterreicher later revised his argument that the eschatological hope described in Romans 9–11 for unity between Israel and the Church should not be interpreted as a covert endorsement of proselytism (a "mission to the Jews"), but rather "expresses simply and solely the belief that at the end of time, God will gather into union with Himself all who profess His name" ([25], p. 193). It is interesting that D'Costa aligns himself with the earlier proselytizing views of Oesterreicher before *Nostra Aetate*, but does not acknowledge Oesterreicher's later abandonment of a mission to Jewish people, as presented by John Connelly.[33]

Still today we might ask ourselves whether or not this legacy has been forgotten altogether, or whether it is still under development. The reigning narrative surrounding the production of *Nostra Aetate* is often placed solely upon Catholics as the unilateral source. For instance, Massimo Faggioli claims that "The story of *Nostra Aetate* is a story of leadership in the Church. It was only indirectly a fruit of a collective process of reflection on the relations between Jews and Christians".[34] Yet in his article, it is only in closing that Faggioli mentions anything about Abraham Heschel.

The ambiguity between forgetting a tradition and a development of it resurfaced during Pope Francis" recent visit to the USA. In September 2015, Pope Francis gave a speech that could be read as an attempt to develop the legacy and teaching of *Nostra Aetate*.[35] In his speech, Pope Francis reminded us that

> the religious dimension is not a private sub-culture. It is part of the culture of any people and any nation. Our various religious traditions serve society primarily by the message they proclaim. They call individuals and communities to worship God, the source of all life, liberty, and happiness. They remind us of the transcendent dimension of human existence and our irreducible freedom in the face of every claim to any absolute power ... Our rich religious traditions seek to offer meaning and direction, "they have an enduring power to open new horizons, to stimulate thought, to expand the mind and heart" (*Evangelii Gaudium* [33], 256). They call to conversion, reconciliation, concern for the future of society, self-sacrifice in the service of the common good, and compassion for those in need. At the heart of their spiritual mission is the proclamation of the truth and dignity of the human person and human rights.

Speaking from Abraham Lincoln's lectern when he gave the Gettysburg address, the Pope develops a central theme from *Nostra Aetate* when he highlighted the goal that all religions share in making it "clear that it is possible to build a society where "a healthy pluralism which respects

---

[33] For more, see [30] John Connelly. "The Catholic Church and Mission to the Jews" In *After Vatican II: Trajectories and Hermeneutics*. Edited by James Heft. Grand Rapids: Eerdmans, 2013, pp. 126–27.

[34] [31] Massimo Faggioli. Nostra Aetate after Fifty Years. Available online: http://www.abc.net.au/religion/articles/2015/10/30/4342407.htm (accessed on 17 March 2016). In this article, Faggioli asks some important ecclesiological questions in light of *Nostra Aetate* and indicates a few positive developments that grew out of it, but largely leaves Rabbi Heschel out of the picture until closing paragraph.

[35] Pope Francis, Religious Freedom speech at Independence Hall (26 September 2015). ZENIT Staff. [32] Pope's Address in Philadelphia on Religious Freedom. Available online: http://www.zenit.org/en/articles/pope-s-address-in-philadelphia-on-religious-freedom (accessed on 17 March 2016). Although it should be stated that these recent speeches by Pope Francis should be read within a broader context, not only *Evangelium Gaudium*, but also all of the documents of the Second Vatican Council, such as *Nostra Aetate*, *Gaudium et Spes*, *Lumen Gentium*, and *Dignitatis Humanae*.

differences and values them as such"" (*Evangelii Gaudium* [33], 255). In this specific context, Pope Francis was referring to the need to welcome immigrants and their gifts as one important way to renew and enrich society. And yet, when he describes the 'spiritual mission" and "the call to conversion", he still employs terms that have a very specific connotation to certain audiences—despite his re-directing the meaning of these terms towards the betterment of society and proclaiming the truth, dignity, and fundamental rights of the human person.

However, if we hear Pope Francis in terms of developing *Nostra Aetate*, we might appreciate the way he draws upon the declaration's assertion that "the Church rejects nothing that is good and holy in those religions" as evidence for the wider religious experience of non-Christians. Likewise, the recognition that non-Catholics can "reflect a ray of that truth which enlightens us all" also points to a knowledge received out of religious kinship. This reinforces an observation made by St Augustine, "No one becomes known except through friendship"[36] and highlights the need to understand the role of religious proclamation in society as that of "becoming known as friends", not proselytism. In this way, we can enrich our own respective traditions through inter-religious dialogue and friendship.

In October 2015, Pope Francis commemorated the 50th anniversary of *Nostra Aetate* by holding an inter-religious audience in Saint Peter's Square, which coincided with an International Congress at the Pontifical Gregorian University where Cardinal Bea once taught. Cardinal Kurt Koch described this commemoration as "an important contribution to further reflection on that "culture of encounter" between persons, peoples and religions that you have very much at heart". Reflecting upon the achievements of *Nostra Aetate* ([1965], n. 4), Cardinal Koch reiterated that

> In the light of this communion that exists between Jews and Christians in the history of salvation, the Council makes evident the Jewish roots of the Christian faith and acknowledges the great "common spiritual patrimony" to Christians and to Jews. Moreover, the Council deplores all hatred and manifestations of violence against the Jewish people, also by Christians, and condemns all forms of anti-Semitism.[37]

Those who know the back-story of Rabbi Heschel's involvement can appreciate how the Cardinal placed these two points in a prominent light. Cardinal Koch went on to illuminate another point—which had been raised by Heschel—but attributes it to the witness of Pope Francis: "In our days, at a time in which unfortunately new waves of anti-Semitism have arisen, you, Holy Father, remind us Christians incessantly that it is impossible to be a Christian and an anti-Semite at the same time". In his own comments, Pope Francis highlighted the various points that *Nostra Aetate* had addressed and said that in our time

> Indifference and opposition have changed into collaboration and benevolence. From enemies and strangers we have become friends and brothers. The Council traced the way with the "Nostra Aetate" Declaration: "yes" to the rediscovery of the Jewish roots of Christianity; "no" to every form of anti-Semitism and condemnation of all insults, discrimination and persecutions that stem from it. Mutual knowledge, respect and esteem constitute the way that, if it is true in a particular way for the relation with the Jews, is also equally true for relations with the other religions [Zenit 2016] [35].

Pope Francis went on to call for mutually "open and respectful" inter-religious dialogue that worked to enhance the "respect of others' right to life, of their physical integrity, of the fundamental liberties, namely liberty of conscience, of thought, of expression and of religion". Concluding, Pope Francis invited all the representatives of the various religions present to pray for one another in

---

[36] [34] Augustine. *De diversis quaestionibus*. 71.5; Augustine. *Eighty-Three Different Questions*. vol. 70, *The Fathers of the Church*. Washington: Catholic University of America Press, 2002, p. 183.

[37] [35] ZENIT Staff. General Audience: On 50 years since *Nostra Aetate*. Available online: http://www.zenit.org/en/articles/general-audience-on-50-years-since-nostra-aetate (accessed on 17 March 2016).

silence reminding them that together the religions can become an important impetus for achieving the common good in society:

Dialogue based on trustful respect can bring seeds of good that in turn become shoots of friendship and collaboration in so many fields, especially in service to the poor, to the little ones, to the elderly, in the reception of migrants, in the care of those that are excluded. We can walk together taking care of one another and of Creation—all believers of all religions. Together we can praise the Creator for having given us the garden of the world to cultivate and protect as a common good, and we can undertake shared projects to fight poverty and ensure to every man and woman fitting conditions of life.

In December 2015, reflecting upon his trip to Africa, Pope Francis gave another general audience that built upon the message he presented during the 50th anniversary of *Nostra Aetate*. Speaking to a group of young people, Pope Francis reiterated the words of his namesake, St Francis of Assisi: the missionary spirit is not proselytizing" but rather that "witness is the great heroic missionary spirit of the Church. Proclaim Jesus Christ with your life!" Pope Francis described the missionary as the one who brings "love, humanity, and faith to other countries. Not to proselytize, no. That is done by those who are seeking something else. Faith is preached first by witness and then through words. Slowly".[38]

4. Concluding Remarks

In light of recent developments pertaining to the 50th anniversary of *Nostra Aetate* and Pope Francis" call for more dialogue between traditions in terms of friendship, it is remarkable that the Commission for Religious Relations issued a document in December 2015 entitled, "The Gifts and Calling of God are Irrevocable".[39] An in-depth analysis of this document about the status of Catholic-Jewish dialogue lies beyond the scope of this essay, but its existence is unthinkable without the legacy of Abraham Heschel.[40] Although the Commission's recent document does not carry magisterial status juridically, the theological reflection it contains upon *Nostra Aetate* does carry juridical weight as reflection upon a Council document. On the other hand, it took about one month for Pope Francis to begin using phrases from this document on his visit to the synagogue in Rome.[41]

The Commission's document recognizes the special status of Catholic-Jewish dialogue on the basis of the Jewish roots of Christianity and the indivisibility of the Word of God and thus "the enduring role of the covenant people of Israel in God's plan of salvation" ([37], n. 43)—despite differing theological interpretations in each tradition. Chapter six is significant especially because it affirms both the Church's responsibility to bear witness to their faith in Christ, but also that the Church repudiates any proselytism, conversion, and mission toward the Jews. The document explicitly says that "the Catholic Church neither conducts nor supports any specific institutional mission work directed towards Jews" ([37], n. 40).

---

[38]   [36] Pope Francis. "General Audience." 2 December 2015. Available online: http://w2.vatican.va/content/francesco/en/audiences/2015/documents/papa-francesco_20151202_udienza-generale.html (accessed on 17 March 2016).

[39]   [37] Commission for Religious Relations with the Jews. The Gifts and the Calling of God are Irrevocable (Rom 11:29). Available online: http://www.vatican.va/roman_curia/pontifical_councils/chrstuni/relations-jews-docs/rc_pc_chrstuni_doc_20151210_ebraismo-nostra-aetate_en.html#6._The_Church\T1\textquoterights_mandate_to_evangelize_in_relation_to_Judaism (accessed on 17 March 2016).

[40]   For more on post-Vatican II developments in Catholic-Jewish relations, see relevant essays in [38] Gilbert S. Rosenthal, ed. *A Jubilee for All Time: The Copernican Revolution in Jewish-Christian Relations*. Eugene: Wipf and Stock, 2014. See also, [39] Michael S. Kogan. *Opening the Covenant: A Jewish Theology of Christianity*. Oxford: Oxford University Press, 2008, chap. 7.

[41]   [40] Vatican Radio. Pope Francis calls on Catholics and Jews to work together for peace. Available online: http://www.news.va/en/news/pope-francis-calls-on-catholics-and-jews-to-work-t (accessed on 17 March 2016). Pope Francis said that "the Declaration *Nostra Aetate*, has indicated the way: "yes" to rediscovering Christianity's Jewish roots; "no" to every form of anti-Semitism and blame for every wrong, discrimination and persecution deriving from it." *Nostra Aetate* explicitly defined theologically for the first time the Catholic Church's relations with Judaism. Of course it did not solve all the theological issues that affect us, but we it provided an important stimulus for further necessary reflections. In this regard, on 10 December 2015, the Commission for Religious Relations with the Jews published a new document that addresses theological issues that have emerged in recent decades since the promulgation of *"Nostra Aetate"*.

The title of the Commission's document is theologically significant because it refers to the integral role that both Judaism and Christianity have currently in the mystery of salvation history. The document defines the goal of dialogue in terms of bringing humanitarian aid together as a blessing to the world that grows out of fraternal dialogue, mutual respect and learning, whilst seeking reconciliation and promoting justice and peace on earth by opposing anti-Semitism ([37], nn. 46–49). The document also calls for Catholic educational institutions and seminaries to integrate into their curricula not only *Nostra Aetate*, but also all subsequent documents regarding the implementation of this conciliar declaration ([37], n. 45). Responding to the Commission's document, Jewish theologian Edward Kessler said

> As a result of a soul change, epitomised by *Nostra Aetate*, the Roman Catholic Church shifted from what was, for the most part, a need to condemn Judaism to one of a condemnation of anti-Judaism. This led not to a separation from all things Jewish but in fact, to a closer relationship with "the elder brother". The new document, which I welcome and commend, reminds Christians of this sibling relationship as it sets out a theological agenda for future discussions.[42]

It is no coincidence that the document issued recently by the Commission maps on directly to the concerns raised by Rabbi Heschel's 1962 memo to Cardinal Bea. In the first part of this essay, I emphasized—against the grain of recent scholarship—how important Rabbi Abraham Joshua Heschel was for the reconsideration of Judaism during the Second Vatican Council and the formulation of *Nostra Aetate*. It is in this particular moment in history that we see Rabbi Heschel explicitly endorsing and bringing about a reform within Catholic theology rooted in the shared prophetic tradition.

In the second part of this essay, I highlighted some recent shifts in Roman Catholic discourse with the papacy of Pope Francis and contextualized these remarks in light of Rabbi Heschel's legacy. Space does not permit to clarify further the links between the story of Heschel's contribution and ongoing development of the directions set in *Nostra Aetate*. However, this could be explored using the theme of "personal encounter" since Rabbi Heschel made such a significant contribution partly through the friendships he had established with Catholics, like Cardinal Bea himself. As we have seen, Pope Francis has recently renewed this emphasis on the role of friendship and personal encounter as central to interfaith and interreligious relations. In this way, this renewed emphasis on friendship and personal encounter underscored by the present pope firms up the link between the back story of Rabbi Heschel's contribution and the ongoing development of *Nostra Aetate*.

As in the past, it would be tempting for Catholic scholars to place the responsibility of this more enlightened form of religious pluralism squarely upon the shoulders of the Pope. But I have suggested that at important junctures in history, it has been non-Catholics that have re-oriented their perspective when it comes to Judaism, and it is only very recently that this is being recognized at the highest levels in Rome. One could think that by endorsing religious pluralism, this might also elicit a further disengagement among the different religions with the world. But the legacy of Abraham Heschel stands as an important testimony to the contrary; because without Heschel's prophetic voice, it would be very difficult to imagine the existence of *Nostra Aetate* and the positive subsequent developments that we are witnessing today. This is something that should not continue to be forgotten by contemporary Catholic scholars writing about the achievements of the Second Vatican Council.[43]

Conflicts of Interest: The author declares no conflict of interest.

---

[42]   [41] Edward Kessler. "Reflections from a European Jewish Theologian." Available online: http://www.ccjr.us/dialogika-resources/documents-and-statements/analysis/crrj-2015dec10/1366-kessler-2015dec10 (accessed on 17 March 2016). For more, see the recent address by [42] Pope Francis to the International Council of Christians and Jews in June 2015. Available online: http://www.ccjr.us/dialogika-resources/documents-and-statements/roman-catholic/francis/1337-address-to-the-international-council-of-christians-and-jews (accessed on 30 May 2016).

[43]   I am grateful for the helpful comments provided by two anonymous reviewers.

References

1. "Nostra Aetate." Available online: http://www.vatican.va/archive/hist_councils/ii_vatican_council/documents/vat-ii_decl_19651028_nostra-aetate_en.html (accessed on 3 June 2016).
2. John T. Pawlikowski. "Defining Catholic Identity against the Jews: Pope Benedict XVI and the Question of Mission to the Jewish People." In *Trialogue and Terror: Judaism, Christianity, and Islam after 9/11*. Edited by Alan L. Berger. Eugene: Cascade Books, 2012, chap. 7.
3. Harold Kasimow. *Interfaith Activism: Abraham Joshua Heschel and Religious Diversity*. Eugene: Wipf and Stock, 2015, esp. chap. 8.
4. Harold Kasimow, and Byron L. Sherwin, eds. *No Religion Is an Island: Abraham Joshua Heschel and Interreligious Dialogue*. Maryknoll: Orbis, 1991.
5. Michael Signer's essay "Body and Soul: Interreligious Dialogue." In *Abraham Joshua Heschel: Philosophy, Theology and Interreligious Dialogue*. Edited by Stanislaw Krajewski and Adam Lipszyc. Wiesbaden: Harrassowitz, 2009, pp. 181–87.
6. Reuven Kimelman. "Rabbis Joseph B. Soloveitchik and Abraham Joshua Heschel on Jewish-Christian Relations." *Modern Judaism* 24 (2004): 251–71. [CrossRef]
7. Gavin D'Costa. *Vatican II: Catholic Doctrines on Jews and Muslims*. Oxford: Oxford University Press, 2014.
8. John Connelly. *From Enemy to Brother: The Revolution in Catholic Teaching on the Jews (1933–1965)*. Cambridge: Harvard University Press, 2012.
9. "Non abbiamo bisogno." Available online: http://w2.vatican.va/content/pius-xi/en/encyclicals/documents/hf_p-xi_enc_29061931_non-abbiamo-bisogno.html (accessed on 3 June 2016).
10. "Mit brennender Sorge." Available online: http://w2.vatican.va/content/pius-xi/en/encyclicals/documents/hf_p-xi_enc_14031937_mit-brennender-sorge.html (accessed on 3 June 2016).
11. John Oesterreicher. "Declaration on the Relationship of the Church to Non-Christian Religions." *Commentary on the Documents of Vatican II* 3 (1967): 1–136.
12. Massimo Faggioli. *John XXIII: Medicine of Mercy*. Collegeville: Liturgical Press, 2014, chap. 4.
13. USCCB. "Statement of Principles for Catholic-Jewish Dialogue." Available online: http://www.usccb.org/beliefs-and-teachings/ecumenical-and-interreligious/jewish/upload/Statement-of-Catholic-Principles-for-Catholic-Jewish-Dialogue-2009.pdf (accessed on 17 March 2016).
14. *Never Revoked: Nostra Aetate as Ongoing Challenge for Jewish-Christian Dialogue*. Edited by Marianne Moyaert and Didier Polleyfeyt. Grand Rapids: Eerdmans, 2010.
15. Edward Kessler's reply to D'Costa in *Theological Studies* 73 (2012): 614–29.
16. David J. Bosch. *Transforming Mission: Paradigm Shifts in Theology of Mission, American Society of Missiology Series No. 16*. Maryknoll: Orbis Books, 1991, chap. 12.
17. Andrew F. Walls. *The Missionary Movement in Christian History: Studies in the Transmission of Faith*. Maryknoll: Orbis Books, 1996.
18. Avery Dulles. "Covenant and Mission." *America*, 21 October 2002, pp. 8–11.
19. *Trialogue and Terror: Judaism, Christianity, and Islam after 9/11*. Edited by Alan L. Berger. Eugene: Cascade Books, 2012.
20. Joseph Fitzmeyer. *Romans*. New York: Doubleday, 1993.
21. Tommaso Federici. "Study Outline on the Mission and Witness of the Church." Available online: https://www.bc.edu/content/dam/files/research_sites/cjl/texts/cjrelations/resources/articles/Federici.htm (accessed on 17 March 2016).
22. "American Jewish Committee Archives." Available online: http://ajcarchives.org/ajcarchive/DigitalArchive.aspx (accessed on 2 May 2016).
23. Edward Kaplan. *Spiritual Radical*. New Haven: Yale, 2007.
24. Marc Tanenbaum. "Jewish-Christian Relations: Heschel and Vatican Council II." 21 February 1983. Available online: http://www.ajcarchives.org/AJC_DATA/Files/Z582.CV01.pdf (accessed on 17 March 2016).
25. Gary Spruch. *Wide Horizons: Abraham Joshua Heschel, AJC, and the Spirit of Nostra Aetate*. New York: American Jewish Committee, 2008.
26. John M. Oesterreicher. *The New Encounter: Between Christians and Jews*. New York: Philosophical Library, 1986.
27. Meir Litvak, and Esther Webman. *From Empathy to Denial: Arab Responses to the Holocaust*. New York: Columbia University Press, 2009.

28. James L. Fredericks, and Tracy Sayuki Tiemeier, eds. *Interreligious Friendship after Nostra Aetate, Interreligious Studies in Theory and Practice*. New York: Palgrave Macmillan, 2015.

29. Doris Donnelly. "Lovingly Observant: an interview with Susannah Heschel." Available online: http://americamagazine.org/issue/618/article/lovingly-observant (accessed on 17 March 2016).

30. John Connelly. "The Catholic Church and Mission to the Jews." In *After Vatican II: Trajectories and Hermeneutics*. Edited by James Heft. Grand Rapids: Eerdmans, 2013.

31. Massimo Faggioli. "*Nostra Aetate* after Fifty Years." Available online: http://www.abc.net.au/religion/articles/2015/10/30/4342407.htm (accessed on 17 March 2016).

32. ZENIT Staff. "Pope's Address in Philadelphia on Religious Freedom." Available online: http://www.zenit.org/en/articles/pope-s-address-in-philadelphia-on-religious-freedom (accessed on 17 March 2016).

33. "Evangelii Gaudium." Available online: http://w2.vatican.va/content/francesco/en/apost_exhortations/documents/papa-francesco_esortazione-ap_20131124_evangelii-gaudium.html (accessed on 3 June 2016).

34. Augustine. "*De diversis quaestionibus*. 71.5; Augustine. *Eighty-Three Different Questions*. vol. 70." In *The Fathers of the Church*. Washington: Catholic University of America Press, 2002, p. 183.

35. ZENIT Staff. "General Audience: On 50 years since *Nostra Aetate*." Available online: http://www.zenit.org/en/articles/general-audience-on-50-years-since-nostra-aetate (accessed on 17 March 2016).

36. Pope Francis. "General Audience." 2 December 2015. Available online: http://w2.vatican.va/content/francesco/en/audiences/2015/documents/papa-francesco_20151202_udienza-generale.html (accessed on 17 March 2016).

37. Commission for Religious Relations with the Jews. "The Gifts and the Calling of God are Irrevocable (Rom 11:29)." Available online: http://www.vatican.va/roman_curia/pontifical_councils/chrstuni/relations-jews-docs/rc_pc_chrstuni_doc_20151210_ebraismo-nostra-aetate_en.html#6._The_Church\T1\textquoterights_mandate_to_evangelize_in_relation_to_Judaism (accessed on 17 March 2016).

38. Gilbert S. Rosenthal, ed. *A Jubilee for All Time: The Copernican Revolution in Jewish-Christian Relations*. Eugene: Wipf and Stock, 2014.

39. Michael S. Kogan. *Opening the Covenant: A Jewish Theology of Christianity*. Oxford: Oxford University Press, 2008, chap. 7.

40. Vatican Radio. "Pope Francis calls on Catholics and Jews to work together for peace." Available online: http://www.news.va/en/news/pope-francis-calls-on-catholics-and-jews-to-work-t (accessed on 17 March 2016).

41. Edward Kessler. "Reflections from a European Jewish Theologian." Available online: http://www.ccjr.us/dialogika-resources/documents-and-statements/analysis/crrj-2015dec10/1366-kessler-2015dec10 (accessed on 17 March 2016).

42. Pope Francis. "Address to the International Council of Christians and Jews." Available online: http://www.ccjr.us/dialogika-resources/documents-and-statements/roman-catholic/francis/1337-address-to-the-international-council-of-christians-and-jews (accessed on 30 May 2016).

![religions logo] *religions*

MDPI

Article

'It's Not the Money but the Love of Money That Is the Root of All Evil': Social Subjection, Machinic Enslavement and the Limits of Anglican Social Theology

Marika Rose

CODEC Research Centre for Digital Theology, Durham University, St John's College, 3 South Bailey, Durham DH1 4NP, UK; marika.rose@durham.ac.uk

Academic Editors: Douglas James Davies and Michael J. Thate
Received: 18 March 2016; Accepted: 5 August 2016; Published: 9 August 2016

Abstract: Maurizio Lazzarato argues that contemporary capitalism functions through two central apparatuses: Social subjection and machinic enslavement. Social subjection equips individuals with a subjectivity, assigning them identities, sexes, bodies, professions, and other markers of identity, along with a sense of their own individual agency within society. Machinic enslavement arises out of the growing reliance of capitalism on what Lazzarato calls "asignifying semiotics"—processes of production that function increasingly independently of human awareness or intention. Drawing on this analysis of the contemporary functioning of capitalism, this paper will explore the concepts of individuals and society at work in recent Anglican social theology. Focusing on two recent texts which attempt to give an overview of Anglican social thinking—Eve Poole's *The Church on Capitalism: Theology and the Market* and Malcolm Brown's *Anglican Social Theology*—it will suggest that, within the contemporary Church of England, mainstream attempts to reckon with political questions tend to understand the role of individual agency and ethical behaviour in ways which prop up existing social, political and economic structures rather than disrupting them.

Keywords: Lazzarato; Anglicanism; Church of England; social theology; capitalism; posthumanism; ethics; politics

1. Introduction

Christianity in the West was deeply involved with the emergence of the Enlightenment figure of the individual, as well as the industrialised capitalist society with which it came into being. The emergence of modernity meant both a new focus on the sovereign individual—modelled, in fact, on the God of classical Christian theology—and also the privatisation of religion, which for Christianity as an institution meant the multiplication of denominations and churches and their increasing relegation to the level of intermediate, voluntary associations.[1] Churches took their place alongside the key intermediary institutions of the emergent democratic states of the West—schools, prisons, hospitals—and were often deeply involved in the emergence, management and reform of these institutions. The processes of the globalization and automation of late capitalist economies, however, marks a crucial shift in the social role and function of the individual, as reflected in the growing body

---

[1] Despite its formal role as the established church, for example, discussions of the social theology of the Church of England in *Anglican Social Theology* repeatedly position the church as an "intermediary" organisation, bridging the gap between the individual and the state ([1], pp. 60, 73, 141).

of work which comes under the umbrella of "posthumanism".[2] The Enlightenment figure of the sovereign individual was always a myth, but in the face of burgeoning ecological catastrophe, the rise of big data and the multiple crises of liberal democracy in the face of the demands of 'the market' its grasp on reality seems increasingly tenuous; our individual lives more complexly entangled in globalized networks of cause and effect than ever before.

This article will explore the changing role of Christianity in the construction of the Western individual, focusing on the one hand on recent accounts of Christianity, the individual and the political within the Church of England; and, on the other hand, on the work of Maurizio Lazzarato, whose work brings together an account of the changing role of the Western individual within a post-Fordist and increasingly automated economy and an account of the role of Christianity in the formation of the individual subject within Western society.

Christianity has always been multiple; and that multiplicity has been exacerbated by the post-Reformation privatisation of religion in the West, which saw a loosening of the connections between churches and states and a multiplication of religious movements and organisations. It has functioned both as an ideological support to the existing order of things and also as a source of political resistance, whether by simply clinging to an older state of things being undermined by capitalism's constant self-transformation or by offering resources for a more radical challenge to the existing order.[3]

It is not then possible, if it ever was, to give an account of *the* role of Christianity in forming Western society's understanding of the relationship of individual and society. What I aim to do here is, instead, to offer a more limited examination of a specific question: how is one Christian institution—the Church of England—responding theologically to the changing role and function of both individuals and institutions within late capitalism? What might this tell us about the ongoing role of Christian institutions in forming, sustaining and disrupting the social order in the contemporary Christian West?

Even this relatively narrow focus leaves us with an institution whose thinking on issues of politics and society is, despite—or perhaps precisely because of—its relatively formal relationship to state power in the UK, more "plural, fluid, contested and unofficial" than that of comparative bodies of thought, such as Catholic Social Teaching ([4], p. 134). Alongside the statements of the General Synod are the numerous more-or-less official statements of the Archbishop of Canterbury, the Archbishop of York, the House of Bishops, the numerous reports of various Church of England bodies and the individual writings of important Anglican thinkers. Here I will focus particularly on two books which seek to wrestle from the contested multiplicity of documents, voices and opinions which make up the Church of England something like a systematic account of Anglican social theology: Eve Poole's *The Church on Capitalism: Theology and the Market* [5] and Martin Brown's edited volume *Anglican Social Theology* [1]. Both of these texts were, importantly, published after the global financial crisis of 2007/8,

---

2   "Posthumanism" covers a range of attempts to move beyond Enlightenment notions of the sovereign individual in order to recognize the complex dependencies and interrelations with other humans, animals, plants, objects, technologies and social orders which constitute human life. While some posthumanist thinkers focus on undermining the myth of the sovereign individual by exposing the ways in which this figure was always dependent on complex networks of relationships with human and non-human beings, others have focused on exploring the specific ways in which the collapse of the myth of the Enlightenment individual is related to technologically-enabled changes in the functioning of power in contemporary Western society. Lazzarato's work belongs within this part of the posthuman turn, alongside thinkers such as Gilles Deleuze, who argues that late capitalism represents a transition from the "disciplinary societies" described by Michel Foucault (in which individuals were formed in enclosed environments such as schools, hospitals and prisons) to "societies of control" which divide not only between but within individuals, blurring the boundaries between formerly distinct social bodies so that "we no longer find ourselves dealing with the mass/individual pair. Individuals have become *"dividuals"* and masses, samples, data, markets, or *"banks"*." ([2], p. 5).

3   For example, see Domenico Losurdo's discussion of the role of Christianity in the simultaneous emergence of liberalism and racial chattel slavery [3]. While many Christians and churches were deeply invested both ideologically and financially in the economy of slavery, Christianity was also the source of resistance to slavery. On the one hand, this resistance emerged conservatively out of the churches' role as part of the ancien régime, which was threatened by the emergence of the new merchant and slave-owning classes ([3], p. 34). But on the other hand, the missionary work of Methodists and Baptists amongst slaves in Jamaica took a more radical turn, as it "furnished them with a culture, consciousness and the possibility of meeting and communicating that clashed irreconcilably with the de-humanization and commodification of human livestock upon which the institution of slavery was based ([3], p. 158).

which they take to mark an opportunity for re-negotiating the relationship between church, society, and the market.[4]

The Church of England is not a monolith; nor is it the only available form of Christianity at work in England today, let alone the world. As an established church, it seems unlikely that it is here that the most radical or disruptive possibilities of Christianity will find expression. This exploration, then, is partial and particular. Yet it begins to examine some questions with global resonance: If Christianity is, in fact, the "special religion of capital", then what happens to Christianities when capitalism itself undergoes radical transformation? [6]. If capitalism is itself best understood as a mutation of Christianity, replacing the divine economy with a money economy,[5] what happens to those institutions which continue to insist on the worship of the God of Christianity, and to grapple with the biblical assertion that "you cannot serve God and mammon"? What is, as Alberto Toscano puts it, "the connection between "the religion of everyday life" (the forms of actual abstraction, belief and fetishism that populate "secular" capitalism) and the institutions and subjectivities thrown up by religions in their specific and contested historical and political existence"? [9].

2. Maurizio Lazzarato: Social Subjection and Machinic Enslavement

In this essay, I will bring the work of Maurizio Lazzarato to bear on these questions. A contemporary European theorist, Lazzarato's work brings together an emphasis on the Christian origins of contemporary capitalism with an attention to the ways in which late capitalism—and the digital technologies which reflect and enable it—disrupts and unsettles existing constructions of the individual and society. It is worth noting at the outset that Lazzarato's work tends to be uncritically Eurocentric. His examples of contemporary work, subjectivity and social organisation are taken overwhelmingly from Western countries. He pays little attention to the persistence not only of earlier forms of capitalist organisation, such as Fordist manufacturing elsewhere in the world, but also of non-capitalist models of production, such as subsistence farming.[6] He tends to ignore the importance of social formation and political struggle in these global contexts, and tends to treat them simply as former stages of capitalism's development, now superseded, rather than as ongoing components of the global political economy.

Lazzarato offers us then, at best, a partial account of the contemporary transformations of the relationship between individual and society under late capitalism. Yet in the context of a largely post-industrial West, deeply shaped by the complex interplay of Christianity and capitalism, Lazzarato's work raises interesting and important questions concerning the ongoing role of Christianity in structuring the relationship between individuals and society. As such, I want to suggest that his work offers valuable tools for taking up the task which Alberto Toscano sets out for critical social theory: to "come to grips with the present 're-enchantment of catastrophic modernity'...to link capitalism as religion with religions in capitalism" [9].

Here, I will focus on the central arguments of Lazzarato's books *The Making of the Indebted Man: Essay on the Neoliberal Condition* [12] and *Signs and Machines: Capitalism and the Production of Subjectivity* [13]. In the former, Lazzarato argues that debt is at the heart of the functioning of the contemporary economy; that debt relies on the social production of individual virtue; that, in the West, Christianity has enabled the development of a society in which ethics and economy are entangled with one another; and that one of the functions of debt in late capitalism is to undermine the sovereignty of nation-states. In the latter, he argues that contemporary capitalism is characterised on the one hand

---

4   While Poole's book focuses on Anglican thinking about capitalism between the fall of the Berlin Wall in 1989 and the
    beginning of the financial crisis it locates itself in the aftermath of this crisis which, Poole argues, represents a crucial
    opportunity for the Church of England to "take its proper place in the reshaping of the global marketplace" ([5], p. 1).
5   This claim is a key element of Lazzarato's work, but is increasingly common amongst continental philosophers of religion,
    exemplarily by Philip Goodchild [7,8].
6   See, for example, the arguments of Ashok Kumar [10] and Silvia Federici [11].

by social subjection—the production of individuals who believe both in their own control over their lives and also in the value of their assigned place in society—and by machinic enslavement—the determination of society by non-human, non-conscious cybernetic processes which treat human beings not as sovereign individuals but as dividuals, a collection of functions which contribute to larger machinic assemblages.

In *The Making of the Indebted Man*, then, Lazzarato argues that the central figure of contemporary capitalism is the indebted man of the book's title. The fundamental opposition of early capitalism, between workers and the owners of the means of production, has been transformed into an opposition between debtors and creditors. This distinction is one that, like the exercise of power, which Deleuze describes in his account of the societies of control, cuts across pre-existing boundaries between employed and unemployed, consumers and producers, working and non-working populations ([12], p. 7). The demand that individuals work on themselves in order to become better employees, better citizens, has been transformed into the demand that individuals take upon themselves "the costs and risks of the economic and financial disaster...the population must take charge of everything business and the Welfare State "externalize" onto society, debt first of all" ([12], p. 9). Of particular importance here is Lazzarato's claim that debt relies on individual virtue. Drawing on Nietzsche's *Genealogy of Morality*, Lazzarato argues that "the task of a community or society has first of all been to engender a person capable of *promising*...of honouring his debt" ([12], pp. 39–40). A person capable of paying their debt is a person with memory, so that they may remember their debt, and a conscience, so that they can be guaranteed to repay it. This means that morality, virtue, ethics are necessary conditions of a debt economy. It means that, in a society which relies so utterly on the circulation of debts as ours, "'ethics' and economics function conjointly"; that economic production is inextricably bound up with the production of virtuous individuals who believe in the necessity of paying what they owe ([12], p. 11). However, Lazzarato insists, if we want to understand the functioning of the world we now inhabit, we must resist the temptation to moralise: what drives the economy is not "an excess of speculation that must be *regulated*...nor an expression of the *greed* and *rapaciousness* of "human nature" which must be rationally *mastered*. It is, rather, a power relation"; it is structural, not moral ([12], p. 24).

Lazzarato also makes a Nietzschean genealogical argument, suggesting that the particular kind of debt that individuals are asked to assume in contemporary capitalism is ultimately reliant on Christianity's affirmation of belief in an infinite God, coupled with its interiorisation of virtue. The individual self to which Christianity gives birth, infinitely indebted to an infinite God is, Lazzarato argues, the essential foundation of the infinite circulation of debt which constitutes contemporary capitalism ([12], p. 78).

Finally, in *The Indebted Man*, Lazzarato argues that the debtor-creditor relationship affects not only individuals but larger social bodies: a crucial consequence of neoliberal policies is the increasing centrality of *public* debt to the functioning of the economy. Not only individual human beings but "entire societies" therefore become indebted, which undermines the sovereignty of individual states, concentrating power into the hands of an ever-smaller group of people and depriving "the immense majority of Europeans of political power" ([12], p. 8).

In *Signs and Machines*, Lazzarato goes on to argue that contemporary capitalism is characterised by two key features: social subjection and machinic enslavement. On the one hand, as individuals we are socially assigned particular characteristics—gender, nationality, race, profession—which tell us what our place in society is and work to keep us in that place. But on the other hand, the increasing reliance of social life on digitised and automated processes means that, despite our socially constructed sense of ourselves as individuals, we are increasingly treated as Deleuzian "dividuals". We are all components of vast machinic assemblages of both human and non-human components, which run both on language and on non-linguistic processes—on "stock market indices, currency, mathematical equations, diagrams, computer languages", which are utterly indifferent to our sense of ourselves as complete individuals in control of our role and function in the world ([13], p. 39). Because they are not linguistic, they are able to "circumvent laws, conventions and institutions" ([13], p. 41): they function automatically and so contribute to a technocratic political culture in which "there is no alternative". Late capitalism works to ensure both that we are constructed as virtuous individuals, with a sense of obligation and a belief that we are in control of our destinies; and also that no individual action or intention can meaningfully control or disrupt the cybernetic circulation of capital.

While Lazzarato offers no exhaustive account of the role of religion in late capitalism (and indeed largely ignores the existence of religions other than Christianity), he does make occasional reference both to Christianity as a source of certain key ideas and ideologies and also to the importance of the churches as institutions with a social and political role. For Lazzarato, both Christianity and the churches (though Lazzarato tends to refer simply to "the church" in the singular) are aligned with capitalism and capitalist modes of subjection. The techniques of the government of the self and others on which the welfare state relies originate with the church ([13], p. 246). The threefold functioning of capital—industrial, commercial and financial—mirrors the Christian theological understanding of the Godhead, Father, Son and Holy Spirit ([12], p. 62). The infinite circulation of debt relies on the Christian theological affirmation of a God who pays our debts with an infinite gesture of self-sacrifice that can never be repaid. It is the Church which first initiates the "capitalization and expropriation" of the peasantry, the destruction of peasant culture within Europe ([13], p. 135). As neoliberalism constantly undermines the social relations on which it relies, it increasingly resorts to "pre-capitalist territories and values, to long-established morals and religions, and to the modern subjectivations of nationalism, racism and fascism which aim to maintain the social ties capitalism continually undermines" ([13], p. 9). For Lazzarato, Christianity and the Christian churches are on the side of symbolic subjection. How does this argument illuminate the social theology of the contemporary Anglican Church?

3. Anglican Social Theology

3.1. The Church of England and the Financial Crisis

In the wake of the financial crisis of 2007–2008, Christianity in the United Kingdom regained a curious prominence. Major newspapers reported on the rise of evangelical Christianity amongst the banking class [14,15]. Christian calls for a more "ethical" capitalism were widely reported [16,17], as was the new Archbishop of Canterbury's "War on Wonga" (and, subsequently, the Church of England's financial stakes in the very company they were criticising for its moral bankruptcy) [18–21]. News outlets repeatedly reported both the Anglican Church's involvement with food bank provision, and official church criticisms of the government cuts to social provision, which created the need for these food banks [22,23].

Many of these media accounts lend superficial support to some of Lazzarato's claims about the role of Christianity and its churches within late capitalism. In them, individual Christians and members of the clergy repeatedly describe the Christianity's importance in strengthening the moral attitudes which enable them to be good members of capitalist society and for shoring up their sense of self within a context of structural uncertainty. Justin Welby argued that Christians should seize the "opportunity" opened up by the welfare state for churches to step in to shore up the social bonds disintegrating as the state increasingly passed on responsibility for social security on to voluntary groups [24]. A vicar argued that in difficult times it was Christianity which gave people working in the banking industry the sense of security that the financial crisis had undermined. Several Christian individuals working in finance made an argument for the centrality of individual morality over structural factors. "'It's not the money but the love of money that is the root of all evil'", said one. Another said that, although the City itself was "amoral", he relied "on prayer to get me through the day." The journalist who interviewed these Christians concluded that "the fundamental tenets of Christianity—charity, humility, forgiveness—are a pretty good moral basis for a human life. Especially a life spent in the City of London" [15]; see also the similar themes in Reference [25].

As discussed above, in order to get a somewhat more systematic perspective on Anglican social theology, I will focus here on two books: Eve Poole's *The Church on Capitalism* and Martin Brown's *Anglican Social Theology*. Both books attempt to give something like a systematic account of the Church of England's approach to social and political issues; but both are also written by authors who are themselves involved in the debates internal to the Church of England about what its social theology *ought* to be. Poole is a frequent commentator in media pieces about the Church of England and currently works for the William Temple Foundation, a key body (as both books acknowledge) in the development of Anglican social theology. Brown works for the Archbishop's Council of the Church of England, and his book gathers together a number of individuals who are involved in various ways in shaping the contemporary thought and practice of the Church of England (with the possible exception of Anna Rowlands, whose work focuses primarily on Catholic Social Teaching). Both books attempt simultaneously to give authoritative accounts of Anglican social theology and also to actively intervene in Anglican debates about what Anglican social theology ought to be and to become; I will attempt to reflect this double positioning by treating them as both describing and enacting Anglican thinking on social and political issues.

Both books explicitly situate themselves in the wake of the financial crisis, which they see as a crucial turning point and an important opportunity. Poole argues that the aftermath of the credit crunch is a crucial opportunity for "the Church to take its proper place in the reshaping of the global marketplace, so that the resulting 'economy'...is genuinely one which benefits the whole household of God" ([5], p. 1). Brown's book is less focused than Poole's on the question of capitalism and the economy and yet, nonetheless, he states that his book "has its origins in the financial and banking crisis of 2007–2008 and in the austerity measures introduced as a result by the Coalition government of 2010", arguing that the shifting of responsibility for social welfare from the state to voluntary organisations and churches necessitates a more robust account of the church's role in providing these services ([1], p. ix).

3.2. Social Subjection and the Virtuous Individual

For Lazzarato, social subjection entails the construction of individuals who believe in their own sovereignty over their lives and yet also the importance of their assigned position within society. The ideal individual of late capitalism is a person who is virtuous—a person who has a strong moral conscience, a person who works hard, who honours their debts, who takes responsibility for their own welfare and their own choices.

Much Anglican social theology wholeheartedly endorses this vision of the individual person. The language of ethics, virtue and morality crops up repeatedly, and is often clearly focused on individual behaviour understood as "private" over more obviously social or political issues. The Church Commissioners of the Anglican church disinvested quickly from BSkyB because of the "adult content" they produce, explaining that this decision was because "this was a simple moral issue" unlike investment in "armaments...breast-milk substitutes...and human rights" ([5], p. 11).[7] Jonathan Chaplin discusses the growing importance of evangelicalism within the Anglican church, and highlights the importance of the evangelical focus on "conversionism"—that is, the religious transformation of individual believers—and its corresponding neglect of structural issues ([26], p. 109).[8]

Sometimes this emphasis on individual morality is explicitly opposed to broader political concerns about the structural functions of institutions and the global economic system. For Bishop Richard

---

[7] Poole suggests that this different response to these issues is "curious" in its "inconsistency"; yet it seems entirely consistent with a privatised understanding of Christianity and morality. Not coincidentally, Poole notes at the same time that the Commissioners are much more willing to take "ethical" stances on investment where to do so "would not destabilise the portfolio".

[8] For a detailed account of the role of this kind of evangelical understanding of individual salvation to the dismantling of systemic support in favour of "moral, pedagogical and punitive interventions into the lives of the poor" in US domestic and foreign policy, see Melinda Cooper ([27], p. 53).

Harries, for example, the church cannot expect individuals to pay attention to its exhortations to moral behaviour at work unless it affirms the basic goodness of industry and commerce: only if "the system is in principle wholesome...which is what the Churches should be saying" is there "some incentive to strive for integrity in the daily operations of buying, producing and selling" ([28], cited in [5], pp. 68–69).

Often this enthusiasm for virtue is explicitly directed at maintaining a virtuous economic subject: the demand for debt relief to African countries is made on the rounds that *"unpayable* debt" is "a contemptible immorality" (italics mine) ([5], p. 16). The General Synod of the Church of England disapproves of "companies offering 'immoral' services such as gambling"; as though late capitalism were not a system entirely reliant on the calculation and manipulation of risk ([5], p. 38; cf. [29]). After surveying the responses of the Synod to a range of issues, Poole concludes that "it is matters of personal morality that tend to attract Synod's 'theological' attention, while those of a public or corporate kind instead attract their "secular political" attention" ([5], p. 39). Moreover, Martin Brown argues, while many within the Church of England were instinctively opposed to the neoliberalising reforms of Thatcherism, it was precisely this focus on morality which rendered the Church unable to offer effective resistance. Anglicanism lacked the theological resources to oppose a programme initiated by people who "saw their political project as profoundly moral (and [even] authentically Christian" ([1], p. 8). The cumulative effect of these arguments is not to undermine but to reinforce the underlying morality of the existing order of things: work is a fundamental good as long as it respects the basic dignity of the individual ([5], pp. 6, 53, 61–65, 66, 73, 75–80; [1], p. 99); the market is virtuous as long as its principles do not replace more properly theological values [5], pp. 1, 4–5, 7, 18, 23, 29, 36, 42, 46; [5], pp. 16, 23, 31–34, 49); the church can address extortionate lending not by reinstating its ban on usury but by offering lending at reasonable rates (it is worth noting that references to usury consistently tend to use it in the sense of lending money at *extortionate* rates rather than the charging of interest on loans per se). As Devin Singh writes concerning recent campaigns for debt relief under the banner of the call for a biblically-inspired "Jubilee" (the Jubilee 2000 campaign had the official backing of the Anglican Synod), such critiques shy away from more radical political claims. They fail to acknowledge that work, markets and debt under capitalism are *inherently* exploitative and fundamentally rely on structural disparities, that (as Lazzarato argues), the problem is not *rapacious* capitalism, *greedy* capitalists or *unjust* markets but capitalism as such. In the absence of these more radical critiques, the call for more moral forms of capitalism, to moderate the "excesses" of capitalism function "as pressure release valves designed to recalibrate the economic system and allow it to persist" [30].[9]

Along these lines, it is significant that a common concern expressed by Anglican thinkers from across the political spectrum is the notion that the way that contemporary capitalism functions is by undermining the social and cultural foundations of morality, coupled with an emphasis on the importance of the church's work in shoring up this morality. Capitalism "takes for granted a moral sub-structure which it tends to undermine" ([5], p. 84);[10] it works to dissolve "traditional moralities" ([5], p. 59).[11] The selfishness decreed by the market undermines the "social cultures and virtues" which are not only good in themselves but also the "preconditions for markets to operate efficiently" ([32], p. 74; [33], p. 16). At the conclusion of her book, drawing together the ideas of the numerous Anglican bodies and individual commentators she has surveyed, Poole argues that "one remedy for the negative effect of moral freedoms...is to educate and prime the moral compass, such that it is not unduly swayed by manipulative advertising or other attempts at economic

---

[9] Much like the liberal political "Third Way", it seems, the "true message" of the much-beloved Anglican "middle way" is "simply that *there is no second way*, no actual *alternative* to global capitalism", such that it is in effect "simply *global capitalism with a human face*, that is, an attempt to minimize the human costs of the global capitalist machinery, whose functioning is left undisturbed" ([31], p. 63).

[10] In this quotation, Poole is describing the thought of R H Preston.

[11] Here Poole is describing the argument of Timothy Gorringe.

persuasion" ([5], p. 143). Anna Rowlands argues that the resurgence of popular and political interest in both Anglican and Catholic social thinking is due to the way that both appeal "to the moral imagination of a post-2007 West" ([4], p. 133). Despite recent conflicts between the Church of England and the UK Government on issues relating to the migrant crisis, Lazzarato's work would suggest that this resurgence is not unconnected to the concurrent rise of racist and nationalist sentiments, often explicitly under the banner of "defending Europe's Christian heritage" from the threat posed by Islam.

3.3. Social Subjection and the Moral Community

Another recurring theme of both *Anglican Social Theology* and *The Church on Capitalism* is the importance of recognising the individual's constitution by the community. Poole highlights a recurring emphasis on the Reformation notion of the "Orders of Creation": the divinely-instituted nature of social institutions such as "marriage and the family, the economic order, the political order, and the community of culture" ([5], p. 44). The freedom of the individual must be held in balance—it is repeatedly emphasised—with the needs of the community as a whole; and it is important to recognise that individuals are shaped not only by their own choices but by the social structures they belong to—family, economic, and cultural structures or, presumably, Lazzarato's gender, race, nationality and profession. For William Temple, arguably the founding figure of Anglican social theology, we must recognise the centrality of these social institutions to the constitution of the individual, the imperative on individuals to serve the communities—the debt we owe to others—yet without undermining the crucial emphasis on the individual's sovereign freedom, which would "remove the very foundation of legal and moral responsibility."[12]

Intermediary social institutions are a recurrent theme of Anglican social theology. Skepticism about the ability of the state to solve social problems has encouraged an emphasis on civil society associations.[13] As Rowlands discusses, this focus has shaped a number of politically influential movements in England in recent years. One example is the emergence of both Blue Labour and Red Tory movements, both of which draw explicitly on Anglican and Catholic social theology, and both of which have gained some degree of influence on party politics ([35], p. 160). Another is the focus on community organising found in the work of Luke Bretherton, which has shaped Anglican involvement with organisations such as the London Assembly. These roles played by Anglican social thinking in British politics are especially significant given the centrality of government language about the "Big Society" and the third sector to the dismantling of social welfare which has taken place in the context of austerity following the financial crisis of 2007–2008, all in the context of—as Chaplin points out—a "declared enthusiasm for the very associational instincts so deeply embedded in evangelical DNA" and, more broadly, in Anglican social theology ([27], p. 129). In the transfer of responsibility from state to individual, these community groups play a crucial role—though it is worth noting here that Anglicans have not been unanimous in their enthusiasm for the Big Society, Rowan Williams in particular having voiced concerns that it might function as "an alibi for cuts, and a way back to the Government just washing its hands" [35].

In keeping with Lazzarato's understanding of social subjection as primarily *symbolic*, relying on language rather than more affective, embodied or machinic forms of communication, it is interesting to observe that Poole notes the tendency of the Church of England's General Synod to engage politically

---

[12] Alan M. Suggate describing the thought of William Temple ([34], pp. 59–61). Neither book engages with the earlier work of Richard Hooker; it is not clear why this tradition is not seen as important for contemporary Anglican social thought.

[13] Brown argues that "a clear grasp of the limits of the state and an equally clear sense of the critical importance of a lively civil society" has characterised Anglican social theology from its inception and must continue to influence its future ([1], p. 188) Rowlands, whilst arguing that Rowan Williams is a "New William Temple" (the founder of Anglican social theology), discusses the development of his thought towards a greater emphasis on "the limits of the state in relation to the importance of civil society" ([35], p. 88); Chaplin speaks of a focus on civil society as "a vital emphasis currently being rediscovered today", and as a characteristic element of evangelicalism ([27], p. 128); Poole notes the significant amount of volunteer time and money Anglican churches and congregants invest in civil society ([5], p. 138).

via issuing written statements requesting the government to draft new legislation: perhaps, Poole suggests, "because Synod is itself a law-making body, it seems keen to use its own tools when recommending solutions" ([5], p. 31).

Finally, it is worth noting that the influence of Anglican theology on society is often mediated by the mainstream media. As I finished the first draft of this article, Justin Welby gave an interview to *PoliticsHome* about the UK's membership of the EU. In the interview, amongst many other things, Welby said both that Britain should take in more refugees from Syria and Iraq and also that "fear" over the consequences of mass migration was "justified" [36]. "Archbishop of Canterbury says it's NOT racist to fear migration", reported the *Daily Mail* [37]; "The Archbishop is right: It's not racist to worry about the migrant effect", concluded *The Telegraph* [38]; and so on and so on. Welby's original statements could arguably be taken either as a challenge or an affirmation of nationalist sentiments concerning migration, but even without Lazzarato's theoretical account of the contemporary political function of the media and civil society institutions in shoring up racist, nationalist and xenophobic notions of identity, it is difficult to be surprised by this outcome.

3.4. Machinic Enslavement

It is more difficult to grasp the ways in which Anglican social theology reflects Lazzarato's machinic enslavement, not least because one of the key points to note is that the importance of these non-symbolic, trans-national, unconscious processes is rarely, if ever, acknowledged. This is, of course, what one might expect from Lazzarato's account of contemporary capitalism as reliant precisely on the disjunction between conscious and symbolic processes of individual and social formation and the unconscious, non-symbolic functioning of economic processes.

Yet there are moments when the Church of England's own entanglement in the machinic processes that Lazzarato discusses can be glimpsed. Brown says that the post-2008 recession has "damaged the reputation of many political and economic institutions" so severely it seems likely that the damage will have permanent consequences; and yet he takes as obvious fact the necessity and inevitability of austerity ([1], pp. 5, ix).

Repeatedly the State is invoked as a force that can limit "the market", yet nowhere is there a discussion of the State's own indebtedness or the implications of this indebtedness for its decision-making processes. The Anglican position is repeatedly presented as a "middle way" between the excessive freedom of the market and the excessive control of the State, as though market and State have not historically enabled one another; it is assumed that the problem with the market is the absence of moral values rather than the complex entanglement of ethics and economics that Lazzarato draws out. Brown concludes his summary of the past, present and future of Anglican social theology by arguing for the need to "eschew on the one hand the kind of ultra-individualism that characterizes certain forms of neo-liberalism and on the other the extreme collectivism that reduces persons to mere cogs in the machine" ([1], p. 187). This places the Anglican church where it seems, on balance, to be most comfortable, in the middle ground between state and market: right at the heart, therefore, of the neoliberal constitution of "a new and foundational stage in the integration of capital and state" [39].

To some extent this account of Anglican social theology has—in an attempt to briefly survey a very heterogeneous assortment of individuals, organisations and groups who are very far from being in perfect agreement with one another—covered over some of the important complexities of Anglican debates about the Church of England's contribution to society and politics. What I have tried to indicate, however, is that in failing to consider itself as part of the machinery of capitalism, the Church consistently fails to recognise the ways in which its statements, actions and assumptions play right into the hand of the very social organisation it considers itself to be challenging. The Christian heritage of the existing social order is occasionally mentioned as a useful resource and a valuable opportunity for the Anglican Church to step into to influence society and politics. Yet it is rarely, if ever, considered that this Christian heritage might be precisely part of the problem, the reason why the church continues not only to fail to escape the contemporary logics of capitalism but to actively enable it. The notions of individual morality, the shared values of communities, and the importance of taking a middle way between excessive state control and an uncontrolled market offered by mainstream Anglican social theology are precisely the themes that, according to Lazzarato, contemporary capitalism most urgently requires from the social institutions which generate symbolic meaning.

4. Conclusions

Both Brown and Poole argue, in the conclusions to their respective surveys of Anglican social theology, that one of the most urgent challenges facing the Church of England today is the need to grapple more seriously with the way that contemporary capitalism works. Brown argues that Anglican social theology must "eschew on the one hand the kind of ultra-individualism that characterizes certain extreme forms of neo-liberalism and on the other the extreme collectivism that reduces persons to mere cogs in the machine" ([1], p. 187). The possibility that social subjection and machinic enslavement might be not two opposed tendencies of contemporary society but two mutually reinforcing aspects of the same economy might be a good place to start.

Conflicts of Interest: The author declares no conflict of interest.

References

1. Brown, Malcolm, ed. *Anglican Social Theology: Renewing the Vision Today.* London: Church House Publishing, 2014.
2. Deleuze, Gilles. "Postscript on the Societies of Control." *October* 59 (1992): 3–7.
3. Losurdo, Domenico. *Liberalism: A Counter-History.* Translated by Gregory Elliot. London: Verso, 2014.
4. Rowlands, Anna. "Fraternal Traditions: Anglican Social Theology and Catholic Social Teaching in a British Context." In *Anglican Social Theology: Renewing the Vision Today.* Edited by Malcolm Brown. London: Church House Publishing, 2014, pp. 133–74.
5. Poole, Eve. *The Church on Capitalism: Theology and the Market.* New York: Palgrave MacMillan, 2010.
6. Marx, Karl. "Theories of Surplus-Value." 1863. Available online: https://www.marxists.org/archive/marx/works/1863/theories-surplus-value (accessed on 8 August 2016).
7. Goodchild, Philip. *Capitalism and Religion: The Price of Piety.* London: Routledge, 2002.
8. Goodchild, Philip. *Theology of Money.* Durham: Duke University Press, 2009.
9. Toscano, Alberto. "Rethinking Marx and Religion." *Marxismes au XXIE Siècle: L'esprit & La Lettre.* Available online: http://web.archive.org/web/20160219205924/http://www.marxau21.fr/index.php/textes-thematiques/religion/5-rethinking-marx-and-religion (accessed on 8 August 2016).
10. Kumar, Ashok. "Interwoven threads: Building a labour countermovement in Bangalore's export-oriented garment industry." *City* 18 (2014): 789–807. [CrossRef]
11. Federici, Silvia. "Women, Land-Struggles and the Valorization of Labour." *The Commoner* 10 (2005): 216–33.
12. Lazzarato, Maurizio. *The Making of the Indebted Man: Essay on the Neoliberal Condition.* Translated by Joshua David Jordan. Cambridge: MIT, 2012.
13. Lazzarato, Maurizio. *Signs and Machines: Capitalism and the Production of Subjectivity.* Translated by Joshua David Jordan. Los Angeles: Semiotext(e), 2014.
14. Bankrollers, Holy. "Evening Standard." 10 November 2011. Available online: http://www.standard.co.uk/news/holy-bankrollers-6366701.html (accessed on 8 August 2016).
15. Preston, Alex. "God's bankers: How evangelical Christianity is taking a hold of the City of London's financial institutions." *Independent*, 23 April 2011. Available online: http://www.independent.co.uk/news/business/analysis-and-features/gods-bankers-how-evangelical-christianity-is-taking-a-hold-of-the-city-of-londonrsquos-financial-2270393.html (accessed on 8 August 2016).
16. Finch, Julia, and Nick Mathiason. "Bankers and morality: Churches turn on the modern moneylenders." *The Guardian*, 25 October 2009. Available online: http://www.theguardian.com/business/2009/oct/25/bank-pay-bonuses-religion (accessed on 8 August 2016).
17. Costa, Ken. "Just the man to preach morality to the City—A Tory banker." *Guardian*, 7 November 2011. Available online: http://www.theguardian.com/world/2011/nov/07/pass-notes-ken-costa (accessed on 8 August 2016).

18. Grice, Andrew. "War on Wonga: We're putting you out of business, Archbishop of Canterbury Justin Welby tells payday loans company." *Independent*, 25 July 2013. Available online: http://www.independent.co.uk/news/uk/home-news/war-on-wonga-were-putting-you-out-of-business-archbishop-of-canterbury-justin-welby-tells-payday-8730839.html (accessed on 8 August 2016).

19. Welby aims to compete Wonga 'out of existence'. *ITV*, 25 July 2013. Available online: http://www.itv.com/news/2013-07-25/welby-aims-to-compete-wonga-out-of-existence (accessed on 8 August 2016).

20. Brown, Andrew. "Welby, Wonga and the moral dilemma of financial investments." *The Guardian*, 26 July 2013. Available online: http://www.theguardian.com/commentisfree/andrewbrown/2013/jul/26/welby-wonga-moral-dilemma-financial-investments (accessed on 8 August 2016).

21. Morton, Cole. "Justin Welby's Wonga revelation." *The Telegraph*, 28 July 2013. Available online: http://www.telegraph.co.uk/news/religion/10206098/Justin-Welbys-Wonga-revelation.html (accessed on 8 August 2016).

22. Church of England bishops demand action over hunger. *BBC*, 20 February 2014. Available online: http://www.bbc.com/news/uk-politics-26261700 (accessed on 8 August 2016).

23. Wintour, Patrick, and Patrick Butler. "Tories seek to avert rift with Church of England over food bank report." *The Guardian*, 8 December 2014. Available online: http://www.theguardian.com/uk-news/2014/dec/08/tories-avert-rift-church-food-bank-report (accessed on 8 August 2016).

24. Bingham, John. "The Church must fill void left by failing state, says new archbishop Justin Welby." *The Telegraph*, January 2013. Available online: http://www.telegraph.co.uk/news/religion/9839866/The-Church-must-fill-void-left-by-failing-state-says-new-archbishop-Justin-Welby.html (accessed on 8 August 2016).

25. Cassidy, Johnny. "Christianity and capitalism: Investing in the Lord." *BBC News*, August 2011. Available online: http://www.bbc.co.uk/news/business-14615704 (accessed on 8 August 2016).

26. Chaplin, Jonathan. "Evangelical Contributions to the Future of Anglican Social Theology." In *Anglican Social Theology*. Edited by Malcolm Brown. London: Church House Publishing, 2014, pp. 102–32.

27. Cooper, Melinda. "The Theology of Emergency: Welfare Reform, US Foreign Aid and the Faith-Based Initiative." *Theory, Culture and Society* 32 (2015): 53–77. [CrossRef]

28. Harries, Richard. *Is There a Gospel for the Rich?* London: Mowbray, 1992.

29. Ramey, Joshua. "Neoliberalism as a Political Theology of Chance: The Politics of Divination." *Palgrave Communications*, 2015. Available online: http://www.palgrave-journals.com/articles/palcomms201539 (accessed on 8 August 2016).

30. Singh, Devin. "Debt Cancellation as Sovereign Crisis Management." *Cosmologics*, 2015. Available online: http://cosmologicsmagazine.com/devin-singh-debt-cancellation-as-sovereign-crisis-management/ (accessed on 8 August 2016).

31. Žižek, Slavoj. *The Fragile Absolute: Or, Why Is the Christian Legacy Worth Fighting for?* London: Verso, 2001.

32. Hughes, John. "After Temple? The Recent Renewal of Anglican Social Thought." In *Anglican Social Theology*. Edited by Malcolm Brown. London: Church House Publishing, 2014, pp. 74–102.

33. Brown, Malcolm. "The Case for Anglican Social Theology Today." In *Anglican Social Theology*. Edited by Malcolm Brown. London: Church House Publishing, 2014, pp. 1–27.

34. Suggate, Alan M. "The Temple Tradition." In *Anglican Social Theology*. Edited by Malcolm Brown. London: Church House Publishing, 2014, pp. 28–73.

35. Blake, Heidi, and Rowan Williams. "Two and a half cheers for the Big Society." *The Telegraph*, 24 July 2010. Available online: http://www.telegraph.co.uk/news/religion/7907830/Dr-Rowan-Williams-Two-and-a-half-cheers-for-the-Big-Society.html (accessed on 8 August 2016).

36. Bond, Daniel, and Justin Welby. "The EU debate is not all about us. It's about our vision for the world." *PoliticsHome*, March 2016. Available online: https://www.politicshome.com/home-affairs-foreign-and-defence/articles/house/justin-welby-eu-debate-not-all-about-us-its-about (accessed on 8 August 2016).

37. Dathan, Matt. "'What took you so long?' Archbishop of Canterbury says it's NOT racist to fear migration but Iain Duncan Smith says his 'rational' comments have come too late." 11 March 2016. Available online: http://www.dailymail.co.uk/news/article-3487444/What-took-long-Archbishop-Canterbury-says-s-NOT-racist-fear-migration-Iain-Duncan-Smith-says-rational-comments-come-late.html (accessed on 8 August 2016).

38. Pearson, Alison. "Justin Welby is right: It's not racist to worry about the migrant effect." 11 March 2016. Available online: http://www.telegraph.co.uk/news/uknews/immigration/12191532/Justin-Welby-is-right-Its-not-racist-to-worry-about-the-migrant-effect.html (accessed on 8 August 2016).

39. Lazzarato, Maurizio. *Governmentality in the Current Crisis*. Translated by Arianna Bove. *Generation online*, 2013. Available online: http://www.generation-online.org/p/fp_lazzarato7.htm (accessed on 8 August 2016).

religions MDPI

Article

The Enlightened Self: Identity and Aspiration in Two Communities of Practice

Erin Johnston

Thinking Matters Postdoctoral Fellow, Stanford University, Palo Alto, CA 94305, USA;
efjohnston@stanford.edu; Tel.: +1-201-572-7915

Academic Editors: Douglas James Davies and Michael J. Thate
Received: 8 April 2016; Accepted: 12 July 2016; Published: 15 July 2016

Abstract: Existing research on religious identity, especially from a narrative perspective, has tended to focus either on accounts of the past (especially occasions of religious change) or on conceptions of religious identity in the present. Religious communities, however, not only provide a sense of identity and belonging in the present—as a "Catholic" or "Buddhist," for example—they also promote a particular vision of the religious ideal: The way of being-in-the-world that all adherents are (or ought to be) striving to achieve. Drawing on fieldwork and interviews, this paper describes and analyzes the identity and lifestyle goals of participants in two communities of practice: An Integral Yoga studio and a Catholic prayer house. I find that the ideal spiritual self in both communities is defined by three key characteristics: A sacred gaze, a simultaneous sense of presence and detachment, and a holistic style of identity management. I suggest that in constructing and transmitting a shared vision of the "enlightened self," these organizations offer practitioners a highly desirable but ever-elusive *aspirational identity*. This study calls attention to religious organizations as important suppliers of possible identities—the identities, either desired and feared, we think we could or might become in the future—and reveals the situated and contextual nature of adherents' religious aspirations.

Keywords: religious identity; possible identities; future selves; narrative identity; aspirations

---

1. Introduction

> "In each kind of self, material, social and spiritual, men distinguish between the immediate and the actual and the remote and the potential"
>
> —William James ([1], p. 200).

While it has been suggested that modern individuals are more like tourists and vagabonds rather than pilgrims with a sense of destination [2], my research in two communities of spiritual practice—an Integral Yoga studio and a Catholic spiritual center—suggests otherwise. Participants at both sites felt their involvement in these communities not only helped them acquire a sense of who they are (in the present), but also provided a clearer sense of who they want to become (in the future). Julia, for example, told me that her participation in a 200-hour teacher training program offered through the Integral Yoga Institute (IYI) changed "how I view the world, how I view myself, and who I want to be." As William James suggests in the epigraph above, Julia distinguished between her present self and a desired future self—the kind of person she hoped to become.

These communities not only encourage practitioners to regard themselves as "yogis" and "Contemplative Catholics," but also to view themselves as *aspirants*: People "earnestly desirous of becoming a certain kind of person, and consciously and continuously in pursuit of that goal" ([3], p. 355; [4,5]). However, what exactly are practitioners, like Julia, aspiring to? Drawing on fieldwork and interviews, I argue that these communities provide a shared conception of the ideal spiritual self: the way of being that practitioners are (or ought to be) striving to embody. In the findings, I describe three key characteristics that mark this collective ideal: A sacred gaze, a simultaneous sense of presence and detachment, and a holistic style of identity management. In constructing and transmitting a shared vision of the "enlightened self," I argue that these organizations offer practitioners a highly desirable yet elusive (and ultimately unattainable) *aspirational identity* [3].

This paper makes several important contributions. First, integrating theoretical work on narrative identity [6–8] and recent work on aspirational identities [3], I draw attention to the future-oriented nature of many religious identities, and outline a set of theoretical and conceptual tools for investigating the structure, content, and consequences of adherents' shared aspirations. In doing so, I highlight aspirational identities as an important means through which religious communities shape individual experience and action. Second, drawing from a multiyear ethnographic study of two communities, I demonstrate how religious organizations actively shape the identity goals of their members, revealing the situated and contextual nature of religious aspirations. Finally, this study calls attention to religion and religious communities as an important source of individuals' *possible identities*—the "positive and negative identities one might hold in the future" ([9], p. 117)—one that has been overlooked in existing psychological research.

Religion, Narrative, and Aspirational Identities

In recent decades, changes in the social and religious landscape—including the expansion of available options and shifting boundaries of identification [10,11]—have fueled interest in the topic of religious identity (see [12,13] for overviews of existing research and calls for more research). How, scholars ask, do individuals construct and maintain a coherent sense of self given the growth and increasing complexity of the contemporary "spiritual marketplace" [11]? How do people integrate their religious identities with other, often competing, social roles and group memberships? Recent reviews have advocated for a narrative approach, suggesting that this perspective can help illuminate how individuals resolve the tensions and complexities associated with identification and meaning in modern social life [12,13]. Narrative identity theorists [6–8] view the self as a reflexively organized and ongoing project defined by the ability to "keep a particular narrative going" ([14], p. 54). Individuals' self-stories, it is argued, help to locate the individual in both time and space [8], providing structure and coherence to complex and changing individual lives. Storytelling and narration then are considered acts of self-formation, practices in and through which individuals construct and maintain their identities. Moreover, these narratives, while personally meaningful, are drawn from available cultural resources: the plot lines, metaphors, and underlying grammar made available in different social and cultural contexts [8].

While a narrative perspective on religious identity is becoming increasingly prominent, existing work has focused primarily on accounts of the past (especially religious change) or on discussions of religious identity in the present. Existing work on religious conversion, for example, focuses on how religious adherents integrate past affiliations and the conversion experience itself into a coherent and continuous self-story. Narratives have been shown to play a role in both accounting for and in accomplishing religious change [15,16]. Other studies have shown how individuals' self-stories are shaped by conventional patterns of telling the story of conversion in their new religious communities [17–19]. More recently, scholars have focused on how individuals understand and describe their religious identities in the present [20,21]. Cadge and Davidman [20], for example, find that both Jewish and Buddhist Americans tell stories which construct their religious identities as simultaneously ascribed (given at birth) and achieved (the result of personal effort and active engagement).

One key element of narrative theory, however, remains underemphasized in existing research: narratives not only "emplot" the past and present—integrating events and experiences into a coherent storyline—but also project forward into the future, suggesting where the storyteller is heading. In fact, the self is defined, from a narrative perspective, as a "working theory of who one is, was, *and will become*" ([9], p. 117), which includes not only "a selective reconstruction of the autobiographical past" but also a "narrative anticipation of the imagined future" ([6], p. 99). A coherent sense of self, then, requires not only an account of "how we have become" but also of "where we are going" ([22], p. 47). A sense of direction and destination is consequential. Starting in the works of Mead [23] and Cooley [24], scholars of identity have suggested that imagined futures inform and shape current self-understanding and individual action just as much as the past. As Bauman writes, "Destination, the set purpose of life's pilgrimage, gives form to the formless, makes a whole out of the fragmentary, lends continuity to the episodic" ([2], p. 22).

Previous work on conversion has clearly demonstrated that the collective identity of the group can provide a sense of destination for novices and newcomers. Religious groups promote a shared understanding of what it means to be a member of the community—the practices, attitudes, and values that define, for example, what it means to be a "Christian" or an "Orthodox Jew"—and existing members serve as prototypical models or templates during the process of initiation and socialization [25–27]. Often, people enter religious communities because of their admiration for existing members and community leaders, driven in part by a desire to emulate their lives. [1] However, in this paper, I aim to make an analytical distinction between the process of initiation—through which individuals become members of the group, adopting an identity as "yogis" or "Catholics," for example—and the ongoing process of spiritual formation—akin to a process of divinization in these communities—that is expected of all practitioners, even the most experienced.

In many religious communities, spiritual formation is considered a continuous and ongoing process [11], and the religious ideal remains an ever-elusive goal for the vast majority of members [4,5]. This requires that we distinguish between the social and aspirational identities provided by religious communities: in other words, being a "yogi" is not the same thing as being "enlightened." Rather, membership in many religious communities is defined, at least in part, by the continuous pursuit of an ideal that is considered unattainable, at least in this lifetime. Armato and Margislio, for example, find that members of the "Promise Keepers," an evangelical Christian movement for men, "have undertaken a *continuous* project of gender identity work to become godly men" ([28], p. 41). Like those in the communities that form the basis of this paper, the Promise Keepers encourage adherents to view spiritual formation as a "never-ending, life-long process" ([28], p. 44). Likewise, in the organizations I studied, spiritual persons—yogis and contemplatives—were marked by their continuous and concerted efforts to move closer and closer to "Enlightenment" (or "Christ-consciousness").

Despite the fact that many religious communities likely encourage adherents to view themselves as aspirants, the content of these aspirational identities, the means through which they are transmitted, as well as their consequences have not been explicitly examined. In this paper, I analyze what precisely teachers and texts in these communities encourage their members to aspire to. In the results section, I describe the content and structure of the ideal spiritual self—what I refer to as the "enlightened self"—constructed and transmitted in these two communities. In the discussion section, I argue that the enlightened self is best understood as an *aspirational identity*, an important and analytically distinct component of the practitioners' religious identities.

2. Data and Methods

The findings outlined below come from a larger ethnographic study examining the process of spiritual formation in two communities of practice: a yoga studio and a Catholic spiritual center. Trinity Prayer House, run by a Sister of Saint Joseph (Sister Nancy) and partially funded by the local diocese, teaches a contemplative approach to religious life. Many of the classes, workshops, and retreats offered at Trinity engage the practice of Centering Prayer. In this form of silent prayer,

---

[1] "As at the modern Orthodox synagogue, an attractive feature of the Hasidic community was that it provided numerous models of caring nuclear families and affirmed the value of family ... The women expressed enormous admiration for the families they met within the religious community and saw them as prototypes for the families they would like to create" ([25], p. 120]).

the individual sits comfortably in a chair or on the floor, with his eyes closed for a period of at least 20 minutes. The practitioner is encouraged to focus on "God's presence and action within in," and, like mindfulness practices, to simply watch his thoughts and feelings but not become engaged in them. Sister Nancy was certified to teach classes on Centering Prayer by *Contemplative Outreach*—an international organization founded by Father Thomas Keating—and she regularly used resources (handouts, books, and DVDs) provided by the organization in doing so. Because of my interest in the role of practice in spiritual formation, my fieldwork at Trinity focused primarily on classes and workshops that actively engaged in and discussed the practice of Centering Prayer. This included participation in the "Intern Program" for those who desired to become Spiritual Directors.[2]

Programs at Trinity ranged in cost from as little as $10 for a one-time workshop to upwards of $250 for a year-long series.[3] Attendance ranged from as few as five to as many as forty participants. In the programs I attended, participants were almost entirely white. I observed only a handful of racial and ethnic minorities, mostly commonly East Asian, Latino, and black participants, during my fieldwork. The majority of attendees were well-educated and were employed (or formerly employed) in professional jobs, such as teachers or nurses. The overwhelming majority of participants were women, and most appeared between 40 and 70 years of age.

The IYI, or Integral Yoga Institute, is affiliated with the broader Integral Yoga tradition developed by Sri Swami Satchidananda. Satchidananda, a disciple of Swami Sivananda, came to the US from India in the 1960s. He led yoga classes, founded an ashram, and was active in the interfaith movement until his death in 2002. The Institute at which I conducted my research was directed by a discipline of Satchidananda (Aadesh). The IYI offers classes and training programs in many aspects of yogic practice and theory. Hatha Yoga classes, however, are the most common, with 2–4 classes offered each day, seven days a week. The average Integral Yoga Hatha practice includes call-and-response chanting in Sanskrit, a series of *asanas* (physical postures), a deep relaxation called *yoga nidra* (yogic sleep), *pranayama* (breathing practices), *mantra japa* (mantra repetition), and a period of silent meditation. In addition to hatha classes, the studio also offered a weekly Bhagavad Gita (a Hindu scripture) study group, as well as a monthly Raja Yoga and Kirtan classes. My fieldwork at the IYI included participant observation at a broad range of classes and workshops, as well as participation in the 200-hour yoga teacher training program that took place between May and August of 2012.

A monthly membership to the IYI cost $60–$70 per month at the time of my fieldwork. A single class or workshop ranged between $10 and $25.[4] Attendance at classes and workshops ranged widely from as few as two to as many as thirty students per class. During my observation period, class participants were predominantly white (approximately two-thirds), with the majority of remaining participants appearing to be of South Asian or East Asian descent. As was the case at Trinity, the gender composition was disproportionately female: Women comprised approximately three-quarters of participants in any given class. Most attendees appeared to be between 30 and 60 years of age.

Data collection for this study included participant observation, review and analysis of assigned texts, in-depth, semi-structured interviews with instructors and practitioners, and a period of participatory immersion. I conducted fieldwork between January 2012 and May 2014. Rather than attending classes at the two organizations simultaneously, I spent 12–15 months focused on each organization in turn. During this period, I spent more than 200 hours in formal classes and training programs at each site, in addition to observing informal interactions among practitioners before and after classes, and at social gatherings in participants' homes. I was an active participant in all of the

---

[2]   Spiritual direction is "help given by one Christian to another which enables that person to pay attention to God's personal communication to him or her, to respond to this personally communicating God, to grow in intimacy with this God, and to live out the consequences of the relationship" ([29], p. 8).

[3]   The year-long series met once per month for 2–5 hours per session between the months of September and May, for a total of 9–10 sessions. A few classes and workshops were offered "by donation."

[4]   These prices were significantly below comparable studios in the area. This is due in part to the fact that the IYI was registered as a not-for-profit community organization, while the vast majority of yoga studios are for-profit businesses.

classes I attended. I practiced alongside others, read the assigned material, completed and submitted written assignments, and participated in collective discussions. I was treated by others, including teachers, as a fellow student although I had no affiliation with or involvement in either community prior to or after the period of my fieldwork.[5] During the yoga teacher training program, I was given permission to audio-record class meetings, resulting in more than 80 hours of recorded interaction. In all other cases, I took notes during classes whenever possible, and wrote more detailed field notes immediately following my time in the field.

In order to get a better sense of practitioners' experiences and interpretations, I also conducted in-depth interviews with 60 teachers and students: 35 Centering Prayer and 25 Integral Yoga practitioners. Interviews were open-ended—seeking to elicit stories and narratives—but clearly structured around several key themes. I asked practitioners about their religious and spiritual backgrounds, how they first came to the practice and organization, how their practice has developed over time, as well as their reflections on religion and spirituality, more broadly. The shortest interview was 45-minutes and the longest more than 2 hours. All interviews were recorded and subsequently transcribed. In addition, I attempted to maintain each practice (Centering Prayer and Hatha Yoga), respectively, for a period of at least one month. During this time, I kept a detailed log of my practice, as well as notes on my experiences, reflections, and observations.

Located just 35 miles apart, Trinity Prayer House and the IYI are both situated in suburban areas within commuting distance of New York City. Despite being rooted in very different religious traditions (Catholicism and Hinduism, respectively), both organizations are dedicated to facilitating the spiritual formation of their members. At Trinity, the ultimate goal of Centering Prayer was said to be "a transformation of consciousness, perception and attention," leading ultimately to divine union and "Christ-consciousness." At the IYI, the goal of practice was said to be "Self-Realization" through the cultivation of "Cosmic Consciousness." At both sites then spiritual formation was considered akin to a process of divinization: Through dedicated and disciplined practice, practitioners sought to uncover and reveal their truest, most authentic (and divine) self. Through fieldwork and interviews, I found that teachers and texts at both sites transmitted a shared understanding of what characteristics and dispositions marked the "enlightened self" practitioners were seeking to cultivate. Below, I describe and analyze three key features of this idealized spiritual self.

3. Results: The Enlightened Self

Sister Nancy began nearly every program, workshop, and group meeting at Trinity with a short prayer. She would quiet everyone down and then sit, with her eyes closed, and reflect for a few moments on the topics we would cover that day. These statements often explicitly referenced what she assumed were participants' motivations for attending. One day, for example, she told us: "I know what you want. [...] You want to find that place within yourself where you and God are one. You strive to never leave the temple and to live from that place." While the descriptions Sister Nancy offered of participants' motivations and desires were always somewhat different, her statements helped articulate key aspects of the kind of life practitioners were (or ought to be) striving to achieve, illustrating the role that she, Trinity, and these classes play in shaping practitioners' future aspirations. Her reflections suggested, more or less explicitly, that a particular set of motivations

---

[5] I began my fieldwork in both organizations with only a very basic understanding of the communities and their requisite beliefs and practices. While I had no prior affiliation with either group, my religious background (I was raised non-religiously), prior experience with the practice of yoga (although not in the IY tradition), and the diversity of religious backgrounds among participants, led me to feel more comfortable with the culture, practices, and discourse at the IYI. At Trinity, I felt more like an "outsider" (the overwhelming majority of participants were Catholic), although this feeling subsided substantially over time. Given my attendance at the majority of classes and workshops, I came to be seen as and treated by many as Sister Nancy's "helper," giving me a clear role and some degree of status among the participants. At both sites, my identity as a white, middle-class, female meant I was very similar to the "typical" participant. At Trinity, however, my age marked me as somewhat of a novelty. I only encountered a participant younger than myself (I was 27 at the time), on one occasion, and I was sometimes asked to speak on behalf of "young people."

and goals are universally-applicable, attributing them to all participants, even while making them sound personalized ("I know what you want"). More, these statements simultaneously reflect a shared understanding of what it means to be a "spiritual person." On another occasion, for example, Sister Nancy explicitly told us: "This is what it really means to be a spiritual person: to live in the moment, to find God in all things [...] to really look for God [...] to be a person of God all the time."

Many of the practitioners I spoke with, like Julia quoted above, told me that their participation in training programs, classes, and workshops at these organizations provided them with a clearer sense of who they wanted to be and how they wanted to live. In addition to learning how to practice then participants also acquired a shared vision of the ideal spiritual self, and a common language for describing and articulating these aspirations.[6] Through fieldwork and interviews, I found that this idealized way of being-in-the-world was marked not by strict behavioral mandates but rather by a set of broad dispositions. In this section, I elucidate three key components of the aspirational identity practitioners were encouraged to cultivate: (1) a sacred gaze; (2) a simultaneous sense of presence and detachment; and finally; (3) a holistic approach to identity management.

3.1. The Sacred Gaze

"Contemplative prayer ... is prayer that sees the whole world through incense—a holy place, a place where the sacred dwell ... [It] leads us to see the world through the eyes of God." ([30], p. 35).

Maria, a 46-year old Centering Prayer practitioner, told me that as she grows and develops spiritually, she has become "more aware" of God's presence and action. In addition, and equally important for her, is the fact that she consciously chooses to be more aware, enacting practices that increase her ability to see, feel, and know God's presence. She links the cultivation of this perceptual and sensual ability to her disciplined practice of Centering Prayer. The practice, she said, helps to bring her to a "place of peace and contemplation" so that when she steps out into the world "the mystery of things and the beauty of things just seem to stand out" more clearly. Maria is motivated to maintain a daily practice, at least in part, by a desire to further develop this awareness: She aspires to notice and appreciate God's presence more frequently and more deeply.

Teachers and texts in both communities argue that all of life—people, objects, events, experiences—is imbued with spiritual meaning. Participants are told that, through practice, they will develop the ability to see and experience that meaning more clearly. This perceptual ability (or sensibility)—similar to what David Morgan [31] has called the *sacred gaze*—is a key component of the ideal spiritual self. The sacred gaze is "a way of seeing [which] invests an image, a viewer or an act of viewing with spiritual significance" ([31], p. 6). To cultivate the gaze, practitioners must display what Morgan calls visual piety: "the constructive operation of seeing that looks for, makes room for, the transcendent in daily life" ([31], p. 6). The spiritual gaze, therefore, is both a practice (something that people do) and a way of seeing (a socio-mental lens [32]).[7] As a socially-acquired way of seeing, the gaze includes norms of attention and disattention, as well as habits of interpretation, acquired through a process of (optical) socialization ([33], p. 33). On the one hand, the spiritual gaze affects *what* is perceived as expectations are translated into selective attention [33]. At the same time, these communities transmit frameworks of interpretations and shared meanings that can be deployed in processing various kinds of observances and experiences. As in the metaphor of seeing things

---

[6] Of course it is important to acknowledge that practitioners come to these communities with a range of different backgrounds, commitments, and identities. Variables such as gender, race, age, and profession, among others, likely affect how each individual navigates, understands, and engages with the discursive and practical resources offered by these organizations. Due to space constraints, this paper is not able to highlight the diversity of experience across individual practitioners, and focuses instead on the counters of the *enlightened self* as it is outlined in the "official discourse" (that put forward by teachers and texts) of these communities.

[7] While perception is a bodily process, it is neither universal and objective nor purely individual. Rather, perception is a process that is structured and shaped by cultural context and social interaction [32].

"through incense," the cultivation of a sacred gaze causes more and more of life to be marked and classified as "spiritually relevant" [34]. Practitioners become more likely to see God's presence and action in the flow of daily events through modified structures of attention and the acquisition of new interpretive frames. The "filter" through which practitioners come to view the world imbues objects, people and events with spiritual meaning, while also transforming the act of looking, itself, into a spiritual practice.

Becoming a member of these communities then requires training the gaze to focus on and read one's surroundings in particular, socially-shared ways. Despite a collective discourse that implies the naturalness of this gaze, practitioners were also told that disciplined practice was necessary both for cultivating the habit of looking and for refining their perceptual abilities. Practices like the Daily Examen,[8] for example, which ask practitioners to give explicit attention to God's presence and action in the course of their daily lives, help practitioners to realize God's presence "by asking [them] to notice where God already exists in [their] li[ves]." Practitioners are told they ought to be looking for God constantly. Sister Nancy told participants to ask, "What is God doing here?" and to "let that be your constant focus." The disciplined practice of Examen helps adherents notice God's presence more and more frequently. It is assumed that eventually they will; come to recognize that God is active in every moment of every day. Examen, then is both a practice of looking and a process through which practitioners refine their perceptual ability, cultivating the sacred gaze.

I found that practitioners at both sites embraced the link between practice and what I'm calling here, the sacred gaze. Many described leaving sessions of Centering Prayer (both collective and private) in a different perceptual and sensual state. Cindy, a Centering Prayer practitioner, for example, told me: "When you come out ... everything is bright, everything is alive—there is so much life in everything." This experience, she says, is qualitatively different from her average mode of being. She continued: "I think it's because all the noise—there's so much noise in the world" which prevents you from focusing on and seeing the beauty of life. However, she noted, "if you can focus your mind on something for a period of time, then your mind just becomes sharper" and you can see more clearly and more easily. The practice of Centering Prayer facilitates changes in practitioners' perceptual experience: they notice different (and more) things about their surroundings, and are more likely to interpret what they notice as spiritually-relevant.

Both the practice of looking and the perceptual ability of seeing are considered markers of spiritual personhood in these communities. Because of this, practitioners in both communities aspire and actively work to cultivate the sacred gaze. In my conversation with Mary, for example, she told me that her awareness of God's presence has "grown considerably." While she used to compartmentalize everything, she has "slowly begun to let the wall down and realize that God is with me all the time. I just have to *open my eyes* and *see*." She sets aside time to work on this in her practice of Examen. She tells me: "I'll look back at the end of the day: Did I see God? Well not quite in everything. Okay, you could have done better there." Drawing on a logic of progressive attainment [4,5], Mary sees the gaze and its deployment as something that has developed over time, but in which she still has considerable room for further improvement.

The sacred gaze is an important part of what it means to "live contemplatively" for members of this community. When I asked Mary what she thinks it means to be a contemplative person, for example, she told me:

> "To be present—to really be present and to notice. To notice. To see, to see. Like behind you, the sunlight on the wall; it's just so beautiful ... it's about experiencing God in everything all the time. You become more and more aware when you live that way—you become more and more aware ... you get drawn into the miracle of everything."

---

[8] Examen is a Jesuit practice, developed by Saint Ignatius of Loyola, which involves prayerful reflection on the day's events in an effort to identify God's presence and to discern his will in regards to the practitioners' life and actions.

Mary's responses clearly ties being a contemplative person to a particular way of seeing and experiencing everyday life. However, Mary's statement also ties the sacred gaze to the cultivation of another important disposition: being simultaneously fully present and relatively detached from the flow of daily experience.

3.2. Presence and Detachment

The ideal spiritual self was also marked by a distinctive subjectivity or relationship to reality: One in which the individual is fully immersed and present in the moment but also somewhat detached, watching themselves and others from the perspective of an external observer. On the one hand, participants were taught the value of being fully present and completely engaged in the flow of everyday life. Being fully present requires not being bogged down by the past (regret, as well as fond recollection) or distracted by worries about the future (anxiety as well as desire). On the other hand, participants were told to cultivate detachment—referred to as "holy indifference" (Trinity) or "non-attachment" (IYI)—a disposition defined by a sense of separation and distance from events and experiences as well as one's thoughts and feelings.

The clearest metaphor for this orientation was described by Ron, an Integral Yoga teacher. During the teacher training program at the IYI, Ron compared this ideal state to the one achieved while watching a really good film. He told the participants:

> "Another example . . . Going to a movie and getting so involved in it that you totally feel for the character and will cry and laugh and identify and find that you've lost any sense of separation from what is going on. You're experiencing it fully. And if it's a good movie, you enjoy it even if it makes you sad . . . In the movie theater, it's easy because your mind knows that I'm not there. You are in this witness place and you know you are sitting in the theater. You are immersed and enjoying it but you aren't attached. Our mistake is thinking that we are the movie."

This metaphor depicts both sides of this idealized disposition: being fully present and relatively detached. Drawing on popular psychological and self-help discourses, the former was described as achieving "flow" [35] or living "in the now" [36]. The latter, referred to as *non-attachment* at the Institute,[9] did not require the individual to give things up—for example, by getting rid of all one's possessions—but rather captured "a certain consciousness" or a "way of being with things." Non-attachment and presence were seen as deeply intertwined. As Ron explained, "You can give yourself to things more fully when you are non-attached." Likewise, being fully present implied a sense of separation from concerns about the past and the future.

At the prayer house, Sister Nancy sometimes described this approach using a proverb she attributed to Buddhist teachings. She told us that we should "look upon our favorite cup as if it is already broken." This proverb encourages both presence and detachment. On the one hand, if we recognize and acknowledge that the things we love will not be around forever, Sister Nancy explains, we are encouraged to be fully present with and enjoy them in the moment. At the same time, recognizing and acknowledging impermanence as an inherent part of human life allows us to avoid devastation when the things (or people) we love break (or leave). Detachment, or what was called "holy indifference" at Trinity, means having only "a light grasp" on our possessions, relationships, and desires. Christ-like persons, practitioners learned, were not bogged down by attachments to roles, places, or even people, but were instead ready and willing to do and go wherever in response to God's will. In fact, Sister Nancy suggested that the cultivation of detachment was correlated with a decline in

---

9   Non-attachment is defined in Sutra 15 of the Yoga Sutras: "The consciousness of self-mastery in one who is free from craving for objects seen or heard about" ([37], p. 20).

the number and variety of things we think we "need" to be happy. At the same time, the number of things that are likely to cause us agitation or "set you off" also shrinks.

Practitioners learned about, practiced, and cultivated this orientation in and through their personal practices of hatha yoga and Centering Prayer, respectively. Yoga practitioners, for example, were instructed to approach the *asanas* (or physical postures) as a "moving meditation." When asked what that meant, Ron explained: "Whatever asana you are doing, that is what your mind is engaged in. Your mind is just fully engaged in doing that posture. That is the meditation ... it is being present with every single action that you are doing." On the other hand, there was a simultaneous emphasis on maintaining a position of relative detachment during practice as well, especially from one's feelings and thoughts. Sister Nancy, for example, suggested that practitioners should imagine themselves sitting on a river bank, watching the different ships and boats (i.e., thoughts and sensations) pass them by. Sometimes, she said, we might find that you have "jumped on a boat and started heading down stream" (i.e., become engaged in a thought). When we realize this has happened, she continued, we should simply acknowledge it, get off boat, and return to our place on the shore, once again observing the ships as they pass. In this analogy, the practitioner clearly takes the position of an observer, envisioning the self (on the bank) as wholly distinct from the movements and fluctuations of the mind (the ships on the river).

The goal of spiritual formation, however, was to embody this orientation not only during practice, but also outside of it: what yogi's referred to as taking their practice "off the mat." When I asked participants how, if at all, they felt the practice had changed them, the cultivation of detachment was the most commonly cited form of progress. Practitioners at both organizations described important changes in how they reacted to and handled the frequent annoyances of everyday life, from traffic jams to unpleasant interactions with colleagues at work. Irene, for example, told me that, in general, things bother her less than they used to. She used "to fly off the handle pretty easily about so many kinds of things," she explains, but "that's the kind of stuff that ... doesn't faze me anymore." Vibha, an Integral Yoga practitioner, described a similar change. She told me that she is "much calmer in the way I deal with things." Before yoga, she said, "I used to be very impatient with many things," but "now I notice that my responses are calm and I don't fly off the handle." Irene and Vibha were both motivated by these results; in fact, a desire to further cultivate this change in demeanor was one of the reasons they cited for maintaining the practices. In classes and interviews at both sites, I heard a broad range of stories that illustrated practitioners' growing ability to remain calm in the face of stressful situations.

At the same time, participants also emphasized their ability to be present. During classes and workshops at Trinity, for example, Sister Nancy often asked participants to share their reflections on the "fruits" (or benefits) of their practice. Participants' responses not only emphasized detachment—being less reactive—but also presence. Sharon, for example, shared that the practice helps her "be more present." Adding that she is "better able to see and feel the movements of the spirit" and feels "more in tune with them," linking presence to the spiritual gaze described above. Likewise, Donna told the group that practicing Centering Prayer made her realize "how not present I am in my daily interactions," and helped her become "more present on average." Similar sentiments were shared at the yoga studio, as well, where participants drew on the language of "being in the flow" to describe an experience of increasingly focused engagement during their daily lives. The ability to be fully present, then, was described as something practitioners *hoped* to embody more often and more fully, translating presence from an in-the-moment experience into an aspirational way of being-in-the-world. Like the sacred gaze, described above, both presence and detachment were arenas in which practitioners said they noticed improvements, but also areas in which they desired additional growth and development.

3.3. Integration

"I don't try to differentiate between the religious, the spiritual and the day-to-day. I think it's all the same"

—Rohit, Integral Yoga teacher and practitioner

"The goal is to live life in awareness of God: to be a person of God all the time."

—Sister Nancy

Early on in the intern program for aspiring spiritual directors, Sister Nancy made it very clear that serving as a spiritual director for others required participants to live their spirituality "twenty-four seven." On the very first day of class, for example, Sister Nancy told us that "spiritual direction is a way of life." This became somewhat of a catch phrase during the program, and by the third meeting when Sister Nancy would begin ("Spiritual Direction is a ... "), the students would complete her sentence (" ... a way of life"). Throughout the course, Sister Nancy made it clear that being a spiritual director is "not a role or identity that you can put on and take off like a hat"; instead, "you really have to *be* that."

While it was especially true for those training to be spiritual directors and yoga teachers, I found that all practitioners, at both sites, were encouraged to view and enact their spirituality as a *holistic identity*. I use this concept to capture an ideal typical style of identity management [38], one in which spirituality is central and highly salient [39] but simultaneously integrated with other roles and obligations. A holistic approach to identity management therefore falls in between two extremes: (1) identities enacted as social roles and therefore tied to particular times, places, or interaction partners; and (2) identities enacted as a master status [40] or master identity [41], in which one identity monopolizes the self-concept, overshadowing and even seeking to displace other sources of self-understanding. A holistic identity, however, resembles the steady hum of background noise: it shapes thought and action in subtle but important ways across many different contexts and social roles.

The spiritual ideal is defined in these communities by "a consistent, fully integrated life of piety, such that one's practice of spirituality is indistinguishable from the rest of one's life" ([42], p. 198). According to texts and teachers, the spiritual identity should be activated not only when the practitioner is on the mat or in the chair, but should be "turned on" throughout their daily lives. Spirituality was described as a way of being, one which not only transcends time and space, but which should ideally filter down and shape how practitioners enact other identities and social roles as well. Treating spirituality as a "way of life" (rather than a bounded social role, for example) implies that all obligations, experiences and other identities are encompassed within and given meaning through their relationship to the project of spiritual formation. The enactment of one's role as a lawyer or mother, for example, was described and experienced as an arena in which to both express and cultivate the ideal spiritual self. This can be seen, for example, in how one reacts to the petty annoyances of co-workers or children: a situation that is transformed from a mundane experience into an opportunity to enact (or fail to enact) the spiritual ideal of presence and detachment. At the same time, the individual's understanding of what is means to be a good mother (or lawyer) may be modified in relation to the spiritual ideal. This "identity spread" ([28], pp. 50–55), or the reevaluation of other identities and social roles in light of their spiritual commitments, was explicitly encouraged in both communities.

To accomplish this goal, it was suggested that practitioners implement structures, disciplines, and routines that could provide the necessary scaffolding for living out their aspirations. Yoga practitioners, for example, were told that they could repeat a mantra, chant Sankrit verses, or practice pranayama (breathing techniques) while doing daily activities like washing the dishes or driving to work. Doing so, it was argued, would help practitioners activate and maintain the idealized way of seeing and of relating to reality described above. Many practitioners followed this advice, and implemented regular schedules of prayer and practice throughout the day. Barbara, a participant at Trinity, for example, uses prayers written by Margaret Guenther [43] to transform daily activities like showering, getting dressed, ironing, and making coffee into spiritual practices. She recalled being encouraged to make a daily schedule of prayer where "morning prayer is 'Thank you God for another day. Help me to live it according to your will.' And noontime is a recollection time: 'How am I doing?' And then nighttime is for a review of the day." And that, she continued, is that "pattern I try to keep in the back of my mind."

Through these practices, individuals continuously "prime"[10] their spiritual identities, encouraging thoughts and actions in line with their ideals.

On the other hand, while all-encompassing, the spiritual identity is not greedy [44]: It does not seek to displace or eclipse other social roles or personal interests. Unlike monastics or clergy who seek to live spiritually-centered lives by giving up all or many of their other commitments (interpreted as potential distractions), these communities do not require that practitioners abandon relationships, give up social roles, or sacrifice their other obligations. At the yoga studio, the teachers often quoted the following Zen proverb in explaining the goal of practice: "Before enlightenment, chop wood, carry water. After enlightenment, chop wood, carry water." In our discussions, it was clear what this proverb was meant to convey: it is not activities or social roles that change in the process of seeking enlightenment but the intention and approach to those activities that are ultimately transformed. The goal then is integration and transformation, not displacement. According to texts and teachers, living a spiritual life did not require withdrawal from social life; rather, practitioners were asked to identify and embrace the spiritual impulse *within* their everyday lives [42].

Holistic identities therefore clearly differ from concepts such as "master status" [40] or "identity lifestyler" [38], terms that have been used to suggest that, in some cases, multidimensionality and balance across identity commitments is either impossible or undesirable. In these cases, the identity in question is not only highly salient but also "determines one's auxiliary characteristics," pushing aside other roles and interests in the process ([38], p. 213). Take for example, the graduate student whose academic obligations and commitments prevent her from participating in previously important hobbies and activities. She may even discover that, over time, as her preferences and identities have shift, she no longer enjoys these activities to the same extent. The spiritual identity, very much like the academic identity, is often enacted as the "essential core" of practitioners' self-understanding: "a way of being and living, and an encompassing meaning of their whole identity, rather than a single aspect within the self" ([38], p. 34). However, with encouragement from others in the community, practitioners strive to maintain their pre-existing roles, relationships, and hobbies, often translating them into tools or arenas for spiritual development in the process.

While many practitioners felt that the ideal of holism would be easier to embody if they lived in a monastery, most felt they could and should actively strive to cultivate this approach in the course of their daily lives. During my conversations with practitioners, many noted evidence of progress in this area as a source of pride and distinction. Irene, for example, told me, "I just find myself automatically thinking about God. Thinking about my interactions with God ... [I feel] like God is more present for me at this point than I ever have. Before, I would have to stop and say, okay, I'll think about God. But now it sometimes just happens—and frequently during the course of the day ... it's more integrated. I don't necessarily have to stop what I'm doing in order for that to happen." Through immersion in these communities, spirituality comes to shape their actions throughout the day, and progress in terms of integration is considered a marker of spiritual growth. While practitioners like Irene felt they had made progress in this arena, they all simultaneously aspired to achieve a point when the spiritual and the everyday were more fully integrated.

4. Discussion: The Enlightened Self as an Aspirational Identity

> "We have a direction, not a destination. We are going East, but you can't get East. You can only go East."[11]

---

[10] Priming is the implicit memory effect in which exposure to a stimulus influences response to a later stimulus. Psychologists often use priming experimentally to train a person's memory both in positive and negative ways. It has also been argued, however, that contexts, people, and objects can "prime" or make salient different identities. More, identity salience has been linked to stronger correlations between identity and behavior [39].

[11] Ramdas, Integral Yoga instructor.

The "enlightened self" was considered by members of these communities to be perpetually out of reach even for the most experienced practitioners [4,5]. This was most clearly conveyed in practitioners' reflections regarding their progress and development. For each of the facets described above, the practitioners I spoke with, regardless of their level of experience, described themselves as simultaneously having undergone meaningful development, yet still a long way away from their final goal. In these communities, the "enlightened self" is something both novice and the most experienced members (including teachers) are striving to achieve. Rather than extant members serving as living models of the community's ideals—people who project the identity, in all its elements—newcomers learn that the full embodiment of the enlightened self is unattainable: something they, and all others, must continuously strive for but will likely never achieve. While it was certainly the case that some practitioners (especially teachers) were thought to more closely embody the ideal than others, no practitioners felt they had achieved it.

This finding suggests the need for an analytical distinction between being a "yogi" (or "Contemplative Catholic") and embodying the "enlightened self." The former is an identity that most practitioners felt they had achieved (and used to describe the self in the present), the latter is an identity that remains perpetually out of reach: a highly desirable yet elusive *aspirational identity* [3]. The enlightened self is never described by practitioners as something they have achieved [20], but only in terms of an ongoing process of becoming. In fact, I found that enacting practices and narratives that convey this sense of continuous striving is an important part of how members construct and perform their identities as "yogi's" and "Contemplative Catholics." In other words, being a "yogi" or a "Catholic" implies positioning oneself as an aspirant: someone "earnestly desirous of becoming a certain kind of person, and consciously and continuously in pursuit of that goal" ([3], p. 355). Yogi's are not those who embody the "enlightened self" but those who exert continuous and concerted efforts to cultivate this way of being-in-the-world.

5. Conclusions

While Bauman [2] has suggested that modern individuals lack a sense of destination, my research in these two communities of practice suggests otherwise. I found that practitioners did in fact have a sense of direction, one shaped by the image of the "enlightened self" depicted by teachers, texts, and fellow practitioners. Above, I demonstrated how this identity was defined not by birth, belief, or practice, but by the embodiment of certain perceptual, affective, and somatic ideals: a sacred gaze, a simultaneous sense of presence and detachment, and a holistic style of identity management. I argued that these communities, in articulating the characteristics and dispositions associated with "enlightenment," transmit a highly desirable but elusive *aspirational identity*. This shared ideal serves as a kind of potentiality: A description of the life practitioners could and ought to lead, a ready-made template for who and what they could be ([45], p. 97).

Aspirational identities are an important component of individuals' self-stories, and can have far-reaching consequences in the present [46–48]. In the case of these communities, the process of *divinization*—or becoming "like God"—structures and gives meaning to the past and present, as well as projecting forward into the future. The past is given meaning in relation to the ongoing process of spiritual formation, tying together disparate experiences with a unifying logic of progressive attainment [4,5]. In the present, the image of the "enlightened self" serves as a kind of compass, motivating and constraining behavior. Practitioners are motivated to undertake lines of action that they believe will move them towards their aspirations. The enlightened self also provides a framework and basis for evaluating the current self [46]. Aspirational identities, therefore, can have important influences on affect and self-esteem: discrepancies between one's ideal self and one's actual self can lead to anxiety, dejection, and low self-esteem [47].

It is important to note that aspirational identities are not the only type of future-oriented identity that may be transmitted in religious communities. Recent psychological research suggests that the *future self*, like the current self, is comprised of many different, and sometimes seemingly contradictory, *possible identities*: the "positive and negative identities one might hold in the future" ([9], p. 117).[12] These imagined future identities include the selves we desire to become [41,47], the identities or roles we think we should or ought to become [27], as well as the people we fear becoming [9,46]. From this perspective then each individual has a "repertoire of possible selves that can be viewed as the cognitive manifestation of enduring goals, aspirations, motivations, fears and threats" ([46], p. 954). Research on religious identity should consider the content and consequences of individual's future self-concepts, the dynamics through which possible identities (both desired and feared) are constructed and transmitted, as well as when, where, and why these imagined futures are brought to bear in deciding on lines of action in the present.

For one, future research can investigate the content of adherents' future-self-concepts and the process through which they are transmitted, identifying similarities and differences within and between communities.[13] Doing so would reveal the situated and contextual nature of religious identities and aspirations, and expand our understanding of how religious communities shape individual identity, experience, and action in the present. Future work might also consider differences in the valence of various possible identities across communities. Religious communities may not only influence what possible identities are available to people, but may also dictate the moral valence, or attractiveness, of the possible identities that are available in the broader cultural milieu. Are the same kinds of identities considered desirable (or negative) across different religious groups? How has the valence of different identities changed over time within the same community? Finally, religious communities would be strategic locations for investigating when and why future self-concepts are brought to bear in deciding on lines of action in the present [9]. When do adherents act in ways that align with their aspirations? When do they fail to do so, and why? Future research on content, structure, and consequences of possible identities, both desired and feared, across religious communities seems promising both as a question of interest in and of itself and as a potential mechanism underlying the impact of religiosity and religious identity on a range of other variables.

Acknowledgments: The author would like to thank Robert Wuthnow, Joanne Wang Golann, and Victoria Reyes for their valuable feedback on earlier drafts of this paper. This manuscript also benefited from the insightful comments and suggestions of participants in the Religion and Public Life workshop at the Center for the Study of Religion at Princeton University. Finally, the author thanks the two anonymous reviewers and the editorial board at *Religions* for helping to improve upon earlier versions of this manuscript.

Conflicts of Interest: The author declares no conflict of interest. The funding sponsors had no role in the design of the study; in the collection, analyses, or interpretation of data; in the writing of the manuscript, and in the decision to publish the results.

Abbreviations

IYI   Integral Yoga Institute

References

1.   William James. *The Principles of Psychology*. New York: Holt, 1890.
2.   Zygmunt Bauman. "From Pilgrim to Tourist—Or a Short History of Identity." In *Questions of Cultural Identity*. Edited by Stuart Hall and Paul du Gay. Los Angeles: SAGE Publications, 1996, pp. 18–36.

---

[12]   Existing research uses a range of different terms to refer to the components of the future self-concept, including: possible identities [4]; possible selves [8], ideal or ought selves [27], and preferred selves/identities [3].

[13]   The study of aspirational (and other possible) identities can be studied from a variety of different angles and methodological approaches. This analysis starts with organizations, and seeks to elucidate and analyze and content and structure of the aspirational identities they transmit. Future work might also start with individuals in order to examine the content of their future self-concepts, before identifying where their various possible identities are rooted, which are most influential, and why. Both approaches can contribute unique insights to our understanding of the sources and consequences of various possible identities. I thank an anonymous reviewer for pointing this out.

3. Thomas Thornborrow, and Andrew D. Brown. "'Being Regimented': Aspiration, Discipline and Identity Work in the British Parachute Regiment." *Organization Studies* 30 (2009): 355–76. [CrossRef]
4. Erin F. Johnston. "Learning to Practice, Becoming Spiritual: Spiritual Disciplines as Projects of the Self." Ph.D. Thesis, Princeton University, Princeton, NJ, USA, 2015. Proquest (3737421).
5. Thomas DeGloma, and Erin F. Johnston. "Cognitive Migrations: Toward a Cultural & Cognitive Sociology of Personal Transformation." In *Oxford Handbook of Cognitive Sociology*. Edited by Wayne Brekhus and Gabe Ignatow. London: Oxford University Press, 2016, forthcoming.
6. Dan P. McAdams. "Narrative Identity." In *Handbook of Identity Theory and Research*. Edited by Seth J. Schwartz, Koen Luyckx and Vivian L. Vignoles. New York: Springer, 2011, pp. 99–115.
7. Paul Ricoeur. "Narrative Identity." *Philosophy Today* 35 (1991): 73–81. [CrossRef]
8. Margaret R. Somers. "The Narrative Constitution of Identity: A Relational and Network Approach." *Theory and Society* 23 (1994): 605–49. [CrossRef]
9. Daphna Oyserman, and Leah James. "Possible Identities." In *Handbook of Identity Theory and Research*. Edited by Seth J. Schwartz, Koen Luyckx and Vivian L. Vignoles. New York: Springer, 2011, pp. 117–45.
10. Robert Wuthnow. *The Restructuring of American Religion: Society and Faith Since World War II*. Princeton: Princeton University Press, 1989.
11. Wade Clark Roof. *Spiritual Marketplace: Baby Boomers and the Remaking of American Religion*. Princeton: Princeton University Press, 1999.
12. Nancy Ammerman. "Religious Identities and Religious Institutions." In *Handbook of the Sociology of Religion*. Edited by Michele Dillon. Cambridge: Cambridge University Press, 2003, pp. 207–24.
13. Arthur L. Greil, and Lynn Davidman. "Religion and Identity." In *The Sage Handbook of the Sociology of Religion*. Edited by James A. Beckford and Jay Demerath. Los Angeles: Sage, 2007, pp. 549–65.
14. Anthony Giddens. *Modernity and Self-Identity: Self and Society in the Late Modern Age*. Stanford: Stanford University Press, 1991.
15. James A. Beckford. "Accounting for Conversion." *The British Journal of Sociology* 29 (1978): 249–62. [CrossRef]
16. Susan F. Harding. "Convicted by the Holy Spirit: The Rhetoric of Fundamental Baptist Conversion." *American Ethnologist* 14 (1987): 167–81. [CrossRef]
17. Erin F. Johnston. "'I Was Always This Way … ': Rhetorics of Continuity in Narratives of Conversion." *Sociological Forum* 28 (2013): 549–73. [CrossRef]
18. Peter G. Stromberg. *Language and Self-Transformation: A Study of the Christian Conversion Narrative*. Cambridge: Cambridge University Press, 1993.
19. Daniel Winchester. "Converting to Continuity: Temporality and Self in Eastern Orthodox Conversion Narratives." *Journal for the Scientific Study of Religion* 54 (2015): 439–60. [CrossRef]
20. Wendy Cadge, and Lynn Davidman. "Ascription, Choice, and the Construction of Religious Identities in the Contemporary United States." *Journal for the Scientific Study of Religion* 45 (2006): 23–38. [CrossRef]
21. Lori Peek. "Becoming Muslim: The Development of a Religious Identity." *Sociology of Religion* 66 (2005): 215–42. [CrossRef]
22. Charles Taylor. *Sources of the Self: The Making of the Modern Identity*. Cambridge: Harvard University Press, 1989.
23. George Herbert Mead. *Mind, Self and Society*. Chicago: University of Chicago Press, 1934.
24. Charles Hoorton Cooley. *Human Nature and the Social Order*. New York: Charles Scribner's Sons, 1902.
25. Lynn Davidman. *Tradition in a Rootless World: Women Turn to Orthodox Judaism*. Berkeley: University of California Press, 1991.
26. Virgil Bailey Gillespie. *The Dynamics of Religious Conversion*. Birmingham: Religious Education Press, 1991.
27. Mary Jo Neitz. *Charisma and Community: A Study of Religious Commitment within the Charismatic Renewal*. Piscataway: Transaction Publishers, 1987.
28. Michael Armato, and William Marsiglio. "Self-Structure, Identity, and Commitment: Promise Keepers' Godly Man Project." *Symbolic Interaction* 25 (2002): 41–65. [CrossRef]
29. William A. Barry, and William J. Connolly. *The Practice of Spiritual Direction*. New York: HarperOne, 2009.
30. Joan Chittister. *Wisdom Distilled from the Daily: Living the Rule of St. Benedict Today*. San Francisco: Harper, 1991.
31. David Morgan. *The Sacred Gaze: Religious Visual Culture in Theory and Practice*. Los Angeles: University of California Press, 2005.
32. Eviatar Zerubavel. *Social Mindscapes: An Invitation to Cognitive Sociology*. Cambridge: Harvard University Press, 1997.

33. Eviatar Zerubavel. "Horizons: On the Sociomental Foundations of Relevance." *Social Research* 60 (1993): 397–413.
34. Ann Taves, and Courtney Bender. "Introduction: Things of Value." In *What Matters?: Ethnographies of Value in a Not So Secular Age*. Edited by Ann Taves and Courtney Bender. New York: Columbia University Press, 2012.
35. Mihaly Csikszentmihalyi. *Finding Flow: The Psychology of Engagement with Everyday Life*. New York: BasicBooks, 1997.
36. Eckhart Tolle. *The Power of Now: A Guide to Spiritual Enlightenment*. Novato: New World Library, 2010.
37. Swami Satchidananda. *The Yoga Sutras of Patanjali: Commentary on the Raja Yoga sutras by Sri Swami Satchidananda*. Yogaville: Integral Yoga Publications, 1990.
38. Wayne Brekhus. *Peacocks, Chameleons, Centaurs: Gay Suburbia and the Grammar of Social Identity*. Chicago: University of Chicago Press, 2003.
39. Sheldon Stryker, and Richard T. Serpe. "Commitment, Identity Salience, and Role Behavior: Theory and Research Example." In *Personality, Roles, and Social Behavior*. Edited by William Ickes and Eric S. Knowles. New York: Springer, 1982, pp. 199–218.
40. Howard S. Becker. *Outsiders: Studies in the Sociology of Deviance*. New York: The Free Press, 1963.
41. Kathleen Charmaz. "'Discovering' Chronic Illness: Using Grounded Theory." *Social Science & Medicine* 30 (1990): 1161–72. [CrossRef]
42. Robert Wuthnow. *After Heaven: Spirituality in America since the 1950s*. Oakland: University of California Press, 1998.
43. Margaret Guenther. *Practice of Prayer*. New York: Cowley Publications, 1997, vol. 4.
44. Lewis A. Coser. *Greedy Institution: Patterns of Undivided Commitment*. New York: Free Press, 1974.
45. Jaber F. Gubrium, and James A. Holstein. *Institutional Selves: Troubled Identities in a Postmodern World*. Oxford: Oxford University Press, 2001.
46. Hazel Markus, and Paula Nurius. "Possible Selves." *American Psychologist* 41 (1986): 954–69. [CrossRef]
47. E. Tory Higgins. "Self-discrepancy: A Theory Relating Self and Affect." *Psychological Review* 94 (1987): 319–40. [CrossRef] [PubMed]
48. Stacey M. B. Wieland. "Ideal Selves as Resources for the Situated Practice of Identity." *Management Communication Quarterly* 24 (2010): 503–28. [CrossRef]

religions

MDPI

Article

The Dilemmas of Monogamy: Pleasure, Discipline and the Pentecostal Moral Self in the Republic of Benin

Sitna Quiroz

Department of Theology and Religion, Durham University, Abbey House, Palace Green, Durham DH1 3RS, UK; sitna.quiroz@durham.ac.uk

Academic Editors: Douglas James Davies and Michael J. Thate
Received: 4 May 2016; Accepted: 2 August 2016; Published: 8 August 2016

Abstract: Based on ethnographic research in the Republic of Benin, this article explores how Pentecostal teachings on marriage and the management of sexual pleasure contribute to shaping converts' moral selves. For Pentecostals, fidelity towards God, when single and fidelity between partners, once married, is presented as the ideal model of partnership to which every "Born-Again" should aspire. In the context where polygamous unions are socially accepted, Pentecostal pastors teach that a satisfactory sexual life restricted to marriage is the means of building successful monogamous unions. However, sexual satisfaction might not always guarantee marital success, especially when people face problems of infertility. The author suggests that the disciplinary regimes that these teachings promote contribute to shaping new modes of intimacy, which are compatible with societal changes but often contradict the extant social norms and ideals of reproduction. Moral dilemmas arising from this tension are the key to understanding how Pentecostal Christianity shapes the moral self. The article addresses how Pentecostals in Benin navigate and negotiate cultural continuities and discontinuities in relation to church authority and family life.

Keywords: Pentecostalism; morality; sexuality; marriage; monogamy; reproduction; infertility

1. Introduction

In recent years, relations of intimacy in Africa have experienced important transformations. These transformations can be considered part of a global trend where emotional intimacy is seen as the source of the "ties that bind" ([1], p. 2). In Africa, as in many other parts of the world, ideas of romantic love, the pursuit of pleasure and the ideal of a companionate marriage have increasingly become paramount attributes of modern relationships and forms of personhood [2,3]. These shifts in contemporary relationships cannot be isolated from broader social, political and economic processes, such as economic liberalization, international migration and the flows of information facilitated by mass media. These factors that have contributed to shaping local aspirations and interpretations of intimacy, based on the cultivation of individualist subjectivities and new forms of consumption [1–3].

The growth of Pentecostal Christianity in Africa, as in other parts of the world, has been part of the processes outlined above. The proliferation of Pentecostal churches in this continent has coincided with the implementation of neoliberal policies and the retreat of state power during the postcolonial and post-cold war era [4–7]. Pentecostalism has been interpreted, on the one hand, as a reaction to a societal environment of fear, deprivation and lack of confidence in the future caused by a retreat of the state [5,8]. These churches have been seen as filling a void left by the state in the provision of social services ([7], p. 53). On the other hand, their emphasis on conversion and the need to break with the past, has been seen as the vehicle by which people, especially the emerging middle classes, articulate aspirations to "modernity" [9–11]. By demonizing anything associated with tradition, they challenge older forms of authority grounded in rural life, as well as in religious and political colonial structures [7,9,12]. In doing so, these churches provide new eschatological, spiritual and moral narratives to re-interpret and predict world events ([7], pp. 63–66) and establish new forms of authority that regulate people's subjectivities and their affects ([7], pp. 65–67).

It is in this area that Pentecostal Christianity in Africa has played an active role in shaping new patterns of intimacy in people's relationships. Indeed, it has been argued that in their efforts to transform society according to a Pentecostal ethos, Pentecostal churches have contributed to shaping ideas of personhood, gender relations and emotions that are compatible with a neoliberal ethic and aspirations [8,13–16] which resonate with the modern ideals of intimacy [1]. One of the key issues is how, in the context of global concerns with the treatment and prevention of HIV, Pentecostal Christians have played an active role in teaching their congregations how to manage their marital and sexual lives. In doing so, they have relied on the introduction of methods such as counseling and the publication and distribution of educational literature on these topics [10,16]. These methods have informed the way in which "born-again" converts learn to express affection in public [17,18], assimilate ideas of romantic love [19] and train their emotions [20] to achieve an ideal of companionate marriage. People in churches are encouraged to speak openly about matters of sexuality, thus transforming local practices of secrecy that prevail in traditional religious contexts [10,17,21,22]. Moreover, these teachings contribute to a moral revaluation of social conditions that in African contexts tend to be stigmatized, such as singleness [23], infertility [24] and the bearing of children outside the marital bond [25].

This article contributes to and extends the body of literature outlined above by exploring how Pentecostal Christians within the Republic of Benin shape their moral selves through practices of discipline and self-discipline in their intimate relationships and the management of their sexuality. I focus on the moral dilemmas that Pentecostal teachings on sexuality bring about and the kinds of moral choices that Pentecostals are confronted with when they try to follow them. Indeed, the analysis of moral and ethical dilemmas has been a key concern in the study of Pentecostalism [26–29]. This is because Pentecostal conversion with its demands to break with the past [11] in order to be "born-again" requires a degree of separation or rupture from former social norms and values and an alignment with new Christian ones [30]. Pentecostal conversion is therefore characterized by an inherent tension between cultural continuities and discontinuities that derive from this process of rupture [29–32]. In his study of Pentecostalism in Ghana, Daswani [29] highlights this tension by bringing together advances in the study of Christianity and rupture with those from the anthropology of ethics and defines Pentecostal transformation in terms of ethical practice. He argues that rupture is always accompanied with ethical disputes and deliberations, where believers try to discern which aspects of their pasts should be left behind and which ones carried forward. They examine the compromises they have to make to remain committed Christians ([28], p. 13). Thus, Pentecostal ethical practice involves three interconnected aspects. The first consists of processes of discipline established by the church to ensure the continuity of a Christian future. The second aspect concerns moments of uncertainty, where converts question the parameters established to define what acceptable Christian practice is and what it is not. The third is what he calls "acts of philosophical labor and critical reflection" that intend "either to alleviate moral ambiguities or to create innovative positions around which new norms eventually develop"([28], p. 469; [29], p. 7). Framing rupture as ethical practice, he suggests allows "for a better understanding of how people respond to an incommensurability of values and practices internal to Pentecostalism" ([28], p. 468).

The moral questioning and dilemmas that happen in the domain of sexuality can be analyzed in the light of some of Daswani's observations and Robbins' [27] theory of morality and social change.[1] In particular, I am interested in the relationship between disciplinary practices, moments of uncertainty

---

[1] I will discuss this process of moral change in relation to Robbins' [16,17] work in the last part of this article.

or ethical deliberations and people's responses to these moments. Moreover, one also needs to consider the relational and emotional qualities of Pentecostal transformation ([29], pp. 20, 27), the way it takes place and is achieved through people's relationships with their kin groups, their immediate family, pastors, church fellows, Jesus and God [28,29,32]. Also, the articulation of emotional expressions that accompany these relationships, such as bonds of affection, love, shame, anger or regret cannot be isolated from the analysis of the process by which converts shape their moral selves. I want to highlight how in cases where people experience conditions such as infertility that bring a sense of "disruption to social and family life" ([33], p. 201; [34]), Pentecostal "ethical practice" provides a sense of continuity and hope. I also show how moral failure and discipline open the possibility of bringing about moral change. At least in matters of sexuality, change is not exclusively the product of moments of philosophical or critical reflection ([29], p. 7). Instead, I suggest moments of moral failure, the disciplinary practices to which converts subject themselves and/or are made subject to and the experience of redemption that results from these, are central to understanding this process. In this case, moral failure and discipline should not be solely seen as negative aspects of a coercive or restrictive moral order; instead, I want to highlight their positive and productive potential.

In Benin, as in other African countries where polygynous[2] unions are prevalent, Pentecostals place an important emphasis on prescribing and teaching how to build monogamous unions where sex is restricted to the context of marriage. These teachings establish disciplinary regimes that also bring about important moral challenges. It is assumed that a satisfactory sexual life plays a crucial role in building and maintaining successful Godly intended monogamous unions. However, in a patrilineal society such as this, where having numerous descendants is highly valued, a satisfactory sexual life does not always guarantee marital success. This is especially the case when monogamous couples face problems of infertility. I argue that the moral and ethical dilemmas of people in these situations reveal certain continuities in the importance of the patrilineage and the value placed on sexual reproduction to secure its permanence. However, in cases when infertility threatens this value, Pentecostal ethical practice can provide a sense of personal continuity. However, this does not mean that the authority of the patrilineage remains unchanged vis-à-vis Pentecostal values. How people experience moral questioning, the choices they make and the way in which they negotiate the tensions between the imperatives of their lineages with those of the church, are key to understanding how Pentecostal Christianity in Benin brings about moral change in social norms and values.

To develop my argument I will first introduce some general characteristics of marital and sexual relationships between men and women in contemporary Benin and some of their historical transformations. Second, I will present the ways in which Pentecostal teachings try to respond to contemporary changes by providing specific moral guidelines. In particular, I describe the kinds of teachings addressed to women and men and the disciplinary regimes that they create. Third, I present the challenges that these teachings bring about, especially when people face problems of infertility. Using the case study of a young couple without children, I present the moral dilemma faced and the tensions between a person's patrilineage and the authority of the church. Fourth, I present what happens in situations where people breach the Pentecostal moral behavior and commit adultery. I suggest that these moments present key opportunities to effect moral change and where disciplinary practices such as public confession play a central role. We will see that these breaches of moral behavior can be considered essential to shaping people's moral selves at individual and societal levels.

The Ethnographic Setting

The material that I present here was gathered during a period of nineteen months of ethnographic fieldwork in the southeast of the Republic of Benin, between 2008 and 2010. The events that I describe

---

2   Polygyny refers to the union of one man with several wives, whereas Polygamy refers to plural unions in general.

happened at the Assemblies of God (AoG), a Pentecostal church in a town that I call here Ipese.[3] Ipese is a semi-rural town situated in the proximities of the border with Nigeria in an area with predominantly Yoruba population. This town has a population of approximately 5000 people and is characterized by the ethnic diversity of its population. Attracted by the burgeoning commercial activity of its two weekly markets, people from different ethnic backgrounds have settled in this town over the years. At the time of my fieldwork, the AoG church in this town had a membership of approximately 300 people, mostly of Gun origin, followed by the Yoruba.

In the Republic of Benin there exist a wide variety of Pentecostal churches with diverse theological approaches. Each of them could be situated somewhere between the continuum of so-called holiness movement or classical Pentecostalism and the increasingly popular prosperity gospel ([35], p. 9). The AoG is the Pentecostal church with most members at a national level. One of the main features of the AoG in Ipese is that its theology could be seen as closer to a classical Pentecostal theology, rather than the prosperity gospel. The pastor and fellowship at the AoG church in Ipese were rather suspicious of prosperity gospel pastors, especially from Nigeria, who emphasized the importance of material wealth as a testimony of God's blessings. Sermons and teachings in this church placed particular emphasis on the need to observe a strict moral conduct. This was particularly the case in relation to sexual practices. I now turn to present some of general aspects of marital relations and sexual reproduction in Benin.

2. Forms of Marriage, Sexuality and Reproduction in the Context of Social Change in Benin

Throughout history, marital relations in Benin, as in many other parts of Africa, have been subject to transformations that reflect broader changes in patterns of power, economic relations, gender inequalities and the assimilation of new cultural ideas [36]. At the beginning of the twentieth century Fadipe [37] described the Yoruba marriage as "one of the social institutions (...) which has been most in a state of flux as a result of the diffusion of foreign ideas and the quick process of economic growth" ([37], p. 91). In this quote, Fadipe referred to the influence of European colonization and Christian missions. Today, this colonial legacy converges with the influence of the internet, foreign films, Latin American and Indian soap operas, the government's legislation in matters of family law, the promotion of women's rights by international organizations and Pentecostal Christianity.

The existence of polygamy in African societies has been subject to contention, debate and study in religious, governmental and academic circles. Nineteenth century Christian missionaries[4] saw polygamy as one of the major obstacles to overcome in their efforts to Christianize the population [38,39]. Many of them condemned this practice as uncivilized, unchristian and immoral ([40], p. 341). Missionary efforts to establish monogamy as the only form of Christian marriage were supported by colonial administrations that justified its enforcement by establishing legal frameworks ([38], p. 55). However, there is also evidence that missionary strategies in establishing monogamy varied across the continent and denominations, some were more tolerant and permissive of polygyny than others ([38,40] pp. 54, 342, 343). This scenario presents some parallels with the current situation in Benin, as will be seen below.

Polygyny has been and continues to be a predominant form of marriage, especially in West Africa ([41], p. 363; [38], p. 56). Neither increasing urbanization, which modernization theories predicted would contribute to its disappearance ([41], p. 365), nor missionary efforts have achieved much to change this predominance. The study of polygamy in patrilineal societies in Africa has been at the center of classical ethnographies [42–45]. One of the main reasons given to explain why men seek to enter polygynous unions is to ensure a large progeny [43], or at least to secure one male child. A large

---

[3] The name of this town and all personal names are pseudonyms. I would like to express my sincere gratitude to all the people in the Republic of Benin whose collaboration made this research possible.

[4] Although the missionary presence in Africa can be traced back to the fifteenth century, it was until the nineteenth century that a systematic approach to missionization took place [30].

number of progeny allows men to establish their seniority and position themselves within the social hierarchy as heads of lineages [46]. It secures a so-called "wealth in people" [45] and the necessary social relations that increase a man's opportunities to access political and/or economic power. Among the Yoruba, Gun and Fon in the southeast of Benin, having numerous children is highly valued despite a trend among younger people to have fewer children. People often say that a person who has many children is a wealthy person, regardless of her economic status. In Yoruba language, children are often described as precious beads and silver ([47], p. 167) and women are praised in traditional oral poetry (*oriki*) for providing their husbands with children ([48], p. 213).

In a society such as this, sexual relations, the means of reproduction, shape marital relations and negotiations of sexuality ([49], p. 159). These are often at the center of power struggles between partners and raise a great deal of concern and dilemma. Due to their capacity to procreate, women play a central role in the perpetuation of their husband's lineage. They are seen both as powerful and dangerous beings that need to be respected and feared ([47], p. 167). As I witnessed in Benin, many women are well aware of the power they hold vis-à-vis their husbands. Sometimes they use their sexuality to their own advantage, in particular to obtain economic rewards from men ([50], p. 153). In turn, men manifest concern about the fidelity of their partners or wives and say that only women know whose child they are carrying in their wombs. A man's decision to take a second or third wife is often a painful emotional experience for women. It brings about feelings of jealousy and creates rivalries between co-wives. Some women in polygamous unions come to terms with their situation, but many others do not. On various occasions I have heard women express with sadness that "the human heart cannot be shared".

Although in Benin monogamy tends to be associated with Christian marriages, religious affiliation alone does not determine the type of marital union. During my fieldwork, I met several Muslim men who were monogamous. Similarly, different Christian denominations hold different views and levels of tolerance towards polygamous unions. It is well known that many so-called monogamous men in Catholic and Methodist churches marry and live with one official wife, but keep clandestine relationships with other women, who are popularly referred to as *seconde* or *troisième bureau* (second or third office). Similarly, the Celestial Church of Christ, one of the largest African Independent Churches in Benin, tolerates polygynous unions on the basis that it is hypocritical to claim monogamous fidelity, while living in concubinage ([38], p. 57). In contrast, Pentecostalism is the only Christian denomination that severely condemns polygamy as unchristian and immoral and shows no tolerance towards "born-again" men who decide to take another wife.

Moreover, in 2004, monogamy became the only form of union legally recognized in the national constitution of Benin. These legislative changes have been promoted by international NGOs promoting women's rights and by the government's efforts to appear "modern" vis-à-vis international donors. The national curriculum in Benin prescribes the teaching in schools of the constitutional law and the declaration of equal rights between men and women. These ideas are debated in the classrooms and young people are asking questions about whether polygyny is something that people should continue practicing. On various occasions, I had conversations with young people who were curious about how monogamy worked in "the West" and the reasons why people had few or no children. Nowadays, young people in Benin become sexually active at a young age and very often a marital union happens because a girl has already become pregnant. Older generations often complain that traditional values such as the importance of virginity at the time of marriage have been lost and they condemn young people's behavior for their lack of morality ([51], p. 964). These local debates reflect how in Benin, as in other parts of Africa, idioms of love and "affective propriety" are used to express generational differences, or assert claims of power or "modernity" ([36], pp. 15, 16). But they also reflect a sense of loss and concern for what people perceive as "lack of moral guidelines" in a context of rapid social change. During many conversations, people said with disapproval that democracy and human rights had only caused disorder, a feeling that seems to be common in West Africa [7].

Pentecostal pastors are well aware of these debates and use their teachings about relationships to offer new moral guidelines. Interestingly, these teachings often draw upon certain "traditional" values to give them Christian meanings. I now turn to explore Pentecostal teachings in relation to sexual and marital relations.

3. Teaching Women and Men to Manage Sexual Desire within the Church

Based on Biblical principles, Pentecostals prescribe the observance of chastity and fidelity towards God while single and fidelity between partners once married. To achieve this, Pentecostal churches teach their congregations how to manage their sexual and marital lives in order to build Godly intended unions and to lead a good Christian life. Single people are taught to practice chastity and to restrain themselves from physical contact until the marriage takes place. However, once married, people are encouraged to enjoy their sexual union fully. Although teachings are directed at both men and women, women's teachings are more prominent. Whereas women's teachings focus on the management of sexual pleasure, teachings for men focus on the development of self-control.

Teachings for women start when they are young and single. Pentecostal young girls are encouraged to keep their "hearts" and bodies pure. Abstinence before marriage holds some attraction for Pentecostal girls. Women consider that Pentecostal churches provide the education that many do not receive at home. In everyday context, people talk and joke openly but indirectly about sex. However, many women told me that they do not necessarily receive sexual education. Beginning marriage as a virgin does not mean that a Pentecostal girl arrives at this point without knowledge. Prior to their wedding day, women who are engaged to be married attend meetings for married women, where the elder women advise them on matters related to their marital and sexual lives [21]. Although the importance of virginity could be considered a form of continuity with "traditional" values, this is not necessarily the case. In the past, virginity was very important because it ensured that children born from a marital union belonged to the husband's patrilineage [37]. However, when a Pentecostal woman keeps her virginity, she is considered to gain God's favor and to receive his blessings in reward. Therefore, the honor of woman's virginity no longer falls upon her patrilineage or her husband's patrilineage. Instead, the blessings and honor fall upon her. Although the value of virginity is pursued, this is regulated under the authority of the church not the patrilineage.

Once a Pentecostal woman is married, she is encouraged to be sexually active and to fully enjoy the sexual union, as long as it happens within the marital bond. In contrast, among non-Pentecostal women in Benin, as in many parts of West Africa, the sexual act within marriage is mostly seen as an act of procreation rather than a pleasurable activity. Women are usually expected to put up with unsatisfying relations for the sake of looking after children and sex is seen as a duty that a woman must endure ([51], pp. 966, 967). Pentecostal women are told that once they are married, the body of a wife belongs to her husband and the body of the husband belongs to his wife. Therefore, they should always be available to their husbands and both partners are entitled to enjoy the sexual act. Moreover, if a woman knows how to please her husband, it will be easier for her to retain him and to maintain a monogamous household. In this sense, Pentecostal teachings reinforce the popular idea that men's infidelity is to be blamed on women's behavior and their incapacity to satisfy their husband's desires ([13], p. 558; [49], p. 173; [50].)

At the AoG church in Ipese, teachings on women's sexuality used to take place during the women group's gatherings every two weeks on Friday. The pastor's wife, maman Jasmine, organized talks (on topics, such as personal care and hygiene, seduction and sexual performance, among others) that helped women to live a Christian life. In relation to personal care, maman Jasmine encouraged women to look after themselves and to be attractive to their husbands. She gave advice in aspects of intimate health and encouraged women to approach midwives and nurses in case they had concerns about either their own sexual health or that of their husbands. She also instructed women in the art of seduction. For example, she advised women to cook their husband's favorite foods and to give variety to what they cooked. She encouraged them to show their affection by feeding their husbands, placing the food in their mouths, removing the bones of their fish and making sure that their husbands had a pleasant time while they shared their meal. Although women are taught to dress very modestly in public, she advised them to reserve and wear revealing clothes in the bedroom. She also encouraged women to be the ones who approached their husbands to have sexual relations, instead of waiting for the husband's initiation. She finally advised women to soothe their husbands by offering their bodies whenever they were sad or angry. More importantly, women were taught to use their sexuality wisely in order to strengthen their marriage and bring their husbands closer to them. Maman Jasmine used to quote Proverbs 14:1 saying, "the wise woman builds her house, but the foolish one pulls it down with her hands." This way, they would prevent their husbands searching for, or justifying their extra-marital sexual liaisons.

There was a very important personal reason why maman Jasmine took these teachings so seriously. She told me that at the beginning of her marriage with the pastor, it had been very difficult for her to be physically affectionate and sexually open. She had grown up in a polygynous household in Togo. Her father had seven wives, of which five lived in the same compound at her village of origin. She had grown up being exposed to the jealousies and discussions between co-wives. Her own mother had left the paternal compound to live in Lome. Therefore, the relationship between her parents was never close. She never knew what conjugal love was meant to be. She feared men's behavior, because she had witnessed domestic violence within her own household. Therefore, once she married, it was very difficult for her to be physically affectionate. As a result, the pastor often felt frustrated because he felt rejected. But maman Jasmine wanted to please God. She was determined to be a good Christian wife. She approached the wife of the pastor in her former church and this woman gave her advice and recommended books to read. Maman Jasmine educated herself by reading the kinds of books that Pentecostal churches produce on these topics and sell to their fellowship. One such book, written by a Christian counselor, is called *Le Banquet du Seigneur. Le Super Sexe* (The Banquet of the Lord. Super Sex). The title refers to the act of marital sex as a banquet, something that is meant to be enjoyable and originally designed by God for that purpose. After having put in practice the things that she had learnt, she noticed the difference that a good sexual union had made to her marriage. She knew that many women in the church could benefit from her own experience and that is why she invested herself in teaching women about their sexuality.

Teachings about the management of sexuality and disciplinary practices for women have a positive and affective quality. They shape women's emotions through the channeling of sexual desire and pleasure ([20], p. 354). Women need to practice abstention when they are single but in the marital context, the sexual union is meant to be both fully enjoyed and key to building a bond of love between husband and wife. Although these disciplinary practices place women under the authority of the church, they are presented and exercised in a way that holds a certain appeal to women. Therefore, women subject themselves voluntarily through "technologies of the self" [52] that involve ways of dressing, self-care and seduction. Women's teachings are complemented by those addressed to men. I now turn to explore the main features of men's teachings.

Teaching Men to Develop Self-Control

Teachings directed to men focus on the development of self-control. In order for a marriage to be monogamous, Pentecostal men need to steer clear of the temptation to seek other women and to avoid succumbing to peer or family pressures. These teachings contradict popular opinions and notions of masculinity based on sexual performance, which predominate in patrilineal societies such as these ([51], p. 966). It is common to hear men say that polygyny is in African men's blood. They justify themselves saying that the desire for more than one woman is a natural need that they have to fulfill ([49], p. 166) and peer pressure encourages monogamous men to seek extramarital affairs ([49], p. 171). Pentecostal men acknowledge these difficulties. However for them, their sense of masculinity is developed in their sense of self-control [53,54]. The Pentecostal men I talked to agreed that the only way they could manage to do this was by being filled with the Holy Spirit, which is achieved and cultivated through practices such as prayer and fasting.

For example, papa Daniel remembered the bad experiences he had while growing up in a polygynous household. He had witnessed the jealousy of his father's co-wives, the discord among their children and subsequent accusations of witchcraft. Even before his conversion to Pentecostalism, he had decided that he wanted to be monogamous. He did not want to repeat what he had experienced as a child. Nevertheless, when he married, he had several secret "girlfriends" and owned a flat where he used to entertain them. However, when he became born-again, he decided to leave this lifestyle behind.

One of the major life changes that he described after giving his life to Jesus was precisely his ability to leave his "addiction" for women. He compared this to other addictions such as alcohol or tobacco. He portrayed peer pressure as having played an important role in his previous life, whereas his current life was one where he was able to withstand this pressure. One of the things that made him change his mind was that the church often preaches that men who have extramarital affairs are more prone to contract HIV, or to die due to spells put on them by the women with whom they sleep. He feared dying young, leaving his wife widowed and his children orphaned. He stressed that it was Jesus in his life that gave him this clarity of thought and the strength to change his lifestyle. He said,

> "You see? Temptations are everywhere, in the job, at home, with friends, in the family [...] but the person who has Jesus is different to the one who doesn't have Jesus in his life. It also depends on the faith and the strength of the faith of each person [...] You always have temptations. It happens among members of the church, and even between pastors and their fellowship. But if you really know The One [Jesus] you have received, then you will be strong [...] Satan will tempt you to see if you are solid, if you can resist. But with prayer and fasting you can always resist, [temptation] will pass." [55]

Resisting temptation is a matter of choice that every Pentecostal has to make and as papa Daniel said, everyone is equally exposed. Similarly, the pastor at the AoG in Ipese admitted that leading a monogamous lifestyle was not easy but it was possible and a man could learn how to do it. I once commented that it must be difficult to lead a monogamous life, especially when polygyny is the norm and most of people have grown up in polygynous households. He agreed, but also said that a person's upbringing does not determine her choices. That is why, he said, it is important to be filled with the Holy Spirit and lead a life of constant prayer and fasting, which are essential to develop self-control. In the case of men, self-discipline, self-control and being sexually satisfied with their wives are key elements that allow men to lead a monogamous lifestyle but more importantly, they constitute the elements by which Pentecostal men develop their sense of manhood, spiritual strength and power ([53], pp. 264, 265; [54], p. 225). Therefore, most men no longer need to define their masculinity based on the criteria of non-Pentecostal men, such as sexual performance.

Teachings directed to women and men establish disciplinary regimes that shape intimate relationships between men and women. In their efforts to build monogamous unions, Pentecostals focus their attention on building bonds of love and affection between partners ([18,19]; [20], p. 31). In doing so, they also seek to address certain dissatisfaction with polygynous unions where emotions such as jealousy and rivalries between co-wives tend to dominate. These teachings demonstrate that we cannot understand Pentecostal ethical practice in the area of sexuality without paying attention to people's relational and affective ties ([29], p. 20). Teachings on marriage, the management of sexuality and channeling of desire are essential to achieving a good Christian life. Although monogamy provides certain advantages such as avoiding jealousies in the household, there is also a downside: when a couple cannot conceive a child. I now turn to explore the challenges and the ethical dilemma of infertility and childlessness.

4. The Challenges of Infertility among Pentecostals in the Republic of Benin

Cross-cultural studies of infertility have demonstrated that this condition is often experienced as "disruption to the anticipated course of life" ([34], pp. 388, 390; [33,56]) and people develop different cultural strategies to cope with and make sense of it [34,56]. In a social context like the southeast of Benin where having a large progeny is important, its opposite, childlessness, bears a great stigma. Although the consequences of infertility affect women and men, it is women who tend to bear most of the negative consequences [33,34,56].

In Benin, parenthood is a marker of adulthood. As a sign of respect, when a person has a child, she will be called mother or father followed by the name of their eldest child or their eldest male child. Those who are unable to conceive are far less respected than those with children; their opinion is hardly valued or taken into account at family reunions. This is particularly difficult when a woman is the first wife of a man, since her position within her husband's family is devalued. Women are severely criticized for being "barren" and not fully accomplished, as well as very often becoming targets of witchcraft accusations. However, men do not carry the same stigma. When a couple is not able to conceive, a man compensates for the lack of offspring by trying to conceive children with other women. Although women are often seen as being victims of their husbands' infidelities, what is less often mentioned is the way in which extended families and peer groups pressure men to engage in sexual encounters outside of the marital bond.

The importance of fertility is such that people engage in different methods to secure offspring, from traditional remedies to Pentecostal prayers. Some people consider that Pentecostal churches are highly efficacious. In some cases, people convert after having obtained the gift of fertility from God but this is not always the case. Once women are pregnant, Pentecostals accompany them in prayer. Miscarriages or hemorrhages during childbirth are attributed to the work of spirits. Deaths that happen during childbirth are considered some of the most spiritually dangerous; therefore it is a moment when women need the most protection via the use of prayer. However, sometimes Pentecostal prayers do not work. Unanswered prayers pose serious challenges to those who cannot conceive. Counter-intuitively, it is probably Pentecostal men who find it more difficult to cope with infertility compared to Pentecostal women ([24], p. 42). I will now show some of these difficulties with reference to the case of Florent and Pelagie.

At the time of my fieldwork, Florent was a man in his mid-thirties and Pelagie was a woman in her late twenties. They were married and attended with commitment the AoG church in Ipese. Florent in particular, was a member of the church committee and helped as a Fon translator. During the five years of their marriage, they had not been able to conceive a child. He indirectly attributed their fertility problems to family jealousy. His wife had been diagnosed with blocked fallopian tubes, a condition that in this context is explained as caused by witchcraft. It is believed that relatives tie a woman's fallopian tubes through "occult" procedures to prevent a woman from conceiving and to block the couple's future. People frequently prayed for the couple for them to be delivered from malign forces. Pelagie often fasted and prayed alone or in company of other women, especially the pastor's wife.

During a conversation, Florent shyly confessed that this situation had been a great challenge to his Christian life. He tried to avoid going to his town of origin, because he did not want to hear criticism. His maternal aunts insisted that he took another wife. He said, "I love my wife very much and hearing these comments makes me feel very sad. Besides, it is a sin! Christians are supposed to attach to one woman and become one flesh". His wife Pelagie faced similar criticism and difficulties, as do other women who cannot conceive. She struggled to come to terms with her situation, however, maintaining virtuous behavior was for her the means to earn God's favor and sustain her marriage. It was clear that they loved each other. They expressed to each other affection, in the ways that were taught and encouraged at church. For example, whenever they gave a testimony in front of the assembly they held hands or, in festive occasions, they wore outfits made of the same fabric.

When I asked Florent in which ways this experience had challenged his Christian life, he said, "In Benin, a person is not complete if they don't have children. When you die and you don't have children, people say that you just die like that! You don't have a future; you don't have someone who will be called 'your son'. Nobody will bury you and represent you after your death". I asked if he was concerned about it and he added:

> "I don't care much about my burial. They can throw my corpse away and let it rot. Those who don't know Jesus are those who worry about the corpse. We Christians know that the flesh is just flesh and it will disintegrate. What matters is the soul that goes to heaven." [57]

In this case, he was not concerned about the funeral ceremony as such, or what would happen if nobody gave him a proper burial. However, he was concerned about not having someone who would be called "his son", someone who would bear his name after his death, or would inherit the house he had built: elements that in this context index the permanence of a patrilineage. When I asked him how he dealt with this situation, he said, "I just pray". He also tried to convince himself that this was not really important. He said, "For people, the honor of this world is what matters most […] I think God will give me a child and if He doesn't, I cannot worry about this honor". Florent was confronted with uncertainty and moral dilemma: to give in to family pressures or to remain loyal to his wife. He critically reflected about his situation and tried to find an explanation for why he was facing this challenge. In this case, judgment and discernment were important in his ethical practice ([28], p. 472). Florent had decided to subject himself to the moral code of the church and to practice self-discipline through prayer and self-control. This gave him and his wife a sense of hope. In cases of infertility, it has been suggested, people develop cultural strategies to reframe their understandings of the self and the world [34]. The "Judeo-Christian ethic" does so, it offers "shifts in vision" that enable people to reframe their understanding of themselves and to re-establish a certain sense of continuity ([34], pp. 401, 402). This happened in the case of Florent and Pelagie.

Florent and Pelagie had chosen to live their lives according to the moral guidelines of the church. Among non-Christian unions, the lack of children justifies the dissolution of a marriage. However, Pentecostal men and women cannot seek divorce in these situations. Those who cannot conceive are encouraged to become stronger in their faith and to use this experience as an opportunity to get closer to God. As a result, Pentecostals shift the focus of the marital union away from its merely reproductive capacity and the patrilineage and instead, place stronger emphasis on its affective role. Thus in principle, the centrality of the patrilineage becomes secondary. However, as I will explain later, this shift is not always achieved. Moreover, because Florent and Pelagie had chosen to focus on cultivating their marital union and relationship with God, they received strong support from the church, particularly in the form of prayers and social recognition. They were considered good Christians. Their social relations within the church offered essential support in moments of struggle and eased their efforts to abide to a moral framework. These relationships gave them a sense of social continuity that counterbalanced the "disruption" in their patrilineal relationships.

The way in which Pentecostals experience these kinds of moral challenges and the kind of choices they make are influenced by a person's gender and his or her position within the patrilineage. For example, Pentecostal women who cannot conceive are usually treated with dignity within the church and their self-worth is not necessarily questioned. However, things tend to be more difficult for men. Monogamy limits men's opportunities to secure at least one male offspring and to secure the permanence of their patrilineage. Florent's anxiety in relation to his death is a clear example of this struggle. It is not insignificant that he expressed concerns in relation to his death. In Benin, people who die without having a child are considered to have lived a futile life, no matter how wealthy, famous, talented or successful they might have been. It is during funerals that most members of the lineage are reunited, where people judge others as to whether or not they lived life to the full and managed to become "successful" in life ([46], p. 362). His testimony conveys a negotiated acceptance of his condition and certain assimilation of Pentecostal ideas of the afterlife. However, his hesitation and concern for not having someone that would be called "his son" after he passed away, conveyed concern for not having someone that would ensure the permanence of his patrilineage.

Many men however, do not manage to overcome the dilemmas of infertility. They end up giving in to family pressures and committing adultery. I now turn to explore these moments of moral failure and the way in which discipline and redemption play a crucial role in shaping moral change.

5. Sin, Discipline, Redemption and Moral Change in Benin

Whenever a member of the AoG church commits a "major" sin such as adultery, they are required to confess in front of the assembly and are subjected to a period of discipline. A person's public confession usually takes place during the Sunday service. The person usually explains the conditions in which such a "sin" happened and manifests his/her repentance. After the confession, members of the assembly pray for the person, to ask for God's forgiveness. During the period of "discipline" the person sits at the back of the church and is suspended from his/her position of responsibility within the church. The length of this period can vary from one month to one year, depending on each individual case, or until the person has demonstrated a complete change in her behavior. When a person concludes the period of discipline, he/she is reincorporated to their former roles and into the life of the church. Most Pentecostal churches in Benin have the same kind of disciplinary practices.

During my fieldwork, there were two cases of adultery committed by men. None of these men decided to marry a second wife. If this had happened, they would have been expelled from the church. Because these two men repented, they were subjected to discipline. One of them was papa Elodie, whose period of discipline lasted for more than one year. Papa Elodie used to be a very devout Christian and an active member of the AoG in Ipese. When I first arrived in Benin, papa Elodie did not live with his wife, he had a concubine and lived with her in another town. After a few months he returned to Ipese to live with his wife, he repented and started a period of discipline. Papa Elodie had one thing in common with Florent: he did not have a male child. He was the father of a young girl with his official wife, who after the birth of their first child could no longer conceive any more children. During one of my conversations with his wife, she confessed that this had caused an enormous strain in their marriage, especially in relation to her in-laws. Her husband's parents had put a lot of pressure on them to conceive a male child. Papa Elodie was also a successful merchant and spent large periods of time away from home. It is common that men with strong economic positions, like papa Elodie, receive strong peer and family pressure to take other wives ([49], p. 167). This must have happened to papa Elodie.

Pentecostal discipline is harsh and committing adultery not only means gaining God's disfavor but mainly losing face among church members. Therefore Pentecostal men think twice before giving in to family and peer pressures, especially if they have achieved a position of respectability within the church. However, having or not having descendants, especially male, has a strong impact on how men in Benin position themselves in relation to the rest of their kin and how they establish themselves as respectable men. In this case, both Florent and papa Elodie were well-respected members of the church, but each of them decided to respond differently to the same moral challenge. One possible reason might be that Florent did not have the same position within his lineage as papa Elodie. Florent was not the eldest son of his father. In contrast, papa Elodie was the eldest male child and a successful businessman, qualities that make him eligible for succession after his father's death. When a man is the eldest male of his father's children, the pressure from the patrilineage tends to be stronger. It is very likely that a person's position within her family, patrilineage and other circles in society influence a person's moral failure. We see here again, a tension between the imperatives of the patrilineage and those of the church.

The assimilation of Pentecostal moral behavior and the tensions that arise when a convert is confronted with the imperatives of opposing moral values is not exclusive of Pentecostals in Benin. Robbins [26,27] describes how the Urapmin Pentecostals of Papua New Guinea experience moral dilemma in quite significant ways, to the extent that they approach most of their lives as a moral torment. Drawing on a Weberian view of social values, Robbins suggests that society is constituted of different spheres, such as the economic, political, esthetic, erotic and intellectual ([27], p. 298), which are hierarchically organized and each one having a dominant value that governs it. Where there is harmony within and between spheres, there exists what he calls a "morality of reproduction", in which most of the moral action happens unquestioningly in everyday life. However, conflict between or within these value spheres lays the ground for a "morality of freedom" and choice, where "people become consciously aware of choosing their own fate" ([27], pp. 299, 300). When a society such as the Urapmin are confronted with a changing hierarchy of values caused by rapid social change, moral conflicts arise because the old or previously predominant values assert their importance in face of the new or formerly subordinate ones ([27], p. 302). The Urapmin live in a constant moral conflict because they have to choose between two different cultural logics with conflicting predominant values: one of Christian individualism that prioritizes individual salvation and one of Urapmin relationalism that prioritizes the creation and maintenance of social relationships. While Christianity has changed ideas in many domains, it has not completely done so in the domain of what Robbins calls "social structure", in other words, it has not completely changed cultural ideas on how society should be organized and how relationships should be carried out ([27], p. 306).

Pentecostals in Benin also live in a context where we could say the hierarchy of values has been disrupted as a result of social change. The experiences of moral questioning that I have explored here demonstrate the tension that exists between the values and authority of the patrilineage and those of the church. Despite changes derived from conversion, the value of reproduction and the principles of seniority maintain a central role in shaping the imperatives of social relations in Benin. However, not every Pentecostal experiences moral conflicts to the same extent or degree. What shapes experiences of conflict and the moral choices they make depend to a large extent on a person's specific social position within her patrilineage. Therefore, moral conflicts need to be understood in relation to a person's generational context, gender and her position within the patrilineage. These conflicts need to be understood in relation to a person's individual position within the broader social structure and her negotiations of different spheres of value.

Although, moral failure constitutes an individual experience it also has a collective transformative potential. When a person confesses publicly, members of the assembly learn the intimate details of people's lives, leaving them exposed to gossip and public surveillance. It is a shameful experience and one could think that it works as a form of coercion ([20], p. 355). However, this is not exclusively the case. Public confession plays an important role in shaping the dynamics of secrecy and disclosure according to a specific moral framework [10,21]. In many Pentecostal circles in Africa, making public what is hidden is seen as a form of "deliverance": it counterbalances traditional forms of spiritual power rooted in secrecy. These are also contexts where words and speech are conceived to be powerful vehicles that bring about the "realization of the subject, more than just being an expression of intentions and motivations" ([10], p. S436). Moreover, for a person to make a public confession, she must first admit her fault and repent. This means that before a person can recognize certain behavior as sin, she must have already internalized certain moral criteria. This assimilation of moral behavior takes place gradually, from the moment of conversion, as a person is socialized into the life of the church, participates in teachings, such as the management of sexuality, and practices disciplines of the self, such as prayer and fasting, as I described above. In turn, the enforcement of disciplinary techniques after a person has committed sin and repented can be seen as ways in which people, collectively, have the opportunity to rethink and later reinforce what they have learnt as part of the new value system. Disciplinary practices such as public confession, prayer and fasting, are techniques by which people can "work on the self" [58] to reinsert themselves into a new moral life. By doing so, they reinforce the importance of the new values to themselves and, through their own experiential example of shame and redemption, to others.

6. Conclusions

In this article I have presented the way in which Pentecostal churches teach their congregations to manage their sexual lives. These teachings play an important role in the project of building Christian monogamous marriages and shaping Christian moral selves. Young people are taught to practice fidelity towards God by remaining abstinent before marriage, whereas married people are prescribed sexual exclusivity and fidelity towards their partners. In the case of married couples, Pentecostals place a strong emphasis on teaching women to please their husbands sexually and men are taught to exert self-control. In this process of shaping and channeling sexual desire people embody a moral behavior through practices of the self, such as prayer and fasting, which help a person be filled by the Holy Spirit that in turn makes possible this self-control.

However, in this society where having numerous children is highly valued, sexual fidelity is hard to maintain when a couple cannot have children. Therefore, this represents one of the areas where Pentecostals in Benin face numerous dilemmas, which sometimes constitute important challenges to their Pentecostal life particularly for men. Pentecostal ethical practice also offers an opportunity to re-establish certain continuity to the personal and social disruption of infertility. This was demonstrated with the case of Florent and Pelagie. Nevertheless, not every Pentecostal decides to abide by it, such as Papa Elodie. Both cases reveal that the way in which a person faces moral choices depends on the social position she occupies, her gender, generational context and personal choice. Moreover, they reveal that sexual reproduction continues to hold prominence in people's marital relations. Although there exists certain continuities in values, such as reproduction, this does not mean that the authority of the patrilineage remains unchanged. The authority of the church plays an important role in molding these values.

Whether a person commits sin through adultery or premarital relations depends on matters of honor, her prestige, social position and personal choice. Moral dilemmas and failures also have the potential to reshape prominent values. After having failed to live up to the principles prescribed; a person can also work on the self. In this case, repentance, confession and discipline by the church served the purpose of re-inserting the person into the new moral system, but also reinforced publicly a stronger sense of morality among its members. Moral dilemmas therefore have an important transformative potential.

Acknowledgments: I would like to thank The National Council for Science and Technology (CONACYT), Mexico, for the generous grant that allowed me to complete this research.

Conflicts of Interest: The author declares no conflict of interest.

Abbreviations

AoG   Assemblies of God

References

1. Jennifer S. Hirsch, and Holly Wardlow. "Introduction." In *Modern Loves. The Anthropology of Romantic Courtship and Companionate Marriage.* Edited by Holly Wardlow and Jennifer S. Hirsch. Ann Arbour: University of Michigan Press, 2006, pp. 1–31.
2. Jennifer Cole, and Lynn M. Thomas, eds. *Love in Africa.* Chicago: University of Chicago Press, 2009.
3. Jennifer S. Hirsch, and Holly Wardlow. *Modern Loves. The Anthropology of Romantic Courtship and Companionate Marriage.* Ann Arbor: The University of Michigan Press, 2006.
4. Jean Comaroff. "The Politics of Conviction: Faith on the Neo-Liberal Frontier." *Social Analysis* 53 (2009): 17–38. [CrossRef]
5. Dena Freeman. *The Pentecostal Ethic and the Spirit of Development: Churches, Ngos and Social Change in Africa.* London: Palgrave Macmillan, 2012.

6. Paul Gifford. *Ghana's New Christianity. Pentecostalism in a Globalising African Economy.* London: Hurst & Company, 2004.
7. Charles Piot. *Nostalgia for the Future. West Africa after the Cold War.* Chicago: The University of Chicago Press, 2010.
8. Ruth Marshall. "Power in the Name of Jesus." *Review of African Political Economy* 52 (1991): 21–37. [CrossRef]
9. Birgit Meyer. "'Make a Complete Break with the Past.' Memory and Post-Colonial Modernity in Ghanaian Pentecostalist Discourse." *Journal of Religion in Africa* 28 (1998): 316–49.
10. Eileen Moyer, Marian Burchard, and Rijk van Dijk. "Editorial Introduction: Sexuality, Intimacy and Counselling: Perspectives from Africa." *Culture, Health and Sexuality* 15 (2013): S431–39. [CrossRef] [PubMed]
11. Birgit Meyer. "Christianity in Africa: From African Independent to Pentecostal-Charismatic Churches." *Annual Review of Anthropology* 33 (2004): 447–74. [CrossRef]
12. Rijk van Dijk. "Pentecostalism, Cultural Memory and the State: Contested Representations of Time in Postcolonial Malawi." In *Memory and the Postcolony. African Anthropology and the Critique of Power.* Edited by Richard Werbner. London: Zed Books, 1998, pp. 155–81.
13. Rekopantswe Mate. "Wombs as God's Laboratories: Pentecostal Discourses of Femininity in Zimbabwe." *Africa: Journal of the International African Institute* 72 (2002): 549–68. [CrossRef]
14. Pierre-Joseph Laurent. *Les Pentecôtistes du Burkina Faso. Mariage, Pouvoir et Guérison.* Paris: IRD-Karthala, 2003.
15. A. Ojo Matthews. "Sexuality, Marriage and Piety among Charismatics in Nigeria." *Religion* 27 (1997): 65–79.
16. Astrid Bochow, and Rijk van Dijk. "Christian Creations of New Spaces of Sexuality, Reproduction, and Relationships in Africa: Exploring Faith and Religious Heterotopia." *Journal of Religion in Africa* 42 (2012): 325–44. [CrossRef]
17. Linda van de Kamp. "Public Counselling: Brazilian Pentecostal Intimate Performances among Urban Women in Mozambique." *Culture, Health and Sexuality* 15 (2013): S523–36. [CrossRef] [PubMed]
18. Linda van de Kamp. "Love Therapy: A Brazilian Pentecostal (Dis)Connection in Maputo." In *The Social Life of Connectivity in Africa.* Edited by Mirjam de Bruijn and Rijk van Dijk. New York: Palgrave Macmillan, 2012, pp. 203–25.
19. Rijk van Dijk. "Counselling and Pentecostal Modalities of Social Engineering of Relationships in Botswana." *Culture, Health and Sexuality* 15 (2013): S509–22. [CrossRef] [PubMed]
20. Tola Olu Pearce. "Reconstructing Sexuality in the Shadow of Neoliberal Globalization: Investigating the Approach of Charismatic Churches in Southwestern Nigeria." *Journal of Religion in Africa* 42 (2012): 345–68. [CrossRef]
21. Naomi Haynes. "Change and Chisungu in Zambia's Time of Aids." *Ethnos* 80 (2015): 364–84. [CrossRef]
22. Vinh-Kim Nguyen. "Counselling against HIV in Africa: A Genealogy of Confessional Technologies." *Culture, Health and Sexuality* 15 (2013): S440–52. [CrossRef] [PubMed]
23. Maria Frahm-Arp. "Singleness, Sexuality, and the Dream of Marriage." *Journal of Religion in Africa* 42 (2012): 369–83. [CrossRef]
24. Tola Olu Pearce. "Cultural Production and Reproductive Issues. The Significance of the Charismatic Movement in Nigeria." In *Religion and Sexuality in Cross-Cultural Perspective.* Edited by Stephen Ellingtom and M. Christian Green. London: Routledge, 2002, pp. 21–50.
25. Julia Pauli. "Creating Illegitimacy: Negotiating Relations and Reproduction within Christian Contexts in Northwest Namibia." *Journal of Religion in Africa* 42 (2012): 408–32. [CrossRef]
26. Joel Robbins. *Becoming Sinners. Christianity and Moral Torment in Papua New Guinea Society.* Berkley: University of California Press, 2004.
27. Joel Robbins. "Between Reproduction and Freedom: Morality, Value and Radical Cultural Change." *Ethnos* 72 (2007): 293–314. [CrossRef]
28. Girish Daswani. "On Christianity and Ethics: Rupture as Ethical Practice in Ghanaian Pentecostalism." *American Ethnologist* 40 (2013): 467–79. [CrossRef]
29. Girish Daswani. *Looking Back, Moving Forward. Transformation and Ethical Practice in the Ghanaian Church of Pentecost.* Toronto: University of Toronto Press, 2015.
30. Matthew Engelke. "Past Pentecostalism: Notes on Rupture, Realignment, and Everyday Life in Pentecostal and African Independent Churches." *Africa: The Journal of the International African Institute* 80 (2010): 177–99. [CrossRef]

31. Liana Chua. *The Christianity of Culture: Conversion, Ethnic Citizenship, and the Matter of Religion in Malaysian Borneo*. New York: Palgrave MacMillan, 2012.

32. Sitna Quiroz. "Relating as Children of God: Ruptures and Continuities in Kinship among Pentecostal Christians in the South-East of the Republic of Benin." Ph. D. Dissertation, The London School of Economics and Political Science (LSE), London, February 2014.

33. Olenja Joyce, and Kimani Violet. "Infertility: Cultural Dimensions and Impact on Women in Selected Communities in Kenya." *Journal of the Pan African Anthropological Association* 8 (2001): 200–16.

34. Gay Becker. "Metaphors in Disrupted Lives: Infertility and Cultural Constructions of Continuity." *Medical Anthropology Quarterly* 8 (1994): 383–410. [CrossRef]

35. Martin Lindhardt. "Introduction. Presence and Impact of Pentecostal/Charismatic Christianity in Africa." In *Pentecostalism in Africa. Presence and Impact of Pneumatic Christianity in Postcolonial Societies*. Edited by Martin Lindhardt. Leiden: Brill, 2015.

36. Lynn M. Thomas, and Jennifer Cole. "Thinking through Love in Africa." In *Love in Africa*. Edited by Jennifer Cole and Lynn M. Thomas. Chicago: University of Chicago Press, 2009, pp. 1–30.

37. Nathaniel Akinremi Fadipe. *The Sociology of the Yoruba*. Ibadan: Ibadan University Press, 1970.

38. Douglas J. Falen. "Polygyny and Christian Marriage in Africa: The Case of Benin." *African Studies Review* 51 (2008): 51–74. [CrossRef]

39. Adrian Hastings. "A Variety of Scrambles: 1890–1920." In *The Church in Africa, 1450–1950*. Oxford: Oxford University Press, 1996.

40. Catrien Notermans. "True Christianity without Dialogue. Women and the Polygyny Debate in Cameroon." *Anthropos* 97 (2002): 341–53.

41. Philippe Antoine. "The Complexities of Nuptiality: From Early Female Union to Male Polygamy in Africa." In *Demography: Analysis and Synthesis, a Treatsie in Population Studies*. Edited by Graziella Caselli, Jacques Vallin and Guillaume Wunsch. Burlington: Academic Press, 2006, pp. 355–71.

42. Ester Boserup. *Women's Role in Economic Development*. London: Allen and Unwin, 1970.

43. Jack Goody. "Polygyny, Economy and the Role of Women." In *The Character of Kinship*. Edited by Jack Goody. Cambridge: Cambridge University Press, 1973, pp. 175–90.

44. Claude Meillassoux. *Maidens, Meal and Money: Capitalism and the Domestic Community*. Cambridge: Cambridge University Press, 1981.

45. Jane I. Guyer. "Wealth in People and Self-Realisation in Equatorial Africa." *Man* 28 (1993): 243–65. [CrossRef]

46. William B. Schwab. "Kinship and Lineage among the Yoruba." *Africa: Journal of the International African Institute* 25 (1955): 352–74. [CrossRef]

47. Taiwo Makinde. "Motherhood as a Source of Empowerment of Women in Yoruba Culture." *Nordic Journal of African Studies* 13 (2004): 164–74.

48. Karin Barber. "Money, Self-Realisation and the Person in Yoruba Texts." In *Money Matters. Instability, Values and Social Payments in the Modern History of West African Communities*. Edited by Jane I. Guyer. London: Heinmann and James Currey, 1995, pp. 205–24.

49. Daniel J. Smith. "Managing Men, Marriage, and Modern Love: Women's Perspectives on Intimacy and Male Infidelity in South-Eastern Nigeria." In *Love in Africa*. Edited by Jennifer Cole and Lynn M. Thomas. Chicago: University of Chicago Press, 2009, pp. 157–79.

50. Douglas J. Falen. *Power and Paradox. Authority, Insecurity and Creativity in Fon Gender Relations*. Lawrenceville: Africa World Press, 2011.

51. Andrea Cornwall. "Spending Power: Love, Money and the Reconfiguration of Gender Relations in Ado-Odo, Southwestern Nigeria." *American Ethnologist* 29 (2002): 963–80. [CrossRef]

52. Michel Foucault. "Technologies of the Self." In *Ethics: Subjectivity and Truth*. Edited by Paul Rabinow. New York: The New York Press, 1997, pp. 135–40.

53. Martin Lindhardt. "Men of God: Neo-Pentecostalims and Masculinities in Urban Tanzania." *Religion* 45 (2015): 252–72. [CrossRef]

54. Adriaan S. van Klinken. "Men in the Remaking: Conversion Narratives and Born-Again Masculinity in Zambia." *Journal of Religion in Africa* 42 (2012): 215–39. [CrossRef]

55. Papa Daniel (member fo the Assemblies of God Chruch, Ipese) in discussion with the author, 15 April 2010.

56. Marcia C. Inhorn. "Interpreting Infertility: Medical Anthropological Perspectives." *Social Science & Medicine* 39 (1994): 459–61. [CrossRef]
57. Florent (member of the Assemblies of God Church, Ipese) in discussion with the author, 12 May 2010.
58. Jarrett Zigon. "Within a Range of Possibilities: Morality and Ethics in Social Life." *Ethnos* 74 (2009): 251–76. [CrossRef]

religions

MDPI

Article

The Apparatus of Belief: Prayer, Technology, and Ritual Gesture

Anderson Blanton

Department of Religious and Ethnic Diversity, Max Planck Institute, Hermann-Föge-Weg 11, 37073 Göttingen, Germany; blanton@mmg.mpg.de; Tel.: +49-551-495-6219

Academic Editors: Douglas J. Davies and Michael J. Thate
Received: 19 April 2016; Accepted: 31 May 2016; Published: 7 June 2016

Abstract: Through a focus on the early history of a mass mediated ritual practice, this essay describes the "apparatus of belief," or the specific ways in which individual religious belief has become intimately related to tele-technologies such as the radio. More specifically, this paper examines prayers that were performed during the immensely popular Healing Waters Broadcast by Oral Roberts, a famous charismatic faith healer. An analysis of these healing prayers reveals the ways in which the old charismatic Christian gesture of manual imposition, or laying on of hands, took on new somatic registers and sensorial attunements when mediated, or transduced, through technologies such as the radio loudspeaker. Emerging from these mid-twentieth century radio broadcasts, this technique of healing prayer popularized by Roberts has now become a key ritual practice and theological motif within the global charismatic Christian healing movement. Critiquing established conceptions of prayer in the disciplines of anthropology and religious studies, this essay describes "belief" as a particular structure of intimacy between sensory capacity, media technology, and pious gesture.

Keywords: prayer; technology; healing; Pentecostal; belief; ritual; transduction; radio

---

> *As if the rite of touching a sacred object, like every contact with the divinity, were not equally a communication with God!*
>
> *Marcel Mauss, On Prayer (1908)* [1].

Every Sunday throughout the 1950s, millions of Americans were tuning-in their radios to hear Oral Roberts' *Healing Waters Broadcast*. In addition to an extensive network of radio stations within the United States, this charismatic faith-healing program encircled the globe via transmitters strategically located throughout Europe, Africa and India. Roberts claimed that he was divinely inspired to name the broadcast after an old hymn that he recalled from his childhood days when he attended brush arbor revivals with his family. In addition, the healing evangelist made an explicit connection between the old camp meeting song and the biblical story from the book of John (5:1–15) that describes how the lame, blind and crippled were healed by dipping into the effervescent waters of the Bethesda pool. The therapeutic currents of this pool were activated at certain seasons of the year when an angel descended to "trouble the waters."

In a special radio issue of his *Healing Waters Magazine*, Roberts summed up the significance of the title of the broadcast: "I thought of the 'Healing Waters,' of waters troubled by an angel, but above all, of the Master standing at the water's edge with His healing touch" ([2], p. 15).[1] A chorus accompanied

---

1   This essay utilizes research methods from the fields of media studies and cultural anthropology to explore the phenomenon of mass mediated healing prayer. I would like to thank Charles Hirschkind, Bruno Reinhardt, Michael J. Thate and two external peer reviewers for insightful comments and suggestions on an earlier draft of this essay. The shortcomings and flaws within this analysis, of course, are entirely my own.

by piano brought the program on the air, and the words of the broadcast's eponymous theme song resounded through a soft haze of static:

> Where the healing waters flow,
> Where the joy celestial glow,
> Oh there's peace and rest and love,
> Where the healing waters flow!

With these liquid resonances in mind, this essay explores how the radio organized new possibilities for the somatic flows of Pentecostal prayer. The phrase *somatic flow* describes the physical sensation of warmth, electricity, tingling, *etc.* that circulates through both the body of the patient and the healer during the performance of charismatic healing touch. With these embodied flows in mind, this essay describes how essential theological and performative elements of charismatic Christian prayer such as the anointing, baptism in the spirit, and the laying on of hands became intimately linked with the radio apparatus in the formative years of mass-mediated healing rituals. By tracing the development of a mass mediated prayer technique, this essay describes how individual religious experience has been organized through an "apparatus of belief" that binds sensory capacities and physical gestures with, and through, media technology.

The most important segment of the *Healing Waters Broadcast* occurred toward the end of the thirty-minute program, when after several songs, some testimonies of miraculous healing by faith, and a brief sermon, Oral Roberts delivered the healing prayer during what was referred to as the "prayer time" of the program. As a specific technique of prayer, the prayer time of the broadcast was structured around what Roberts termed "the point of contact." Now a ubiquitous term in the global language of Pentecostal and charismatic Christian healing prayer, Oral Roberts developed this technique specifically in relation to the radio apparatus.[2] According to Roberts, the radio as a point of contact allowed the patient to "turn loose" or "unleash" a kind of standing reserve or potentiality of faith that resided within the interior of the religious subject. Throughout his ministry, Roberts used technological metaphors to explain this charismatic technique of prayer:

> A point of contact is a means of sending your faith to God. A point of contact is something tangible, something you do, and when you do it you release your faith toward God. All sources of power have a point of contact through which they can be reached or tapped. You flip a light switch, and what happens? The light comes on. You step on the starter of your automobile and the motor hums. You turn a hydrant and the water comes out. In each case, whatever you do to start the flow of energy becomes your point of contact [5].[3]

Once again, it is not mere coincidence that Roberts was constantly invoking metaphors of technology to describe the point of contact, as the first explicit formulation of this new prayer-gesture emerged within the context of his popular radio broadcast. In his article entitled, "The Story Behind Healing Waters," Roberts explains the basic ideas behind the radio as a point of contact:

> I conceived the idea of placing my hand over the microphone while people put their hands on the radio cabinet and by these two actions forming a double point of contact. From the very beginning of the *Healing Waters Broadcast*, I have felt led to offer a healing prayer at the close of each program...My preaching is to help people reach a climax in their faith and then I bring the sermon to a quick close and offer the healing prayer. At this time people gather around their radios and place their hands on their radio cabinets while I place mine over the microphone *as a point of contact in lieu of placing my hands upon them*...It has been amazing how many thousands of people have caught on to this idea and have turned their

---

[2] For a contemporary ethnography of the radio as a point of contact see: [3,4]. (see the comments in the References)
[3] For more explanations and instructions on the point of contact, see Roberts' famous treatise on faith healing: [6].

faith loose. They have believed while I prayed and in their believing, have been healed. Some very powerful miracles have been wrought through the broadcast and still even greater miracles are being wrought from week to week [1].[4]

In its earliest formulations, the point of contact was imagined as a technological supplement to the charismatic sensations of tactility and the communication of healing power actuated through the ancient ritual gesture of handlaying. Throughout the history of Christianity, the ritual gesture of placing or pressing the hand upon various parts of the body has been practiced as a form of political initiation, consecration and miraculous healing.[5] As millions of listeners tuned-in to the "prayer time" of the broadcast, audiences began to experience the distanced voice-in-prayer on a new somatic register (Figure 1). The radio loudspeaker translated the praying voice into a series of warm vibrations that were manually experienced as listeners laid their hands upon the "radio cabinet" as a point of contact between the everyday and the sacred. In this way, technical reproduction allowed for a new tactile sensation of the warm vibrations of the voice through the hand, signaling a shift in the pious sense of "touching-hearing" attuned through the practice of prayer. Thus, the early Christian ritual of handlaying (*manus imposito*) for the efficacious communication of healing virtue, prestige and power was, quite literally, interfaced with the apparatus [9]. In addition to the somatic vibrations of language, the large glass tubes of the older model "radio cabinets" would have created a warm electromagnetic field that also enlivened the mediated reverberations of prayer with an auratic presence. In this way, the ecstatic "climax" of prayer that was previously referred to by Roberts is intimately related to the visceral sensations of sound generated through the apparatus itself.

Transcriptions from the prayer time of the Healing Waters Broadcast will help evoke the specific textures of what Bruno Reinhardt, in his analysis of the pedagogical practice of "soaking in tapes" in a Ghanaian seminary, aptly terms the "haptic voice" [10]. These visceral testimonies, in turn, will shed light on the specific implications of this tactile radio voice for Pentecostal rituals of faith healing.[6]

1. *Healing Waters Broadcast, 25 May 1952*

[25:30] Heavenly father, in the name of Jesus of Nazareth I come to thee for the deliverance of every man, woman and child who is believing thee around their radio cabinets right

---

[4] As is often the case with faith healers, it is likely that Roberts was refining a practice that was actually pioneered a decade earlier by Sister Aimee McPherson. From her powerful radio station KFSG, located within the Angelus Temple in Los Angeles, Sister Aimee would instruct her pious audience: "listeners kneel by the radio and place [your] hands on it to receive long-distance cures...As I lay my hands on this radio tonight, Lord Jesus, heal the sick, bridge the gap between and lay your nail-pierced hand on the sick in Radioland..." (Quoted In [7]). Although Roberts did not pioneer this practice, he was the first to explicitly formulate this technological prayer-gesture as the centerpiece of the ritual form. The somatic force of this new technique was quickly adopted by other prominent faith healers such as A. A. Allen and become so ubiquitous a phenomenon in the landscape of popular culture that the American funk band Parliament mimicked this faith healing technique in the song "Make My Funk the P-Funk" from their influential album, *Mothership Connection* (Casablanca Records, 1975):

Now this is what I want y'all to do:
If you got faults, defects or shortcomings,
You know, like arthritis, rheumatism or migraines,
Whatever part of your body it is,
I want you to lay it on your radio, let the vibes flow through.
Funk not only moves, it can re-move, dig? [8]

We see in this album a powerful transduction of the poetic force of Charismatic Christianity.

[5] *Cf.* James 5:14 "Is any sick among you? Let him call for the elders of the church; and let them pray over him, anointing him with oil in the name of the Lord."

[6] I would like to thank Steve Weiss and the archival technicians at the media laboratory of the Southern Folklife Collection at the University of North Carolina at Chapel Hill for their generous assistance in digitizing these rare radio transcription discs. In terms of the basic infrastructure of the *Healing Waters Broadcast*, hundreds of large vinyl discs had to be sent out to individual stations throughout the world after they had been initially "cut" at a radio studio in Tulsa, Oklahoma. In turn, each station broadcast the pre-recorded program during a scheduled time each Sunday. Based on the thousands of listener testimonies that were sent to the Oral Roberts organization, the fact that these programs were "re-broadcast" does not seem to have detracted from the sense of immediacy and "presence" produced by this faith healing program.

now. Father, I believe God. I believe that you can do for us what no man can do. And that right now, there is no power like the power of God. Grant me this miracle according to the power of God in heaven, that every single one of them shall feel the healing presence of God going through every fiber of their mortal bodies, through their soul and mind. And that right now they shall be made whole from the crown of their head to the soles of their feet. Father heal this little girl; heal this little boy. Heal this dad, this mother. Let them feel the presence of Jesus; let it go through them to heal them in the name of the Lord. Now father I command the diseases to go: in the name of Christ **COME OUT** of them. And now neighbor, be thou made **WHOLE**! In the name of Jesus, be thou made **WHOLE** from **HEAD** to **TOE** by the **POWER** of Jesus Christ and through the name of the son of God. Glory to his precious name. Believe and believe right now. Right now. And God doth make thee whole from the crown of your head to the soles of your feet. In Jesus' name, Amen.

[27:02] song "Only Believe"
Only believe, only believe,
All things are possible, only believe.
Only believe, only believe,
All things are possible, only believe.

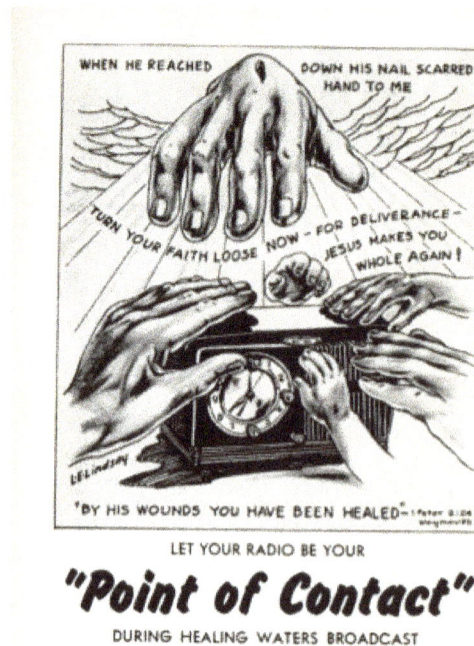

Figure 1. Illustration from *Healing Waters Magazine*.

At that pivotal moment during the performance of prayer when the healer commands the disease to leave the body of the patient, Roberts enunciates specific words with a percussive punch. These percussive poetics are indicated in the textual transcription through the use of bold, capital letters. The development of this percussive inflection during special sections of the performance is part of a long tradition of charismatic poetics of breath that signals to the congregation that the "anointing," or power of the Holy Ghost, has possessed the speaker's faculties of vocalization.[7] What I want to emphasize here are the specific ways in which this anointed poetics of breath is transduced through the radio loudspeaker. Expanding upon the work of cultural historian Jonathan Sterne and anthropologist Stefan Helmreich, I define transduction as the transformation of "sound into something else and that something else back into sound" ([12], p. 22).[8] Like a percussive instrument in a rite of passage, the electromagnetic diaphragm of the radio loudspeaker becomes a drum, sounding out the curative technique in disjointed bursts [14].

In this way, a charismatic technique of breath is transduced into a series of percussive pressures that literally resonated upon the hand of the patient. The radio apparatus affects the anointed voice-in-prayer in specific ways that cannot be abstracted from the medium of sound reproduction. In these formative years of mass-mediated ritual, the radio is not merely a passive instrumentality for the transmission of a discretely self-contained religious message, but the apparatus itself enlivens the performance of charismatic prayer with an auratic presence in excess of any stable representational content. The sound of prayer is translated into a tactile sensation of heat, pressure, and undulation; and thus the healing waters flow at that miraculous point where the capacities of the hand are augmented through the loudspeaker (Figure 2). One might summarize the ritual inversions and sensory disjunctures inherent in this performance of mass mediated healing prayer in the playful rhyme:

The mouth of the speaker allowed the hand to hear,
And the patient touched the radio to bring the healer near.

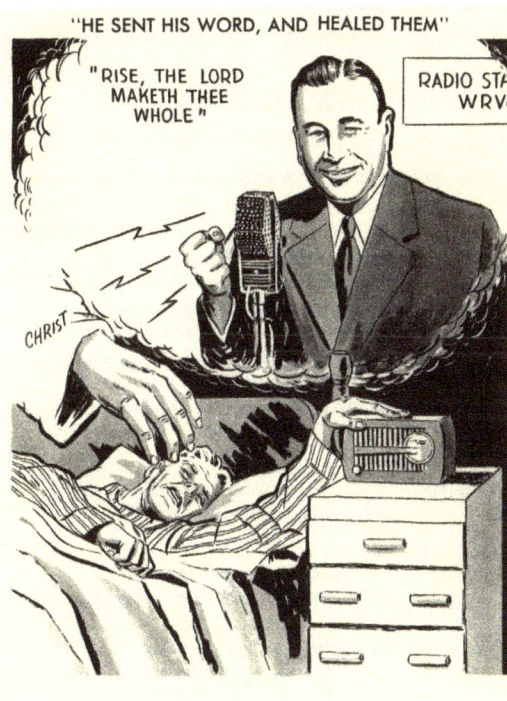

Figure 2. Cartoon illustration from *If You Need Healing Do These Things*.

---

7 For an excellent account of a charismatic technique of breath, see: [11].
8 For an anthropological analysis of the phenomenon of transduction, see also: [13].

Note how the ritual preparations and prayer itself repeatedly invoke an awareness of bodily boundaries, both in terms of a proprioceptive sensation of "wholeness from the crown of their heads to the souls of their feet," and the demonic egresses of disease through the "mortal body." Moreover, the miraculous quickening of the body resounds at precisely that moment when the sensory capacities of the mortal flesh are extended and attuned by the augmentations of the radio apparatus. It is at this "point" where the body is able to feel the reverberations of prayer-through-the-hand that the excess of "healing presence" inundates the patient. Or, to put this another way, the body is exorcised of illness-causing demons and achieves a sensation of wholeness in the curative moment when the hand is placed upon the radio and the boundaries of the mortal body are augmented by a technological prosthesis.

2. *Healing Waters Broadcast, 15 March 1953*

[23:33] And now comes that wonderful moment of prayer in the Healing Waters Broadcast when something like two million people this time each week gather around their radio cabinets for my healing prayer. You come too, unsaved man, unsaved woman. You sick people come. Some kneel, some raise their hands, some touch their radio cabinets as a point of contact. But I'm going to pray for God to save ya, for God to heal ya. Believe now. Just after they sing "Only Believe" I'm going to pray.

[24:07] song "Only Believe"
Only believe, only believe,
All things are possible, only believe.
Only believe, only believe,
All things are possible, only believe.

[24:32] Now Heavenly father, thousands and thousands of people are gathered around their radio cabinets for this healing prayer, for thy salvation, for thy healing, for thy deliverance. Grant me the miracle of their salvation. Grant me the miracle of their souls being transformed from sin, saved by thy power. And now father grant me the miracle of healing for the mortal bodies of every man, woman and child who is looking to thee right now with faith in God. Here father is a man who's been sick for years, a woman who's been bedfast, a little child who is crippled and afflicted. Hear my prayer, and grant their healing in the name of Jesus. Thou foul tormenting sickness, thou foul affliction and disease, I come against you in the name of the savior. In the name of Jesus of Nazareth, not by my name, but by the name and power of the son of God. And I take authority over you in the name of Jesus; and I charge you loose them. **LOOSE THEM! COME OUT! COME OUT** in the name of Jesus of Nazareth! And now neighbor, be thou made whole. Be thou made **WHOLE**! In the name of Jesus, be thou **LOOSED** from thy **AFFLICTIONS**! Rise and praise God and be made whole. Amen, and amen. Believe now with all your heart.

[26:02] song "Only Believe"
Only believe, only believe,
All things are possible, only believe.
Only believe, only believe,
All things are possible, only believe.

Like the rituals of entry and exit described by Hubert and Mauss in their classic work, *Sacrifice: Its Nature and Function* [1898], it is interesting to consider why the performance of healing prayer is bracketed by the repetitions of the song "Only Believe." In other words, why must the proscriptions of the curative technique exclude the material exigencies of the point of contact in the selfsame performance wherein these material conduits are essential elements for the opening of communicative relays between the everyday and the sacred? Why the insistence on an abstracted and spiritual practice of Protestant "belief" when the material point of contact is a crucial aspect of the performance and its curative efficacy? At the very heart of the curative technique, this performance of revelation and concealment discloses the *objectile* dimension of prayer. The objectile of Pentecostal prayer connotes an irreducible materiality that is necessary for the appearance of faith, yet denied or disavowed during the ritual enactment of healing (hence the term objectile also resonates with the words projectile and abject). As the crucial performative and experiential dimension of prayer, the objectile can neither be attributed to a Pentecostal hypocrisy or anxiety in the face of "things of this world," nor to an instrumental interpretation that describes the way credulous audience members are duped through the technological artifice of the healer. Instead of these typical explanations, the objectile of prayer suggests that the force or efficacy of the ritual hinges upon this simultaneous revelation and concealment of the material medium [15]. In other words, the objectile is not some anxious appendage or qualification to the performance of prayer, but intrinsic to the organization of ritual efficacy itself.

The concept of ritual efficacy is here limited to a description of the opening or organization of specific experiential frameworks in-and-through the performance of prayer. In this way, the efficacy of prayer emerges from its specific attunements of the senses. This organization of somatic experience, in turn, "heals" or enframes bodily experience, the classification of suffering, and the structures of everyday life in a profoundly different frequency. The proscriptions that characterize the objectile of prayer "set-up" the religious subject to experience the ritual environment—an environment that emerges, or is structured by material objects and media technologies—in a particularly compelling, perhaps even shocking, way. To deny or dismiss the very medium that is structuring an appearance of sacred presence amplifies the basic sensory experience of technological mediation with an even greater immediacy or actuality. This is not simply a logic of oscillation between two poles, of explicit awareness of the material infrastructure of healing on the one hand, or forgetting on the other, but a doubled awareness, that, like the objectile itself, experiences an excessive presence through the material medium precisely because it is a reproduction. In this ritual milieu, presence becomes doubled—simultaneously immediate and actual within the private space of the home or automobile, yet emerging from a displaced space *somewhere else*. The objectile of prayer thematizes this doubled awareness of the material infrastructure, and through this ritual performance organizes new structures of awareness and embodiment.

Since the beginning of the *Healing Waters Broadcast* in 1947, hundreds of thousands of letters were sent to the Oral Roberts headquarters in Tulsa, Oklahoma by listeners claiming to have been miraculous healed during the prayer time of the program. Many of these testimonies were reproduced in Roberts' popular *Healing Waters Magazine*, and were intended to help cultivate a sense of belief in the reading audience. The following testimonies have been selected from the healing magazine and are representative of the general spirit of the healing narrative and its relation to the prayer-gesture of the radio as a point of contact (Figure 3).

PLACES HAND ON RADIO AND HEARS AGAIN

Dear Brother Roberts,

During your healing campaign in Jacksonville I was listening to your radio program. As you prayed for the sick I laid my hand and head upon the radio, and was healed of deafness in my left ear, which I had not heard out of in thirty years. I do praise God for what he has done for me. You may use this testimony in any way that others might believe God still hears.

L.D. Lowery,

3019 Dillon St.,

Jacksonville, Fla. ([16], p. 9).

THERE IS NO *Distance* IN *Prayer*

By ORAL ROBERTS

bourg in Europe. A woman in Norway, who couldn't understand a word I was saying, felt God's power in my voice and was instantly and completely healed.

There is no distance in prayer. God was with me in Tulsa when I prayed, was in Luxembourg in Europe when the program was released, was in Norway with the woman who couldn't understand English. God is everywhere; therefore, there is no distance in prayer.

A man in South Africa, a high church official, heard my voice on our broadcast over Radio Lorenco Marques. He was healed of an incurable kidney disease. He immediately became one of the instru-

Figure 3. Illustration from the *Healing Waters Magazine*.

NAZARENE MINISTER HEALED THROUGH BROADCAST

Dear Brother Roberts:

For years I have been bothered with bad tonsils. I had been holding a revival near Mineral Wells, Texas and had developed a serious case of tonsillitis. I had been taking Sulfa drug but to no avail. My fever was high, pulse irregular and my throat was swelled so inside until I could hardly swallow.

I was driving home that night after services and was suffering considerably. Brother Roberts' program was coming over my car radio and when he asked those in radio-land to lay their hand on the radio if they wanted healing, I did so. As he prayed, I prayed, and suddenly it seemed that something turned loose in my throat, and I swallowed and found the swelling was all gone. My temperature was normal and my pulse was regular. That has been nearly four years ago, and I have never had a sore throat since that time. Praise God for his healing power!

Rev. J. Royce Thomason

Nazarene Minister

Eldorado, Oklahoma ([17], p. 9).

HIGH BLOOD PRESSURE HEALED

Dear Brother Roberts:

I want to write and tell you how God wonderfully healed my body through your prayers. I have been troubled with high blood pressure for years and I also had a bad kidney ailment. I had to go to bed as I was so sore I could not rest day or night. I was taking fourteen doses of medicine a day but, hallelujah to Jesus, I put my hand on the radio Sunday as you prayed for the sick and the healing power of God surged through my whole body and I was instantly healed! I arose in the name of Jesus and have not had any pain since. I do praise God for healing me. Enclosed is an offering to help on the broadcast.

A sister in Christ,

Frances Baker,
Fuquay Springs, N. C. ([18], p. 9) [Figure 4].

Many have testified that God saved and healed them as they listened to the evangelist over radio.

Figure 4. Image from a pamphlet issued by the *Oral Roberts Evangelistic Association*.

I Danced With Joy

Although I have been a minister of the gospel in England for 30 years, I have been unable since 1954 to follow my calling. In that year rheumatic fever struck me twice leaving me with locked joints in my shoulders and arms. I became almost helpless and my wife had to assist me even to dress. We listen to your radio program here in England over Luxembourg, 208 meters, at 11 p.m. each Tuesday and it has become the highlight of the week for us. One Tuesday night in April this year, as you were praying for the sick, I placed my still locked arms on the radio and claimed the healing power of Jesus Christ. The power of God swept through my body—I was drenched with perspiration as the poisonous acids left me. My joints were instantly loosed and set free. I threw both arms above my head and danced with joy for complete liberation. Now, at 64 years of age, I am in perfect health and re-entering the ministry. I have purchased a piano-accordion for my work and since my glorious healing I play it lustily without the slightest twinge of pain. May God continue his blessings upon you and your wonderful work for Him.

Rev. Robert Williams, Walton-on-Naze, Essex, England [19].

With these somatic surges of divine power and miraculously loose body parts in mind, I would like to contrast the description of radio prayer I am here elaborating with Thomas Csordas' ground breaking work on practices of Charismatic Catholic healing. Because of the relevance to the current analysis, Csordas' Presidential Address to the Society for the Anthropology of Religion (2002) is worth quoting at length.

This intimate alterity appears again in the Charismatic practice of "resting in the spirit," in which a person is overwhelmed by divine power/presence and falls, typically from a standing position, into a sacred swoon...I also suggested that the experience is constituted in the bodily synthesis of preobjective self processes. This is to say that the coming into being of "divine presence" as a cultural phenomenon is an objectification of embodiment itself. Consider the heaviness of limbs reported by people resting in the spirit. Quoting Plugge,

R. M. Zaner points out that "within the reflective experience of a healthy limb, no matter how silent and weightless it may be in action, there is yet, indetectably hidden, a certain 'heft'" [20], p. 56. This thing like heft of our bodies in conjunction with the spontaneous *lift* of customary bodily performances defines our bodies as simultaneously belonging to us and estranged from us, and hence the alterity of the self is an embodied otherness. While resting in the spirit, the heft is always there for us indeterminately and preobjectively is made determinate and objectified. Its essential alterity becomes an object of somatic attention within the experiential gestalt defined as divine presence ([21], pp. 169–70).

As a specific technique of charismatic healing, the radio as a point of contact marks an "exteriorization" of the "intimate alterity" and "primordial aspect of the self" described by Csordas. As a bodily prosthesis that extends the capacities of hearing into the field of touch (a kind of supra-sensitive hearing), the point of contact, like the Charismatic Catholic healing practices described by Csordas, also thematizes an embodied doubling; yet, this alterity resonates at the interface between everyday sensory capacities and their extension through material objects and media technologies. Indeed, given the etymological resonances of the term "prosthesis" with the Eucharistic elements and the theme of miraculous transformation, we might substitute Csordas' "preobjective" with "prosthetic" in our description of the production of divine presence [22].

This term, moreover, foregrounds the concern of charismatic Christianity with the gift (*charism*) of discernment, or an infilling of the Holy Spirit that allows the subject to register that which eludes the everyday sensory capacities. Troubling the subject with a presence that persists just beyond capacities of the 'natural' or 'unarmed' sensory faculties, in an age of mass-mediated ritual sacred presence is revealed at that "point" between the body and its technological attunements.

This technological artifice at the heart of the curative technique recalls "the moment of prestidigitation" described by Mass and Hubert in their classic work, *A General Theory of Magic* (1902):

> Imagine for a moment—if you possibly can—the state of mind of a sick Australian Aborigine who calls on a sorcerer...Beside him the shaman dances, falls into a cataleptic fit, has dreams. His dreams take him up into the other world and when he comes back, deeply affected by his long journey into the world of souls, animals and spirits, he cunningly extracts a small pebble from the patient's body, which he says is the evil spell which has caused the illness. Obviously there are two subjective experiences involved in these facts. And between the dreams of one and the desires of the other there is a discordant factor. Apart from the sleight of hand at the end, the magician makes no effort to make his ideas coincide with the ideas and needs of the client. These two individual states coincide only at *the moment of prestidigitation.* There is, then, no longer at this unique moment a truly psychological experience, either on the side of the magician, who cannot delude himself at this point, or on that of the client, because the alleged experience of the latter is no more than an *error of perception*, beyond a state of critical resistance, and thus beyond being repeated if not supported by tradition or by and act of constant faith [23].[9]

Mauss and Hubert's analysis of the curative rite need not be limited to the "primitive" procedures of the Australian Aborigine, but is directly relevant to the current description of the therapeutic environment organized through the radio as a point of contact. Here, the moment of prestidigitation (pesto = quick/nimble, digit-us = finger: sleight of hand, legerdemain, delusion, illusion), and the coincidence of two disparate individual states that it marks, seems *en route* to an account of religious experience and its relation to technologically mediated "special effects" that are constantly outpacing the everyday structures of awareness [25]. Moreover, the "error of perception" described in this classic account evokes the sensory disjunctures and extensions that are orchestrated in mass-media ritual

---

[9]   The second portion of this translation is taken from: [24].

contexts such as the prayer time of the *Healing Waters Broadcast*. The radio as a point of contact is a moment of prestidigitation that "quickens" the force of ritual language with a presence in excess of its representational content. This sensory disjuncture between the sound of language and its tactile resonances facilitates a therapeutic transformation into a new mode of somatic awareness and understanding of illness, disease, and suffering.

Roberts often emphasized the temporal dimensions organized through the point of contact. For example, in the popular instructional book, *How to Find Your Point of Contact with God*, he describes how this particular prayer-gesture "sets the time" of the miraculous cure:

> If I said, "I'll meet you," and you said, "When?" and I said, "Anytime," and you said, "Where?" and I said, "Anywhere," more than likely we would never meet. But if I said, "Meet me tomorrow at 2:00 PM at the front entrance of the main post office in your town," then we would have set the time and the place, and we would expect to meet. When you set a time for something to take place, you reach of point of expectation. The bible teaches you to expect a miracle if you want it to happen ([5], p. 8).

Like the clocks that were often built into the radio sets of the time, the radio as point of contact instantiated a specific charismatic temporality by cultivating a sense of immediacy for the patient. Yet, this temporal awareness actuated by the radio as a point of contact is not merely a stable and fixed time signaled by a clock. To be sure, the point of contact "sets the time," however, this charismatic temporality organized through the apparatus is sustained by what Victor Turner, in his analysis of the disproportionate, grotesque, and off-kilter elements of the ritual form, terms "anti-temporality" [26]. This ritual anti-temporality connotes a rupture in the habitual rhythms of everyday life. Thus, the sense of immediacy produced during the "Prayer Time" of the *Healing Waters Broadcast* is doubled, both in terms of a distant and public voice resonating within the private space, and as a special effect of sound-prayer registered through the hand [27]. In this disjointed ritual environment, sensations of divine presence and miraculous healing are organized through the radio apparatus.

As a comparative foil to the specific claims I am making about the off-kilter temporalities of radio ritual and the concomitant shifts in the performance and sensation of healing prayer structured therein, let us briefly turn to another crucial objectile in the history of Pentecostal prayer, the "anointed handkerchief." Since the early days of Pentecostalism, these fragments of anointed fabric (also termed "prayer cloths," "blest cloths," "faith cloths," *etc.*) have been circulated through personal exchanges of hand and postal relays for the purposes of divine healing, protection, and miraculous accumulation. Following the etymological accounts of the ancient term "belief" (*cred/credo*) by de Certeau and Benveniste, the "belief" organized through the circulation of prayer cloths follows a classic economic model of temporal articulation [28]. More specifically, through a series of exchanges, deferrals and delays, the circulation of the prayer cloth structures a particular experience of belief for the patient.

In contradistinction to this temporal articulation of belief through exchange, the radio as point of contact articulates its miraculous temporality through a technologically produced special effect, or particular attunement of the sensory faculties. In this way, the radio inaugurated a new apparatus of belief that parasitically subsisted upon the specific sensory disjunctures of prayer through the radio.

Concepts such as the "apparatus of belief" and the "objectile" that I have employed to describe formative moments in the history of mass-mediated healing challenge longstanding and entrenched understandings of prayer in the disciplines of anthropology and religious studies. Emerging during the formative years of these disciplines circa 1900, these influential accounts describe prayer as a history of progressive abstraction from the material world into the silent recesses of a cognitive interiority.[10] I have deployed these concepts as a critique against this model, one which persists and continues

---

[10] For a representative example of this logic of abstraction see for instance: [29] Marcel Mauss, whom I have invoked throughout this essay, is not immune to this narrative of progressive intellectualization and spiritualization from the world of material devotion. See for example certain sections of his early work *On Prayer*:

to orient many of the basic assumptions behind the academic study of prayer.[11] The organization of new prayer-gestures such as the radio as point of contact suggest a new direction in the study of prayer that attends to the particular material and technological "exteriorizations" that sustain and enliven the contemporary performance of belief. Indeed, Oral Roberts maps these new technological orientations quite well when he emphasizes that the prayer of faith can only be "loosed" when the subject makes tactile contact with an apparatus that extends the limited sensory faculties. In this way, "belief" itself is literally made sensible through an apparatus that interfaces media technology with older forms of ritual healing gestures and performances of prayer. This essay has demonstrated how the undercurrents of flow that orient key elements in the Pentecostal and charismatic Christian performance of prayer (the communication of power through handlaying, the poetic capacities of the anointing, the sensation of immersion, *etc.*) are enlivened in special ways through modern media technology (Figures 5 and 6). From the dark electro-magnetic depths of the radio cabinet, the angel of transduction troubles the healing waters.

> Thus by tracing the development of prayer, it is possible to discern all the great trends which have influenced religious phenomena as a whole. It is known in fact, at least generally, that religion has undergone a double evolution. Firstly, it has become more and more spiritual. Whereas religion originally consisted of mechanical rites of a precise and material nature, or strictly formulated beliefs composed almost exclusively of tangible images, it has tended in the course of its history to give greater place to consciousness. Rites have becomes attitudes of the soul rather than those of the body and have become enriched by mental elements, sentiments and ideas. Beliefs for their part become intellectualized and, growing less and less material and detailed, are being reduced to an ever smaller number of dogmas, rich and varied in meaning ([1], pp. 23–24).

How different an account of prayer and its relation to the body Mauss delivers during his famous lecture (1934) on "Techniques of the Body"! It should be noted, however, that Mauss was already struggling with this question in his doctoral dissertation *On Prayer*. This is revealed in a more robust quotation of the passage that commenced this essay:

> For Sabatier, prayer is the essence of religion. "Prayer," he says, 'there you have religion in action'. As if every rite did not have this characteristic! As if the rite of touching a sacred object, like every contact with the divinity, were not equally a communication with God! Thus 'the inner bonding of the soul to the God who is within', such as takes place in the meditative prayer (ρρητοσ νωσισ) of an ultra-liberal Protestant, becomes the generic type of prayer, the essential act of every religion ([30], p. 31).

I read the emphasis on these sentences with the use of exclamation marks as indicative of Mauss' struggle with technology, materiality and the body in his early work.

[11] Of course, important exceptions can be made to this general narrative of abstraction. The work of scholars such as Asad, Morgan, Meyer and Hirschkind, among others, and the burgeoning group of scholars in the field of anthropology and religious studies who have been influenced and inspired by their work, have begun the long process of bringing attention to the role disciplinary practices, body techniques, and material/media objects play in the organization of religious "belief." For an useful reading list on this material turn in anthropology and religious studies, see David Morgan's syllabus available on the *Material and Visual Cultures of Religion Website* (under the directorship of Sally Promey): [31]. For more explorations of prayer and its intimate relation to media technologies and devotional objects, including actual sound recordings from the *Healing Waters Broadcast*, see my curated *Materiality of Prayer Collection* within the *Reverberations* website sponsored by the Social Science Research Council: [32].

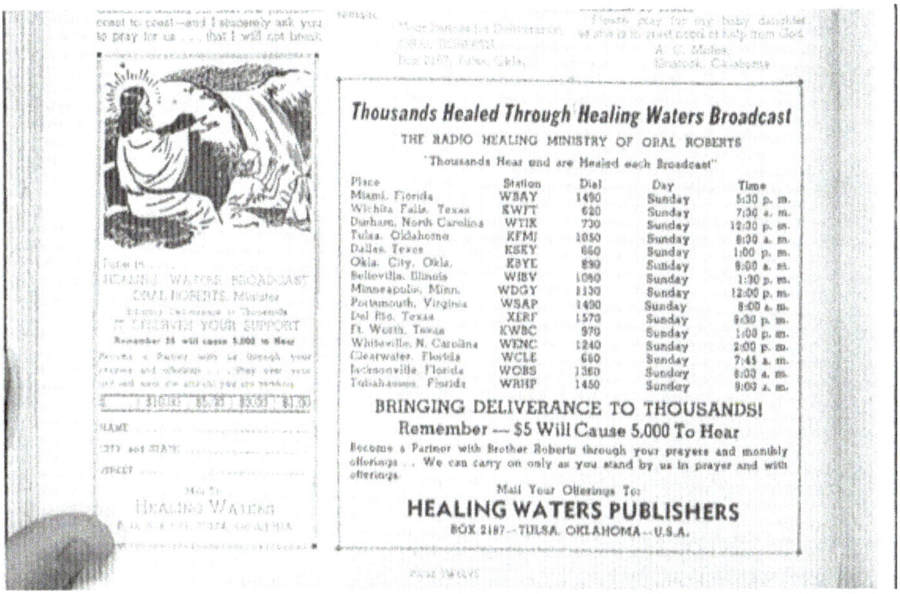

Figure 5. Advertisement from the *Healing Waters Magazine*.

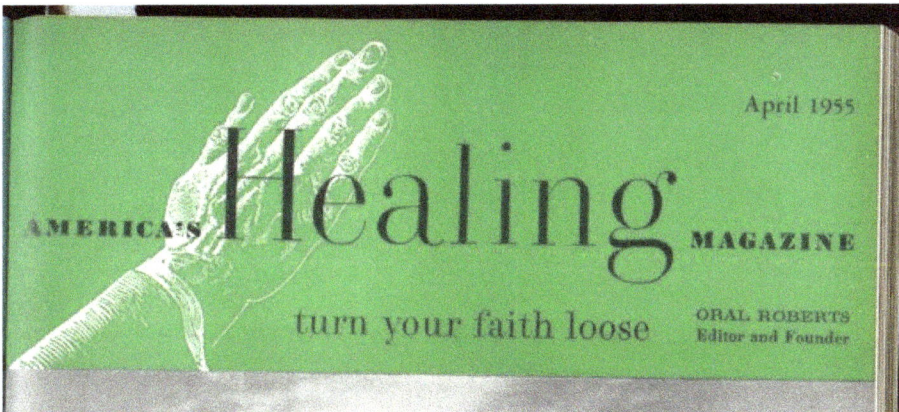

Figure 6. This image of a spectral hand was featured on many of the front covers of *America's Healing Magazine*.

Conflicts of Interest: The author declares no conflict of interest.

References

1. Mauss, Marcel. *On Prayer*. New York: Berghahn, 2003.
2. Roberts, Oral. "The Story behind Healing Waters." *Healing Waters Magazine*, June 1952, p. 15.
3. Blanton, Anderson. "Radio Prayers in Appalachia: The Prosthesis of the Holy Ghost and the Drive to Tactility." In *Radio Fields: Anthropology and Wireless Sound in the 21st Century*. Edited by Lucas Bessire and Daniel Fisher. New York: New York University Press, 2012.
4. Bessire, Lucas, and Daniel Fisher. *Radio Fields: Anthropology and Wireless Sound in the 21st Century*. New York: New York University Press, 2012.

5. Roberts, Oral. *How to Find Your Point of Contact with God*. Tulsa: Y&N Publications, 1962.
6. Roberts, Oral. *If You Need Healing Do These Things*. Tulsa: Oral Roberts Evangelistic Association, 1950.
7. Hangen, Tona J. *Redeeming the Dial: Radio, Religion, and Popular Culture in America*. Chapel Hill: University of North Carolina Press, 2002.
8. Parliament. *Mothership Connection*, Casablanca Records, 1975. Casablanca Records, 1975.
9. Whitehouse, Michael. "Manus Impositio: The Initiatory Rite of Handlaying in the Churches of Early Western Christianity." Ph.D. dissertation, University of Notre Dame, 4 April 2008.
10. Reinhardt, Bruno. "Soaking in tapes: The haptic voice of global Pentecostal pedagogy in Ghana." *Journal of the Royal Anthropological Institute* 20 (2014): 315–36. [CrossRef]
11. De Abreu, Maria José A. "Goose Bumps All Over: Breath, Media, and Tremor." *Social Text* 26 (2008): 59–78. [CrossRef]
12. Sterne, Jonathan. *The Audible Past: Cultural Origins of Sound Reproduction*. Durham: Duke University Press, 2003.
13. Helmreich, Stefan. "An Anthropologist Underwater: Immersive Soundscapes, Submarine Cyborgs, and Transductive Ethnography." *American Ethnologist* 34 (2007): 621–41. [CrossRef]
14. Needham, Rodney. "Percussion and Transition." *Man New Series* 2 (1967): 606–14. [CrossRef]
15. Taussig, Michael. "Viscerality, Faith, and Skepticism: Another Theory of Magic." In *Magic and Modernity: Interfaces of Revelation and Concealment*. Edited by Birgit Meyer and Peter Pels. Stanford: Stanford University Press, 2003.
16. Lowery, L. D. "Testimony Section." *Healing Waters Magazine* 2 (1949): 9.
17. Thomason, Royce. "Testimony Section." *Healing Waters Magazine* 15 (1952): 9.
18. Baker, Frances. "Testimony Section." *Healing Waters Magazine* 4 (1949): 9.
19. Williams, Robert. "Testimony Section." *Abundant Life Magazine* 5 (1957): 9.
20. Zaner, Richard M. "The Context of Self: A Phenomenological Inquiry Using Medicine as a Clue." Athens: University of Michigan Press, 1981.
21. Csordas, Thomas. "Asymptote of the Ineffable: Embodiment, Alterity and the Theory of Religion." *Cultural Anthropology* 45 (2004): 163–85. [CrossRef]
22. Buck-Morss, Susan. "The Cinema Screen as Prosthesis of Perception: A Historical Account." In *The Senses Still: Perception and Memory as Material Culture in Modernity*. Edited by Nadia Seremetakis. Chicago: University of Chicago Press, 1996.
23. Mauss, M. *A General Theory of Magic*. New York: Norton, 1975 *(my italics)*.
24. Crapanzano, Vincent. "The Moment of Prestidigitation: Magic, Illusion, and Mana in the Thought of Emile Durkheim." In *Prehistories of the Future: The Primitivist Project and the Culture of Modernism*. Edited by Elazar Barkan and Ronald Bush. Stanford: Stanford University Press, 1995.
25. De Vries, Hent "Of Miracles and Special Effects." In *Religion and Media*. Edited by Hent de Vries and Samuel Weber. Stanford: Stanford University Press, 2001.
26. Turner, Victor. "Images of Anti-Temporality: An Essay in the Anthropology of Experience." *Harvard Theological Review* 75 (1982): 243–65.
27. Adorno, Theodor W. *Current of Music: Elements of a Radio Theory*. Frankfurt am Main: Suhrkamp, 2006.
28. De Certeau, Michel. "What We Do When We Believe." In *On Signs*. Edited by Marshall Blonsky. Baltimore: Johns Hopkins University Press, 1985.
29. Marett, Robert Ranulph. "Spell to Prayer." *Folklore* 15 (1904): 132–65. [CrossRef]
30. Mauss, Marcel. *Techniques, Technology and Civilization*. New York: Durkheim Press, 2006.
31. Material and Visual Cultures of Religion. Available online: http://mavcor.yale.edu/sites/default/files/Morgan-Syllabus-Religion-and-Materiality_0.pdf (accessed on 15 March 2016).
32. Reverberations. Available online: http://forums.ssrc.org/ndsp/category/materiality/ (accessed on 15 March 2016).

religions

MDPI

Article

Towards an Existential Archeology of Capitalist Spirituality

George González

School of Humanities and Social Sciences, Monmouth University, 400 Cedar Ave, West Long Branch, NJ 07764, USA; ggonzale@monmouth.edu

Academic Editors: Douglas James Davies and Michael J. Thate
Received: 3 April 2016; Accepted: 24 June 2016; Published: 29 June 2016

Abstract: Throughout his career, Michel Foucault sustained a trenchant critique of Jean-Paul Sartre, whom he accused of arguing that the subject "dispenses (all) significations". In contrast to existentialism's interests in subjective consciousness, Foucault pursues an archaeological method which he later develops into a genealogical approach to discourse that emphasizes the institutional practices and forms of knowledge/power that undergird historical epistemes. Taking contemporary networked Capitalism, the discourse of "workplace spirituality", and the life history of one management reformer as its case studies, this paper turns to the cognitive linguistics of George Lakoff and Mark Johnson in an effort to historicize experiences of neoliberal "spirituality", as an archaeology of knowledge might, while also attempting to account for intentionality and biography, as existential approaches would. Turning to work in contemporary critical theory, which associates strident anti-humanism in social theory with the rise of neoliberal discourse, I argue that sustained attention to the ways in which personal and social history always entail one another and are mutually arising makes not only for better phenomenology but makes for better critical scholarship as well.

Keywords: workplace spirituality; critical theory; archaeology of knowledge; existentialism; philosophy of the subject; ethnography of capitalism; cognitive linguistics; neoliberalism; religious studies; management theory; religion and capitalism

1. Introduction

In a previously published article, I explore the discursive formation of neoliberalism at the level of dominant patterns of social metaphor. There, I argue that contemporary management theory provides a window into the cultural logic of post-Fordist Capitalism, wherein the sharply delineated bureaucracies and iron-clad factories (we can also add to this list union collectives and social safety nets) of the modern industrial imaginary are being torn asunder, replaced by the cybernetic, plasmic and circular metaphors of an explicitly emotive, probabilistic and increasingly immaterial global Capitalism [1]. I conclude that discussion with the suggestion that what we might call "existential deconstruction" can serve the purposes of the social criticism of "corporate spirituality". However, there, the suggestion remains theoretical and is not supplemented by a concrete ethnographic application which describes some of the ways in which social and personal histories are always mutually arising and embedded within existing historical, institutional arrangements. The present discussion provides such an application and articulates an ethnographic methodology, what I call *existential archeology*, for tracking the conditioning power of "cultural" rules, on the one hand, and the subjective intentionality and biographical inflections according to which history is always personalized, on the other hand.

Today, networked Capitalist cosmology has substituted the breezy feedback loop for Max Weber's iron-cage and the *mentalité* of the system takes its ideological cues from complexity theory rather than Newtonian physics.[1] The movement towards a "real economy" characterized by service and ritualization but shepherded and disciplined by a strongly abstracting finance has implied accompanying shifts in the conceptual contours of both "religion" and "economy". A cybernetic "spirituality" is today the going ideology of the post-secular bourgeoisie, having supplanted, at least in the North Atlantic postindustrial context, the celebration of "machine production", which dominated the Fordist economy.[2] If Weber associated the ideal-type of a specifically Capitalist rationality with a formal disinterest in psychological life, traditional values and religion, *postindustrial* Capitalism, as evidenced by the rhetorical strategies and practices of marketing and management discourse, actively covets the disciplinary effects and trust-enhancing power of ritual, pre-conscious psychic attachment, the poetic imagination, and religious metaphor.[3] As this paper will detail, behind the celebrations of the service economy, the sharing economy, and a branded world stands a more primary metaphorical grammar which emphasizes recursive connectivity, performativity and the dissolution of the once vaunted boundaries of official modern metaphysics. As I will describe, amidst these linguistic fissions whereby a postindustrial cosmology takes historical shape, key methodological questions of special interest to this volume on the theoretical status of the individual also present themselves.

First, if what is implied is a shift in what Michel Foucault refers to as *episteme*, how exactly is the shift in the cultural logic of a historical context accomplished at the level of practice, biography and experience? Following C.W. Mills [6], how might we seek to elucidate the dynamic interplay between biography and history? Second, what is to be made of the religious "ghosts" that rise up from the spaces of tension, contradiction, resistance and anxiety characteristic of the neoliberal age and its attendant forms of ephemerality and social precarity? How do these specters make themselves known in the interstices between the shifting conceptual platelets of historical displacement and what Jan Rehmann refers to as, "the contested space of social institutions and attitudes," especially when it comes to the socialization of the individual by organizational apparatuses ([2], p. 38)? However, since, as Michael Jackson writes, following Theodor Adorno, the gap between word and world can never be elided, it ought to be noted that the spaces of intersubjective tension that comprise the "force fields" of lived discourse are never dependent for their reality on modes of active resistance (see [7]).

2. The Cybernetic Ideology of "Spiritual Management"

In their landmark work, *The New Spirit of Capitalism*, the sociologists, Luc Boltanski and Eve Chiapello, suggest that contemporary management theory is marked, in the end, by its celebration of spontaneity and "rhizomorphous capacity" [8]. In contrast, the machine, mechanization, and objectivity

---

[1] Weber is often read as a historical sociologist who, within the context of his comparative studies of religion and society, describes the ways in which the modern West transitioned from a traditionalistic social order to one characterized by "legal-rational" rationality and a formal separation of spheres. However, in contradistinction to this normative reading of Weber, Jan Rehmann reads him as an "organic intellectual" of the modern, industrial bourgeoisie whose work anticipates and benefits the passive revolution of Fordist modernization [2]. Complexity theory, a theoretical science of complex adaptive systems, is primarily associated with the pioneering work of the Santa Fe Institute, which was founded in 1984. As I will discuss in this paper, some of the core principles of complexity theory anticipate the discourse of "new management" which would develop later. However, as would be anticipated by an archeological analysis, we can also note the emergence of complexity discourse within the purview of other social institutions (such as the architectural theory of Robert Venturi, see [3]).

[2] Jan Rehmann's overview of theories of ideology is a very helpful reference [4]. Following Rehmann's discussion, I understand ideology theory to both identify objective interests (e.g., objective measures of social security) and to explore the ways in which the turn to values and attitudes, "can go hand in hand with the loss of collective and individual agency." There is an interest in the voluntary subjection to forms of domination but a facile and reifying account of "false consciousness" is resisted. As Rehmann suggests, "A *theory* of ideology begins at the moment when its social genesis, functional necessity and efficacy becomes the object of reflection" ([4], pp. 5–6).

[3] Of course, Weber's account of ideal-types, or average cases, needs to be supplemented by genealogies which demonstrate the ways in which historical moments and historical change are characterized by messy counter-examples and accompanied by cross-purposes. Often, surprising examples turn out to be as much the rule as the exception. Ideas of neat "linear progress" pertain to the ideological and metaphysical repertoire of Western modernity and are confounded by historical details. Within religious studies, a classic study which unsettles many of the assumed secular trajectories and directions of American religion and modern Capitalism is Liston Pope's *Millands and Preachers—A Study of Gastonia* [5].

were compelling tropes of the imaginary of industrial American Capitalism; machine metaphors also underwrote the literary and journalistic production of the late-nineteenth and early-twentieth centuries in addition to its management theory (see [9]). An industrial aesthetic attached to the work of the organizational philosopher, Fredrick Winslaw Taylor, and, later, to the cosmology of Fordism. According to the management scholar Mauro Guillén, the scientific management philosophies that rose to prominence at the turn of the twentieth century tended to share in a fascination with "machinery, technology, factory aesthetic, [and] mass production" and conceived of the worker's body as a "living machine" [10]. At the time, simple managerial hierarchies, specialization and routinization were also common.[4]

One effect of the epistemic movement away from the imaginary of modern industrial Capitalism in which industrial machine metaphors abounded to the imaginary of a cybernetic "postmodern" Capitalism in which digital and organic metaphors are increasingly dominant is the construction of explicitly capitalist concepts of "spirituality" and related ideas like "mysticism" (e.g., [12], p. 35). With a unifying interest in the inculcation of company narratives and workers' self-legislation of shared, corporate values, the discourse of "spiritual management" can be understood to be "a holistic, monistic, markedly Western, and mainly Christian rooted discourse of universalism and globalism" [13]. As Boltanksi and Chiapello explain, the networked organization is held together by processes of self-organization and self-monitoring. In its primary interests in accepting, predicting and managing *excess* (or that which overruns the linear horizons of instrumental control), posing reality as a series of closed loops, and deconstructing the perceived rigidities of the "unliberated" firm, "spiritual management" has recourse to an eclectic and definitively "postmodern" potpourri of ideological resources in its work.

According to Boltanksi and Chiapello, not only are managers ascribed explicitly monastic qualities according to which they catalyze and inspire human potential but it also the case that, "the transmission of operational modes for organizing firms is, in the work of some authors, glorified by a lyrical, even heroic style, or defended by numerous heteroclite references to noble and ancient sources such as Buddhism, the Bible, and Plato" (e.g., [8], p. 59). For example, the exceedingly influential management philosophies of Robert Greenleaf, Margaret Wheatley and Peter Senge [14–16] all trade in religious metaphor, making use of them to mark cybernetic phenomena. In the process, the body of labor is reconfigured in "new management" as a complex and dynamic node. The dissipation of the tangible heaviness of the body of labor mirrors the dissolution of state bureaucracy that is the *sine qua non* of neoliberal discourse. A basic premise of this paper is the idea that the deregulating currents of contemporary "workplace spirituality" are, in part, reproduced at the level of lived social metaphor. Through their mundane speech-acts, I will argue, individuals play a necessary role in the active re-formation and re-inscription of the *ontological shape* of capital.[5] One central modality and register of neoliberalism has to do with the ways in which its cosmography is inculcated by workers (and consumers) and, in Daniel Dubuisson's terms, gets "incarnated within our own existences" ([19], p. 212).

The discourse of "spirituality" within organizational management, of course, necessarily emerges within broader structural contexts and discursive histories. First, it is an extension of the human relations revolution in North Atlantic management (see [10,20]). It is also nested within the institutionalized logic of neoliberalism as a whole. Neoliberalism is, according to David Harvey, in the first instance a theory of political practice which posits that human well-being is best enhanced through the liberation

---

[4] Religious horizons were, already, from the start, imbricated in the cosmology of Fordist production. For a discussion of the ways in which "interwar religious visions trafficked in secular futures", disrupting our analytical categories of the religious and the modern, (see [11]).

[5] In *Being and Time*, Heidegger seems to suggest that acts of superficial classification, which would include speech acts, sediment and constitute our world and its overarching taxonomical structures (see [17]). In my monograph [18], an extension of what I propose here, my ethnographic accounts of everyday speech and ritual at the workaday worlds of two organizations involved in the "workplace spirituality" movement are indebted to this kind of account of what Heidegger calls a "hermeneutic circle".

of entrepreneurial energies supposedly occasioned by market liberalization and strong private property rights ([21], p. 2). It is, of course, in turn, necessary to understand neoliberalism according to its policy commitments and the structural adjustments enacted in its spirit (cuts in top-tax rates, reductions in social welfare programs, resistance to union power, the regional and global integration of economies, and the loosening of government controls of "cross-border investment") ([22], p. 164). A Hayekian critique of collectivism and "planned economies" and an attendant celebration of the "*spontaneous social order*" is baked into the very core of neoliberal economics ([4], p. 278). Of particular importance to the present discussion, it is also the case, however, that ideological work beyond the rationality of economics is required to actually maintain the neoliberal consensus on the ground

As Bethany Moreton has argued, a central paradox of neoliberal ideology is that it cannot actually be sold to "living hosts" according to the unvarnished autism of economic rationality [23]. Neoliberalism engages the existential desire for association and the spirit of service towards anti-collectivist ends, as a structural matter. Neoliberal forms of labor are sanctioned and sanctified by religious enthusiasm even if, as Moreton argues, religious ideas and practices can always, in turn, shape economic ideologies of work [23]. The spiritual care provided by industrial chaplains and "enlightened" managers speaks to what Winnifred Fallers Sullivan writes is the "ongoing indeterminacy about where to locate religious work in the late modern period" ([24], p. 53). In keeping with Moreton's now classic analysis of the strongly Christian Evangelical "soul of neoliberalism", Sullivan associates the proliferation and ubiquity of chaplains with the "leftover business" which the state and its proxies still have to do, ministering to constituents who need and demand "practices of presence" despite their ostensibly secular and laissez-faire institutional contexts ([24], p. 185).

The discursive space of early twenty-first century American "capitalist spirituality" is rife with the suggestion that the phenomenal world, including organizational life, is best (that is, most efficiently) understood according to the tone of pattern, the language of poetry, the mathematics of probability, and the form of spirit. Since she argues that, today, understanding requires a "poetic" grasp for transitive phenomena, Margaret Wheatley exhorts managers to incorporate, "any process...that encourages nonlinear thinking and intuition, and uses alternative forms of expression such as drama, art, stories, and pictures. The critical task is to evoke our senses, not just the grey matter" ([15], p. 143). "Workplace Spirituality" is one with the self-understanding of contemporary management theory writ large in its critique of the Newtonian focus on stable identities and separable parts and in its concomitant insistence upon the singular importance of recursive, self-regulating interrelationships. In fact, even in the most influential and popular organizational philosophy of the neoliberal age, "trust" in the final order of seeming chaos is often indexed in cybernetic, "spiritual" terms (e.g., [25]). Wheatley makes use of the metaphor of the "dark night of the soul" ([15], p. 170) and the insights of "Sufi teaching" ([15], p. 10), for example, while Peter Senge argues that in order to understand the "circle economy" and its "system wide interrelationships", one must master a discipline of intuitive processing whose roots, "lie in both Eastern and Western spiritual traditions, and in secular traditions as well" ([16], p. 7). For his part, in his effort to reconnect organizational life to matters of cosmic concerns, Robert Greenleaf calls upon the power of "religion" to, at its root, "rebind" society and turns to Jesus, Confucius, the Buddhist eightfold path, Abraham Heschel, the Torah, Reinhold Niebuhr and Harvey Cox, among others, to inspire his servant leadership philosophy [14]. We might well consider these great luminaries in the management world to be "organic intellectuals" of the postmodern, postsecular bourgeoisie.[6]

In this marshalling of religious symbols to help teach and organize the art of immaterial intuition, contemporary "workplace spirituality" participates in what Scott Lash and John Urry refer to as the, "aesthetic reflexivity [that] is the very stuff of post-organized capitalist economies of signs and

---

[6] Prompted by Rehmann's Gramscian analysis of Weber as an unwitting apologist for Fordist production, I mean here that all of these popular and influential theorists of postmodern work look to connect the interests of working persons to the corporatist level and to the needs of postindustrial management.

space" ([26], p. 59). The signs of the "spiritual" bind workers to one another, to the master narratives of their organizations, and to the material conditions of their labor. Wheatley suggests that, "the era of the rugged individual has been replaced by the era of the team player" ([15], p. 39). No longer strictly unencumbered, self-intending and invested in the heroic powers of pure reason, the bourgeois *intraviduals* of networked workplaces [27] ooze the "religious aroma" that marks the misty scent of what the critical theorist, Eduardo Mendieta, refers to as "the crystallization of ideology" ([28], p. 125). Aided by a ghostly furtiveness, the "capitalist spirituality" of organizational management participates in the evasive tactics of power under what Zygmunt Bauman calls conditions of "liquid modernity" [29]. Rather than an "iron-cage", today we might speak of capitalist organization in terms of shape-shifting ameba which are able to manage and control excess not according to the categorical exclusions of clear lines of demarcation but, instead, according to the managed play of statistical *difference*. In this movement of statistical power, modernist boundaries between the secular and the sacred (boundaries that were ideological if also never fully realized on the ground) grind and continue to transform.

If modernization and industrialization transformed "the processes of becoming human and the human itself", according to Michael Hardt, capitalist postmodernization has implied a thoroughgoing informanization of production which privileges the work of service and symbolic manipulation to such a degree that *immaterial labor* now claims the highest value in the marketplace as a "symbolic-analytic service" which produces an "immaterial good such as a service, knowledge, or communication" ([30], p. 94) Following Fredric Jameson's claim that, today, "the word processor replaces the assembly line in the mind's eye"([31], p. 389), Hardt argues that "we increasingly think like computers, and the interactive model of communication technologies becomes more and more central to our laboring. Interactive and cybernetic machines become a new prosthesis integrated into our bodies and minds and a lens to redefine our bodies and minds themselves" ([30], pp. 94–95).

3. Existential Horizons at the Crossroads of Archaeology

In many ways, Michel Foucault is the obvious theorist with whom to think through moments of discursive transformation. According to Gary Gutting, in his archaeological work, "...a set of conceptions, along with the conception of knowledge they entail, constitutes what Foucault calls the *episteme* of a period" ([32], p. 140). If Foucault's analyses in *Madness in the Age of Reason*, *The Birth of the Clinic*, *The Order of Things*, and the *Archaeology of Knowledge* formed his archaeological corpus, the publication of *Discipline and Punish* in 1975 is often considered to mark his turn to genealogy. As Gutting explains,

> In order to analyze the development of bodies of knowledge out of systems of power, Foucault employs a new historical method that he calls genealogy. Genealogy does not replace archaeology, which is still needed to uncover the discursive rules that constitute bodies of knowledge. But genealogy goes beyond archaeology by explaining (through the connections with power) changes in the history of discourse that are merely described by archaeology ([32], pp. 6–7).

In his genealogical work, Foucault is very keen to trace the relationships between "discursive knowledge and the power structures" of society, making use of the now ubiquitous concept of power/knowledge to describe how discursive and institutional practices reinforce one another through processes of social discipline. While Foucault's recognition of the fact that systems of thought are never autonomous and interests in the role of language in self-constitution are to be applauded, many contend that he never went far enough in his recovery of the subject.

Of course, Foucault's work comes as a response to the, "unfortunate division between "society" and "culture" that had emerged out of social scientific theories and social histories that proposed mechanistic, causal models wherein "cultural" phenomena were finally flattened out by a thoroughgoing economic functionalism. In response to the hegemony of Marxian economisms among the French left in the 1960s, Foucault was only one of several celebrated representatives of the "linguistic turn" who, in the 1960s, 1970s and 1980s, "turned to linguistic theories to help it carve out an autonomous realm for "culture," now understood as a "self-enclosed, non-referential mechanism of social construction that precedes the world and renders it intelligible by constructing it according to its own rules of signification" ([33], p. 8). In the strongly structuralist articulations of Foucault's archaeology, Ferdinand de Saussure's linguistics and Pierre Bourdieu's early sociology, the unconscious operations of discourse are privileged over and against "conscious, purposive individual activity" ([33], p. 6).

According to Jan Rehmann, "structuralism might roughly be described as the endeavor of identifying general (and therefore ahistorical) signifying structures that undergird human speech utterances, social practices or 'culture' in general" ([4], p. 211). Radicalizing structuralism's "linguistic turn", poststructuralist theories, in turn, often associated the later work of Foucault, Derrida, Julia Kristeva, Jacques Lacan and Roland Barthes, question, "the assumptions of fixed, ahistorical dichotomies, which are therefore to be deconstructed (Derrida)" ([4], p. 211). In Foucault's genealogies and his work in ethics and governmentality, power is understood to always produce effects, including the creative possibilities for resistance. The reversibility and generativity of relations of power, introduces surplus and excess into the system.

For some, the question of whether Foucault, despite his turn from archaeology to genealogy and ethics, still reproduces a closed system in important ways remains. According to the American historian, Gabrielle Spiegel, a growing number of voices have joined the British economic historian, Gareth Steadman Jones, in wondering out loud whether theories and methods heavily indebted to Foucault (and especially to the readings of his many celebrated readers and interpreters) might be creating, in their single-minded focus on discourse, a "deterministic fix" in which cultural history's linguistic approach is now (somewhat ironically) combined with "the undead residue of historical materialism"([33], p. 10). For some of even Foucault's otherwise friendly readers, the result is an understanding of discourse which buries and renders invisible the historical effects of subjective agency.[7] Subjects are still variable subject *positons* and, at the end of the day, according to Foucault, "any given society is constituted through a multiplicity of dynamic, fluid, and ever-changing systems of meaning (discourses), which create regimes of practical rationality and actions as well as regimes of truth" ([33], p. 11). This "supplemantariness" is still attributed to the dynamism of power and discourse rather than to the carnal existences of diverse and different human agents.

According to Spiegel, Foucault's poststructuralist progeny have generally viewed the subject "not only as discursively constituted but also as controlled, ultimately, by the social as hegemonically, that is, discursively thought (knowledge/ power)" ([33], p. 12). In the words of the poststructuralist historian Joan Scott, being a subject means "being 'subject to' definite conditions of existence, conditions of endowment of agents and conditions of exercise" ([33], p. 12). At the extreme end, Judith Butler argues that subjection is always and already subjectivization: that is, the very possibility of subjectivity is founded on a primary submission to interpellations of power [35]. In light of this strong suspicion of the subjective perspective, the historian Gary David Shaw argues that the poststructuralist "self" is so "divested of autonomy and control that it can't really operate as a cause, as an agent ([33], p. 12). The sociologist Anthony Giddens writes, "Foucault's 'genealogical method', in my opinion, continues the confusion which structuralism helped to introduce into French thought, between history without a *transcendental subject* and history without *knowledgeable human subjects*" ([36], pp. 221–22). In other

---

[7]   One of the most erudite and persuasive readers of Foucault in religious studies today is Mark Jordan. In *Convulsing Bodies—Religion and Resistance in Foucault,* he argues that one of Foucault's central interests lies in somatic rather than voluntary refusals of pastoral power (see [34]). To the degree that recoveries of agency in theory are tempted to look past these non-voluntary expressions of power, they ought to be chastised by the kind of reading Jordan offers. On the other hand, within the context of a critique of postmodern Capitalism, given the ways in which forms of collective bargaining have proven to be the sharpest tool in labor's resistance to domination, it seems patent that due emphasis on *voluntary* as well as involuntary resistance is warranted and necessary.

words, if the subject is always conditioned by history, this does not therefore imply that historical subjects are simply *determined* by discursive conditions.

According to the historian Judith Newton, even if it is true that subjects are socially and historically determined, this does not imply that the subject is "dead" or that human agency is, at base, illusory ([33], p. 12). Rehabilitations of the subject can focus precisely on the ways in which actors affect change and are also shaped by the social world in turn. In precisely this vein, neo-phenomenological practice theories, "tend[s] to focus on the adaptive, strategic, and tactical uses made of existing cultural schemes by agents who, in the very act of deploying the elements of culture, both reproduce and transform them" ([33], p. 12). According to Gabrielle Spiegel, these approaches highlight the ways in which "the individual agent's perception is mediated and constrained but not wholly controlled by the cultural scaffolding or conceptual schemes within which it takes place" ([33], p. 13). It is admitted that, as Jacques Revel argues, the choices of individuals are "inseparable from the representations of relationships, space, the resources which it places at their disposal, [and] the obstacles and constraints which [this] imposes on them" ([33], p. 13). However, practice theory refuses to settle at the extremes and understands "culture" and "experience," neither of which are self-evident, sui generis or a-historical categories, in terms of the irreducibility of practical activity. The relationship between the subject and history approached in this way, ethnography becomes situational sociology and shines a direct light on the social semantics whereby structuring structures are reproduced by socially competent actors.[8] As a descriptive matter, methodologies able to trace the ways in which agency and history are mutually arising and always entail one another is warranted. In what follows, I will therefore provide

---

8   The work of Jacques Derrida has exercised a profound impact on the study of religion given deconstruction's patent successes as a tactic and strategy for challenging and undoing the boundaries and parameters of identities and practices traditionally policed by religious institutions and authority. Of his celebrated notion of "différance", Derrida writes: "Différance is the systematic play of differences, of the traces of differences, of the *spacing* by means of which elements are related to each other. This spacing is simultaneously active and passive (this *a* of différance indicates the indecision as concerns activity and passivity, that which cannot be governed by or distributed between the terms of this opposition) production of the intervals without which the "full" terms would not signify, would not function" ([37], p. 27). Logocentrists, Derrida insists, believe that "writing should erase itself before the plenitude of living speech ([37], p. 25). In other words, the "I" precedes my embodiment and adoption of it as a possible position for me (and one that is dependent on the spacing of différance such that I assume that my dog, Clover, can never embody that same position given the humanistic pretensions of Western metaphysics) but I conveniently disavow this reality as a speaker. The problem with Derrida's approach is that he almost inverts the switch such that living speech is forced to erase itself before the primacy of writing.

  In *Writing and Difference*, Derrida proposes to further radicalize Freud's concept of the unconscious via the *trace*, which, "is the erasure of selfhood, of one's own presence, and is constituted by the threat or anguish of its irremediable disappearance, of the disappearance of the disappearance" ([38], p. 230). For existential anthropologies and practice theories like my own existential archeology, Derrida, like Freud, swings the pendulum too far in the direction of involuntary forces. The binary itself between speech and writing is itself a red herring, in the end. We cannot speak of one without the other since in the world of human meaning they mutually imply one another.

  Derrida's poststructuralist challenge would also hold that metaphor is always and already performative. There is no discourse, for Derrida, that does not always and already *show* rather than *state* (see [39]). In a society in which global Capitalism depends as much as it does on marketers and corporate managers' exceedingly well-funded *science of metaphor*, the empirical and political onus remains on the view which holds that metaphor is always and already performative and, as such, not amenable to any intentional organization and utilitarian appropriation whatsoever. Of course, none of this implies that attempts to mark, freeze, and understand metaphor will not also always be haunted by that which slips through the grasp of science and unsettles its ambitions to control the fluidity of lived phenomena. We need not revert to an a-reflexive empiricism, naïve phenomenology or vulgar positivism. Nevertheless, my approach stands in contrast to Derrida's unrelenting critique of *logocentrism*, or his damning association of the idea that persons intentionally manipulate words to make meaning with the hierarchies of a Western metaphysics of presence. Neoliberalism is not conceptually underwritten by the metaphor of structure in the way Derrida suggests modern Capitalism was. It does not disavow the *fluid* movement of metaphor, as Derrida argues modernism does, but, rather, hopes to control and exploit the liquid power of language as a shifting, embryonic sac. Nor does neoliberalism overvalue the powers of the rugged individual, constructing persons, as it does, as iterations and instances of complexity driven discourses.

  Ken Surin explains that for Derrida the subject, "arises from a "space" of responsibility that is antecedent to the subject's emergence and its identification with the self" ([40], p. 167). That is, the self can only always and already be identified to itself only via alterity and the traces of différance. According to Surin, the problem Derrida poses any critical theory of Capitalism is that within a Derridean account, "there is no way of (actually) inserting the subject into the domain of the political" ([40] p. 195). How to concretize Derridean ethics within extant institutional contexts is never self-evident and, unsurprisingly, Derridean deconstruction suffers from a certain sociological poverty when it comes to analyses of Capitalism ([4], p. 54).

some empirical textures to what I mean by "existential archeology", or the ethnographic study of how institutionalized epistemic codes are brought into being in overdetermined ways by agents who are simultaneously mediated by irreducibly particular biographical histories. However, it is important to note that the oft-assumed line between description and politics is, from the start, overdrawn and dangerous. To the degree that methodologies fully bury existential horizons under the weight of archaeology and discourse, they are structurally complicit with the politics of the neoliberal order.

With Michael Jackson and other practitioners of forms of existential anthropology critical of the "sociological reductions" which place the scholar in the role of "hierophant or seer" and depict other persons "one-dimensionally", as simple instantiations of "social processes" ([41], p. 4), I am partial to what Michael Herzfeld writes is the new "ethnographic attempt to reverse the usual ethnographic emphasis of pattern over experience, the collective and the cultural over the range of idiosyncrasy that the members of a society are prepared to tolerate"([42], p. 14). While an approach like Foucauldian archaeology gives important stress and importance to the codes which provide historical limits to what can be thought and experienced, it can, like the totalizations of historical materialism Jean-Paul Sartre took issue with, dissolve the individual into history, burying her within the deep structures of society (see [43], p. 8).[9] I proceeded with my own investigations of the "new spirit of Capitalism", empirically, as an ethnographic history of the present or existential archeology, precisely in an attempt to mitigate against the absorption of living human praxis by a system of concepts, structures and Ideas.

4. Biographical History at Seeing Things Whole

4.1. Seeing Things Whole and Landry's Bicycles

The ethnographic field sites for my fieldwork, conducted between 2007 and 2011, were two related organizations, Seeing Things Whole (STW) and Landry's Bicycles. The former is a business roundtable comprised of small to medium-sized businesses that have traditionally met in the Boston, Minneapolis-St. Paul Twin Cities, and Chicago metro areas to engage in ritualized group reflection on pressing organizational quandaries. Several of the group's officers have also written extensively on what they call a "theology of institutions," establishing intellectual kinship with the work of Robert Greenleaf, who popularized servant leadership in the 1970s and 1980s. They trace their organizational history back to the Metropolitan Associates of Philadelphia (MAP), an action-research project from the 1960s sponsored by several Christian Protestant denominations, itself inspired by the World Council of Churches's (WCC) study of the "Missionary Structure of the Congregation."

Founded in 1993, though indebted to a rich intertwining of much older organizational and personal histories, STW is, according to its mission statement, a "community of business leaders and scholars dedicated to exploring the intersection of spirituality, values and organizational life and performance." The group is "drawn by a vision of a world in which the performance of organizations is measured no longer on the basis of a single bottom line, but rather on multiple bottom lines which together more fully reflect the health and impact of the organization on the world around it" [46]. According to the group's published organizational history, one stream for the idea of a "theology of institutions" developed out of initiatives and collaborative research undertaken at the World Council of Churches (WCC), the American Baptist Church (ABC), and six Protestant denominations in the 1950s and 1960s [47].

---

[9] While his influence over my own thinking is strong, I do not turn to, in any immediate way, Pierre Bourdieu's work to frame the present analysis. While Bourdieu looks to attend to this impasse in his later work (see [44]), I agree with Michael Jackson's assessment that even the concept of the "habitus" is mired in a reductive expectation of a "quasi-perfect" coincidence between the objective tendencies of "structuring structures", on the one hand, and subjective expectations and the living out of freedom "at the margins" of history, on the other hand (see [45], p. xxi). Similarly, Foucauldian ethics (e.g., the concept of "care of the self") fails to concretize the relationship of the self to the discourses of social institutions at the level of *lived* relations, which are, at least in part, biographically mediated by personal histories.

Under the leadership of Jitsuo Morikawa, there was an attempt to make good on the "powerful call to address the Reformation mandate to recover the ministry of the laity" that came out of the 1954 Evanston meeting of the WCC. In 1964, Morikawa invited Dick Broholm to join the staff of the "Division of Evangelism" of the ABC. At the time, the division had been considering "the possibility of establishing an American model of the German Evangelical Academy—a center for theological dialogue between theologians and leaders in government, business, media, etc." [47]. Harvey Cox, who was then on Morikawa's staff, urged the group to instead "consider the option of establishing an American mission within a major metropolitan city [which] rather than serving as a center for dialogue... would seek to engage in a mission to the city" [47]. According to Broholm and David Specht, the idea would be to develop an urban mission that would "serve as a signpost to the denomination about what it might mean for Christian laity to take seriously their ministry in the workplace" [47].

Metropolitan Associates of Philadelphia (MAP) grew out of the idea and, eventually, five denominations joined ABC in signing on to the project: the Episcopal Church, the United Church of Christ, the United Methodist Church, the Presbyterian Church (USA), and the Missouri Synod of the Lutheran Church. MAP oversaw different but related ministries. It oversaw the work of eight "worker ministers," "clergymen, who, like the worker-priests in Germany and France, found employment in a variety of secular occupations in the political, business, social service, and educational sectors of the city" [47]. In addition to these "worker ministers," MAP also salaried six clergy to work as "urban agents" who served as "roving reporter(s)—seeking to be present whenever significant events were occurring" [47]. MAP also designated one hundred and twenty-five "lay associates" who were charged with thinking "reflectively about what might constitute "ministry" in their workplace" [47]. The stated mission of MAP was to "engage in experimental missionary action for the sake of a common witness to and participation in Christ's work or renewal in the city" [47]. As an "action-research project for the church," the aim was to "learn how decisions are made affecting the city's life and suggest how Christians can help institutions realize their God-given role in the society" [47].

In the end, MAP was active between 1964 and 1974. However, its commitment to the idea that, in Jitsuo Morikawa's words, "biblical faith finds change and revolution basic to the way God acts in the world and enables men and women to be free to enter into that challenge," [47] lived on through important publications like *A Strategy of Hope* and Dick Broholm's work at Andover-Newton Theological School. In 1974, Dick Broholm returned to Andover, his alma mater, to help the seminary pursue similar work. There, he worked closely with the president of the seminary, George Peck, and with the theologian Gabe Fackre, Broholm led a center that was eventually "institutionalized as the Center for the Ministry of the Laity" in the early 1980s. The Center's efforts revolved around "an action research effort involving six local congregations" [47]. The pastor and five members of each congregation would meet with faculty once a month for five years, working to identify forces that enabled and blocked the work of the laity within their particular institutions. Broholm and Specht write that it was at this time that it became crystal clear that what was missing in the work of the center was a "theology of institutions" that would assist the team in thinking theologically about businesses [48]. Dick Broholm, who also collaborated closely in the 1980s with Robert Greenleaf, the father of servant leadership management theory, eventually rediscovered in Greenleaf's work resources for developing the group's theology, which was designed to provide the theoretical and ethical grounding for its interdisciplinary work. After the Center for the Ministry of the Laity closed its doors in 1982, Broholm was instrumental in the resurrection of the work under the auspices of STW.

At the time in which I completed my fieldwork with the group, the members of the Boston roundtable, which I attended, were Landry's Bicycles, the Xenon Corporation, beingmeta, Zoar Outdoor, The Society for Organizational Learning, and a small consultancy group called Executive Soul. The members of the Twin Cities area roundtable included Quality Bicycle, Reell Precision Manufacturing, World Servants, Hilleren and Associates, and Integris. In 2014, roundtable meetings at the Divinity School of the University of Chicago were also developed. Traditionally, the typical member of the roundtables has been a small to medium-sized company that is not publicly traded.

Landry's Bicycles, an independent bicycle retail company with strong roots in the biking advocacy world and the member organization I came to know best given my ethnographic work there, brings in about $10 million in revenue and at the time of my research operated four retail locations in the greater Boston area—a number which has recently grown to five. Logistically, the meetings have generally been held at the offices of the host organization, the group presenting an organizational quandary for purposes of shared reflection. Programmatically speaking, "the host organization presents a real-time, unresolved challenge it is facing, and participants serve as temporary trustees who work for half a day with the hosts on this dilemma." As of 2015, STW's circle of gravity has shifted to Augsburg College and St. Thomas University in the Minneapolis/St. Paul area, where a professor of leadership studies and Catholic social thought, respectively, have been exploring a "fee-for-service" consultancy model. The Boston wing of STW, for its part, has now turned its focus to "next generation leadership" work with young professionals.

Many of the members of STW relate the work they do to a larger need they observe in society to reintroduce "spirituality" and "religion" back into the workplace. For example, through the membership, scholarship, and activism of Margaret Benefiel, who had been Adjunct Professor of Spirituality and Congregational/Organizational Leadership at the Andover-Newton Theology School and is currently Executive Director of the aforementioned Executive Soul and of the Shalom Institute for Spiritual Formation, STW has maintained an institutional voice at the Management, Spirituality and Religion (AOM MSR) special interest unit within the American Academy of Management—a professional subgroup with over 600 members. Margaret, who also maintains an active membership with the American Academy of Religion (AAR), has chaired the group as recently as 2008. A journal associated with the group, *The Journal of Management, Spirituality and Religion* (JMSR), currently issued by Routledge Press, has been publishing on "spirituality" and what it considers to be the rise of the "moral organization" since 2004 [49]. As I discovered through my interviews, key members of STW consider the work of the AOM MSR to be very much in line with the mission of their own organization. In any event, through the ideological influence of Robert Greenleaf's work and the later adoption of Peter Senge and Margaret Wheatley's associated management theory, on the one hand, and through the practical organizational connections to the AOM, on the other hand, STW clearly participates in, reproduces and is informed by the discourse of "new management" and its attendant form of "cybernetic", capitalist spirituality. Of course, as Michael Jackson writes, every story told is *janus-faced*, continuously shifting between collective and idiosyncratic levels of meaning ([50] p. 139). Ethnographic histories can be narrated in this fashion, stitching together personal and social modalities of experience. In the present case, the wider and nested histories of cybernetic Capitalism, the "workplace spirituality movement" and STW are woven together by the irreducibly particular threads of ethnographic history.[10]

4.2. Tom Henry

Tom Henry is currently the general manager of Landry's Bicycles; at the time I was doing my ethnographic work, he co-owned Landry's along with his older brother Peter and late sister-in-law, Jeanne. Believing that profit must be socialized, Tom and Peter have transitioned the company to an Employee Stock Ownership Plan (ESOP) and, as of 2014, the ESOP owned 28 percent of the company.

---

[10] While there is no "unmediated" account of the "real", Sartre nevertheless does recognize the important (if also necessarily insufficient) role non-dialectical, analytical knowledge plays in the progressive development of what he calls *comprehension*. Non-ethnographic, analytical knowledge (e.g., the institutional history of STW) can always, "be integrated into a more comprehensive dialectic" ([51], p. 275). What Sartre calls "dialectical reason" implies an empirical methodology which inserts the scholar "feet first" into the historical field and highlights the lived, intersubjective qualities of ethnographic relationships, framing scholarship, in the process, as a form of shared labor (see [52]). As Sartre notes, highly discursive projects tend to eschew the issue of the scholar's relationship to history. I do not mute my voice when I narrate ethnography precisely because my own actions, choices and feelings are to be included within the scope of empirical data to be reflected on and theoretically reconsidered at the back end of "fieldwork" (see [18]).

Tom is a well-known fixture in the local and national biking worlds, especially in activist circles. Much like "workplace spirituality," biking activism began to grow in the 1990s, only to explode, comparatively, in recent years. According to Tom, when he and others decided to establish "the first industry-wide lobbying effort in Washington" in 1999, there were only twelve members of the biking community who "went to share our vision with Congress" about the need to increase bike lanes and to improve the social infrastructure for biking, more generally. A decade later, upwards of 700 activists converged on Washington, compelled by a passion for biking and the conviction that the world would be a far better place if we biked more and drove our cars less.

Tom's résumé in the biking universe is as impressive as his accomplishments are very concrete. Tom served as the president of the Massachusetts Bicycle Coalition, MassBike, for three years. Among other advocacy successes, MassBike has successfully lobbied for the expansion of hours during which bikes can be brought onto Boston subway trains and for the creation of "safe bicycle routes for students" ([53], p. 45). Margaret Benefiel profiles Tom in one of her books, *The Soul of a Leader: Finding Your Path to Success and Fulfillment*. She writes:

> Tom also invited partners to help strengthen the National Bike Summit, held annually in Washington, D.C. Founded in 2001, the National BikeSummit lobbies legislators regarding cycling issues. At the Bike Summit, sponsored by the League of American Bicyclists, industry representatives can attend presentations dealing with legislation affecting cycling. They can also take the opportunity to lobby legislators and to recognize government officials who have helped improve conditions for cycling in America. For example, in 2005, Sen. John Kerry, in accepting the National Bicycle Advocacy award, spoke about how honored he felt to receive it, having been a bicycle enthusiast since childhood ([53], p. 45).

It was under the rubric of these efforts that Tom reported to the STW membership gathered around one of the roundtable meetings that he and his fellow advocates had a successful meeting with the first Obama secretary of transportation, Ray Lahood, whom Tom reported was very open to the group's talking points and overall vision regarding the environmental and health benefits of bicycling, especially as a mode of everyday transportation. During my interviews with Tom, it became clear that he hopes to affect history on both state and national levels through his biking advocacy and spiritual activism.

Tom was fifty-six at the time I began my fieldwork with STW and Landry's. Tom was born in Gloucester, MA and moved to Exeter, NH when he was very young. His family was Congregationalist and attended a United Church of Christ (UCC) congregation. There was no crucifix, he recalled, only an "abstracted cross." The white church only had clear glass. Along with Herbert Blau, Tom's former theater troupe director, and Dick Broholm, Tom considers the minister, George Booth, to be one of the three most important mentors in his life. He recalled that Pastor Booth "preached sermons that revolved around the world, about justice, civil rights, and the Vietnam War." Pastor Booth, Tom qualified, was a critic of the war but he was not an "uncritical protestor" either. For his part, Tom is not entirely uncritical of his religious upbringing in Pastor Booth's church. Tom once explained that when he was a boy growing up, one of his best friends was Catholic and that he remembers thinking the stained glass windows and the incense of this boy's world seemed "weird" and "cultish." Now, he chalks this attitude up to his own parochial Protestant upbringing. Tom admits that his religious education was thick, though progressive and mainline. Taking stock of the good and the bad, he realizes that he was from his childhood "informed by that kind of mainstream Protestant tradition" that trained him in biblical exegesis at an early age and exposed him to liberation theology early in life.

While away at college at Oberlin, Tom worked in theater with the late Herbert Blau, a luminary in American experimental theater, an iconoclastic scholar of performance studies and interpreter of Jacques Derrida's work for the theater. Tom also signed on to work with his professor's theater group after college and very much enjoyed his life as an actor. When Blau disbanded the group, however, Tom explained that he had felt lost and "didn't know what to do." He briefly went to work for his brother, Peter, who was already in the bicycle business even though he found the world of sales and profit-making strongly unappealing. At first, Tom said, "I couldn't stand it!" "This is horrible!" Tom recalls that one day he was "just standing at a work bench and I was *showing wheels* and standing under these florescent lights and I was in so much grief about the end of the theater work. I think I was angry in those days." It was at that moment, a moment which to him felt absurd, that Tom decided to go to seminary, just as his father had once predicted, and despite the fact that he lacked traditional theological commitments, preferring instead to think metaphysics by way of the "spirituality" of theater and poetry. Once there, his fellow students at Andover-Newton sometimes accused Tom of "not having faith" because he could not confidently speak about God. Tom recalls that in those days he simply felt the urge to "flip off" these detractors, many of whom he felt were "anti-intellectual." While at Andover-Newton, Tom met and studied under Dick Broholm, who challenged his students to understand society itself, including its business and government institutions, as the "mystical body of God incarnate". Under Dick's sustained mentorship, Tom has spent the next quarter-century making good on the exhortation to work in the world with a servant heart. In the process, he has developed an appreciation for business and a passion for the biking industry. However, as I discovered through my relationship with him over time, leadership is an extension and prolongation of his scope as an actor. Time and again, Tom wove together connections between the work of STW and his experiences in the theater.

The actor's craft, Tom will readily tell you, has everything to do with the dialectic between presence and absence. For example, he once described an actor's presence as "that something that we can't quite define where you begin to see yourself in the other person and to feel something larger than the person who is there." He called this "some kind of knowing, some kind of awareness," adding that this is "what you look for in great art and certainly in great theater." *Presence* for Tom, though, is "directly relational; it's in a direct relationship to their absence." Tom recalled that one of his theater directors once went to see Marlon Brando in *The Iceman Cometh* and had described to Tom the ways in which Brando had literally become "an icicle" because he was "that frozen, that absent." Continuing, Tom said that what he finds beautiful about acting, poetry, and the work of the imagination is "an absence *cycled* through presence, death and life, living, breathing and dying all coexisting." "Theater," he once said, "is in many ways a spiritual discipline because it's a kind of confession, a kind of revelation, a kind of prayer." Tom added, "theater acting at its best is fundamentally about revealing something. How do you come to know true love of God, self, and other? Most theater is about that. The failure of that. The tragedy of that. The success of that." During our conversations, I noted the ways in which Tom contextualized acting as a play of form and formlessness accomplished by "self-emptying." "One part of the actor," he said, "has to do with the teleology, the goals and objectives of the scene, the larger arc of the movement." Tom continued, asking, "What is the arc of this play? *The arc of history*. The movement towards justice and love. Every play has an arc. You have to also track that. But you also have to be present to the thing as it is." While reality shifts for Tom, there is a core that persists and orients the dynamism of life. At several points in my ethnographic work with Tom, he referred to this center as Love. Linking different arcs of justice and history, Tom also talks about his commitment to socially enlightened business as a practice of Love.

"The ability to let yourself be possessed" is a necessary part of the spiritual discipline of theater, Tom once explained. However, "spirit" possession, Tom argues, is also a key aspect of life at work. The *demonic*, a word Tom uses a lot, is, for him, the power of unconscious possession. Companies and organizations can become trapped by what he calls "*cycles of power*" in which certain destructive behaviors are reinforced without conscious thought or moral awareness. Institutional "cultures" take on lives of their own, he explains. The competitive free market, Tom explains, says that "there is *no central control* but it says you can save, accumulate money whoever has the idea, find the need this wild, competitive, free-ranging kind of thing. Some people have a faith in that." Tom does not. Our strengths need to be brought back together and made "*whole*," Tom says, if we are going to have any chance at all to withstand the demonic forces that allow corruption to become endemic of commercial culture.

Tom credits his work with STW in guiding him to take a principled stand against a destructive industry trend that he thinks was driving a "race to the bottom" and which he believes would have wreaked havoc upon independent bike retail.[11] Corporate and industry cultures themselves need to be reformed, Tom is one with STW in believing, so that what comes to possess us is virtuous rather than "demonic" in nature. Good habits must become what Tom calls *"momentum wheels"*; they also imply "possession" by our light demons or better angels. Tom explains that *"feedback loops"* and *"reinforcing cycles,"* terms that also pervade the management theory of Margaret Wheatley and Peter Senge, imply "being played by the music, the music playing us." It is akin, he will say, to being "in a mantra state." The proper goal for any company, he believes, is to create a "culture" that will inspire and give rise to virtuous rather than demonic action. For Tom Henry, I discovered during our many conversations, music, dramaturgy, poetry and dance provide the most apt and adequate metaphors for experience, even our experiences at work, because they imply the semi-circular and interminable movement of presence into absence and back again.

Within contemporary "cycles of power", Tom Henry is fond of suggesting that bicycling has a special and positive role to play. If fear and unconscious possession by destructive systems fuels the demonic aspect of capitalist life, conscious reform that leads to unconscious possession by fair and balanced systems is what will save the world, Tom Henry explains, echoing management theory but speaking it by way of his own life story. For Tom, biking is a bodily, spiritual practice that one practices, driving towards a destination one might never see. Even if his Christian Reformed pessimism inflects his performance theory, Tom speaks about the need for "spiritual" reform with enthusiasm. He speaks of the "urgency of biking to save the world systems" and he does so because he notes an elegant symmetry between bicycle and human body, on the one hand, and spiritual cycles, on the other hand. The bicycle, he says, "is in perfect balance with the human body. It fits the body very nicely." "To this day," Tom adds, the bike is "the most efficient means of transportation on the earth." Tom likes to quote the head of the Transportation and Infrastructure Committee, who argues that the bicycle can help us "turn the hydro-carbon economy into the carbohydrate economy." In a productive, *self-regulating loop*, this would also increase fitness levels and improve overall health, Tom says. Biking can also, he argues, wean us from fossil fuels and the destructive geo-politics that feed our addiction to carbon-based energy. In this, or any Justice seeking we might do at work, Henry argues that it is important to practice the actor's craft of self-emptying in order that we might finally allow ourselves to be played by virtuous rather than destructive "cycles of power." We must allow the good scripts to guide us.

During one of our interviews, Tom made a point that I later understood differently than I did at the time. Tom explained that there was a new book out that discussed the fate of the biosphere after humans. "It's an interesting experiment," Tom suggested. "If I am the perceiver, what happens if I am not there perceiving it? What is there?" At the time, I was not at all sure what to make of Tom's odd talk of "perceiving perceivers." For my purposes in this present discussion, it makes sense to pause and consider a few things. Until I began to research the work of Margaret Wheatley and other creativity-inspired management theorists, I had little awareness of the deep and profound ways in which major principles from "new science" were being actively introduced into organizational science. When Tom made the comment about "perceiving perceivers" over lunch at Legal Seafood, I took it simply as an extension of his interest in the dynamism of poetry and performance theory. Now, in

---

[11] When Specialized, one of the major American bicycle retailers, accounted plans to go "big box" and expand the market within the likes of Wal-Mart, its then CEO told industry leaders that more profit could be made all around. To the independent bike shops, like Landry's, he said that "big box" bikes would mean a greater demand for bike repairs. With a wink and a nod, the CEO of Specialized smiled and laughed while the industry leaders gathered around him and did the same. For Tom, this moment has become the paradigmatic example of "demonic possession" at work. The people in the room did not even realize, he says, that they were suggesting that they wanted to provide worse products and put people at risk all for the sake of profit. Tom stood up and gave a damning speech that, he will proudly tell you, has become part of urban lore in the bike industry. He says he took his stand from a position of "whole self," a concept which resonates with themes in the management literature of the STW universe. Tom's view won the day and Specialized and the industry, he explained, went in a different direction that resisted a "big-box" model for bicycle retail.

retrospect, I realize that, given the particular influence which the work of the leading organizational theorists Margaret Wheatley, Robert Greanleaf, and Peter Senge have had on the discursive world of STW, I also need to consider it to echo the quantum idea that the observer evokes reality, an idea popularly expressed by the principle of "Schroedinger's cat."

In her now classic manifesto, *Leadership and the New Science: Discovering Order in a Chaotic World*, Wheatley writes:

> A live cat is placed in a box. The box has solid walls, so no one outside the box can see into it. This is a crucial factor, since the thought experiment explores the role of the observer in evoking reality. Inside the box, a device will trigger the release of either poison or food; the probability of either occurrence is 50/50. Time passes. The trigger goes off, unobserved. The cat meets its fate. Or does it? Just as an electron is both a wave and a particle until our observation causes it to collapse as either a particle or a wave, Schroedinger argues that the cat is both alive and dead until the moment we observe it. Inside the box, when no one is watching, the cat exists only as a probability wave ([15], p. 61).

For my part, I am sure that the life or death of the cat would matter to whatever kittens it might have or would matter to its loving caretakers in ways that are quite different from the supposed impact that the steely gaze of the quantum scientist, who has come to think of cats like wave particles, might have on its reality.

Here, though, what I want to highlight is the fact that Tom Henry's question might simultaneously represent a cultural dominant, the popularization of quantum scientific principles, what Foucault might speak of in epistemic terms, and also speak to his personal background in theater and love for poetry. In other words, "power" operates in misty ways that achieve sociological solidity (as what Michael Jackson calls "patterns of intersubjective experience") but which can also allow Herbert Blau and Jacques Derrida through him to wed Margaret Wheatley in or as the mystical Body of Christ. Symbolic conflations, psychic history, and the personalization of social metaphor work together to defy the neat categorizations and definitions in which we often put much stock. As it is enacted and lived, "power" is, in other words, liquid. It is, in life, *existential* rather than *analytical*.[12]

5. Towards an Existential Archeological Methodology

"New Management" is rife with talk of self-regulating feedback loops, circle economies and metaphors that mark the embodied, co-creative processes of communication and cultural production that are endemic to contemporary work. The fissions that have attended the deregulation of heavy industry in favor of immaterial labor are often marked in the management literature by religious and poetic metaphor. As a longstanding and visible member of STW and consistent participant at the roundtables, Tom Henry absorbed and was shaped by this discourse. However, it would be both empirically and politically myopic to conclude that Henry is merely a passive effect of discourse. In fact, as is the case for all persons, Henry's social reality is always mediated by his existential history.[13]

---

12 Management discourse, like any other limiting structures of history, is never simply conserved and reiterated but always brought to new places through the mediations of intersubjectivity. As Michael Jackson writes, "As Sartre argued, the conscious projects and intentions that carry us forward into the future are grounded in unconscious dispositions, accumulated habits, and invisible histories that, taken together, define our past. Accordingly, any essay in human understanding requires a progressive-regressive method that both discloses the preconditions that constrain what we may say and do, while recognising that no human action simply and blindly conserves the past; it goes beyond it" ([50], p. 293).

13 Political and ethical considerations are central to Sartre's concept of *choice*. We are never simply passive vessels of limiting structures but are held to ethical account by our moral responsibility to choose. We are defined not by any essence but according to the ways in which we respond to the exigencies of messy existence. We can adopt a life-project which is characterized by chosen values which totalize the scope of our biographical history, as a whole. While Sartre understood well the need to change the structures that shape and constrain choice (and argues that the intellectual must commit to this goal), unlike Foucault, he did so according to an account of a biographically inflected freedom which does not collapse discursive and existential histories.

Social metaphor is particularized by the vagaries of biography and is always, in practice, intersubjective in nature. As Sartre argued, it is not simply the case that the world makes us. We, in turn, remake the world though our acts, living steps and spoken words. In their classic study, *Metaphors We Live By*, George Lakoff and Mark Johnson argue that metaphoricity acts through the body, giving rise to ways of knowing and experiencing the world:

> The concepts that govern our thought are not just matters of the intellect. They also govern our everyday functioning, down to the most mundane details. Our concepts structure what we perceive, how we get around the world, and how we relate to other people. Our conceptual system thus plays a central role in defining our everyday realities, and what we do is very much a matter of metaphor ([54], p. 3).

As I detail in *Shape-Shifting Capital—Spiritual Management, Critical Theory, and the Ethnographic Project*, the STW roundtables represent attempts to *reframe* what STW calls "organizational stories" by synergistically reading these in tandem with and through the lens of an assortment of texts and images culled and mined from diverse religious traditions, humanistic disciplines, the "new science" discourse, and literary traditions ([18], pp. 35–81).

What Lakoff and Johnson call *ontological metaphors* (a metaphor which views "events, activities, emotions, ideas, etc. as entities and substances") are evident in the group's desire to *reframe* organizational stories to begin with. For STW, to reframe organizational stories is precisely to redraw the boundaries of business around the metaphor of "concentric circles held together by tension and informed by one's deepest values" [48]. Within the group's "Theology of Institutions", circles are metaphorical containers within which spirit (e.g. creativity) flows *dynamically*, that is, in creative tension, but ultimately in harmony and coherently because the circles are understood to exist under Christ's good providence [48]. Flexible circles capture the recursivity of cybernetic movement without forsaking the management interest in order and control. The nature images sometimes displayed on a screen during the group's ritual meetings weave the natural world into this circular pattern of divine creativity and purpose, connecting sacred and market time.

If we are often not consciously aware of the "conventional metaphors" that pattern experiential gestalts and shape lived realities, Lakoff and Johnson note that we do sometimes actively and quite self-consciously attempt to create "new meaning" by creating new relationships of similarity. New metaphors, they write, "make sense of our experience in the same way conventional metaphors do: they provide coherent structure, highlighting some things and hiding others" ([54], p. 139) In the end, STW's "spiritual" reform principally consists of the creation of new meaning and new relationships of similarity.' The ritual work of forging new meanings through the inscription of "new metaphor" was the dominant focus of the STW roundtable meetings I attended. The question of *how* new meanings are constructed was less patent.

Following up on Lakoff and Johnson's pioneering work, Gilles Fauconnier and Mark Turner develop the argument that "creativity involves bringing together elements from different domains" ([55], p. 37). What they call "conceptual blending" speaks not simply to the intentional juxtaposition of conceptual matrices but, in the end, to its ubiquitous and pre-conscious operation in "everyday thought and language." Human networks of meaning integrate cognitive blends that are at once cultural and personal. In short, to the degree that theological and management frames are formative for persons, these blends are already shaping experience more broadly, whether or not persons take it upon themselves to *do theology* or *talk management*, as it were. Theological reason, like internalized management discourse, exists, from the start, *as a blend*. Cybernetic metaphors are alive for Tom as existentially mediated *metaphorical complexes*. Discourse is never "internalized" in the same way; we do not deploy language outside of the vagaries of biographical and empirical contexts. With his talk of "cycles of power", Tom personalizes the group's theology and reads himself into it. In doing so, he reproduces management ideology and participates in social history and the epistemic turn to immaterial labor and global, cybernetic Capitalism. Importantly, Tom makes history, psychically, at varying and shifting degrees of metaphorical inchoateness and conscious intentionality.[14]

In his masterful review of theories of ideology, alienation and subjection, Jan Rehmann argues that one consequence of poststructuralist thought's unique attention to the discursive power of language is that the project of de-naturalizing fixed identities always remains "at risk of morphing into an overall de-*materiali*sation of social life" ([4], p. 218). The radicalization of the linguistic turn, whatever else its obvious ethical fruits are, can be understood to reproduce a postmodern variant of "what Marx has analysed as "fetishism", namely the alienating rule of abstract value over use-value, of abstract average labour over concrete labour" ([4], p. 217). Indeed, while poststructuralism's strident anti-humanism is often lauded as a radical critique of Enlightenment liberalism and for being a check on the latter's inordinate celebration of reason and autonomy, in an important recent volume on the relationship of the thought of Michel Foucault to the rising neoliberal tides of his day, Daniel Zamora argues that, in many ways, Foucault's later work in ethics and governmentality, especially, dovetail, as an ideological and historical matter, with anti-statist austerity programs, the deregulation of the welfare state, the abstracting finacialization of social life, and the celebration of the ultimate sovereignty of the market [56]. In short, given his own libertarian anxieties regarding the institutional regulation and control of conduct, Foucault found common cause with neoliberalism's "anthropological economism" and anti-bureaucratism.[15] However, amidst Foucault's critiques of the "rigidities" of the security state, he, "...neglects the function of finance, debt, and money. This is because he is unable to think about economic relations per se and the mediation of relations of power through money and value" [59]. In the process, in Foucault's late work, Capitalism acquires ontological status as a saturating and pervasive "invisible reality" ([56], p. 75). Understood in the way Zamora does, Foucault falls prey to precisely the kind of unchecked symbolic conflations and political slippages which the critical theorist, Russell Berman, warns against:

> Both the neoconservatives and the new social movements have, in addition to their critiques of the state, their respective cultural programs. These however are less interesting than the repetition of the antibureaucratic discourse of deregulation in the postmodernist cultural programs in terms like polyphony ([60], p. 134).

To assume, without contextualizing our ideas about subjectivity within the currents of neoliberal Capitalism, that any attempted recovery either of the subject or of biographical history is necessarily retrograde is to tread similar waters.[16]

---

[14] Whenever we speak of word clouds or data clouds, we mirror the networked imaginary of contemporary Capitalism, while also, at the same time, reproducing these broader social formations at the level of lived experience. Recently, I have caught myself using the increasingly common idiom "having the band-with to" as in the question "do you have the bandwith to take care of this right now?" I do not intend to cite a subject position when I use this Internet metaphor, but, despite myself, such a statement contextualizes my life within the digital age and in important other ways as well.

[15] The work of Bruno Latour represents a watershed moment in Western social theory that privileges politics over and against existence. However, unlike Latour, whose "principle of generalized symmetry" assigns equal agency to persons as non-persons, including social structures and sedimented history, I am loath to go down Latour's path of "Actor-Network Theory" on political grounds [57]. Systems very much express the agencies of individuals even if they also cannot be reduced to human agency. No doubt, some actors working for multinational corporations and in global finance work hard to support and maintain the "impersonal" structures of global neoliberalism because the paradigm enhances their financial and political power. The difference is that, as Sartre suggested, some individuals have more leverage than others and the processed materiality of history supports agency and human well-being in differentiated and unequal ways (see [43,51]). It is also not the case that the solidarity of the dispossessed can be ever be simply assumed at a distance, either. Choice always remains central to relationships of solidarity. Hence, both the constitutive instability of social solidarity and its very possibility are, in part, a consequence of a recalcitrant and at times politically inconvenient human freedom. For thorough discussions of the defining features of Sartre's existential Marxism, see [52,58].

[16] Nor can we assume that desire and *eros* are the great antidotes capable of undermining utility's system. Jean-Joseph Goux provides a useful discussion of the ways in which Georges Bataille misrecognizes the ways in which affect and the inner life are not other than or separate from the systemic coherence of Capitalism but, rather, constitutive and generative of it (see [61]).

As anthropologists of Capitalism, such as Karen Ho [62], Melissa Fisher [63] and Caitlin Zaloom [64], describe, even the most highly abstracting finance Capitalism is still ultimately constructed through practice. For example, in her brilliant ethnography of Wall Street, Ho argues that since it is the case that "part of the discursive power of the financial market is precisely its representation as abstract," ([62], p. 37) the deployment of ethnographic methods renders "concrete" the ways in which financial decisions and the experiences of financiers (in this case, investment bankers) are "thoroughly informed by cultural values and the social relations of race, gender, and class" ([62], p. 37). She demonstrates the ways in which "the *personal biographies* of investment bankers play into, and converge with, job status and workplace experiences to shape a commonsense understanding of the righteousness of Wall Street analyses and recommendations" ([62], p. 11). To the degree that the social construction of corporate "spirituality" ratchets up the power and scope of abstraction, ethnographic descriptions of its construction through practice can prove to be powerful, *critical* counterweights. Existential archeology highlights what Robert Orsi calls the memories, relationships, desires, fears, inheritances and attachments that attach to the redoubling of power and the iteration of social codes (see [65]).[17]

Of course, this kind of approach stands in contrast to "orthodox" poststructuralist methodologies which too often underplay the role of social semantics in the construction of ideology. According to David Graeber, performativity, or the reduction of all human action to politics and the idea that power creates its own truth, came into its own as a hegemonic theory between 1980 and 2008 [67]. Its prominence coincided with the increasing *financialization* of the economy and the "confidence games" that attend to the creation of market bubbles wherein value simply becomes what we think it is or what we can be convinced it is. Criterion of truth outside of the performative gestures of the market assemblage disappear and, in their place, there is a, "widespread assumption of no meaningful distinction between the nature of reality, the techniques of knowledge designed to analyze and interpret that reality, and the forms of institutional power within which knowledge is produced" [67]. In a neoliberal age, market logic *makes things so by saying so* and no alternative accounts of reality are admitted to cross-witness.

According to Jan Rehmann, Foucault constructs just this very kind of ideologically closed loop in his studies of governmentality. Foucault, he writes, insisted that neoliberalism's leadership techniques and pastoral philosophies must be investigated in a positive way. Rehmann adds: Foucault's "Governmentality studies", "reproduce the view of management which looks at employees from the perspective of managerial leaders and dissimulates the domination and alienation in neoliberal capitalism behind the smokescreen of motivational incentives and appeals to teamwork" ([4], p. 314). Put another way, "since its interpretation is restricted to the programmatic interpellations of management literature without investigating their encounter with real subjects, the distinctions between techniques of self-conduct and domination becomes obsolete" ([4], p. 314). In other words, the subject is uncritically and too simply identified with the discourse that shapes it. *An existential archeology of contemporary postindustrial "workplace spirituality" will track the contours of the neo-hegemonic discourse, on the one hand, and will also exploit the spaces of contradiction wherein biographical history simultaneously reproduces and resists—both as a voluntary matter or not—identification with this discourse, on the other hand.* As a type of practice theory which self-reflexively aims to bridge existentialist and poststructuralist insights, it specializes in the investigation of the ways in which the discursive rules that constitute knowledge *across multiple social institutions* are reproduced at the level of intersubjective history. It attempts to make good on Mark Poster's suggestion that critical theory must, with Sartre,

---

17 Focusing on social semantics or the space of intersubjectivity between self and discursive world does not in any way preclude supplemental, complementary or even antagonistic foci on something of what Jasbir Puar has in mind: "The assemblage, as a series of dispersed but mutually implicated and messy networks, draws together enunciation and dissolution, causality and effect, organic and non-organic forces" ([66], p. 211). My argument is not that we ought to privilege existentially mediated speech acts but, rather, that we cannot summarily dismiss them altogether from our analyses.

attend to the "dialectical interplay of men and things" and simultaneously follow Foucault in his considerations of the "systematized rules of formation" according to which the subject is linguistically constituted ([68], p. 275).[18]

In contrast to the Foucauldian collapse of the distinction between technologies of self and domination occasioned by the artificial removal of the "contradictions of socialization under the antagonistic conditions of neoliberal capitalism," ([4], p. 315) an existential archeology of contemporary "workplace spirituality" gives voice to these tensions and gains critical leverage in doing so. In *Shape-Shifting Capital*, I provide thick ethnographic accounts of the biographical mediations which attach to the reproduction of management discourse for *deconstructive* purposes. While Tom Henry is a vocal champion of STW's "Theology of Institutions", which itself bears a strong family resemblance to the broader ideology of "new management", his existential history resists a full and final identification with the discourse and, at times, points to sites of viscerally felt tension as a charismatic salesman who also believes that wealth must be socialized and as a former actor whose first love will always be the theater rather than the boardroom. In these ways, what Michael Jackson calls "existential deconstruction" (see [7], p. 3) meets the demands of "a critical ideology-theory (which) needs to grasp the contradictions between neoliberal discourses of self-activation and the submission to alienated relations of domination" ([4], p. 318).

Ethnographies of "spiritual management" must also always remain attentive to the differing milieus of their reception. As Rehmann argues, "the appeals to creativity and initiative might play a mobilising and constructive role in the formation of identities if they correlate to labour-conditions that actually require and bolster a certain (relative) autonomy and freedom; they tend to destroy agency and subjectivities if there are no, or very restricted possibilities to act" ([4], pp. 317–8). As I describe in the monograph, the lower-end workers I met at Landry's tended not to adopt the STW framework and sometimes actively resisted many of its most basic assumptions. They also often worked with competing accounts of the "spiritual" (see [18], pp. 119–55). At an even more radical political and epistemological distance, we might compare and contrast the "spirituality" of leadership ideology and the lived religion of populations not afforded the same "new management" niceties—religious life and religious conversion within the prison-system and police surveillance complex, for example (see [4], p. 317). In all cases, even in these days of assumed performativity and the lingering popularity of poststructuralist accounts of the subject in the study of religion, a methodology appropriate to the study of religion and Capitalism must take "seriously the agency of individuals and their attempts at self-socialisation and self-conduct. The emergence of capacities to act is not to be equated beforehand with subjection" ([4], p. 318). As Zygmunt Bauman argues, "conflict, is no longer between classes, but between each person and society. It isn't just a lack of security, but a lack of freedom" [71]. Critically exploiting the gap between the discursive say-so and the empirical do-so, an ethnographic existential archeology can draw important contrasts between "neoliberalism's attractive promises of individualization and its practical reductionism" ([4], p. 318).

6. Concluding Reflections

Capitalism has not drowned out the "heavenly ecstasies of religious fervor," as Marx predicted ([72], p. 206). It is in the business of generating its own distinct variety of "religious fervor." Networked Capitalism is characterized by its misty ephemerality. Its R&D units, dark money, dark pools,

---

[18] For a discussion of the ways of the false oppositions, which tend to confuse understandings of the relationship of Sartrian and Derridean accounts of subjectivity see Steve Martinot, *Forms in the Abyss: A Philosophical Bridge Between Sartre and Derrida* [69]. Martinot writes, "Subjectivity does not manifest itself as writing in the Derridean sense, any more than writing manifests itself as subjectivity in the Sartrean sense. One can no more say that consciousness produces writing as its thought than that writing produces consciousness as its text. They are homological, which means these are not oppositions between Sartre and Derrida" ([69], p. 248). In a similar vein, I appreciate the ways in which Amy Hollywood's Derridean readings, attentive to the "perversion" inherent to Derrida's thought itself, resist a new, poststructuralist orthodoxy of the subject and make room for active, intentional work (see [70], p. 269).

dark data and shadow banking reveal its increasingly penumbral quality. Increasingly, "spirituality" is an explicit and public aspect of Capitalism's present archeological form. The battle over religious metaphor is, Derrida writes, all encompassing: "the war for the "appropriation of Jerusalem" is today the world war. It is happening everywhere, it is the world" ([73], p. 73). Both Max Weber and Karl Marx believed that "enchantment would disappear". And yet, according to Jean and John Comaroff, today, "more and more ordinary people see arcane forces intervening in the production of value, diverting its flow toward a new elect: those masters of the market who comprehend and control the production of wealth and contemporary conditions" ([74], p. 25).

According to the Comaroffs, "epochal shifts in the constitutive relationship of production to consumption, and hence of labor to capital" as well as the rampant explosion of digitally mediated forms of casino Capitalism have resulted in what they call the "ontological conditions-of-being under millennial Capitalism" ([74], p. 25). "Occult economies" can provide existential hope to persons when social conditions place them in danger. As the late ethnographer of Capitalist magic, Galina Lindquist, writes, magical practices, "thrive where power is brutal and overwhelming, where the rational channels of agency are insufficient or of limited value" ([75], p. 2). Unauthorized ghosts and forms of spectral assault can aid in the resistance of Capitalist discipline (see [76]). Magical techniques can also mark the utter primitivism of financial chicanery.[19]

The "spirituality" of contemporary management theory never has the final word. The members of STW are not alone in turning to "extrasocial" sources in an effort to manage the many crises of Capitalism. Many are conjuring forth specters, ghosts, and spirts from the borderlands, in search of hope and spectral assistance. In addition to "religion" as it has been sequestered to meet the totalitarian demands of Capitalist domination, religion has also become, "the privileged, if not primary form in which the impoverished masses...articulate their hopes as well a critique of the world ([28], p. 51), At all times, we are all always haunted by other, elusive "spirits" that populate the limits of what we can do and know.[20] In a society so thoroughly suffused with the alienating logic of capital, we participate in this religious history whether we like it or not. However, this is not the "timeless time of creation," as one of the STW roundtable meetings suggested. We are tethered to history. It is also our perpetual task in life to remake it. We ourselves help write the history of "spiritual Capitalism", not as pawns in a progressive unfolding of purpose, but through the everyday things we say and the little steps we take. We who labor in the study of religion must reckon with the new, ancient, and revenant spirits of Capitalism.[21]

---

[19] Indeed, in 2008, the *New York Times* reported that following the economic collapse of that same year, psychics and tarot card readers saw a spike in business as day traders looked to occult techniques to help them predict and manage the increasingly chaotic financial markets (see [77]).

[20] In her masterful, *Politics Out of History*, Wendy Brown queries: "are ghosts and spirits what inevitably arise at the end or death of something—an era, desire, attachment, belief, figure, or narrative?" There, she suggests that the mourning of modernity's many certainties has given rise to the furtive specters which Derrida then conjures forth ([78], p. 114).

[21] As Robert Orsi reminds, modern, Western criticisms and naturalistic reductions of the "real presence" of religious agencies necessarily participate in racial, colonial, gendered and class histories which have traditionally made much of modern, secular taxonomies according to which religious societies have been understood to exist at primitive stages of socio-cultural evolution and religious persons who insist on the reality of religious "presence" have been deemed some version of ignorant, psychotic or delusional. These histories necessarily breathe down the back of the critic of even highly commodified and bourgeois forms of "capitalist spirituality" (see [79], pp. 3–5). Capitalist spirituality places religious studies in a difficult but productive "double-bind". There are simply no intellectually defensible reasons for concluding that it is appropriate to glibly write-off "capitalist" forms of "spirituality" on account of the charge that they are somehow "unreal" or not the kind of "religion" that is worthy of our best efforts as religion scholars. The kinds of lived experiences of "presence" which accompany self-help techniques ought to matter to us and to our scholarly projects. At the very same time, to eschew criticisms of the inequalities and social suffering that underwrite bourgeois capitalist spirituality is to seek refuge in an apolitical, phenomenological refuge of the scholar's own making. Fortunately, a better understanding of how Capitalism is viscerally "religious" can only improve our social criticisms of contemporary conditions. Criticism and phenomenology are in no way opposed to one another.
According to Amy Hollywood, the question of the limits of the "real" antecedes modern discourse and is, for example, constitutive of Medieval periods in which she works. It is also the case, as Hollywood suggests, students of religion are perhaps *inescapably* and especially confronted with the problem of critical reason's constitutive limits (see [70], p. 135). Hollywood marshals the "apparently uncritical readings" of Medieval, women mystics traditionally marginalized for their

Acknowledgments: Portions of this essay and aspects of the argument appeared in my monograph, *Shape-Shifting Capital—Spiritual Management, Critical Theory, and the Ethnographic Project.* © Lexington Books. I want to thank the publisher for granting permission to reprint this material.

Conflicts of Interest: The author declares no conflicts of interest.

References

1. González, George. "Shape-Shifting Capital: New Management and the Bodily Metaphors of Spiritual Capitalism." *Journal for the Theory of Social Behaviour* 42 (2012): 325–44. [CrossRef]
2. Rehmann, Jan. *Max Weber—Modernisation as Passive Revolution.* Chicago: Haymarket Books, 2015.
3. Venturi, Robert. *Complexity and Contractiction in Architecture.* New York: The Museum of Modern Art, 1977.
4. Rehmann, Jan. *Theories of Ideology—The Powers of Alienation and Subjection.* Chicago: Haymarket Book, 2013.
5. Pope, Liston. *Millhands and Preachers—A Study of Gastonia.* New Haven: Yale University Press, 1958.
6. Mills, Charles Wright. *White Collar: The American Middle Classes.* New York: Oxford University Press, 2002.
7. Jackson, Michael. *Minima Ethnographica: Intersubjectivity and the Anthropological Project.* Chicago: University of Chicago Press, 1998.
8. Boltanski, Luc, and Eve Chiapello. *The New Spirit of Capitalism.* London: Verso, 2007.
9. Cook, Jennifer Carol . *Machine and Metaphor: The Ethics of Language in American Realism.* New York: Routledge Press, 2006.
10. Guillén, Mauro. *Models of Management: Work, Authority and Organization in a Comparative Perspective.* Chicago: University of Chicago Press, 1994.
11. Curts, Kati. "Temples and Turnpikes in 'The World of Tomorrow': Religious Assemblage and Automobility at the 1939 New York World's Fair." *Journal of the American Academy of Religion* 83 (2015): 722–49. [CrossRef]
12. Neal, Judith. *Edgewalkers: People and Organizations That Take Risks.* Westport: Praeger Publishers, 2006.
13. Goldschmidt Salamon, Karen Lisa. "Going Global From the Inside Out: Spiritual Globalism in the Workplace." In *New Age Religion and Globalization.* Edited by Mikael Rothstein. Aarhus: Aarhus University Press, 2001.
14. Greenleaf, Robert. *Servant Leadership: A Journey into the Nature of Legitimate Power and Greatness.* New York: Paulist Press, 2002.
15. Wheatley, Margaret. *Leadership and the New Science: Discovering Order in a Chaotic World.* San Francisco: Berrett-Koehler Publishers, Inc., 2006.
16. Senge, Peter. *The Fifth Discipline: The Art and Practice of the Learning Organization.* New York: Currency Doubleday, Inc., 1990.
17. Broggi, Joshua. *Sacred Language, Sacred World.* New York: Bloomsbury, 2015.

---

purported bodily and affective excesses (readings which are bound to specific times and places but which can, whether "then" or "now", ignite new meanings). While I am generally partial to this kind of Benjaminian dialectic, it must be *contextualized* within the movements of a post-secular discourse which generates much of its power by grinding its axes against a fetishized, "dead" and "unhip" secularism. While I agree that we cannot assume that religion is inherently uncritical, today, this kind of understanding must be contextualized within a sociology of "spiritual Capitalism" in which economic reason does not outright reject and disavow religious and theological reason but, instead, hopes to strategically manage, predict and control "religious", "poetic", linguistic and psychic borderlands through forms of statistical power. Today, Capitalist reason seeks not to disavow but rather to don the trappings of "excess". This is precisely how fire walking corporate training exercises and shamanic rituals have become some of the favored technologies of today's surfing CEOs and poet CFOs (see [18], pp. 1–34). Can the sacred past "blaze up" today the way Benjamin would have us hope when, in the contemporary context, the ideology of Capitalism itself covets the disciplinary power of ancient, religious metaphor and looks to mine penumbral spaces and liminal states in search of profitable creativity?

As Hollywood's Derridean readings would seem to suggest and I argue, from a slightly different angle in my monograph, our situation is marked by *contestations* over already overdetermined forms of "religious" metaphor. A double-movement is needed—the "religious" (or attendant forms of the poetic, the affective, spirituality and mysticism) cannot be opposed to the rational; instead, competing accounts of the "religious" (and the "poetic") can be conjured forth, forced to coexist in generative tensions which might explode the possible horizons of meaning. In my own work, the ethnographic details resist the totalizations of management discourse and its ideological, capitalizing accounts of "spirituality". They also resist the totalizations of critical reason. Politics is informed by phenomenology and phenomenology is framed by sociology but the connective circles are never closed. Detailed archival work can also accomplish something akin to this kind of open critique always at odds with itself so long as, in my view, intersubjectivity is not collapsed into a generalizing account of discourse.

18. González, George. *Shape-Shifting Capital—Spiritual Management, Critical Theory, and the Ethnographic Project.* London: Lexington Books, 2015.
19. Dubuisson, Daniel. *The Western Construction of Religion: Myths, Knowledge, and Ideology.* Baltimore: Johns Hopkins University Press, 2003.
20. Rose, Nikolas. *Governing the Self: The Shaping of the Private Self.* London: Free Association Books, 1999.
21. Harvey, David. *A Brief History of Neoliberalism.* Oxford: Oxford University Press, 2005.
22. Steger, Manfred. *The Rise of the Global Imaginary: Political Ideologies from the French Revolution to the Global War on Terror.* Oxford: Oxford University Press, 2009.
23. Moreton, Bethany. "The Soul of Neoliberalism." *Social Text* 25 (2007): 103–24. [CrossRef]
24. Sullivan, Winnifred Fallers. *A Ministry of Presence—Chaplaincy, Spiritual Care, and the Law.* Chicago: University of Chicago Press, 2014.
25. Fukuyma, Francis. *Trust: The Social Virtues and the Creation of Prosperity.* New York: Free Press, 1995.
26. Lash, Scott, and John Urry. *Economies of Space.* London: Sage, 1994.
27. Conley, Dalton. *Elsewhere, U.S.A.—How We Got from the Company Man, Family Dinners and the Affluent Society to the Home Office, Blackberry Moms, and Economic Anxiety.* New York: Vintage Books, 2010.
28. Mendieta, Eduardo. *Global Fragments: Globalizations, Latinamericanisms, and Critical Theory.* Albany: SUNY Press, 2007.
29. Bauman, Zygmunt. *Liquid Modernity.* Malden: Polity Press, 2000.
30. Hardt, Michael. "Affective Labor." *Boundary 2* 26 (1999): 89–100.
31. Jameson, Fredric. *Postmodernism, Or the Cultural Logic of Late Capitalism.* Durham: Duke University Press, 1991.
32. Gutting, Gary. *Michel Foucault's Archaeology of Scientific Reason.* Cambridge: Cambridge University Press, 1989.
33. Spiegel, Gabrielle. "Introduction." In *Practicing History: New Directions in Historical Writing After the Linguistic Turn.* Edited by Gabrielle Spiegel. New York: Routledge, 2005.
34. Jordan, Mark. *Convulsing Bodies—Religion and Resistance in Foucault.* Palo Alto: Stanford University Press, 2014.
35. Butler, Judith. *The Psychic Life of Power: Theories in Subjection.* Palo Alto: Stanford University Press, 1997.
36. Giddens, Anthony. *Profiles and Critiques in Social Theory.* Berkeley: University of California Press, 1982.
37. Derrida, Jacques. *Positions.* Chicago: University of Chicago Press, 1981.
38. Derrida, Jacques. *Writing and Difference.* Chicago: University of Chicago Press, 1978.
39. Cazeaux, Clive. "Living Metaphor." *Studi Filosofici* 34 (2011): 291–308.
40. Surin, Kenneth. *Freedom Not Yet.* Durham: Duke University Press, 2009.
41. Jackson, Michael. *Lifeworlds—Essays in Existential Anthropology.* Chicago: University of Chicago Press, 2013.
42. Herzfeld, Michael. *Portrait of a Greek Imagination: An Ethnographic Biography of Andreas Nenedakis.* Chicago: University of Chicago Press, 1998.
43. Sartre, Jean-Paul. *Search for a Method.* New York: Vintage Books, 1963.
44. Bourdieu, Pierre. *Pascalian Meditations.* Palo Alto: Stanford University Press, 2000.
45. Jackson, Michael. *Existential Anthropology—Events, Exigencies and Effects.* New York: Berghahn Books, 2005.
46. Seeing Things Whole. "Mission." Available online: http://www.seeingthingswhole.org/1003/who-we-are/mission (accessed on 1 October 2010).
47. Seeing Things Whole. "Trustees of the Universe." Available online: http://www.seeingthingswhole.com/PDF/STW-TrusteesoftheUniverse.pdf (accessed on 6 December 2010).
48. Seeing Things Whole. "Toward a Theology of Institutions." Available online: http://www.seeingthingswhole.com/PDF/STW-toward-theology-of-institutions.pdf (accessed on 6 December 2010).
49. The Journal of Management, Spirituality, and Religion. Available online: http://www.tandfonline.com/loi/rmsr20#.V3GQ_LgrLIU (accessed on 27 June 2016).
50. Jackson, Michael. *The Politics of Storytelling—Violence, Transgression, and Intersubjectivty.* Copenhagen: Museum Tusculanum Press, 2002.
51. Poster, Mark. *Existential Marxism in Postwar France: From Sartre to Althusser.* Princeton: Princeton University Press, 1975.
52. Sartre, Jean-Paul. *Critique of Dialectical Reason Vol. 1-2.* London: Verso, 2004.

53. Benefiel, Margaret. *The Soul of a Leader: Finding Your Path to Success and Fulfillment*. New York: Crossroads Publishing Co., 2008.
54. Lakoff, George, and Mark Johnson. *Metaphors We Live By*. Chicago: University of Chicago Press, 1980.
55. Fauconnier, Giles, and Mark Turner. *The Way We Think: Conceptual Blending and the Mind's Hidden Complexities*. New York: Basic Books, 2002.
56. Zamora, Daniel. "Foucault, the Excluded, and the Neoliberal Erosion of the State." In *Foucault and Neoliberalism*. Edited by Daniel Zamora and Michael C. Behrent. Cambridge: Polity Press, 2016.
57. Latour, Bruno. *Reassembling the Social: An Introduction to Actor-Network-Theory*. Oxford: Oxford University Press, 2007.
58. Flynn, Thomas. *Sartre and Marxist Existentialism*. Chicago: University of Chicago Press, 1984.
59. Dean, Mitchell. "Foucault, Ewald, and Neoliberalism." In *Foucault and Neoliberalism*. Edited by Daniel Zamora and Michael C. Behrent. Cambridge: Polity Press, 2016.
60. Berman, Russell. *Modern Culture and Critical Theory: Art, Politics and the Legacy of the Frankfurt School*. Madison: University of Wisconsin Press, 1989.
61. Goux, Jean-Joseph. "General Economics and Postmodern Capitalism." *Yale French Studies* 78 (1990): 206–24. [CrossRef]
62. Ho, Karen. *Liquidated: An Anthropology of Wall Street*. Durham: Duke University Press, 2009.
63. Fischer, Melissa. *Wall Street Women*. Durham: Duke University Press, 2012.
64. Zaloom, Caitlin. *Out of the Pits: Traders and Technology from Chicago to London*. Chicago: University of Chicago Press, 2010.
65. Orsi, Robert. "Afterward: Everyday Religion and the Contemporary World." In *Ordinary Lives and Grand Schemes—An Anthropology of Everyday Religion*. Edited by Samuli Schielke and Liza Debevec. Oxford: Berghahn Books, 2012.
66. Puar, Jasbir. *Terrorist Assemblages: Homonationalisms in Queer Times*. Durham: Duke University Press, 2007.
67. Graeber, David. "The Sword, the Sponge, and the Paradox of Performativity—Some Observations on Fate, Luck, Financial Chicanery, and the Limits of Human Knowledge." *Social Analysis* 56 (2012): 25–42. [CrossRef]
68. Poster, Mark. *Critical Theory and Poststructuralism: In Search of Context*. Ithaca: Cornell University Press, 1989.
69. Martinot, Steve. *Forms in the Abyss—A Philosophical Bridge between Sartre and Derrida*. Philadelphia: Temple University Press, 2006.
70. Hollywood, Amy. *Acute Melancholia and Other Essays—Mysticism, History*. New York: Columbia University Press, 2016.
71. De Querol, Ricardo. "Zygmunt Bauman: 'Social Media Are a Trap'." *El País*, 25 January 2016. Available online: http://elpais.com/elpais/2016/01/19/inenglish/1453208692_424660.html (accessed on 7 June 2016).
72. Marx, Karl, and Friedrich Engels. "The Communist Manifesto." In *The Portable Karl Marx*. Edited by Eugene Kamenka. New York: Penguin Books, 1983.
73. Derrida, Jacques. *Specters of Marx: The State of the Debt, the Work of Mourning and the New International*. London: Routledge, 2006.
74. Comaroff, Jean, and John Comaroff. "Millennial Capitalism: First Thoughts on a Second Coming." In *Millennial Capitalism and the Culture of Neoliberalism*. Edited by Jean Comaroff and John Comaroff. Durham: Duke University Press, 2001.
75. Lindquist, Galina. *Conjuring Hope: Magic and Healing in Contemporary Russia*. New York: Berghahn Books, 2006.
76. Ong, Aihwa. *Spirits of Resistance and Capitalist Discipline: Factory Women in Malaysia*. Albany: SUNY Press, 2010.
77. LaFerla, Ruth. "Love, Jobs, and 401(k)s." *New York Times*, 21 November 2008. Available online: http://www.nytimes.com/2008/11/23/fashion/23psychic.html (accessed on 11 April 2015).
78. Brown, Wendy. *Politics Out of History*. Princeton: Princeton University Press, 2001.
79. Orsi, Robert. *History and Presence*. Cambridge: Harvard University Press, 2016.

religions

MDPI

Article

"Show Us Your God": Marilla Baker Ingalls and the Power of Religious Objects in Nineteenth-Century Burma

Alexandra Kaloyanides

Ho Center for Buddhist Studies, Department of Religious Studies, Stanford University, 450 Serra Mall, Stanford, CA 94305, USA; akaloyan@stanford.edu; Tel.: +1-650-723-0465

Academic Editors: Douglas James Davies and Michael J. Thate
Received: 16 April 2016; Accepted: 30 May 2016; Published: 23 June 2016

Abstract: This essay examines the unusual evangelical work of Marilla Baker Ingalls, an American Baptist missionary to Burma from 1851–1902. By the time of her death in Burma at the age of 75, Ingalls was known as one of the most successful Baptist evangelists among Burmese Buddhists. To understand the extraordinary dynamic of Ingalls' expanding Christian community, this essay focuses on two prominent objects at the Baptist mission: A life-sized dog statue that Ingalls kept chained at the edge of her property and a massive banyan tree covered with biblical illustrations and revered by locals as an abode of divine beings. This essay argues that these objects transformed Ingalls' American Baptist Christianity into a kind of Burmese religion that revolved around revered objects. Through an examination of the particular shrine practices that pulled people into the Baptist mission, this essay reflects on the larger context of religious encounter, conflict, and representation in modernizing Burma.

Keywords: Christianity; Buddhism; missions; Burma; United States; visual culture; material culture

1. Introduction

Over three hundred feet tall and covered in gold, Shwedagon Pagoda is the most famous religious monument in Burma. The massive shrine glitters atop a hill in the port city of Yangon, attracting locals and tourists to circumambulate the central structure said to house sacred Buddha relics. When American Christian missionaries began journeying to this Southeast Asian country in 1813, the towering pagoda and its swirling pilgrims captured their attention even before they were ashore. The evangelical Baptists had heard that this kingdom across the Bay of Bengal from India was full of what they called "heathen superstition," and when they finally arrived and saw the countless pagodas and Buddha statues that filled the land they began to name the country's religion "Buddhism." By identifying it as such, the Baptists categorized Burma's royally-sponsored religion as a part of the larger Asian tradition starting to be understood in the West as a phenomenally popular world religion.

For these American missionaries, Shwedagon Pagoda quickly proved a powerful symbol of the rival religion. But the monument was not simply an emblem of the strongly held beliefs of the Burmese, it was also an active object, continually animating religious practice. This practice was particularly problematic for the Christian evangelists, who saw it as idol worship. Because the people of Burma were so devoted to the Buddha, whose relics are said to be enshrined in this pagoda, and to the merit-making practices performed at this sacred site, the Baptists declared that they were constantly committing the sin of worshipping a false god. The Protestant operation sought to bring the country's people toward the teachings of Christ by turning them away from pagodas and Buddha statues.

Shwedagon Pagoda is "one of the proudest monuments of superstition in Burmah," ([1], p. 78) exclaimed Marilla Baker Ingalls, an American Baptist missionary to the country from 1851–1902. Ingalls worked as a single female missionary in a remote region without any American male missionaries, an unprecedented arrangement in the Baptist mission.[1] Whereas her colleagues in large, urban mission stations interacted with people from a variety of the country's ethnic groups as well as from British colonial society, Ingalls became immersed in a community of Burmese people, that is, a community comprised of people from the country's Bamar majority population.

Ingalls' 1857 book on her adopted country, *Ocean Sketches of Burmah*, described the "long-established sway of the Burmese religion" ([1], p. 77). Ingalls explained that the pervasive power of Burmese Buddhism was evident in how "the Burmans have filled the land with idol gods, Pagodas, and temples, served by their yellow-robed priests" ([1], p. 77). Like the country's multitude of Buddha statues and monasteries, pagodas proved to the American how the Asian religion had "interwoven itself with political and civil life" ([1], p. 77). And the magnitude and prestige of Shwedagon Pagoda represented how resistant Burmese Buddhism was to rival theologies. For missionaries "to assail such a system with mere arguments," Ingalls contended, "would have been like attempting to overthrow that solid Pagoda itself" ([1], p. 78). Tried as it might, the American mission to the Burmese could not topple Buddhism with its Christian theology. After the first few decades of the Baptist mission to Burma, so few Burmese had converted that the mission shifted their resources away from that dominant population. They turned instead to ethnic minorities in the country—especially the Karen—who had shown much more interest in joining Christian communities.[2]

Even after the American mission began reallocating resources to Burma's minority groups in the mid-nineteenth century, Ingalls remained committed to converting the Burmese. In 1859, Ingalls settled in Thonze, a remote village in southern Burma where she worked as a single female missionary until her death at the age of 75 in 1902. After over forty years of evangelical work, Ingalls was said to have converted more than one hundred Buddhist priests.[3] These unmatched numbers earned her a reputation as America's most successful evangelist among the Burmese. Given the Baptist mission's failures among Burma's majority group, how are we to understand Ingalls' extraordinary conversion record?

This essay argues that Ingalls' career was distinguished by creative responses to her realization that Burmese Buddhism would not be overcome by "mere arguments." To bring about religious change in Burma, Ingalls turned to objects that had material strength, objects that were just as solid as Yangon's Shwedagon Pagoda. To make Christianity appeal to the Burmese, Ingalls created idols of her own.[4]

There were two key objects that dominated Ingalls' work: A life-sized dog statue that she kept chained at the edge of her property and what she called her "great sign tree," a large banyan covered with pictures and revered by locals as the abode of divine beings. The cast-iron canine attracted visitors every day to Ingalls' mission, and some days the visitors numbered in the hundreds. Her nearly as famous sign tree fascinated the local community with the Biblical illustrations, photographs, and American medicinal advertisements that hung on its massive trunk.

---

[1] Women were leaders in the Burma mission from the time of its inception, but their role was seen in the early period as primarily that of wives of male missionaries. After the first wave of missionary couples and single men settled in Burma, single female missionaries were occasionally appointed to the country with the expectation that they would marry an American missionary working in the country, often a widower. For more on the role of women in the Burma mission, see [2].

[2] During the first two decades of the Burma mission, the entire operation focused on the Burmese majority group. By the 1840s, only about half of the staff was dedicated to the Burmese. Even with so many resources going to the Burmese, the mission was far more successful among the Karen. For example, in 1836, the mission recorded a total of 729 baptized Karen as compared to 207 Burmese since the inception of the mission ([3], pp. 129–32).

[3] The *Baptist Missionary Magazine* obituary for Ingalls provides an example of how the Baptist community celebrated Ingalls as having converted over one hundred Buddhist monks. In that obituary, Reverend Edmund F. Merriam wrote that "Mrs. Ingalls was particularly successful in her labors among the Burman priest, who are a class of people extremely hard to reach by the influences of Christianity; but by her tact and enthusiasm, aided largely by her ingenuity of approach, she was permitted to see more than a hundred of these bigoted priests throw off the yellow robe and become humble and faithful followers of the Lord Jesus Christ, many of them becoming preachers of the gospel. This must be considered one of the most prominent features of Mrs. Ingalls' work" [4].

[4] I am using the term "idol" here in the lexical sense of "images that represent superhuman beings." I include Burmese spirits (nats) in this category of "superhuman beings."

This essay examines the role these objects played in Ingalls' career not only to understand the work of an exceptionally creative missionary, but also to consider the larger dynamic of religious confrontation in the American Baptist mission to Burma. To tell the story of Marilla Baker Ingalls is to tell a story about a more pervasive atmosphere of religious encounter, exchange, representation, and conflict in colonizing Burma. In addition, this story of objects-based evangelism suggests that among the most powerful catalysts of religious change in the Christian-Buddhist encounter were objects themselves. While Ingalls continued to incorporate theology into her religious discussions and to distribute tracts that made arguments against Buddhism, her most popular methods relied on the metal dog she called "America" and her adorned tree shrine. By examining these two objects and the work they did for (and perhaps to) Ingalls, this essay argues for the power of "things" in the religious life of nineteenth-century Burma.[5]

This investigation into the central objects in Ingalls' missionary work asks: To what extent did this American evangelist adopt local material culture and its attendant practices to promote Protestantism? And, to what extent did local religious practices convert Ingalls? In other words, did Ingalls use Burmese-style objects as a kind of gimmick to draw people into Christianity or did the country's popular, image-based practices transform Ingalls' Christianity into a Southeast-Asian "religion"?[6] This investigation finds that while Ingalls saw her work as a kind of gimmick in the service of God, the extraordinary popularity of her mission station was the result of her ideas- and texts-based evangelism changing into an evangelism of multi-sensory communal activities. Ingalls' mission transformed to become more familiar and attractive to those who affiliated themselves with it. In this way, Ingalls' Baptist Christianity became a kind of Burmese religion.[7]

1.1. Marilla Baker Ingalls, 1827–1902

Marilla Baker (pictured in Figure 1) was born in Greenville, New York on 25 November 1827. She came of age during a time when Protestant newspapers and magazines all over the northeast were publishing regular accounts of foreign missions. Stories of pioneering evangelists, exotic landscapes, and foreign cultures filled front pages and sparked imaginations.[8] Among the home and foreign missions in operation in the first half of the nineteenth century, the Baptist mission to Burma was one of the most, if not *the* most, publicized on account of being the very first intercontinental mission, featuring the celebrity missionary couple Ann and Adoniram Judson. The Judsons initially gained attention by establishing the mission in 1813 after being turned away from India; they came to fame in the 1820s through stories of Adoniram's imprisonment during the First Anglo-Burmese War of 1824;

---

[5]   This essay's attention to the power of objects is informed by scholarship on visual and material cultures of religion—specifically the work on American religious history by Sally Promey and David Morgan and the work on Asian religions by John Kieschnick and Richard Davis—as well as by Arjun Appadurai's scholarship on things as social networks. See [5–8].

[6]   The Burmese language has no direct equivalent to the term "religion." The language of the country's sacred Buddhist texts, Pali, has the term "*sāsana*," which is often translated as "religion," but as Alicia Turner's study of religion in colonial Burma shows, the two terms "were distinct, if overlapping, categories operating at the same time." Turner defines *sāsana* "as the life of the Buddha's teachings after he is gone...the condition of possibility for making merit and liberation." By focusing on this Buddhist term, Turner is able to demonstrate how, in colonial Burma, "religion as a category was not static but a moving container for a variety of discourses and projects that was itself undergoing continuing redefinition" ([9], pp. 1, 9, 10).

[7]   This argument for the combinatory nature of Ingalls' missionary methods builds on the work of Catherine Albanese, a historian of North American religions who argues that religious Americans have always been practitioners of changing religions that combine elements from earlier traditions with those adopted through contact with new forms. See her essay "Exchanging Selves, Exchanging Souls: Contact, Combination, and American Religious History" in [10].

[8]   The most prominent Baptist newspaper in the first half of the nineteenth century was *The Macedonian*, a publication dedicated to the coverage of missions, especially the Burma mission. *The Macedonian* not only featured columns on Baptist efforts and foreign religions, but it also showcased illustrations of various religious cultures that foreign missionaries encountered. For an analysis of *The Macedonian*'s illustrations, see ([11], pp. 85–109). For more on the broader landscape of print technology and American evangelism, see [12].

and their deaths—Ann's in 1826 and then Adoniram's in 1850—were mourned in print by Baptist and mainstream publications.[9]

Figure 1. Marilla Baker Ingalls, 1827–1902 [4].

Around the time of Adoniram's highly publicized death, Marilla Baker met Reverend Lovell Ingalls, a colleague of Adoniram on furlough in the States. Reverend Lovell Ingalls had returned from Burma after his first wife's death, and he met Marilla at a missionary gathering in Racine, Wisconsin. "At that time," remembered Rev. Edmund Merriam, a prominent Baptist writer and editor, Marilla "exhibited all the characteristics of personality which all who knew her so well remember. She was vivacious and enthusiastic, and it was remarked that she seemed the last person in the world fitted for the exacting duties of a missionary. But," Merriam continued, "her very buoyancy and vivacity were in a large degree the qualities which made her missionary career so eminently useful and successful" [4]. The ebullient Marilla was only twenty-two when she married the then forty-two year old Lovell. Seven months later, in July 1851, the couple set sail for Burma, where Marilla would begin her study of Burmese religion and culture. Close, sensitive, and creative participation in local communities combined with her lively personality would come to distinguish her in the missionary field. In a photograph of Marilla (Figure 1) featured alongside Merriam's obituary, she is portrayed with a steady gaze and modest dress, suggesting her maturation from a young missionary's wife into a dignified missionary in her own right.

After only five years of being married to Marilla and working with her as a Rangoon-based missionary, Lovell died. Lovell left behind a school-age daughter from his first wife, and so Marilla returned to the States to arrange for the girl to have an American education. During her time aboard The Hornet, the ship that took her from the Bay of Bengal to the English Channel over the course of three months, the newly widowed Marilla Ingalls wrote the book that would become her first published account of the peoples of the Southeast Asian country: *Ocean Sketches of Burmah*.[10] Over three-hundred pages long and exhibiting forty-two illustrations, *Ocean Sketches of Burmah* gives lively accounts of Burmese and Karen culture that speak to how much she had learned in her first years of field work. Ingalls addressed the book to her "dear young friends" and presented it as a collection of colorful children's tales. But its rich descriptions of Buddhist philosophies and practices, its insights into Burmese court intrigues and British colonial politics, and its celebration of the virtues of Burma's newly converted Christian communities appear constructed to appeal to adult readers. Using the frame of a children's book, Ingalls managed to showcase a sophisticated portrait of a complex Buddhist society with scarce, but hopeful, opportunities for Christian conversion [1].

---

[9] For more on the Judsons and their relationship to American Protestant print culture, see [13].

[10] *Ocean Sketches of Burmah* was the first of many texts Ingalls published. In addition to English-language publications, Ingalls also published in Burmese, including an 1883 Burmese-language book on the life of Christ with the English title *Narrative of Jesus* [14].

During her 1857–1858 trip back to the States, Ingalls made arrangements with the American Baptist Missionary Union to go back to Burma, this time as an independent missionary. Ingalls returned to Rangoon in 1859, but rather than stay at the large urban mission station there, she decided to venture to the remote village of Thonze, on the border of the Tharawaddi District. At that time, Thonze could only be reached by a two-day boat trip from Rangoon along the Hlaing River. Baptist authorities in the Burma mission discouraged Ingalls from going to such an isolated location without a husband or American male colleague. However, Ingalls went anyway, and stayed there working as an independent missionary for forty-three years. During her life in Thonze, Ingalls cultivated a large Christian community that produced Burmese preachers and missionaries, but she never had any American male missionaries in residence.[11] It was in this unorthodox arrangement in far-flung Thonze, that Ingalls' unique objects-based evangelism emerged.

In addition to her relative missionary sovereignty, the national conditions in Burma shaped Ingalls' distinct methodology. Over the course of her long and storied missionary career, Ingalls watched as Burma transformed from a Buddhist kingdom into a British colony. When she first arrived in Burma, the country was on the brink of the Second Anglo-Burmese War, which resulted in the British occupation of all of Lower Burma and in the newly crowned King Mindon building a new capital city in Mandalay. Three decades later, in 1885, the Third Anglo-Burmese War delivered the final blow to the Konbaung Dynasty and subsumed the entire country into British India.[12] These wars do not simply mark Burmese military and political history; they are also significant for Burma's religious history, as the country had, up to this point, a millennium-old tradition of Buddhism being dependent on a patron king. As the Burmese kingdom became weakened over the course of the nineteenth century, the Buddhist people of Burma were concerned with how the Buddha's teachings would survive without royal support for monks and the maintenance of shrines. Once the final Konbaung king was deposed by the British, lay communities began taking over the religious work previously assigned to royalty, thereby transforming the dynamic of patronage and practice in Burmese Buddhism. As Alicia Turner has shown, the shifting of religious responsibility from kings onto non-ordained men and women gave rise to the development of new technologies—such as print media and voluntary associations—which helped promote the classic Buddhist traditions of preserving the Buddha's teachings and regulating the ethical conduct of monastic and lay communities [9]. In addition to these changes to Burmese Buddhist culture, the empowerment of the British in Burma lent new political and economic value to Christian affiliation. The British Raj, for example, began military recruitment in Christian Karen communities. And those educated in mission schools learned English and the etiquette of Western society—skills attractive on the new colonial job market.[13]

The colonization and modernization of Burma was most visible to Ingalls and her fellow townspeople when the British laid the country's first rail line through Thonze in 1877, turning the village into a bustling station town. Once Thonze became a stop on the Irrawaddy Valley State Railway, it was only a few hours from Rangoon. The new train line quickly connected Thonze to the urban centers powering the British occupation. Sir Dietrich Brandis, the renowned German tropical forester who worked with the British Imperial Forestry Service in Burma and elsewhere in colonial India,

---

[11] Rather than posing a threat to the male leadership in the American Baptist mission to Burma, Ingalls' work as an independent female missionary seems to have served as a model for single women in the field. In a letter to the Executive Committee of the American Baptist Missions held in the archives of the American Baptist Historical Society, Abram Rose—a leader in the mission to the Pwo Karen—wrote, "If young ladies wish to be independent like Mrs. Ingalls and do as they like, I have not the least objection. Only but they like Mrs. Ingalls go by themselves to a new field and carry on the work as does Mrs Ingalls..." [15]. Rose is using the example of Ingalls to respond to the development of organizations dedicated to the support and promotion of female missionaries. Clearly, there was a concern among the American Baptist male leadership about women's missionary work. Ingalls, however, did not seem to compound that concern, but rather she was an example of what the male leadership saw as acceptable work for single women: solitary labor in a new mission field.

[12] For more on the religious influences on Burma's last kingdom, the Konbaung Dynasty, see [16].

[13] An example of British colonial strategies regarding the Karen is found in a text published right after the Third Anglo-Burmese War by Donald Mackenzie Smeaton of the Bengal Civil Service that argues why the Karen are suitable British allies [17].

recalled how Ingalls responded to the arrival of the railway by creating "two circulating libraries, with their reading rooms well supplied with the latest literature" [18]. Brandis remembered how she had "arranged for lectures to them, delivered by missionaries and others," and wrote that her circulating libraries "remain as monuments of her loving interest" in the "English and Eurasian station masters, guards and other employees of the railway" [18]. Brandis concluded that Ingalls was "greatly missed and mourned by the railway servants of Lower Burma" [18]. His remarks hint at Ingalls having taken the new British railway and transformed it into a missionary machine with the same evangelical drive and creative approach that reshaped her Thonze mission into a popular center of powerful religious objects.

1.2. Situating Ingalls in an Academic Landscape

The story of Marilla Baker Ingalls and her objects-based evangelical work is a part of larger story of encounter told by scholars of the religious histories of North America and Burma. While no other historian of American religion or Burmese Buddhism has studied Ingalls' legacy, work in these fields has explored important related issues such as the appeal of Buddhism in nineteenth-century America, missionary theories of Christ and culture, and religious developments during Burma's transition from a Buddhist kingdom to a British colony. Before diving into Ingalls' writings, I pause here to reflect on the important scholarship on which this paper builds and to suggest how Ingalls' story contributes to, and occasionally challenges, that scholarship.

North American communities first started learning about Buddhist teachings and history in the mid-nineteenth century through academic reports on Asian texts and popular writing enchanted by Indian religions. The groundbreaking study of this earliest period of interest in Buddhism is Thomas Tweed's *The American Encounter with Buddhism, 1844–1912* [19]. Tweed reveals how Americans who favored Buddhism saw themselves as dissenting from American culture, but that their engagement with the religion ultimately consented to basic Victorian values such as individualism, optimism, and activism. Tweed's study dismisses missionaries outright because he contends that that missionaries, unlike the Buddhist sympathizers and adherents at the center of his study, produced almost entirely hostile interpretations of the Asian religion. While it is certainly true that many missionaries, including Ingalls, penned antagonistic descriptions of Buddhist practices and philosophies, this is only part of the story. As the first Americans to spend time in Buddhist cultures and observe living Buddhist practices, missionaries expressed a wide range of attitudes toward the Asian religion. Ingalls' writings about Buddhists peoples and practices form a case study in which a foreign evangelist develops keen knowledge of Asian religions and in which an Asian community transforms an expression of American Christianity.[14]

Whereas the study of Buddhism in nineteenth-century America has not yet taken missionary materials into full consideration, these materials have been explored by scholars of American evangelism. Foremost among them is William Hutchison, whose *Errand to the World* analyzes debates about Christian missions and their attendant cultural transmissions [21]. Hutchison shows how the nineteenth-century missionary movement was driven by both a passion for Christian expansion and a zealous belief that Americans had a distinct responsibility to save the world. Hutchison focuses on theoretical debates among American-based, male theologians and omits analysis of the writings of foreign missionaries. When we begin to explore writings of American missionaries in the field—writings that circulated widely through the popularizing Protestant press—we see that foreign evangelists' approaches to promoting Christianity vibrantly engaged the discussions about

---

[14] At the same time as the Americans in Tweed's study were encountering Buddhism in scholarship and popular writing, Europeans were working to define "Buddhism" as a world religion alongside Christianity. As Tomoko Masuzawa has demonstrated, Europe's discovery of Buddhism was primarily through texts and their attendant philological labors. Masuzawa argues that the form of Buddhism that was constructed during this encounter was caught up in Europe's concern for its "own standing in the spiritual topography...of the world" ([20], p. 143).

methodology at the center of Hutchison's study. Furthermore, by taking seriously the work of female missionaries like Ingalls, we see that women in Burma were at the forefront of the exploration of evangelical possibilities that Hutchison casts as the work of male, home-based promoters.

The final area of scholarship upon which this article builds is the area covering religious innovations in Burma around the turn of the twentieth century. This was a time of great cultural change as the country navigated its new colonial situation. Two recently published monographs have significantly opened up this area—Alicia Turner's *Saving Buddhism* and Erik Braun's *Birth of Insight* [9,22]. These works reveal how Burmese leaders and communities drew on Buddhist traditions to renegotiate the conditions of British rule and create new religious resources suited to modernizing Burma. *Saving Buddhism* and *Birth of Insight* form a part of a growing field of scholarship on Burmese Buddhism that has focused on politically influential documents such as royal chronicles, monastic productions, and urban newspapers.[15] There certainly remains important work to be done with these documents, but the American Baptist mission to Burma offers a previously unstudied wealth of evidence of other forms of religious activity in the country. This evidence provides rare glimpses into everyday life not seen in court histories or colonial records. Missionary archives have preserved an abundance of detailed accounts of cultural interactions at far-flung Baptist posts and along itinerant preaching tours. These conversations feature elderly village women with strong Buddhist convictions, young city men curious about white foreigners, and families on their way to make merit at local pagodas. We must keep in mind that the vast majority of these missionary interactions were translated into English and further filtered through the process of their American authors penning them for diaries, letters to friends back home, or official accounts to be published in Baptist periodicals. Even with this Protestant rendering, this large collection of social history documents still contains evidence of how religious ideas and practices were expressed by the peoples of Burma who interacted with the Baptist mission. Ingalls' writings are a prime example of a missionary archive revealing a unique perspective on religious conflict, collaboration, and change in nineteenth-century Burma.

Let us now turn to those writings and the story they tell about how the Baptist mission celebrated as the most successful converter of Buddhist monks relied on an enshrined dog statue and a worshipped sign tree.

2. Ingalls' Dog Statue

On festival days, Ingalls' dog statue would have hundreds of visitors. Even on regular days, the dog was bound to attract at least a few passersby who had come to see the strange creature at the edge of the American religious woman's land. The way Ingalls told it, the life-size dog statue would gather people around it because it seemed, at first glance, to be real. The missionary would stand by as new visitors recoiled in fear or approached the dog to offer food. When they got close enough to see it was made of cast iron, they would ask Ingalls why she kept the dog. This was when the Baptist missionary would launch into a lesson on the folly of idol worship. Just as her dog statue could not chase away thieves, Ingalls argued, lifeless Buddha statues could not help devotees who came to the statues with prayers and offerings. She called the dog her "dumb teacher," because, she said, it wordlessly instructed countless Burmese visitors on the uselessness of venerating images [25].

Ingalls' writing about her dog statue can read like a stereotypical evangelical tale of a Christian missionary enlightening ignorant heathens about their superstitions. However, when we study her accounts in the religious and political context of her Burmese mission, a more complex story emerges. This story tells of the power of religious objects to attract attention and inspire activity in nineteenth-century Burma. While Ingalls presented the dog statue as a device to demonstrate the

---

[15] This field of scholarship on Burmese Buddhism includes key works such as Patrick Pranke's study of Buddhist history writing, Michael Charney's work on the Buddhist literati in the Konbaung Dynasty, and Jason Carbine's analysis of stability and disruption in Burmese Buddhist monasticism [16,23,24].

powerlessness of idols, her essay also reveals how local image practices became a part of Ingalls' missionary work, transforming it from aniconic, text-based evangelism to religious activity that centered on venerated objects. While Ingalls may have intended for her dog to teach people to stop worshipping false gods, the dog seems to have also joined a local pantheon of religious figures.

To investigate the work the canine did for Ingalls and for its Burmese visitors, let us turn to "My Dumb Teacher," Ingalls' most detailed account of her famous dog and the only publication that included a photograph of the statue (Figure 2). In this essay for the May 1896 issue of the *Baptist Missionary Magazine*—the premier publication of the American Baptist Missionary Union—Ingalls wrote about a day when she was at her home in Thonze and heard outside a half-dozen people approaching her dog. She recognized one of the men, so she invited the group onto her land. The man she knew, another man, and a woman accepted her invitation. As they got closer to the dog, they exclaimed "He haw!" [25]. the woman "seemed timid," so Ingalls told her, "'though he is chained up to that post, give him something to eat and he will not harm you'" [25]. Ingalls then wrote that the woman, who was carrying a tray of dried meat and vegetables, "walked up and put down the tray at the feet of the dog, but then she crouched back and looked up into the face of the dog and saw that it was a dumb image and picked up her tray" [25]. The Burmese visitors asked why the dog was there, and it was at this point that Ingalls "put questions to them" about the power of statues. Here is their exchange, according to Ingalls:

> "Is he not here to guard me from thieves and *dacoits*, and help me in various ways?"
> "But he cannot do anything," they replied.
> "Don't deride my American dog," I continued. "See, he has ears and eyes and feet," and then we got up and peered into those ears and eyes. It all came back to me. They smote upon their breasts a little and put up their hands to me in a respectful attitude.
> "We do not like to dispute the great teacheress but it is impossible for this dumb image to hear you or see you, or do anything for you." [...]
> "I am only following out your customs if I trust in a dumb image, and you are right. It cannot hear me when I ask for protection and it cannot guard me while I sleep."
> "Ah! That is good," said the man, "your words are now true and wise and good."
> I continued "It cannot do anything for you or any other person," and then I told them that I had brought it here to show up their false customs of making an idol, calling it a god and trusting in it for help. They said their god was consecrated, but I told them it was not changed in power after it came from the maker's hand, and that my old dog passed through a *fire-consecration* when he was made, but he had no life or power [25].

Figure 2. Ingalls' Dog Statue [25].

We can see how this episode might have amused the American readers of the *Baptist Missionary Magazine*. The anecdote depicts unnamed Asian individuals being tricked into thinking a cast-iron dog is real. Readers also might have delighted in the image of Ingalls craftily suggesting the protective power of the dog, thereby putting her visitors in the position of explaining that a statue cannot hear commands or chase away thieves. From this point of view, Ingalls cleverly got the Buddhists to make the very argument that Christian missionaries were making against treating Buddha statues as though they were mighty beings able to respond to prayers.

Another point of view, however, is glimpsed by the story's inclusion of the Burmese explanation of the difference between her dog statue and their enshrined Buddhas. The visitors told Ingalls that their statues were consecrated, by which they meant that their Buddha images had gone through a special ritual in order to bring the power of the Buddha into the objects. This consecration argument draws from a Buddhist understanding of what makes an object sacred: a special ritual process executed by a religious specialist that infuses the statue with the extraordinary capacities of the Buddha.[16] This Burmese explanation of how statues that begin as mundane sculptures become sacred objects counters the Baptist's equation of her dog with their Buddhas. It also suggests that there is more going on in their way of approaching the dog than a simple mistake. Specifically, it pushes us to ask why the woman might have gone to place dried meat and vegetables in front of the dog in the first place and then decided against it.

Ingalls suggested that the Burmese woman really believed her statue was a living, breathing, dangerous dog that she could pacify with something to eat. But then when she got close enough to see it was made out of cast iron instead of flesh and bones, she knew it would be pointless to feed it. But what if we posit that the woman knew that the dog was metal the whole time? What if she was not so easily fooled into thinking that a dog statue was a real dog? In that case, what would be the point of offering real food to a dog statue? Ingalls' typical American reader may not have understood this as anything besides ignorant superstition, but those with knowledge of Burmese culture would have immediately recognized this action as a common ritual.

Throughout the country, Buddhist statues and shrines to the local spirits known as "nats" continue to attract edible offerings. It is an especially common tradition to present food to nats because they are understood to cause mayhem when upset. Nats are said to do things like flood a village's crops if its villagers fail to show signs of respect as they pass the nats' abode.[17] But regular offerings of food and signs of respect are meant to pacify nats and coax them into helping their devotees by doing things like bringing about good fortune or curing an illness. Even when we put to the side questions of how much these Burmese people really believed in spirits, it is important to keep in mind how their community had a tradition of presenting food to images and objects recognized as special. This act of generosity and sacrifice is a venerable and well-established practice in Burma and in other cultures with Buddhist traditions. One gives up a portion of one's possessions in order to benefit the larger Buddhist tradition, the local community, one's family, or oneself. The common Burmese practice of making offerings at holy sites is understood as a wholesome ("kusala" in Pali, "kutho" in Burmese) act that generates merit ("puñña" in Pali, "pon" in Burmese). Americans in the nineteenth-century mission were especially interested in this particular offering practice and often asked Burmese people about it. The most common response Burmese informants gave was a simple explanation that they

---

[16] Kate Crosby's overview of Buddhist consecration practices in Theravada cultures summarizes the practice of consecrating a Buddha statue as one in which the statue "is empowered not through the Buddha himself being immanent in the statue, but through a process of empowerment, in which the Buddha's powers are transmitted into the statue" ([26], p. 53).

[17] One of the most famous nat stories in Burma is about Min Mahagiri, a renowned blacksmith in the Pyu kingdom. In this story, the Pyu king marries Min Mahagiri's sister, Taunggyi Shin, so that he can lure the famous blacksmith to enter his city and then have him executed by fire. Taunggyi Shin is so upset when this happens that she throws herself onto the flames engulfing her brother's murdered body. Their angry spirits then live in a tree, so the king orders that tree cut down and thrown in the Irrawaddy River. The tree trunk washes up in the kingdom of Pagan, and the Burmese king there—inspired by a dream—carves their images onto the trunk and establishes the trunk on the sacred Mount Popa so that the nats can be appeased there. For more on this particular nat story and the Burmese nat tradition at large, see [27].

were performing these image-focused acts because this is what their ancestors did. Presenting food at shrines, they told the Americans, is understood to be traditional, virtuous, and meritorious conduct.[18]

Returning now to the Burmese woman's behavior in front of the dog statue, let us consider a scenario in which she goes to present food because she thinks it is a kind of nat shrine. In this mindset, the woman sees a statue at the edge of the land belonging to a religious leader and determines that she should make an offering there as she would at other sacred shrines. But once she gets close enough to see that the statue does not have other food offerings in front of it, she realizes that it is not sacred and therefore not fit for an act of sacrifice.

Unlike her American readers, Ingalls would have been familiar with this scenario of a Burmese person offering food to a statue. She even gave explicit evidence of her knowledge of the particularities of Buddhist image worship when she said that her dog "passed through a *fire-consecration*" [25]. By using Buddhist ritual terminology, Ingalls worked to equate her dog to Burma's sacred Buddhas.[19] She then tried to contend that even after going through a fire ritual, her dog did not have any agency. Burmese Buddha statues, Ingalls wanted to demonstrate, are just as powerless as a metal dog, and therefore people should stop worshipping them and become followers of Jesus Christ. However, is this the only message coming across? Was Ingalls not also posing her dog as an enlightened being with an extraordinary way of connecting people to a powerful god? By resembling Burmese shrines and being said to have gone through a fire-consecration, was the Baptist's dog proving idols powerless or was it taking on the power of an idol?

Ingalls added one more detail that exhibited her extensive knowledge of Burmese religious traditions and her recognition that her dog had become a kind of local shrine. Ingalls wrote that the dog stood "in front of a group of crotens and roses, sun or rain, night and day" [25]. We might dismiss this mention of the roses and the flowering shrub more commonly spelled "croton" as a simple literary technique meant to enchant readers with a colorful picture of the Southeast Asian landscape. However, the juxtaposition of the religious authority's statue with a collection of flowers mirrors Burmese image practices. Just as Ingalls would have been very familiar with Burmese food-offering rituals, she also would have known that the other common ritual offerings are flowers. Buddhist sacred spaces have been marked by blossoms as far back as the historical record will take us. Early Buddhist texts regularly describe the pilgrimage sites housing the Buddha's relics as adorned with flowers, and anthropological evidence features artwork illustrating Buddhist statues in front of flowers.[20] By putting flowers in front of her dog statue in this Burmese Buddhist context, Ingalls must have known the dog appeared as an adorned, venerated image.

What was the result of all this religious mimicry? Ingalls wanted to say that it ultimately led to Burmese people abandoning idol-worship and converting to Christianity. She wrote that "God, the living God, is able to use various means to bring light to his creatures" [25]. Here she suggested that she was serving this God by means of the dog statue. In this kind of ends-sanctify-the-means argument, Ingalls presented her unconventional evangelical work as eventually resulting in Christian conversion.

---

[18] For more on moral conduct and merit-making in Theravada Buddhism, see Kate Crosby's chapter "The Good Buddhist" in her book on Theravada Buddhism [26].

[19] Just as Ingalls was familiar with Buddhist fire consecrations, Ingalls also knew about the lowly status of dogs in Burma, and therefore how insulting it would be to compare the Buddha to a dog. Ingalls wrote that "the name of 'dog' is a little offensive to the Burmans, so I often qualify and explain the comparison used" [25]. Ingalls is not only telling her readers something about this relevant point of Burmese language and culture (that the Burmese term for dog, "hkway," was used derogatively), but she is also explicitly saying that she does more to contextualize her methods and tailor them for the Burmese community than the example in her essay might suggest. Ingalls therefore makes sure to publicly acknowledge that the exchanges she reports omit parts of the interaction between her and her Burmese interlocutors. This point about Burmese attitudes towards dogs also raises the question about how the Burmese identified the statue. Perhaps those that performed reverential acts toward it saw the cast-iron creature as something other than a common canine. Perhaps it looked to the Burmese like a more esteemed animal, such as a tiger or a lion. Unfortunately, we do not have the evidence necessary to support this hypothesis.

[20] Bilinda Devage Nandadeva's study of Sri Lankan manuscript covers, for example, demonstrates the importance of flower offerings in Theravada ritual traditions [28].

Indeed, her essay features a follow-up scene in which the man from the group returns to Ingalls' property to "show up the dog and convince his other friends of the folly of idol-god worship" [25]. Ingalls reported that the man told her "that he and the other couple had never gone to the idol-god since that day" [25]. Ingalls was clearly suggesting that the Christian teachings she gave with the aide of her dog statue eventually led people to abandon idol worship.

However, rather than leave it to Ingalls to tell us the meaning of her work, let us look again at the evidence of the religious encounters embedded in the essay. In the follow-up scene with the man described as trying to persuade his friends of the foolishness of image veneration, that man accepted a few theological leaflets from Ingalls and then made a telling exclamation: "*That* has done more for me than these kinds of books!" [25].

Ingalls replied to the man's praise for the dog statue by inviting him back to "get lessons from the dumb teacher" [25]. The man said he would accept her invitation and stated that "at the great festival last year I heard the dog had over three hundred visitors, men, women and children" [25].

"This was true," Ingalls told her readers. "On great occasions, many of the district people come in to look at him, and there is not a day but what he has some visitors" [25].

In the end, the man seemed most impressed with the hundreds of people who came out to visit the dog. It was the dog's power to attract visitors that helped win the man over. To understand more about why the popularity of a statue on a religious site would have been so impressive to the local Burmese community, we must consider the larger context of Baptist encounters with Burmese image practices.

Ingalls and the Headless Buddha

Ingalls' famous dog and its messages about idols were the result of the missionary's decades of interactions with Buddha images and their worshippers. Like other American evangelicals in the country, Ingalls went to popular gathering places such as bazaars and pagodas to distribute texts and discuss religion. Her essay "My Dumb Teacher" opens with a scene of Ingalls out at a pagoda conversing with people about the statues occupying the shrine grounds. "I found that everyone believed in idols," Ingalls wrote [25]. At the pagoda, Ingalls read Christian material aloud and talked for a long time about its messages, "but," she concluded, "they were joined to their idols" [25]. Ingalls felt "tired and hoarse" and sat down on a bench in front of a niche [25]. When she saw that there was a locked door in front of the alcove, she asked about it. Her interlocutors explained that "a crazy man had knocked off the head of the god" [25]. This prompted a discussion about what Ingalls described as "the dumb idol" [25].

The Buddhists "insisted that although it was not Gautama himself, it was a holy object, and must be ranked as a god" [25]. Ingalls said that she "tried to tell them of Jesus the Savior, but it was no new story to them, and they only listened to [her] out of respect" [25]. A woman explained to Ingalls that "you are our old friend, and we know that you love us and believe what you say" [25]. The woman then "looked into a niche, and her eyes brightened with pride, and she continued: 'Our forefathers called these *gods*, and in some way or other they must be sacred'" [25]. Ingalls responded to the woman's insistence on the sacredness of the statues by arguing, that "they cannot do anything for you" [25]. In this account, the Buddhist woman politely assured the American of the community's affection for her and respect for her Christian convictions. She then gazed at the holy statue and explained how her ancestors had designated the statues divine, which meant that the statues were also divine for this woman and her community.

After her day of talking about Buddha statues at the pagoda, Ingalls finally got up to leave, taking one last look before she left. She saw "the proud woman...saying her prayers before the locked-up door of the headless image" [25]. Ingalls explained that she had "talked with this woman very much for over twenty-five years" in an effort to convert her, and therefore when Ingalls "sat down to rest in [her house,] [she] meditated and was very sad" [25]. However, while she "was sitting there, [she] heard a jabbering and looked out and saw half a dozen men and women looking at [her] New York dog" [25]. Ingalls then followed this story of being sad about the venerated headless Buddha with her story of being gratified by her popular teaching dog.

Ingalls reported these scenes of religious statues for the *Baptist Missionary Magazine*. We can imagine how, writing for that particular American Protestant audience, she wanted to stress the Burmese people's love for her and portray them as somewhat simple in the way they followed the religious habits of their ancestors. With those readers in mind—readers interested in missionary work and targeted for financial and political support of foreign evangelism—Ingalls may have revised the exchange to make herself look hardworking and respected and the Burmese look ignorant and clearly in need of the teachings of Christ. I intend to suggest here that I do not think we can take missionary accounts as missionary fact. Scholars working with missionary materials should always take care to examine evangelical accounts for the ways they might have been manipulated to promote missionary concerns, such as the concern with portraying the Burma mission as a noble operation worthy of financial support. But this does not necessarily mean that the Burmese people depicted in this exchange are fictional characters created out of some evangelical fantasy of rescuing heathens with the message of Christ. We should recognize that there were real Burmese people that engaged missionaries and influenced the way the Americans understood Asian religious practices. These people were not in the habit of keeping journals, writing letters, or publishing essays, so, unfortunately, we do not have their versions of these exchanges. But even through the filter of Ingalls' writing, we can detect expressions of resistance, debate, and edification on the part of the Burmese.

When we look for those Burmese expressions in Ingalls' essay on her dog statue, we learn something about the ways that people who engaged with Ingalls' mission understood the American, how they related to her methods, and how they challenged her assertions. Her kind of ethnographic reporting allowed for expressions of dispute from the people she was trying to convert. Ingalls tried to equate her dog statue to their Buddhas, but her Burmese interlocutors explained the crucial ritual process that their Buddha statues had gone through in order to be channels to the power of the Buddha. Ingalls replied by suggesting that her dog, too, was consecrated. She did this to try to diminish the power of the consecration ritual. Perhaps this line of argumentation worked for some people. Indeed, she told the story of the man to show how he gave up his practices of venerating Buddha statues. But we must also ask how the suggestion of the dog's consecration helped infuse her dog with power rather than disempower the revered Buddha statues. Furthermore, the dog's extraordinary popularity seems to have been the most impressive thing about it. By being the center of so much attention, the dog attracted unprecedented numbers of people to the Christian mission. But by using a statue to assemble a religious community and connect it to a higher power, Ingalls transformed her foreign American Baptist religion into a more familiar form—a religion of fascinating objects that pulled devotees together onto a holy site.

Thus, when we return to the central questions of this article—when we ask again why Ingalls was considered such a successful converter of Burmese Buddhists and what that teaches us about religious life in nineteenth-century Burma—we begin to see that Ingalls' success was linked to the way her religion was reshaped into a kind of Southeast Asian religion with its powerful objects and associated practices. But it was not just the famous dog statue that helped reshape Ingalls' mission station. A large and elaborately adorned banyan tree also rooted the Christian site in a tradition of Burmese shrine practices.

3. Ingalls' Sign Tree

Ingalls called it her "great sign tree." It was a massive banyan tree on the missionary's property in Thonze. Tacked all around its wide, ropey trunk were biblical illustrations. One featured a tall, bearded Jesus standing next to his disciples in bright-white robes. Alongside these Christian visuals, Ingalls hung other images, including advertisements for American medicines and portraits of Queen Victoria. Passersby, noticing the adorned tree, would approach it to find a black-and-white photograph of that Empress of India in profile, wearing a voluminous gown, medals of honor, a white lace veil, and a miniature diamond crown. Next to her was a Burmese translation of John 3:16: "For God so loved the world, that he gave his only begotten Son, that whosoever believeth in him should not perish, but have everlasting life" [29].

Before Ingalls' sign tree showcased biblical quotations about everlasting life and Christian imagery, it was revered for the great spirits who were said to live in its branches. Locals coming to pay homage to it explained to the Baptist that "this tree was more than a hundred years old; that the great *nats* (spirits) had their headquarters up in the tree, and if they did not revere them and present offerings, they would send great calamity upon them" [29]. This banyan tree, like so many trees, rivers, and rocks throughout the country, was treated as an abode of spirits and a place to propitiate them. According to Ingalls' 1897 essay on the tree, entitled "Our Great Sign Tree" and featuring a photograph of the banyan (Figure 3), the Burmese people who approached the tree had always, "taken off their sandals, closed their umbrellas, and had their heads bowed down in the attitude of Buddhist worshipers" [29]. It was not just their bared feet and respectful postures that signaled to Ingalls that they treated the tree as a sacred object. They also "emptied their trays of rice under the tree," making the kinds of offerings Ingalls had seen in front of spirit shrines [28]. In her earlier essay on her dog statue, published a year before "Our Great Sign Tree," Ingalls omitted mention of this food offering practice even as she described Burmese people giving dried meat and vegetables to her "dumb teacher." Ingalls seems to have wanted to keep the image of Burmese people giving food to a cast-iron dog comical, to keep it a scene of ignorant Asian people mistaking a statue for a living being. But in her later essay, Ingalls shared her knowledge of Burmese food rituals to illustrate the tree as a non-Christian religious site about to be dramatically transformed into a Christian object. By examining the origin story she tells in "Our Great Sign Tree" and then investigating particular signs she featured on the tree's trunk, we will consider how the shrine might have attracted Burmese people to the Baptist mission because it was adorned as a conduit to the divine powers of a foreign god. And we will also reflect on how much of Ingalls' appeal as a religious leader may have come from her possession of magical things.

Figure 3. Ingalls' Decorated Banyan Tree [29].

Ingalls' encounters with the tree and its worshippers started with her using it to wager theological arguments for Christianity. Ingalls wrote how she "began to tell them about the holy and good God who created the tree, when [she] heard 'Ahem!' and 'Ahem!'" [29]. She was interrupted by the Buddhist monk who ran the adjacent monastery. He was old and blind, but aware enough to notice

Ingalls at the base of the banyan tree, talking to local people about Jesus Christ. The very name of this foreign god was "an offence to his ear," Ingalls explained, and caused a "scorn on his face" [29]. But "Our Great Sign Tree" depicts how the intrepid evangelist Ingalls boldly followed the disapproving monk back into his monastery. Ingalls wanted to assure him she was a friend, so she reached in her bag for a gift. All she had were her smelling salts. She gave them to the monk to sniff until tears came to his eyes, and he asked if the salts might be able to cure his blindness. Ingalls explained that she "cannot do what Jesus Christ did while he was here on earth" [29]. The monk was not interested in hearing about Christ, so she told him instead about her grandfather who had gone blind in old age.

Ingalls vividly described how her grandfather would find pleasure through his working senses by petting his dog and cat, playing with his grandchildren, eating sweet apples, walking amongst singing birds. Into this scene of sensory pleasure, Ingalls incorporated Christian teachings. She added that she read to her grandfather "out of a good book which had a gold edge and beautiful pictures" [29].[21] The monk asked about the words in the adorned book, so Ingalls made a deal with him: if he would stop handling his Buddhist prayer beads, she would tell him. The monk agreed, and Ingalls proceeded to recite Romans 5:7–8, "for scarcely for a righteous man will one die, yet peradventure for a good man some would even dare to die. But God commendeth his love toward us in that while we were yet sinners Christ died for us" [29]. First, she recited the verse about her foreign god dying for poor wrongdoers in the Buddhist canonical language Pali and then in Burmese. Ingalls wrote that the monk "was too proud to say he liked to hear the text," but as she continued to visit him over the course of the year he would ask her "to 'repeat [her] Pali,' and would then add, and 'now the Burmese'" [29].

Although this monk enjoyed hearing her recite scripture in Burma's sacred Buddhist language and in the common vernacular, he never became one of Ingalls' converts. Ingalls wrote that she "had no evidence that he felt that he was a sinner. He was a Buddhist priest, and rested on that" [29]. Ingalls may not have gotten him to think of himself as a man in need of Christian salvation, but she did earn his affection. Ingalls' visits to the monk and his spirit tree continued until the elderly monk's remaining senses finally gave way and he prepared to die. Ingalls wrote that "as he knew the Christians needed a better ground for [her] house, he called up witnesses and made his monastery and place over to [her]...the head man of [their] village came and planted the flags at the four corners, and this was how [she] came into possession of this tree and the land for [their] chapel and mission house" [29]. Ingalls took care to note the flag-staking process by which land was measured and transferred to a new owner in Thonze, implying that she only ended up with the nat tree because it happened to be within those property lines. Perhaps she wanted to assure readers that she did not actively acquire a local spirit shrine. However, we should also recognize that she explicitly states that the monk never converted to Christianity. Surely she could have suggested as much if she was interested in recasting the story to improve her reputation as a successful converter of Buddhist monks. If the story is not designed to spotlight Ingalls transforming dedicated Buddhists into enlightened Christians, how else might we read it?

As with Ingalls' writings about her dog statue, we can see how the account of her tree works to entertain the American audience that supported foreign mission work—the readers whose donations and public encouragement of international evangelism allowed the Burma mission to continue through the hardships of the American Civil War and Reconstruction.[22] Ingalls' essay complements the

---

[21] By describing the bible as a book with "a gold edge and beautiful pictures" Ingalls may have been intentionally drawing a comparison to the Burmese *Kammawa* ("*Kammavāca*" in Pali), a Theravada Buddhist ritual text that has a tradition in Burma of being highly ornamented with lavish elements such as gold paint and exquisite illustrations. The American Baptist mission to Burma collected several Burmese *Kammawa*, including one that Marilla Baker Ingalls obtained from the chest of King Thibaw, the last king of Burma. That *Kammawa* is held in the American Baptist Historical Society and features the gold paint, red lacquer, and nat illustrations emblematic of Konbaung-era *Kammawa*. An attached note explains how Ingalls took the manuscript from the king's chest with "permission of a Court Minister" [30]. For more on the Burmese *Kammawa* see ([11], pp. 52–72).

[22] For more on the history of the Baptists in the United States, see [31].

mission's claim that the Burmese are in need of salvation and that the Americans there are uniquely suited to help them find it. The old, blind monk and the tree-worshipping locals are presented as almost comically ignorant. However, while her writing does not deviate from the ways in which the Burma mission justified its presence, we also see a kind of carefree delight in the way she tells her stories. Ingalls, after all, turned seventy years old the month "Our Great Sign Tree" was published. She was a renowned senior missionary, a woman who had spent over four decades living an extraordinary life in Asia and had the stories to prove it. Like her dog article, Ingalls' tree essay is one of these stories. It therefore offers less guarded glimpses of the strange religious transformations happening in Thonze. Two glimpses are particularly illuminating: Ingalls's gift to the monk and the medicinal advertisements her tree showcased.

Let us look again, then, at the exchange about the smelling salts. How might her gift of the pungent compound hint at other assumptions at play in the relationship between the missionary and the monk? Ingalls may have included the monk's question about curing blindness with a substance used for far simpler conditions like faintness to help caricature the Buddhist as naive. But we should also question why else this monk would think that Ingalls would have a powerful medicine in her bag. Did Ingalls have a reputation as a purveyor of curative substances? Ingalls took care to add that she told the monk that she could not do what Jesus had done. She surely did not want her readers to think she was going around Burma claiming the ability to cure blindness. Yet her writings do depict her telling Christian miracles stories and charming people with her foreign ways and adventurous spirit.[23] Furthermore, why were smelling salts the only thing she had in her bag? Did she have a fainting problem? Or did she find that they worked to both help people with alertness and to get their attention?

We know that Ingalls used other medicines in this way—to bring people physical relief and to attract them to Christian evangelism. She even hung advertisements for the specific medicines that missionaries would hand out alongside Christian texts. She wrote how the trunk of her banyan tree featured "the bright, flashing notice of the Perry Davis Pain Killer, and...the more modern one of Dr. Jaynes' medicines. They are a blessing to Burma, and go packed off with our Bible and tracts" [29]. Both Perry Davis's Pain Killer and the medicines of Dr. Jayne would have been familiar to Ingalls' readers, as they were popular remedies in North America. Dr. Jayne brand medicines were common treatments for a range of conditions from tapeworm and goiters to coughs and bruises. But even more popular, especially in Ingalls' mission, was Perry Davis's cure-all drug boldly called "Pain Killer."

Pain Killer was an analgesic made with opiates and ethyl alcohol. The medicine was common in North American pharmacies and homes and also with American foreign mission movements in the mid and late nineteenth century. Perry Davis' Pain Killer had multiple print ads, including text-only ones that ran in *The Baptist Missionary Magazine* declaring Pain Killer "The Most Popular Medicine Extant" [33]. Among the most popular of the medicine's illustrated advertisements at the time of Ingalls' sign tree, and the one that seems to match Ingalls' description of it as "bright" and "flashing," was an advertisement that showed a fleet of six fair-skinned cherubs carrying a brown glass medicine bottle over the globe. The largest ad copy reads "Joy to the World" above smaller type branding it "Perry Davis' Vegetable Pain Killer." The message is obvious: this medicine from Providence, Rhode Island (the only place marked on the map) delivers heavenly relief the world over. We also find a similar visual in a common advertisement for Dr. Jayne's medicines in which a porcelain-skinned boy angel carrying a white lily leans through a window into an advertisement for "The Best Blood Purifier for Scrofula, Cancer, Epilepsy, Dropsy, Skin and Liver diseases." Chubby baby angels were a visual

---

[23] One of the more charming of Ingalls' accounts is her journal entry from her visit to the royal city of Mandalay. There she visited the women's quarters of the palace and befriended a queen and a princess. Ingalls writes about their interest in her as a white women who could speak Burmese and who possessed such curios as a stereoscope and geographies. In particular, her conversation with the queen (who was clearly well educated in Theravada scriptures) gives us a specific image of the kind of attraction Burmese people had to this odd Christian woman [32].

trope in nineteenth-century medicinal advertisements in the U.S., but what could these images have signaled to a Burmese audience?

I would like to suggest that the figures on the medicine advertisements appeared to Burmese visitors as a kind of foreign nat. Nats are commonly depicted in Burma as winged creatures, and Ingalls was certainly familiar with this key feature of nat iconography given how much time she spent evangelizing in places like pagodas that housed nat sculptures. It is possible, then, that Ingalls intentionally made the visual connection between the cherubs and the nats that the Burmese told her had resided in the venerable banyan tree. Ingalls' shrine tree, her professed connection to a foreign god, and her possession of powerful medicine may have positioned her as a kind of holywoman with extraordinary powers.[24] This is just conjecture, as we do not have any evidence of local people describing her posters in terms of nat imagery or explicitly saying that Ingalls wielded magical objects. Unfortunately, we do not have any records of anything that people thought about Ingalls' shrine other than Ingalls' own accounts of what brought people there and what they said about it.

In one of these accounts, there is a comment attributed to a Burmese woman that connects Pain Killer to the images on Ingalls' tree. This account suggests a link between the medicine Ingalls distributed and the way the posters on her tree brought about religious transformation. In an 1877 essay, "A Morning at Thongzai," Ingalls strung together a series of vignettes showing various people discussing religion with the missionary [35]. In one, a woman approaches Ingalls to ask, "Have you any Pain Killer? My boy has cut his foot; your medicine once cured my brother in two days so that he went about his work. I came for this, but I want to see those big pictures. The women who came the other day say they understand your doctrines much better since they saw Jesus and the man out of the grave, and those blind and deaf people" [35]. The Burmese woman's point here about visuals being more effective than doctrine echoes the argument made in Ingalls' dog shrine article by the man who said that the dog had done more for him than all of the texts he had received from the missionaries. By publishing two stories in which Burmese characters state that images are more persuasive than theology, Ingalls worked to demonstrate to her readers how valuable her religious objects were. To be sure, her cast-iron dog and her decorated banyan tree might have seemed like strange—perhaps even inappropriate—gateways into the Baptist mission, but Ingalls indicated that she had ingeniously used these objects to bring the Burmese to a Christian god. Harder to determine, though, is what all of this combinatory, objects-based evangelism meant for the Burmese who visited the mission and for those who joined its Christian community.

What we do know is that Ingalls' sign tree, just like her dog statue, developed a reputation in the local community, attracting people to gather at the mission station. These material and visual religious objects animated Ingalls' Christian community, making it known as a site of more converted Burmese Buddhist monks than any other Baptist mission station in the country. Certainly Ingalls' unique, ebullient personality and extraordinary commitment to a Burmese community were partially responsible for the expansion of Thonze's Christian population. The history of evangelism is replete with portraits of especially capable missionaries. Ingalls' writings beg alternative readings for her success, however. They suggest that her famous dog and decorated tree were catalysts for religious change in the Baptist mission that were even more powerful than her particular gifts of personality.

4. Conclusions

The Baptist mission to Burma always had an image problem. In a land densely populated with Buddha statues, spirit shrines, and ornamented pagodas, American evangelists struggled to draw attention to a god that could not be pictured. This contrast between the aniconism of Baptist

---

[24] Ingalls may even have been seen as a kind of *weikza-do*, a Burmese wizard. Patrick Pranke defines the Burmese *weikza-do* as "a master of esoteric arts and possessed of extraordinary magical potency," ([34], p. 467) who "can be supplicated for protection, for spiritual advice, and for mundane boons as well" ([34], p. 474). The key difference, however, is that *weikza-do* are considered Buddhists, whereas Ingalls explicitly identified as a Christian.

Christianity and the abundance of Burma's Buddhas was a persistent issue for the Protestant operation. The pioneering missionary Edward Stevens described this concern as one of the top three Burmese objections to the Baptists' religion. The primary objection, according to Stevens, was "the recent appearance of Christianity" in Burma; the second objection was "the invisibility of God, while their objects of worship are before their eyes;" and the third was that Christianity permits "killing animals for food," a stark contrast with the Buddhist vow to refrain from killing all beings, including those slaughtered for meat [36].[25] As Stevens pointed out, the number one argument Burmese missionaries heard against Christianity was that it was the religion of newly arrived foreigners whereas Buddhism and nat worship were the long-established traditions of their ancestors. Second to the problem of being alien was Christianity's problem of centering on an invisible god.

Protestantism's image problem was so pervasive that we even find it highlighted in one of the few extant accounts from the point of view of one of Ingalls' converted Buddhist monks. When this man was baptized into Ingalls' Christian congregation in Thonze in 1892, he spoke about his journey from Buddhism to Christianity. While he was sharing his experiences with those gathered for his baptism, Ingalls "abridged them down," on a bit of paper she found in her bag, and then sent that text to the *Baptist Missionary Magazine* [37]. Taking on the first-person voice of the convert, Ingalls' article tells how he had encountered Christians and their theology at several points throughout his life, but that he had always argued against Christianity. This account specifically notes that his most successful argument was that the Christian god was invisible, whereas Burmese gods and Buddhas could be seen everywhere in the form of sacred statuary and other artwork. As the convert put it in the article, he "could always bring the people to [his] side by the question, 'Show us your God'" [37]. This man continued to encounter Christian communities and teachings, but it wasn't until he joined a Baptist prayer circle after the death of his Christian brother-in-law that he said he put himself "in the hands of Jesus Christ" [37]. This conversion story is distinct in its scene of religious surrender during a funeral service, but it is familiar in its emphasis on the predicament Protestants faced when they could not show their god to the Burmese.

Like her fellow missionaries and those they sought to convert, Ingalls was well aware of the problem of proselytizing for an invisible god. She knew that Buddhist statues and nat shrines helped bind Burmese communities. But rather than simply sound arguments against idol worship, Ingalls found objects of her own to form her alternative Christian congregation. With its famous statue and adorned banyan tree, this congregation, then, must have seemed both familiar and new, both a religion with revered images *and* a religion of recently arrived and increasingly powerful foreigners.

After Ingalls' death in 1902, the American Baptist mission to Burma continued for another half-century. The British occupation that Ingalls witnessed winding its way through Burma along new rail lines, economic networks, and military campaigns lasted until the country gained independence in 1948. Christian evangelists continued their operations under British rule and into independence, but in 1966 the Socialist Republic of Burma expelled all foreign missionaries. Even after the Americans were sent home, Baptist communities carried on. Today, Baptist Christianity is one of the, if not *the*, most popular religions in Burma outside of Buddhism.[26] The country's Baptists, however, are almost entirely found among ethnic minorities, underscoring how extraordinary Ingalls' effect was on a community from the Burmese majority. During her forty years in Thonze, Ingalls' cast-iron dog and

---

[25] This does not mean that Burma's Buddhist communities were vegetarian. Animals, especially fish, were (and still are) common in Burmese diets, and monks are not forbidden from accepting offerings of prepared meat. But many Burmese Buddhists vow to refrain from killing animals themselves and instead buy butchered meat and previously caught fish.

[26] The World Religion Database counts 74.4% of Myanmar's population as Buddhist, 8.2% as Christian, 3.8% as Muslim, 1.7% as Hindu, 1.5% as Confucianists, and 9.5% as Ethnoreligionists [38]. The majority of the country's Christians are Baptist, but reliable demographic studies detailing the country's various Christian denominations do not exist. The "The World Factbook" published by the Central Intelligence Agency of the United States of America calculates a relatively low estimate for Myanmar's Christian population, 4%, and breaks that population down into Baptists, which it counts as 3%, and Roman Catholics as 1% [39].

sign tree drew many Burmese into her Baptist mission. However, in the end, there proved no way to compete with Shwedagon Pagoda and its Buddhism. The golden shrine still towers above Yangon, reflecting the persistent power of the country's religious objects.

Conflicts of Interest: The author declares no conflict of interest.

References

1. Ingalls, Marilla Baker. *Ocean Sketches of Life in Burmah*. Philadelphia: American Baptist Publication Society, 1857.
2. Robert, Dana Lee. *American Women in Mission: A Social History of Their Thought and Practice*. Macon: Mercer University Press, 1996.
3. Shwe Wa, Maung. *Burma Baptist Chronicle*, Judson sesquicentennial ed. Rangoon: Board of Publications, Burma Baptist Convention, 1963.
4. Merriam, Edmund. "Gone Home: Mrs. Marilla Baker Ingalls." *Baptist Missionary Magazine*, February 1903, pp. 59–61, 76.
5. Morgan, David, and Sally M. Promey. *The Visual Culture of American Religions*. Berkeley: University of California Press, 2001.
6. Kieschnick, John. *The Impact of Buddhism on Chinese Material Culture*. Princeton: Princeton University Press, 2003.
7. Davis, Richard H. *Lives of Indian Images*. Princeton: Princeton University Press, 1997.
8. Appadurai, Arjun. *The Social Life of Things: Commodities in Cultural Perspective*. New York: Cambridge University Press, 1986.
9. Turner, Alicia. *Saving Buddhism: The Impermanence of Religion in Colonial Burma*. Honolulu: University of Hawai'i Press, 2014.
10. Tweed, Thomas A. *Retelling U.S. Religious History*. Berkeley: University of California Press, 1997.
11. Kaloyanides, Alexandra. "Baptizing Buddhists: The Nineteenth-Century American Missionary Encounter with Burmese Buddhism." Ph.D. Dissertation, Yale University, New Haven, CT, USA, 2015.
12. Brown, Candy Gunther. *The Word in the World : Evangelical Writing, Publishing, and Reading in America, 1789–1880*. Chapel Hill: University of North Carolina Press, 2004.
13. Brumberg, Joan Jacobs. *Mission for Life: The Story of the Family of Adoniram Judson, the Dramatic Events of the First American Mission, and the Course of Evangelical Religion in the Nineteenth Century*. New York: Free Press, 1980.
14. Ingalls, Marilla Baker. *Narrative of Jesus*. Rangoon: American Baptist Mission Press, 1883.
15. Rose, Abram. "Letter to the Executive Secretary of the American Baptist Missionary Union." In *Rev. A. T. Rose*, American Baptist Historical Society. American Baptist Foreign Mission Society Records, Missionary Correspondence Files: 17 December, 1892. Courtesy of the American Baptist Historical Society.
16. Charney, Michael W. *Powerful Learning: Buddhist Literati and the Throne in Burma's Last Dynasty, 1752–1885*. Ann Arbor: Centers for South and Southeast Asian Studies, The University of Michigan, 2006.
17. Smeaton, Donald Mackenzie. *The Loyal Karens of Burma*. London: Kegan Paul, Trench and Co., Ltd., 1887.
18. Brandis, Dietrich. "Mrs. Marilla B. Ingalls." *The Standard*, 6 June 1903, p. 8.
19. Tweed, Thomas A. *The American Encounter with Buddhism, 1844–1912: Victorian Culture & the Limits of Dissent*. Chapel Hill: University of North Carolina Press, 2000.
20. Masuzawa, Tomoko. *The Invention of World Religions, or, How European Universalism Was Preserved in the Language of Pluralism*. Chicago: University of Chicago Press, 2005.
21. Hutchison, William R. *Errand to the World: American Protestant Thought and Foreign Missions*. Chicago: University of Chicago Press, 1987.
22. Braun, Erik. *The Birth of Insight: Meditation, Modern Buddhism, and the Burmese Monk Ledi Sayadaw*. Chicago: The University of Chicago Press, 2013.
23. Pranke, Patrick Arthur. "Treatise on the Lineage of Elders (*Vaṃsadīpanī*): Monastic Reform and the Writing of Buddhist History in Eighteenth-Century Burma." Ph.D. Dissertation, University of Michigan, Ann Arbor, MI, USA, 2004.

24. Carbine, Jason A. *Sons of the Buddha: Continuities and Ruptures in a Burmese Monastic Tradition*. New York: De Gruyter, 2011.
25. Ingalls, Marilla Baker. "My Dumb Teacher." *Baptist Missionary Magazine*, May 1896, pp. 137–39.
26. Crosby, Kate. *Theravada Buddhism: Continuity, Diversity and Identity*. Malden: Wiley Blackwell, 2014.
27. Brac de la Perrière, Bénédicte. "Sibling Relationships in the *Nat* Stories of the Burmese Cult to the 'Thirty-seven'." *Moussons. Recherche en sciences humaines sur l'Asie du Sud-Est* 5 (2002): 31–48.
28. Berkwitz, Stephen C., Juliane Schober, and Claudia Brown. *Buddhist Manuscript Cultures: Knowledge, Ritual, and Art*. New York: Routledge, 2009.
29. Ingalls, Marilla Baker. "Our Great Sign Tree." *Baptist Missionary Magazine*, November 1897, pp. 602–4.
30. "Abbreviations of the Sacred Books of Gautama (of the Buddha)." Burmese Kammawa manuscript held by the American Baptist Historical Society. Courtesy of the American Baptist Historical Society.
31. Leonard, Bill. *Baptists in America*. New York: Columbia University Press, 2005.
32. Ingalls, Marilla Baker. "Visit To Mandelay: The Royal Household." *Baptist Missionary Magazine*, September 1873, pp. 339–44.
33. "Perry Davis' Vegetable Pain Killer." *Baptist Missionary Magazine*, August 1883, p. 1.
34. Pranke, Patrick. "On saints and wizards—Ideals of Human Perfection and Power in Contemporary Burmese Buddhism." *Journal of the International Association of Buddhist Studies* 33 (2012): 453–88.
35. Ingalls, Marilla Baker. "A Morning At Thongzai." *Baptist Missionary Magazine*, June 1877, pp. 139–40.
36. Stevens, Edward. "Shway Dagong, At Rangoon: Description." *Baptist Missionary Magazine*, February 1876, pp. 34–36.
37. Ingalls, Marilla Baker. "Thongze Work Notes." *Baptist Missionary Magazine*, August 1892, pp. 364–67.
38. Johnson, Todd Michael, and Brian J. Grim, eds. *World Religion Database International Religious Demographic Statistics and Sources*. Leiden: Brill, 2008.
39. "The World Factbook: Burma." Central Intelligence Agency of the United States of America. Available online: https://www.cia.gov/library/publications/the-world-factbook/geos/bm.html (accessed 25 May 2016).

religions

Article

Mothers and Spirits: Religious Identity, Alcohol, and Death

Candi K. Cann

Baylor Interdisciplinary Core, Baylor University, Waco, TX 76798, USA; candi_cann@baylor.edu;
Tel.: +1-254-710-3379

Academic Editors: Douglas James Davies and Michael J. Thate
Received: 17 April 2016; Accepted: 6 July 2016; Published: 19 July 2016

Abstract: Mothers and Spirits examines the intersection of women, alcohol, and death through a comparative analysis. Offering a brief history of the study of drinking, followed by a short analysis of drinking in European and Chinese cultures, Cann examines two religious texts central to the roles of women and alcohol in Chinese religious thought and Christianity. Finally, Cann utilizes the historical and textual background to contextualize her ethnographic study of women, alcohol, and death in Mexican Catholicism, Chinese religions, and American Southern Baptist Christianity. Cann argues that both alcohol and temperance are used as a way to forge, cement, and create gender identity, constructing alternate discourses of power and inclusivity.

Keywords: women; Mary; Mulian; alcohol; Baptist; Santa Muerte; death; female; drinking; temperance

---

"Let beer be for those who are perishing, wine for those who are in anguish!

Let them drink and forget their poverty and remember their misery no more."

—Proverbs 31:6,7

1. Introduction

Examining the intersection of women, alcohol, and death through a comparative analysis of both text and practice reveals that alcohol and gender intersect in such a way as to create an alternative discourse of, and access to, agency. Alcohol and temperance are used as a way to forge, cement, and create gender identity, constructing alternate discourses of power and inclusivity. Through an analysis of texts, historical analysis, and ethnographic case studies of Mexican Catholicism, Chinese religions, and American Southern Baptist Christianity, it becomes evident that alcohol and motherhood intersect to provide women with alternate economies to power. In the Chinese and Mexican Catholic cases, alcohol and the symbolism of motherhood is utilized as a way to circumnavigate traditional claims to power, creating alternate routes to legitimation and recognition. In the Southern Baptist case, women also receive power from alcohol, but through its regulation and an emphasis on temperance, rather than its consumption. Baptist women, particularly Baptist mothers, enforcing abstinence, are able to assert their claims as virtuous and moral leaders of church and home through the absence of alcohol. In all three cases, images of motherhood and the power of women are made stronger through alcohol, whether through its presence or absence.

The three cases are deliberately chosen—seemingly disparate and different, all three reveal a deeper connection between symbols of motherhood, death, and alcohol, constructing alternate discourses of belonging and exclusion in images of the afterlife and in everyday religiosity. Utilizing examples from Asia, Latin America, and the contemporary United States also allows one to consider the possibility that perhaps the relationship between women and alcohol is not merely coincidental, but possibly universal.[1] In both Chinese and Mexican Catholic religious folk practices, alcohol—symbolic blood, and giver of life—is a transformative mediating agent that links people in life to those in death. The alcohol offerings in Chinese religious practice are given at the gravesite, and are meant to counter the polluting effects of childbirth blood in afterlife, purifying mothers, while simultaneously linking them to their children through the consumption of the bloodbowl (symbolized by wine). Tequila offerings to Santa Muerte (Saint Death) reinforce both local and national identity, while challenging more traditional and patriarchal discourses of state and church, and granting alternate access to spiritual power. I examine the prayers and practices of Santa Muerte as both a literal and figurative inverse of Mary, Catholic Mother of God.[2] Here, the Mother of Life has been turned into the Mother of Death, but all women, as mothers, introduce their babies to death by bringing them into the cycle of life. These two examples are contrasted to Southern Baptist religiosity, in which both alcohol and symbols of death (the crucifix) are missing from the sanctuary, and mothers are charged with the responsibility of keeping the values of the home through temperance. In the Southern Baptist example, women become distinct from men by becoming guardians of family morality through the denial and governance of alcohol. The absence of alcohol in the Southern Baptist church corroborates the equally absent corpse of the dead Jesus, yet women (not men) remain responsible/liable. The three examples offer, through entirely different models, similar conclusions—that alcohol offers women not merely an alternate economy, but an alternate access to agency, in both the sacred and profane realms.

The fermentation of alcohol makes it a dangerous and powerful drink—a drink that provides access to shamanic states while challenging mortality. Since alcohol can be preserved without going bad (and in fact, often becomes better with preservation), it has long been viewed as a drink that defies death, and early names given to alcohol across cultures bear this out (e.g., the Greek term *nectar*, or the Indo-European version, *mead*, etymologically defined as "immortal drink") [3]. More recent descriptors, such as *whiskey* or *brandy*, were equally optimistic, derived from the Latin *aqua vitae*, or water of life.[3] Alcohol is powerful and dangerous not merely because it creates alternate states of mind, but because it challenges mortality itself. Women, particularly in their roles as mothers, are equally dangerous—as guardians of both past and future, birth and death, mothers both give life, yet introduce their children into death. Mothers and (alcoholic) spirits both mediate life and death, sacred and profane, this world and other world, situated as they are on the boundaries of church and home.

2. A Brief History of Drinking

One of the oldest drinks in the history of humankind, alcohol has traditionally been associated in many cultures with a rich symbolism of water, milk, and blood [5]. Historically, alcohol was one of the safest drinks to consume, as many places in the world did not have voluminous or potable water supplies, and alcohol could be made, stored, and drunk when water was not readily available. Alcoholic beverages in the ancient world, with their antimicrobial qualities and relatively low alcohol content (generally 1% in contrast to the higher alcohol content of 7%–20% found in beer, wine, and liquor of today) were relatively easy to produce, preserve, store, and transport, and offered quantifiable health benefits in contrast to water.

---

[1] While I realize it has somewhat fallen out of fashion to offer universal constructs, I do this by relying heavily on William Paden's notion of "aspectual focus," while also remaining cognizant of J.Z. Smith's emphasis on difference, examining a comparison of seemingly disparate phenomena through a focal lens of alcohol, women and death. See [1,2].

[2] I have focused on the Santa Muerte example (rather than an example from mainstream Catholicism and the many examples related to the Virgin Mary) for two reasons: (1) focusing on the intersection between women and alcohol in Santa Muerte reveals a paradigm in contemporary folk Catholicism in which Santa Muerte reflects the internal double of the Virgin Mary; and (2) the recent work on Santa Muerte tends to focus on the practices of folk religiosity, somewhat neglecting the textual evidence, and I wanted to provide the reader (initial and brief) access to this rich body of material.

[3] See ([4], p. 169) more on this. Liebmann's history of alcohol—sixty years old this year—remains one of the better cultural histories of alcohol in the field today.

Mary Douglas's seminal text, *Constructive Drinking*, first published in 1987, examined the role of drinking in society and communities from an ethnographic viewpoint [6]. Douglas argued for three functions of drinking—as a way of creating and reinforcing existing social bonds, introducing the symbolism of an idealized world, and drinking as an alternative economy.[4] Drinking, like eating, is an inherently social practice that has been incorporated into various religious rituals, and is so basic to human survival that the dearth of studies regarding drinking symbolism may reflect our assumptions that because it is so common, it cannot possibly have symbolic meaning. But the choice of drink, like food, is important, and reflects many things, from the broader societal infrastructure to class, status, gender, age, and religious identity. What we choose to drink is as much an indicator of identity as our foods, the homes we live in, and the cars we drive. Examining the function of drinking and, more specifically, alcoholic beverages in funerals and memorialization rituals, reveals much not just about the world of the living, but also about conceptions of the afterlife.

Alcohol creates both social cohesion and social disruption. It has been known to foster homosocial bonds and provide a counter-discourse against domestic narratives,[5] and in times of temperance or prohibition, consuming alcohol can be viewed as one way to formulate counter-narratives against the state or dominant cultural narrative. Precisely because of its inebriating qualities, alcohol has served historically as a drink offering an escape and reassertion of the individual self against some of the more restrictive aspects of society and social control. Throughout the history of the world, alcohol has cycled through periods of acceptance and periods of prohibition, but its close association in nearly all cultures with festivals, holidays, and celebrations means that alcohol has often been associated with folk movements and traditions. Alcohol, thus, functions simultaneously as a drink that encourages social cohesion, while offering an anti-structural discourse that challenges authority. It is no surprise then that alcohol has been so closely tied with both narratives surrounding death and death rituals themselves. Both death and alcohol occupy a liminal space in the everyday world, offering a counter-narrative to traditional roles, time, control and gender. Both the presence of, and specific proscription against, alcohol provide clues into notions of the afterlife, relationships between the living and the dead, and the intersection between life and death from a religious viewpoint.

Historically, in Europe, alcohol has been considered a product of the domestic arts that both women and religious clergy not only had access to, but utilized and capitalized upon to help them enter into the everyday market economy. Like many quotidian consumables, the various kinds of alcohol were classified and typologized to signify particular classes and genders. Until the last two hundred years or so in Europe, beer-making was considered to belong to the realm of women's work, while wine-making was generally relegated to the realm of men.[6] Beer was regularly consumed by both genders, and for many years was the primary source of hydration, particularly since the process of making beer generally involved boiling water, thus eliminating microbials and other water-borne pathogens, such as typhus. Wine, on the other hand, was viewed as a drink of the upper classes, with

---

[4] One of the more interesting aspects of Douglas' study of alcohol is its use as an alternative economy. Alternative economies are those systems that use other sources as a form of currency. In this case, food and drink became part of a popular barter system that allowed one to exchange food commodities for other goods. This included all sorts of foods, grain staples, and alcohol. Alcohol could be stored and preserved which made it a consistent commodity on the barter market. Since Douglas, the history and study of drinking has remained somewhat marginal in academia, and the majority of studies on drinking analyze it from the perspective of behavior or health outcomes. The Drinking Studies Network is an interdisciplinary group of contemporary scholars who are conducting work on alcohol from a historical or cultural perspective [7].

[5] "The rituals of male drinking and socializing together in coffeehouses and bars, although emphasizing masculinity, are directed toward obscuring male dependency on the female members of their family. By excluding women from coffeehouses men reinforce a doubtful female subordination." ([8], pp. 7–8).

[6] Judith Bennet's study notes that beer brewing and selling was largely located in the realm of women's work until 1350, but by 1600 beer brewing and selling transitioned to men's work. Bennet relates these changes in part to society's shifting views of the role of women. She writes that a marriage contract was viewed as a socially secure way to enforce broader social contracts involving money (in other words, the husbands could be counted upon should the wife somehow evade her legal and contractual responsibilities), and that in this way, beer brewing gradually shifted to the realm of men's work. For more, see [9].

ale and beer more common and accessible. As religious communities developed in medieval Europe, these (mostly male) communities gradually co-opted beer-making, relegating women's work to the domestic arts, and beer-brewing as a more male-dominated activity.[7] This continues to be the case today, where judging by most advertising campaigns, beer is primarily considered to be a man's drink, and wine is primarily relegated to the realm of women.[8] Thus, the types of alcohol consumed, the ways in which they are viewed, and the process associated with alcohol-making has shifted across various times and cultures. The important point here is that alcohol, like death, is a cultural and social construction, and the social status, attitudes, consumption patterns, and laws and regulations regarding alcohol shift and change with time.[9] Alcohol production in Europe—beer made first by women in their homes, then by religious monastics in their religious communities—and finally moving to the slave plantations of the new world (where they made rum from sugar cane or gin from juniper berries)—belonged to the liminal populations who did not have traditional occupations and career paths.[10] The importance of alcohol as an alternative economy is central here, as alcohol production allowed for those on the fringes of traditional market economies access to, and freedom from, the constraints of traditional hierarchical systems. This also may be why alcohol has cycled in and out of favor with state authorities, as it threatens traditional authority and economies, granting access to those that the government seeks to exclude.

In Asia, where wine-making from grapes was traded for the fermenting of rice and a much stronger rice wine (with an alcohol content from 40–65%), alcohol production remained within the realm of men, and women were generally banned from the process, especially in the fermentation process, as they were considered to be a pollutant to the spiritual, healing, and medicinal qualities of alcohol. In both Chinese religion and medicine, the idea of achieving a balance between Yin and Yang is essential to maintaining not only equilibrium and harmony in the cosmos, but also the health of the body. Since women are considered to be fundamentally Yin, and alcohol, essentially Yang, women could not be involved with the making of alcohol as they could dilute the Yang strength found in spirits. As Li Shizehen wrote in *The Bencao Gangmu* (Compendium of Materia Medica): "Wine is pure yang in nature, and pungent and sweet in flavor, thus it has the effects of invigorating vital function and dispersing pathogens. Wine is dry and hot in property, and is thus used to expel dampness and cold" [13]. Uses of wine in Chinese medicine were generally geared towards "cold" diseases caused by too much Yin and, thus, requiring balance through Yang, and the heat-generating properties of wine. Thus, wine was considered to be effective for those diseases such as arthritis, chest pain, and post-partum injuries, as well as impotence and infertility, diseases also caused by an overabundance of Yin [13].Wine, in moderation, is believed to invigorate the body, reducing stagnation and stimulating the body. Thus, alcohol in the Chinese context was traditionally associated not only with Yang, and properties of male characteristics, but was also fairly strictly relegated to the world of men—to produce, to consume, and to regulate. Women were generally banned from drinking, except in rituals and religious ceremonies, or to partake in wine drinking for medicinal purposes [14]. Having given a brief analysis of both the study of drinking as a field, and a short history of the importance of alcohol in Christian and Chinese cultures over time, I turn now to an analysis of wine and women in Christian and Buddhist scriptures. I want to link the practices, and these models to their texts and, thus, I offer

---

[7] Early monastic communities offered beer and ale to travelling pilgrims visiting their monasteries, considering it an act of hospitality, gradually developing the sale of alcohol as a powerful alternate economy. For more on the history of this, see [10].

[8] In fact, according to a study conducted by the Wine Market Council, 80% of all wine purchases in the United States today are made by women. For more, see [11].

[9] Even notions of "drunkenness," and definitions of inebriation are subject to cultural and societal interpretation.

[10] The production of alcohol by slave economies and plantations did not merely aid the slaves, but added to the wealth of the plantation owners. However, it also gave slaves a marketable skillset that allowed some slaves access to an alternate economy that added value to their everyday lives, which (some) plantation owners recognized also kept slaves tied to their land and increased their loyalty. For more on alternate slave economies see [12].

the reader a brief hermeneutic exploration of the Buddhist and Christian texts regarding mothers and alcohol as a way to situate the practices and interpretations that emerge out of them.

3. Women and Wine in Christian and Buddhist Scriptures: Mary and Mulian's Mother

The importance of the link between the role of motherhood and alcohol is found in both Christian and Chinese scriptures. In both stories, the motherhood of the female characters—Mary, as the mother of Jesus, and Mulian's mother—is central to the story. The bond between mother and son in each story is the compelling bond that puts the narrative in action. The demand for wine—either as first miracle that reveals Jesus' mission on earth, or as purifying agent for the pollution of childbirth—is made by women to their male child, and becomes the narrative pivot through which death is overcome. It is no mistake that the transformation of water into wine at a wedding feast is the first recorded miracle in the New Testament, and is done so at the request of Jesus' mother,

> When the wine was gone, Jesus' mother said to him, "They have no more wine." "Woman, why do you involve me?" Jesus replied. "My hour has not yet come." His mother said to the servants, "Do whatever he tells you." Nearby stood six stone water jars, the kind used by the Jews for ceremonial washing, each holding from twenty to thirty gallons. Jesus said to the servants, "Fill the jars with water"; so they filled them to the brim. Then he told them, "Now draw some out and take it to the master of the banquet." They did so, and the master of the banquet tasted the water that had been turned into wine. He did not realize where it had come from, though the servants who had drawn the water knew. Then he called the bridegroom aside and said, "Everyone brings out the choice wine first and then the cheaper wine after the guests have had too much to drink; but you have saved the best till now"[11]

It is important to note that it is through Mary (both physically as a mother giving birth to Jesus, and symbolically, through her insistence that Jesus transform water) that Jesus actually fulfills his duty as messiah. The association of Mary as mother with the first miracle of transforming the water into wine is significant, as it is Jesus' first public act as miracle worker, and the miracle is put into motion at Mary's behest. The miracle in the wedding feast symbolizes the notion that salvation is meant for everyone, not simply the first guests, and the observations made by the host of the wedding feast affirm this fact. The "good wine" is served last, revealing that even those who come to the feast later can not only still enjoy the wine, but have even better wine.[12] The story of transforming water into wine can be contrasted to the story of Moses, who turned waters of the rivers of Egypt into blood. And the symbolism of transforming water into wine is not lost on the Jewish and Christian reader—Jesus is transforming water into blood, symbolized by wine (we see this symbolism again later through the Christian Eucharist). Mary is essential to the story as she operates not only as the dual symbol of woman who brought Jesus into the world and implored him to perform his first miracle, but also as a foil of Eve, and the nativity. Just as in the passage of Mulian and his mother (below), it is not merely Mary's role as woman that is emphasized, but mother. It is through Mary as mother that Jesus is brought into the world, redeeming the world from its fallen state, and it is in Mary's role as mother, that Jesus is requested to perform the transformation of water into wine. The passage underscores the importance of Mary as mother, as creator, and the transformation of the world and the water through her relationship to Jesus.

Similarly, in the Chinese Buddhist canon, the desperate cries of Mulian's mother as a hungry ghost implores Mulian to descend into the depths of hell to rescue her from the Blood Pool Hell,

---

[11] John 2:3–10, NIV Bible.

[12] This passage also parallels Matthew 20:1–16, the Parable of the Workers in the Vineyard, in which a master pays all those who work in the field the same pay—even those who arrive later in the day. The message in both of these reveals that the fruits of salvation do not vary, those "late to the party" also receive the good wine.

When Mu-lian heard this [that his mother was trapped in the Blood Pool Hell], he was very sad and he asked the warden, How can we repay (bao da) our moms (a niang) for the kindness of giving birth to us in order that they may leave the blood-pool hell?" The hell warden answered, "Teacher, you only need to carefully be a filial son or daughter, respect the Three Jewels [the Buddha, the Sangha, and the Dharma], and for the sake of your mom, hold Blood Bowl Feasts for three years, including organizing Blood Bowl Meetings (xue peng sheng hui) to which you invite monks to recite this sutra for a full day, and have confessions (chan hui). Then there will be a prajna boat to carry the mothers across the River Nai He and they will see five-colored lotuses appear in the blood pool, and the sinners will come out happy and contrite and they will be able to take rebirth (chao sheng) in a Buddha Land ([15], p. 206).

When Mulian remembers his mother through drinking a bowl of wine, meant to symbolize the blood of childbirth that his mother shed for him in her birth, Mulian is able to offer, through ingestion, a reciprocal gift of blood repaying his childbirth debt. Like Jesus in the Christian story, Mulian is also called to action by his mother (albeit in a very different way) through the reminder of how she has already paid her debt for his life, and now he must return the favor through the drinking of wine. Chinese women who have given birth during their lifetime are generally believed to be trapped in a pool of blood following their death, because the polluting effects of childbirth blood have not been counteracted ([16], pp. 89–90). The post-partum period after a woman gives birth is considered to be a period of imbalance and heavily Yin, and the "solution" to counterbalance this post-partum stage is to eat chicken, eggs, chicken broth soup, and wine, all believed to help the woman regain her strength, and recover from her childbirth; they are also foods and drinks considered to be heavily Yang. However, these foods counter the woman's Yin state in life, and do not extend to her death when she is expected to pay off her debt for the childbirth blood. Mulian, as male and yang element, and the offering of wine, also heavily yang, balances out the yin/female/childbirth blood, with a debt repayment and reenactment of life, rebalancing the cosmos. While the mother gave birth to her son, it is the son who must now rescue his mother from death. The story of Mulian illustrates the complex role women play in the Chinese religious cosmology, and why wine remains one of the central components for both Chinese funerals and memorialization rituals. Mulian's mother is a considered to be a hungry ghost,[13] and it is only through the son's remembrance of her life that she can be redeemed. The balance, thus, is asserted in this passage between male and female, parent and child, life and death, wine and blood.

Both the story of Jesus' first miracle and Mulian's descent into hell tie together women and wine to relay larger messages about their respective religious traditions, and offer insights into conceptions of the afterlife. In the miracle story of Jesus, the transformation of water into wine reminds readers of past Biblical narratives,[14] while foreshadowing the sacrificial offering of blood on the cross. The story emphasizes the inclusive nature of Christian salvation—even latecomers can benefit from the blood sacrifice of Jesus. Mulian's story also democratizes the afterlife—emphasizing the bodhisattva ideal and offering a simple Chinese ritual that allows equal access to Buddhist heaven, for women as well as men. One overlap that cannot be overlooked here is the role of motherhood in both scriptures. In both

---

13   In Chinese religion, hungry ghosts (餓鬼 èguǐ, the Chinese translation for the Sanskrit preta) are beings that reside in one of the six Buddhist realms of existence (Buddhist hell). Literally depicted as beings with pinhole openings for necks, and cavernous bloated stomachs, hungry ghosts can never satiate their desires and are metaphorical representatives of beings who have deep desire, addictions, or obsessions. Hungry ghosts are believed to come back to haunt the living when the rituals for the deceased have not been properly observed, and in this way the story of the hungry ghost is really about the ties between the living and the dead. For more on hungry ghosts see [17].

14   In Exodus 7:20, Moses turned the waters of the Nile into blood, signifying the arrival of the first plague on the Egyptians and the Jews' status as God's chosen people; the turning of water into wine both serves as a reference to this act, while also signifying the future sacrifice to come. "Moses and Aaron did just as the LORD had commanded. He raised his staff in the presence of Pharaoh and his officials and struck the water of the Nile, and all the water was changed into blood" (NIV Bible).

stories, the motherhood of the female characters is central to their voice—in fact, in both stories it is the bond between mother and son that seems to compel the action in both stories to even occur and, in both stories, the women demand wine—whether transformed from water, or offered at the altar as a repayment for childbirth. The intersection between women, wine, motherhood, and death cannot be underscored enough. Now that I have given a brief background of the intersection of women and wine in Christian and Buddhist scriptures, I turn now to a few ethnographic analyses of the intersection of death, wine and women in contemporary rituals in Mexico, China, and the United States.

4. From Text to Ethnography: Women and Spirits in Mexico, China, and the United States

Comparing actions around alcohol, gender, and death in three ethnographic studies of China, Mexico, and the United States helps to give a picture of the ways in which alcohol and women intersect and influence understandings and conceptions of death and the afterlife. More importantly, though, alcohol and its presence or absence in rituals for, to, and about the dead has been used to define, demarcate, and reinforce gender roles in religious communities and understandings of the afterlife. Mexican folk practices involving Santa Muerte reveal a counter-narrative regarding alcohol and traditional Catholicism, utilizing the role of motherhood to critique, challenge, and invert the traditional views of death. The Chinese blood-bowl ritual offers a performative transformation of ties between mother and child through the drinking of wine that places the role of motherhood front and center in this life and the next. Finally, in contrast to both of the Mexican and Chinese practices, the absence of alcohol and Baptist branding through temperance, marks a decidedly different interpretation of gender, with women defined by their denial of alcohol and the practice of death rituals and funerals in spaces that have been publicly declared as alcohol-free.

4.1. Mexico

Like the scriptural passages of both Mary/Jesus and Mulian's mother/Mulian, Santa Muerte, or Saint Death, both capitalizes on and benefits from her role as mother. The popularity of the mother goddess figure originates in pre-Columbian religiosity, and the association of motherhood symbolism and death were existent before the arrival of colonial Christianity. Santa Muerte strongly resembles the pre-Columbian goddess Coatlicue, in her fierceness and associations with both death and maternity.

> All of the earth-mother goddesses were associated both with exuberant fertility and horrifying death, the earth as both womb and tomb of life ([18], p. 422). [De] Sahagun records the Aztec belief that Cihuacoatl, despite being the patron of women giving birth, walked at night "weeping and wailing, a dread phantom foreboding war" ([19], p. 3). Coatlicue, the divine mother who gave birth to gods and humans, was also thought to feed on human corpses and was called the "dirt devourer" ([20], p. 269; [21], p. 23).[15]

Coatlicue paved the way for the emergence of Santa Muerte, in tandem with the popularity of the virgin prototype in Mexican Catholicism. Ranked higher than saints, martyrs, angels, and even the Virgin Mary, by her followers, Santa Muerte is viewed as directly below God, in her ability to hear and answer prayers ([25], p. 59). She is given this place because she performs God's handiwork in both restoring life and bringing death, and is believed to be able to protect her adherents from death since she controls it. Santa Muerte is not officially sanctioned by the Roman Catholic Church, in part because she seems to be threatening the official pantheon of recognized and sponsored saints, and in the last five years or so, Santa Muerte has grown in both attention and adherents. Not to be confused with the more joyful and playful Calavera Catrina, the Mexican folk icon of the Day of the Dead celebrations,[16] Santa Muerte is believed to be a Mexican incarnation of the European "Grim Reaper," and Argentine

---

[15] For more on this, see ([22], pp.31–32).
[16] For a background on the history of Mexico's Day of the Dead, see [23,24].

San Muerte. She is distinct, however, in that unlike the European and Argentine versions, Santa Muerte appears as a female ([25], p. 189). To the outside and uneducated eye, however, Santa Muerte may look very similar to either Catrina or the Grim Reaper, as she is a skeleton, dressed in long robes, and carrying a scythe, and like the Virgin of Guadalupe,[17] Santa Muerte's roots are distinctly local and indigenous.

Prayers to Santa Muerte often appropriate prayers to the Virgin Mary, either replacing Santa Muerte's name in places where the Mary's would generally be, or tacking on Santa Muerte to the already established church hierarchy of God and saints. In the most obvious example, Santa Muerte followers frequently pray the rosary, replacing the name of Mary with the name of Santa Muerte, symbolically uniting the two through ritual as well as role. The relationship between Santa Muerte and the Mary cannot be underscored enough, as Santa Muerte is, like Mary, described as mother, creator, life-giver, and patron saint of the disenfranchised and marginalized. To the outsider it may seem as though Santa Muerte is replicating Mary, supplanting Mary, or simply aiding Mary in her role as patron to the peripheral. Robinson Hererra writes, however, that Santa Muerte seems to have a dialectical relationship with the Virgin Mary:

> In my mind, the dialectical relationship resembles something like this: Mary forgives us for the very things we ask Santa Muerte to do and Santa Muerte protects us when doing the very things for which Mary forgives. Seen in the light of Marx's dialectic the prayers that include both Mary and Santa Muerte make sense, the two deities don't threaten each other, rather they co-exist, each covering and guarding their specific divine territories, leaving it to supplicants to navigate the complicated paths that lead to a Catholicism that encompasses the gospel of prosperity, however one cares to define that prosperity.[18]

Santa Muerte and Mary work together in tandem—Mary forgiving the deeds that Santa Muerte performs, and Santa Muerte performing miracles that Mary cannot (or rather will not) perform. Supplicants refer to Santa Muerte with the same names given to Mary—Holy Mother, Saint, Protector, Mother of Mine, Mother of Tears—and anyone hearing these titles may at first confuse them with Mary. However, one aspect that stands out among prayers to Santa Muerte is the assertion by Santa Muerte followers that her power is stronger than even God, something that is never seen or read in prayers to the Virgin. In the Prayer to Santa Muerte, for example, titled "Mother of Tears," petitioners pray the following: "In the name of the All-powerful God, more powerful is the mother of tears. I ask for your help, I beg you to cease the bad luck [surrounding] my house. Give me money, work, and good luck. Mother of tears, protect me from danger, protect me from evil, mother of tears, rescue me from this abyss where I find myself and give me protection from all affliction and evil. I dedicate myself to you today; hear the prayer I place at your feet. Amen."[19] The name given here to Santa Muerte—the Mother of Tears—begins like many prayers to Mary, tying together the role of mother as one who both suffers (in tears) and comforts (the suffering). However, it soon becomes quickly apparent that this Mother of Tears is not Mary, because we are told that she is even greater in power than the all-powerful God. The prayer is at once both an invocation for, and an inversion of, the traditional understanding of Mary, with gender, death, and power all shifting places in Santa Muerte. In another prayer, the "Prayer to Saint Death," (see below) there is a similar inversion of this power—when the petitioner at

---

[17] Patrizia Granziera's article does a nice job of explaining the relationship between the maternal symbolism of Coatlicue to the more contemporary images of the Virgin. See [26]. For more on the later development of this symbolism to current Santa Muerte iconography, see [25].

[18] Email exchange with Robinson Herrera, 28 March 2016.

[19] "En nombre del Dios Todopoderoso más poderoso, madre de las lágrimas, yo invoco tu ayuda, te pido para quitar la mala suerte de mi casa. Dame dinero, trabajo y buenasuerte.Madre de las lágrimas, protégeme del peligro, protégeme de todo mal, madre delas lágrimas, clamo a ti en este abismo donde me encuentro y te pido que me protegede toda afflición y el mal. Consagrarme a ti en este día y poner mi petición a tus pies(estado su petición) Amén." [27].

first prays to All Powerful God for placing Santa Muerte in her path, and then shifts audiences to Saint Death, requesting forgiveness, patience, protection, and guidance.

> All Powerful God, I give thanks to you for putting Saint Death in my path. Holy Mother of mine, I give thanks to you for your help that delivers me and for giving those of us who are lost, your love, I beg you not to leave me, to watch over my path and over all of my family and over all that I love and care for. Mother of mine, please forgive me if occasionally, I am confused, have doubts, or do not trust [you]! It is not you, but [caused by] the people that surround me, forgive me if occasionally I do not trust in your great power. Teacher, I will attend to you when my enemy is near or when the sadness I feel becomes very great. Teacher, I will never forget that you exist, and that your presence is always with me in all ways and in all places, defend me from all things that want to harm me, Mother of mine, [and] I hope that even in my dreams I will be able to see you, and that no matter how hard it seems to see you, feel you, and hear you, I will never forget that you are nearer now and this gives me a happier life than the Creator that gave life. I give thanks to you, Mother of mine for watching over me and for all of mine, in the name of the Father, the Son, and the Holy Spirit. Amen.[20]

It is apparent in the end of the prayer, that when the petitioner says "I will never forget that you are nearer now and this gives me a happier life than the Creator that gave life," that the traditional hierarchy of Mary below God as Father, Son, and Holy Spirit, has been reversed, and Santa Muerte may, in fact, be more powerful. What is invoked in this prayer is Santa Muerte's role as mother, as creator and giver of life, the role traditionally given to Mary.

Similarly, just as Mary is viewed as the patron to the disenfranchised, and especially popular to women, Santa Muerte is also popular with the more marginal groups of Mexican society, and has been particularly noted in the news as a popular saint with undocumented immigrants, police workers, drug cartels, transgendered peoples, and the poor. What she seems to be most popular for in everyday life, however, is in preventing death, and repairing relationships—though her methods of doing this seem quite dissimilar from those of the Virgin Mary. Santa Muerte represents, in some ways, the anti-hero to the Virgin's hero—a saint who is known for getting the job done any way she can. She is known for wreaking vengeance and justice, and will kill, hurt, and destroy to keep her supplicants safe and happy. Hence, her reputation as a somewhat dangerous saint. Promises made to Santa Muerte must be kept, and altars to her likeness need be replenished, cleaned, and regularly maintained, or else she is known to wreak havoc. Offerings at her altar are quotidian and common: e.g., the everyday vices of tobacco and alcohol, and the popular foods and sodas consumed by the working class.

> Offerings at her altars, as well as her nicknames and wardrobe, reveal a saint that is cosmically Mexican. In other words, adherents view her as in some ways a supernatural version of themselves. Tequila, beer, cigarettes, and chocolate are placed at her altars in the belief that the White Girl likes consuming the same food, drink, and smokes that devotees enjoy. And like her adoring followers, she occasionally drinks to excess. In Morelia cult leader Vicente Pérez Ramos claimed that his skeleton saint likes to "get hammered," sometimes drinking her favorite brand of tequila, Rancho Viejo ([25], p. 56).

---

20 "Dios Todopoderoso, te agradezco haber puesto en mi camino a mi Santísima Muerte. Santísima Madre Mía, te agradezco toda tu ayuda que me brindas y nos das a todos los que te lo pedimos con amor, te pido que no te apartes de mí, cuida de mi camino y el de toda mi familia y el de todos los seres que amo y quiero. Madre mía, perdóname si algunas veces me desespero, dudo o desconfío, ! No de ti¡ sino de las personas que me rodean, perdóname si alguna vez desconfío de tu gran poder. Maestra, a ti acudiré cuando mi enemigo este cerca o cuando el dolor que siento sea muy grande. Maestra, nunca olvides que existo, has que tu presencia siempre este conmigo en todas partes y en todo lugar, defiéndeme de todos aquellos que quieran hacerme daño. Madre mía, concédeme que aunque sea en sueños yo te vea y nunca olvidare que lo que yo creía tan lejano como es el verte, tenerte y escucharte, ahora esta tan cerca y eso me hace el mortal mas feliz que el Creador le hay dado vida. Gracias te doy, Madre mía por cuidar de mi camino y el de todos los míos, en el nombre Padre, del Hijo y del Espíritu Santo. Amen." [28].

This is another area where Mary and Santa Muerte both intersect and diverge; while Mary drank wine, and was both present and encouraging in Jesus' first miracle of the transformation of water into wine, it is not wine that Santa Muerte prefers. She favors alcohol that symbolizes ethnic and cultural Mexican identity—tequila, made from Mexican agave, locally produced, and popularly consumed, along with beer, is the drink of choice among Santa Muerte followers, and the drink of choice among the middle and lower classes. Chesnut argues, "A glass of chardonnay or cabernet sauvignon at the altar of Santa Muerte would seem like an overly effete offering for this rather earthy saint" ([25], pp. 72–74). It is no accident that the drink of choice for Santa Muerte is not the wine of the upper classes, but the everyday beverages of the working class. In Santa Muerte, and the altars devoted to her, alcohol and gender combine to form a religious response to restrictive and normative everyday values, through the worship of embodied death. The alcohol is not the church-sanctioned wine of communion or the vintage of the upper classes, but the alcohol most symbolic of both Mexican identity and the working class. The motherhood figure found in Santa Muerte is the opposite of the Virgin Mary, patiently and kindly suffering and waiting for her reward. Santa Muerte, as motherly icon, is fiercely protective of her children and has no problem seeking vengeance and retribution for her children if they have been wronged. I would argue, though, that Santa Muerte is not a reaction against the church, per se, but rather an internal critique against the church's (and symbolically, the Virgin Mary's) passiveness in the face of corruption, elitism, and patriarchy. Women and alcohol in rituals concerning Santa Muerte combine in a way that is not dissimilar to the story of Mary at the wedding feast—just as Mary invokes the beginning of the ministry of Jesus through the transformation of water into wine, Santa Muerte responds to the suffering of her followers through the offering of alcohol, demanding protection for those that the contemporary world seem content to ignore. Mary, traditionally viewed as the passive virgin female, is the one who initiates action, and works balance into a socially fragile and risky situation. She restores and protects those in socially exposed situations. The parable of turning the water into wine demonstrates an internal double of Mary that comes to the surface in comparison with the contemporary Santa Muerte.[21]

4.2. China

The intersection of motherhood and alcohol is similarly found in Chinese death rituals, particularly in the blood bowl ritual. In China, because kinship lineages are traced through patrilineal bloodlines, a woman was traditionally not given her place in the family ancestral tablet unless she had given birth to children, securing her place not only in her husband's family, but in the afterlife as well [31]. However, though she may have earned her rights as a legitimate ancestor in the Chinese afterlife through giving birth to children, the polluting effects of childbirth remained, and the blood that polluted the earth from giving birth in life, needed to be ritually countermanded following death. The mother cannot be released from the "blood bowl hell" without ritual aid from the living, neatly tying the realms of the living to the realm of the dead through the mediating agent of alcohol.[22] The functional purpose of this ritual is to aid the deceased in their transition from earthly spirit to afterlife ancestor, while giving grieving children a ritual that, like praying the rosary for one's mother following her death, allows them to feel as though they are helping their mother in her transition. The blood bowl ritual simultaneously unites and unties the realms of the living and the dead, with alcohol serving as the mediating agent that reinforces and transforms the bonds between mother and child.

Maxine Miska, in her fieldwork in a Hakka village in contemporary China, describes the "blood bowl" ritual:

---

[21] Two additional sources that offer excellent and interesting insights into the development of Santa Muerte are [29,30].
[22] See [15,32] for an extended overview and analysis of the Tale of Mulian.

The ritual, as I saw it performed, involves setting up a small stool in the courtyard, under which sand is piled. Painted duck eggs and colored pennants are arranged in the sand. A bowl filled with wine is placed in the corner of the sand pile beneath the stool. This stool with its flags and sand represent a fortress guarded by demons of the underworld. Imprisoned within the fortress is the soul of the dead woman, wallowing in a pool of blood, represented by the bowl of wine. In order to secure her release, her descendants drink the bowl of wine, symbolically drinking the blood in the pool of hell. Once done, her soul is released from this torture, and her passage through the underworld to rebirth is expedited ([16], p. 90).

The ritual utilizes wine as a way to ensure that the deceased has been fully transformed into an ancestor, and can no longer come back as a spirit to harm the living.[23] Both Miska and Ahern assert the danger of mothers in the Chinese kinship system—women who are considered outsiders to the families they marry into—who are needed to extend kinship lineages, and yet through their relationships with their children, are also viewed as possible threats to the very family they are responsible for extending [16,34]. The tie, then, of the polluting effects of childbirth blood with the dangers of vengeful mothers seeking retribution on their families as spirits after death, is believed to be muted through the blood bowl ritual of drinking wine. The ritual both affirms and negates the relationship between mothers and their children—viewing these relationships as both dangerous and polluting—while also affirming the strong bonds and kinship ties between them.

Wine becomes the mediating and transformative agent—mediating through its link between life and death, spirit and ancestor, mother and child—and transformative through its ability not only to negate, but also to bridge and change. Wine is essential to transform the polluting effects of childbirth so they are no longer dangerous, and to transform the deceased mother from a spirit who can haunt the living into an ancestor who can help her relatives. It is wine that marks the change from child into adult—symbolized here in the shift from the mother who gave birth to the child to the dutiful child who now helps release the mother from the bonds of hell, and transforms the mother from earthly person to otherworldly ancestor, no longer bound by the bonds of their earthly existence. Alcohol shifts the marginal ghost mother into a legitimate ancestor, one that can now be brought within the official (state and familial) pantheon, no longer representing a possible danger or threat to society or person. Just as mothers are marginal in everyday Chinese society, so are ghosts to Chinese afterlife, and the blood bowl ritual allows for a way to routinize this danger. In the offerings to Santa Muerte, and in the wine drunk on behalf of ghosts, alcohol not only mediates, but transforms—in Mexico beyond the state religion, and in China, to bring the ghosts back into its confines. Now, I turn to American Southern Baptists and their temperance movement to demonstrate the ways in which the absence of alcohol also became not merely a source of identity, but also a form of branding, for Baptist women, and more specifically Baptist mothers.

5. The United States: Baptist Branding and Temperance

In contrast to both of the Mexican and Chinese practices, the absence of alcohol and Baptist branding through temperance, marks a decidedly different interpretation of gender, with Southern Baptist death rituals and funerals in spaces that have been publically declared alcohol-free. Baptists were not always publically against alcohol. In fact, in the 1700s, a Baptist minister named Elijah Craig invented bourbon, while another Baptist minister opened one of the first commercial bourbon distilleries in the United States, considered by many to be the quintessential Southern drink in the

---

23 The distinction is an important one in Chinese religion, and marked by ritual differences: Wolf writes, "Gods are contrasted with ghosts and ancestors; ghosts are contrasted with gods and ancestors; and ancestors are contrasted with gods and ghosts. For example gods are offered uncooked (or whole) food, ghosts and ancestors are offered cooked food [because they were at one time human]; ghosts are worshipped outside homes and temples; gods and ancestors are worshipped inside; ancestors are given an even number of incense sticks; ghosts and gods are given an odd number of sticks" ([33], p. 7).

United States [35]. About a hundred years later, however, in 1896, the Southern Baptist Convention denounced alcohol, declaring that anyone who sold and/or drank alcohol should be excommunicated from the Southern Baptist church.[24] The resolution prohibited fellowship to anyone who engaged in alcohol trade or who indulged in drinking, declaring that anyone who engaged in liquor "traffic" was engaged in a sin against God [36]. The public denunciations of alcohol demarcated clear expectations of both gender roles and social spaces—with women expected to participate in social roles defined by sanctity found in the alcohol-free space of the church and the home. The Southern Baptist female ideal is, and continues to be, framed by the notion that the ideal Christian woman is a homemaker, whose primary goal and identity is geared to the family. This gender aspiration has been confirmed by the 1987 Southern Baptist Convention resolution stating, "Full-time homemakers have shown dedication, diligence, and unwavering commitment to their families and to the Lord who has ordained the home as a workplace" [37]. The role of a "good" mother, according to Southern Baptists, is a woman who, as homemaker and moral guide, steers her family away from the consumption of alcohol. Six years earlier, in 1981, the Southern Baptist Convention tied the role of mother and alcohol together in a clear message stating that the two should not meet:

> WHEREAS, Families bear the responsibility for rearing healthy and loving children, providing creative life styles free from stress and all drug dependencies; and the family is the main target of the alcohol beverage industry with massive home advertising campaigns; and Family life is under increasing stress due to the use of alcohol in the home, resulting in more divorce, battered women, child abuse, birth defects; and Over 561 alcohol related deaths occur each day; ...and seven and a half million youth between the ages of fourteen and seventeen who have alcohol related problems; and Expectant mothers need to be aware of the dangers of consuming alcoholic beverages during pregnancy; ...Be it therefore RESOLVED, That we challenge families to consider what alcohol is doing to them, and to be aware of the uncritical way alcohol is accepted in society with little attention given to it as America's number one drug problem; and Be it further RESOLVED, That we educate the children in our churches to abstain from use of alcoholic beverages and the abuse of drugs; and...That Southern Baptists renew their commitment to minister compassionately to those who have drinking problems and to relate to their families in redemptive ways [38].

While the resolution placed the responsibility of abstinence on families, it is the effects of alcohol on children and mothers that are the central focus in this resolution, with alcohol posed as the problem for family structures and the breakdown of family in society. Long past prohibition, the resolution (this one was passed in 1981, though there are a total of 69 resolutions on alcohol alone from 1886 to 2006) is clear on its proscription on alcohol. In an interview with a local female Baptist pastor, who was raised in the Southern Baptist tradition, the attitudes regarding alcohol were confirmed. She told me, "I was raised that drinking alcohol is a sin. It was such a big deal. You never know if you are an alcoholic, so if you take just one sip, that could be the end of it."[25] Garret Peck confirms this attitude, quoting Tim Johnson, "in Baptist congregations that tend to encourage a detachment from mainstream values, the stigma is greater. This is generally true of congregations in poorer and more rural communities...The

---

[24] "That we, the members of the Southern Baptist Convention, reassert our truceless and uncompromising hostility to the manufacture, sale, importation and transportation, of alcoholic beverages in any and all their forms. We regard the policy of issuing government licenses for the purpose of carrying on the liquor traffic as a sin against God and a dishonor to our people. We furthermore announce it as our conviction that we should by all legitimate means oppose the liquor traffic in municipality, county, State, and nation. Furthermore, we announce it as the sense of this body that no person should be retained in the fellowship of a Baptist church who engages in the manufacture or sale of alcoholic liquors, either at wholesale or retail, who invests his money in the manufacture or sale of alcoholic liquors, or who rents his property to be used for distilleries, wholesale liquor houses, or saloons. Nor do we believe that any church should retain in its fellowship any member who drinks intoxicating liquors as a beverage, or visits saloons or drinking places for the purpose of such indulgence" [36].

[25] Interview with anonymous source, 24 March 2016.

Southern Baptist Convention equates alcohol with drug use and even calls alcohol a gateway to other drugs" ([39], p. 188). What is interesting, though, is that this banishing of alcohol has functioned to serve as a sort of branding for Southern Baptist Christian identity, but even more importantly, abstinence and its enforcement are carried out by women. This is particularly challenging, however, when the inconsistencies regarding alcohol consumption carried out in social contexts are generally performed by men. In one study carried out in a Southern Baptist church in Alabama, the author found that, "Of the fifty-four cases of 'excessive drinking,' 'too much drinking,' 'intoxication,' and 'whiskey-making,' all involved males and all but one were lodged against white males" ([40], p. 40). In this context, then, the consumption of alcohol in the home becomes a transgressive act that reinforces homo-social behavior, reasserting men's control over women. The banning of alcohol in public worship spaces relegates alcohol consumption to the domestic sphere, making private and/or hiding those behaviors regarding alcohol consumption, forcing women to turn to public methods (shaming) to regain the control they are expected to maintain over their domestic spaces.[26]

These suspicions of alcohol in the church act at odds with the role of alcohol in the Christian text of the first miracle, and subvert the notion of alcohol as a symbol of blood sacrifice, alcohol as material evidence of sacred miracles, or even alcohol as mediating agent through which Christ's ministry is first realized. The function of alcohol in Southern Baptist terms is a symbol of the world and its vices, not as symbol of God's potential to save through sacrifice and mystery. Unlike the text of Mary and the first miracle in which alcohol brings new life through motherhood and sacrifice, in Southern Baptist culture, alcohol serves to separate and segregate. Abstinence in the Southern Baptist context mediates Baptist identity through a counter-cultural response to society. Alcohol's banishment from both the church sanctuary and the home serves to replicate the banishment of the crucified Christ on the cross and the sacramental theology of the Eucharist. Just as the dead body of Christ does not hang on the cross and wine is not served in the Baptist sanctuary, death itself has disappeared from Southern Baptist churches. Instead, a cross, empty of the tortured body, hangs in the front of the sanctuary, and grape juice, devoid of its alcoholic content, is served to the monthly (or sometimes, yearly) congregants. Corresponding to the elimination of alcohol (and death) from the Baptist sanctuary, many Baptist publications and websites argue over the supposed "fact" that Jesus didn't actually transform water into wine but into grape juice, giving extended explanations of the difference between alcohol contents of ancient world wines and today.[27] In Southern Baptist Christianity, the emphasis is not on death, but the resurrection;[28] thus alcohol—that symbolic beverage mediating life and death, sacred and profane—is equally missing. Alcohol, symbolic blood, is not the transformative mediating agent that we see in Chinese religion and Mexican Catholic folk practices. The rejection of transubstantiation may be evident in social and cultural identity that extends beyond the church and family[29]. Both alcohol and temperance are used as a way to forge, cement, and create gender identity, constructing alternate discourses of belonging and exclusion both in afterlife conceptions, and everyday religious identity.

6. Conclusions

Offerings of tequila to Santa Muerte in Mexico serve to reinforce local and national identity, while challenging traditional discourses of state and church, providing supplicants with an alternate religiosity that utilizes established prayers and rituals and playing on the tensions between the two

---

[26] Pevey, Williams and Ellison confirm similar findings with their sociological study of women's bible classes. See [41].

[27] The alcohol content was reduced, but not negligent; this is evident not just in archeological explorations of sediment in wine jars, but also in the many writings of Paul, who argued that consumption of wine should be for the stomach (i.e., its antimicrobial properties), rather than its ability to induce an altered state. The wine in Jesus' time, then, was indeed alcoholic. For examples of the typical construction of the argument against Jesus' turning water into alcoholic wine, see [42] Boatman argues that, "The wine, or grape juice used in the New Testament by the Lord would be the same as us drinking sodas, tea, or Kool-Aid instead of water."

[28] Andrew Stern offers an excellent analysis of the symbolism of cross vs. crucifix in afterlife conceptions. See [43].

[29] See [44] for more on Baptist identity.

"mothers" of Mary and Santa Muerte. Santa Muerte offers a challenge to the more traditional role of the Virgin Mary as a suffering (i.e., passive) mother, while giving access to a feminist discourse of power that capitalizes on the dangers of death and violence. Wine from the blood bowl ritual in Chinese religions provides a link between this world and the afterlife, allowing for children and mothers to transform their relationships in such a way to safely shift spirits into ancestors. Access to the mother is granted through a symbolic reverse participation of childbirth itself, and the participation of the male child in "undoing" his own pollution, simultaneously binding mother and child and establishing the continuing importance of the mother's role, even in death. Mothers can haunt the living if they are forgotten. Finally, Southern Baptist temperance operates as a form of religious branding, distinguishing women from men as the guardians of family morality and church values in the home, while inverting the role of alcohol and banishing it from the religious landscape, both metaphorically and in practice. Even in the Southern Baptist example, it is through alcohol that women, and especially mothers, gain their power—not through the consumption or offering of alcohol, but through their denial and governance of alcohol. The marginality of both women and alcohol operate together in each of these three examples to offer an alternative economy—not of currency, but of power. Through the production, consumption, and even policing, of alcohol, women access alternate discourses of agency that capitalize on images of motherhood and death, inverting and/or challenging traditional, hierarchical, and patriarchal notions of life, morality, and afterlife.

Conflicts of Interest: The author declares no conflict of interest.

References

1. Paden, William E. *Interpreting the Sacred: Ways of Viewing Religion.* Boston: Beacon Press, 2003.
2. Smith, Jonathan Z. *To Take Place: Toward Theory in Ritual.* Chicago: University of Chicago Press, 1992.
3. Thompson, Stith. *Motif-Index of Folk-Literature: A Classification of Narrative Elements in Folktales, Ballads, Myths, Fables, Mediaeval Romances, Exempla, Fabliaux, Jest-Books and Local Legends.* Bloomington: Indiana University Press, 1960, vol. 4, p. A1427.
4. Liebmann, Alfred J. "History of distillation." *Journal of Chemical Education* 33 (1956): 166–73. [CrossRef]
5. Elvin, M. Jellinek. "The symbolism of drinking; a culture-historical approach." *Journal of Studies on Alcohol* 38 (1977): 852–66.
6. Douglas, Mary. *Constructive Drinking.* New York: Routledge, 2013, vol. 10.
7. Drinking Studies Network. "Members." Available online: https://drinkingstudies.wordpress.com/members-2/ (accessed on 16 April 2016).
8. Gefou-Madianou, Dimitra, ed. *Alcohol, Gender and Culture.* New York: Routledge, 2002.
9. Bennett, Judith M. *Ale, Beer, and Brewsters in England: Women's Work in a Changing World, 1300-1600.* Oxford: Oxford University Press, 1996.
10. Poelmans, Eline, and Johan F. M. Swinnen. "From monasteries to multinationals (and back): A historical review of the beer economy." *Journal of Wine Economics* 6 (2011): 196–216. [CrossRef]
11. Atkin, Thomas, Linda Nowak, and Rosanna Garcia. "Women wine consumers: Information search and retailing implications." *International Journal of Wine Business Research* 19 (2007): 327–39. [CrossRef]
12. Wood, Betty. *Women's Work, Men's Work: The Informal Slave Economies of Lowcountry Georgia.* Athens: University of Georgia Press, 1995.
13. Shen-Nong. "Traditional Chinese Medicine." Available online: http://www.shen-nong.com/eng/lifestyles/tcmrole_health_maintenance_habits.html (accessed on 7 July 2016).
14. Spirits of the Harvest. "Development History of Rice Wine Brewing Technology." Available online: http://www.spiritsoftheharvest.com/2014/03/chinese-alcohol-rice-wine-technology.html (accessed on 20 March 2016).
15. Cole, R. Alan. *Mothers and Sons in Chinese Buddhism.* Palo Alto: Stanford University Press, 1994.
16. Miska, Maxine. "Drinking the Blood of Childbirth: The Reincorporation of the Dead in Hakka Funeral Ritual." In *Bodylore.* Edited by Katharine Young. Knoxville: University of Tennessee Press, 1993, pp. 88–110.

17. Weller, Robert. *Unities and Diversities in Chinese Religion.* Seattle: University of Washington Press, 1987.
18. Nicholson, Henry B. "Religion in Pre-Hispanic Central Mexico." In *Handbook of Middle American Indians: Guide to Ethnohistorical Sources.* Edited by Robert Wauchope. Austin: University of Texas Press, 1976, vol. 10.
19. De Sahagun, Bernardino. *Florentine Codex: General History of the Things of New Spain. Book I: The Gods.* Translated by Arthur J. O. Anderson and Charles E. Dibble. Salt Lake City: University of Utah Press, 1950.
20. Hultkrantz, Ake. *The Religions of the American Indians.* Translated by Monica Setterwall. Berkeley: University of California Press, 1979.
21. Hellbom, Anna-Britta. *La Participation de las Mujeres Indias y Mestizas en el México Precortesiano y Postrevolucionario.* Stockholm: Ethnographical Museum, 1967.
22. Harrington, Patricia. "Mother of death, mother of rebirth: The Mexican Virgin of Guadalupe." *Journal of the American Academy of Religion* 56 (1988): 25–50. [CrossRef]
23. Viqueira Alban, Juan-Pedro. "La Illustracion y las fiestas religiosas populares en la Ciudad de Mexico (1730–1821)." *Cuilcuilco (Revista de la Escuela Nacional de Antropologia e Historia)*, July–December 1987, pp. 14–15.
24. Brandes, Stanley. "Sugar, colonialism, and death: On the origins of Mexico's Day of the Dead." *Comparative Studies in Society and History* 39 (1997): 270–99. [CrossRef]
25. Chesnut, R. Andrew. *Devoted to Death: Santa Muerte, the Skeleton Saint.* Oxford: Oxford University Press, 2011.
26. Granziera, Patrizia. "From Coatlicue to Guadalupe: The image of the great mother in Mexico." *Studies in World Christianity* 10 (2004): 250–73. [CrossRef]
27. La Santa Muerte. "Madre de Lagrimas." Available online: http://www.santamuerte.org/santamuerte/5733-madre-de-lagrimas.html (accessed on 24 March 2016). (Translation mine).
28. La Santa Muerte en Pueblo. "Oraciones." Available online: http://santamuerteenpuebla.galeon.com/oraciones.html (accessed on 25 March 2016). (Translation mine).
29. Roush, Laura. "Santa Muerte, Protection, and Desamparo: A View from a Mexico City Altar." *Latin American Research Review* 49 (2014): 129–48. [CrossRef]
30. Thompson, John. "Santísima Muerte: On the Origin and Development of a Mexican Occult Image." *Journal of the Southwest* 40 (1998): 405–36.
31. Sangren, P. Steven. "Myths, Gods and Family Relations." In *Unruly Gods: Divinity and Society in China.* Edited by Meir Shahar and Robert P. Weller. Honolulu: University of Hawaii Press, 1996, pp. 150–83.
32. Grant, Beata, and Wilt L. Idema. *Escape from Blood Pond Hell: The Tales of Mulian and Woman Huang.* Seattle: University of Washington Press, 2012.
33. Wolf, Arthur. "Gods, Ghosts and Ancestors." In *Religion and Ritual in Chinese Society.* Edited by Arthur Wolf. Palo Alto: Stanford University Press, 1974.
34. Ahern, Emily M. "The Power and Pollution of Women." In *Women in Chinese Society.* Edited by Margery Wolf, Roxane Witke and Emily Martin. Palo Alto: Stanford University Press, 1975, pp. 193–214.
35. Hailey, David J. "Beverage Alcohol and the Christian Faith." *Search* 22 (1992): 53–59.
36. Southern Baptist Convention. "Untitled." 1896. Available online: http://www.sbc.net/resolutions/46/untitled (accessed on 17 April 2016).
37. Southern Baptist Convention. "Resolution on Honor for Full-Time Homemakers." 1987. Available online: http://www.sbc.net/resolutions/533/resolution-on-honor-for-fulltime-homemakers (accessed on 1 April 2016).
38. Southern Baptist Convention. "Resolution on Alcohol Awareness." 1981. Available online: http://www.sbc.net/resolutions/90/resolution-on-alcohol-awareness (accessed on 1 April 2016).
39. Peck, Garrett. *The Prohibition Hangover: Alcohol in America from Demon Rum to Cult Cabernet.* New Brunswick: Rutgers University Press, 2009.
40. Flynt, Wayne. *Alabama Baptists: Southern Baptists in the Heart of Dixie.* Tuscaloosa: University of Alabama Press, 1998.
41. Pevey, Carolyn, Christine L. Williams, and Christopher G. Ellison. "Male God imagery and female submission: Lessons from a Southern Baptist ladies' Bible class." *Qualitative Sociology* 19 (1996): 173–93. [CrossRef]

42. Boatman, Dan. "The Bible and Alcohol." *Independent Baptist*, 2 July 2014. Available online: http://www.independentbaptist.com/2014/07/the-bible-and-alcohol/ (accessed on 16 April 2016).

43. Stern, Andrew Henry. *Southern Crucifix, Southern Cross: Catholic-Protestant Relations in the Old South.* Tuscaloosa: University of Alabama Press, 2012.

44. Leonard, Bill J. *Baptist Ways: A history.* King of Prussia: Judson Press, 2003.

religions

MDPI

Article

Messianic Time and Monetary Value[1]

Michael J. Thate

Center for the Study of Religion, Princeton University, 5 Ivy Lane, Princeton, NJ 08548, USA;
mthate@princeton.edu

Academic Editors: Douglas James Davies and Philip Goodchild
Received: 30 May 2016; Accepted: 9 August 2016; Published: 27 August 2016

Abstract: In this essay we return to Walter Benjamin's notion of messianic time as outlined in his _Theses on the Philosophy of History_. Messianic time is read with Benjamin's _Sonnette_ as a "divestment" from historical time. That is, messianic time is a relinquishing of historical time's formation of identities within late capitalism. Messianism represents that opening which whispers the possibility of bringing asymmetrical accumulation and subjective formation to a standstill. The aim of the essay is thus to push a rereading of Benjamin's notion of messianic time as subjective divestment from historical time which in turn breaks the uneven distribution of time, accumulation, and the monetary value of market time at work in our current world of global finance.

Keywords: Walter Benjamin; messianism; time; money; value

> We need to fetch back the time they have stolen from us.
>
> Milky Chance [1].

> Every line we succeed in publishing today—no matter how uncertain the future to which we entrust it—is a victory wrested from the powers of darkness.
>
> Walter Benjamin ([2], p. 262).

1. Introduction

In his recent volume, _Flashboys_, Michael Lewis narrates the complex ways in which our current moment within global finance capitalism in general, and the evolution of high-frequency trading (HFT) in particular, have compounded longstanding inequalities by refashioning both the time-value of money and the monetary value of time [3]. There are remarkable amounts of money to be made, for example, in trading futures in Chicago against the list prices of individual stocks in New York and New Jersey. Every day there are thousands of moments when price discrepancies between these geographies are leveraged by those with quicker access to both markets ([3] p. 8).[2] In this simple arbitrage between cash and futures, Larry Tabb suggests that "if a single Wall Street bank were to exploit the countless minuscule discrepancies in price between Thing A in Chicago and Thing A in New York, they'd make profits of $20 billion a year" ([3], p. 15). What is more, with the creation of dark pools [4], where private stock exchanges are run by big brokers who are not required to inform the public of what happens inside of them, a broker's traders might trade against their own customers in the pool ([3], p. 86). Though it may only take 100 milliseconds to blink your eyes, in a fraction of that blink, "vast market consequences" exist between those with and those without access to these

---

[1] Für Hind Lakhdar, die mich überzeugt hat, dass die Zeit tatsächlich angehalten werden kann.
[2] "In a paper published in February 2013, a team of researchers at the University of California, Berkeley, showed that the SIP price of Apple stock and the price seen by traders with faster channels of market information differed 55,000 times in a single day" ([3], pp. 98–99).

market milliseconds ([3], p. 49). If person B arrives even a millisecond after Person A, the market has vanished for the former ([3], p. 53). As one expert in the HFT business put it, "people are getting screwed because they can't imagine a microsecond" quoted in ([3], p. 52).

What is distinct about our moment within the sprawling enclosure of global finance capital is that the market is increasingly becoming a "pure abstraction" ([3], p. 52). Moreover, the U.S. American stock market, as Lewis suggests, is "now a class system, rooted in speed," differentiated between the haves and have-nots:

> The haves paid for nanoseconds; the have-nots had no idea that a nanosecond had value. The haves enjoyed a perfect view of the market; the have-nots *never saw the market at all*. What had once been the world's most public, most democratic, financial market had become, in spirit, something more like a private viewing of a stolen work of art ([3], p. 69).[3]

High-frequency traders make their money by digesting publicly available information faster than others; while their dark pools hide order information from the wider public ([3], p. 122).[4] By the summer of 2013, global financial markets evolved "to maximize the number of collisions between ordinary investors and high-frequency traders—at the expense of ordinary investors, and for the benefit of high-frequency traders, exchanges, Wall Street banks, and online brokerage firms" ([3], p. 179); cf. [5]). These trades happen at unsafe and unfair speeds, as well as hedged by shrouds of secrecy. The same system that sold us subprime mortgages which collateralized debt obligations few investors understood, has now fashioned a stock market that trades at fractions of a penny at the unsafe speeds of nanoseconds, that no investor can possibly understand ([3], p. 233).

This is just one instance—a very particular instance, to be sure—of the ways in which long-standing inequalities are becoming compounded in our current moment of global finance capitalism. It is not the intention of this essay to say anything specific about HFT, cf. [6], or the "unsafe speed" of the nanosecond at which markets move for a small group of hidden elites. Nor is the aim of this essay attempting to narrate the old tale of the growing monetary inequalities of our age. This essay's aim, rather, and its governing anxiety, relates to the distinct ways in which time itself has become classed (as well as gendered and racialized). The interest of this essay is in the distinct manners of temporal inequality released and compounded by global finance capitalism.[5] Sadly, though extreme, the example of HFT is hardly an aberration to what this essay will phrase the production of *unequal access to time*. It is the rule.

It is this anxiety that I hope to merge with the mounting interest in the so-called "return of religion" within Continental philosophy in general, and the turn to messianism and the rising attention paid to St Paul and time in particular. In lieu of a conclusion, at the end of this essay an attempt is made to appropriate this new legibility of the first-century Apostle within contemporary critical thought into a comparative analysis and critique of *time* and *value*. The majority of this essay, however, pays little attention to the texts of the Apostle. Instead, we return to one of his more enigmatic interpreters, viz., Walter Benjamin and the notion of messianic time outlined in his *Über den Begriff der Geschichte* ([8], vol. 1, pp. 691–704). Benjamin's notion of messianic time, however, will be read with his brief sketch, *Kapitalismus als Religion* ([8], vol. 7, pp. 101–3), as well as his *Sonnette*—which were, in a sense, programmatic reflections put to verse after the suicide of his close friend, Christoph Heinle. Read together, I suggest the messianic in Benjamin's thought as a longing for a *divestment* from historical time. It is the removal of oneself from sovereignty's accumulation, packaging, and trading off

---

3   Emphasis original.
4   Lewis gives the following example: "Say, for instance, that the market for P&G shares is $80–80.01, and buyers and sellers sit on both sides on all of the exchanges. A big seller comes in on the NYSE and knocks the price down to 79.98–79.99. High-frequency traders buy on NYSE at $79.99 and sell on all the other exchanges at $80, before the market officially changes. This happened all day, every day, and generated more billions of dollars a year than the other strategies combined" ([3], p. 172).
5   Here, cf. the discussion of scientific paradigms and the capitalistic framing of time [7].

of what I will refer to as the *vested self*—that form of life produced by capital's standardized meaning, value and relationality through precise renderings of space, time, and being. That is, messianic time is a relinquishing of the *self* from historical time, a disburdening from historical time's plasticity. Messianism is the possibility for an opening or rupture within sovereignty's enclosure, and threatens to bring sovereignty's asymmetrical accumulation to a standstill. The expectation and longing for messianic time is thus for a *divested existence*.

Divestment, of course, may connote several meanings within a corporate context and business strategy. Carolin Decker and Thomas Mellewigt have helpfully surveyed the diverse range of meanings and strategic methods, which have historically been classified as "divestment" [9]. In addition to surveying important literature on the topic of divestment, Decker and Mellewigt structure divestment strategies into two general types. The first, "status quo-preserving," is when a business unit's divestiture happens without any systemic change in the firm's prior strategic trajectory; the second, what they call a "strategic business exit," involves systemic reorientation [9]. It is this second sense of divestment that I appropriate here. Divestment carries with it the potential for triggering strategic reorientation ([9], p. 2; cf. [10]). Divestment is read as a kind of reorientation and removal of the self from the current operations within historical time. The aim of the essay is therefore to press a rereading of Benjamin's notion of messianic time *as divestment from historical time* which in turn breaks the uneven distribution of time, accumulation, and monetary value of market time at work in our current world of global finance in its packaging of forms of life. And it is this reading of Benjamin's messianic time which, I will suggest at the end, provides a political lens through which to reengage with St. Paul.

2. Time, Life and Walter Benjamin

In the summer of 1913, Walter Benjamin (1892–1940) returned to Freiberg after studying abroad in Berlin. While in Berlin, Benjamin read philosophy at Friedrich Wilhelm University, attending the lectures of, among others, the sociologist Georg Simmel (1858–1918). It is from this period where Benjamin's exposure to Simmel's thought, especially his essay on "The Metropolis and Mental Life," and his students, (e.g., Ernst Bloch, Georg Lukács, and Ludwig Marcuse), began to shape Benjamin's own developing views on social life and the so-called "problem of historical time."[6] The return to Freiburg was in some measure the result of a failure to secure reelection to the steering committee of the Berlin Independent Student's Association on which he had invested significant political energies, cf. ([8], vol. 3, pp. 75–90). Gustav Wyneken (1875–1964), whose radical pedagogy of awakening youth would considerably influence the early Benjamin ([12], pp. 24–28, 35–39), urged him to take leadership of the School Reform Unit upon his return to Freiburg. The group held its meetings on Tuesday evenings to discuss various readings and works of art, and was led by Philipp Keller at the time. It was during this period Benjamin formed an "intense intellectual friendship" with the young poet Christoph Friedrich Heinle (1894–1914), which would leave a distinct and lasting influence on Benjamin throughout his life ([12], p. 53). In particular, I want to suggest the influence of Heinle's death on Benjamin's developing articulation of the problem of historical time.

2.1. "Disburden Me from Time"

On the morning of 9 August 1914, Benjamin would awake to an express letter written in Heinle's hand, which read: "You will find us lying in the meeting house" ([13], vol. 2, p. 605). The ominous "us" referred to the self-abandoned bodies of Heinle and his partner, Rika Seligson—killed through inert gas asphyxiation. The significance of this event, and its effective force upon Benjamin's thought and life, rests in no small measure in the distinct manners in which the deaths were represented and interpreted. Local newspapers portrayed the event as a kind of show of tragic love and the follies of

---

6   The phrase itself comes from Simmel, though, of course, Benjamin expressed deep reservations toward Simmel's articulation of the problem, cf. ([11], pp. 14, 103–24).

youth. Benjamin and the social circle of the School Reform Unit, however, refused this explanation and interpreted the act as "the most somber of war protests" ([12], p. 70); a final act against their collective fears of conscription and internment.

The "shattering effect" of Heinle's suicide on Benjamin would manifest itself throughout his life and writing ([12], p. 70; cf. [14]). Benjamin would take charge of Heinle's poems and manuscripts and attempted, unsuccessfully, over the next several years to have them published. In addition, he penned a cycle of fifty sonnets, and added others through the years as a way to grieve the loss of Heinle—or, perhaps better, to give that loss signification. In his own writings, though cryptic, the corpse of Heinle factored in the opening pages of *One-Way Street* and *Berlin Childhood around 1900* [15,16]. He referred to his first literary-philosophical essay, "Two Poems by Friedrich Hölderlin," as a reflection in memory of his departed friend ([8], vol. 2, p. 921).[7] Though the text itself did not survive, Benjamin would repeatedly assert "that his most important work" up to 1922 was his editor's introduction to Heinle's writings and poetry which themselves proved a kind of foreground for Benjamin's own concerns ([12], p. 169). Moreover, the poems of Heinle became a significant social marker within Benjamin's circle of relationships. Those around Benjamin spoke of the cult-like veil he maintained around the poems, both in terms of their public reading and his guarding of the physical texts themselves ([18], p. 64). One's proximity to the poems revealed one's social standing with the aloof and guarded Benjamin. These points converge in Benjamin's own *Sonnette* and provide an important lens through which to view his complex notion of *time* articulated in the later *Über den Begriff der Geschichte*, and of course, the added dimensionality provided by *Kapitalismus als Religion*. Though presented in a form of mourning the death of Heinle,[8] the *Sonnette* carry in addition to this mourning a cipher through which to read Benjamin's anxieties over the political situation in which he felt entrapped.

Benjamin begins the *Sonnette* with an impassioned plea to be released from the burdens of time lived without his friend, Heinle. The register of time here carries a specific sense. The experiences of life since Heinle's suicide have been enclosed within a temporality of loss and ruin. The specificity of Heinle's death worked within Benjamin a wound inflicted in some general sense by the world—a "Bleeding openly from wounds inflicted by the world" (*Aus Wunden bluten die die Welt gegeißelt*) ([21], p. 103). The particularity of the loss of Heinle loosed a feeling of estrangement and alienation, and gave rise to Benjamin's expression for a desire to be *released* from time. Benjamin's philosophy of history and messianism were formed through his own personal sense of loss and despair, cf. ([22], p. 313). He was, in the elegant words of Wendy Brown, "the consummate theorist (poet) of political despair who mines a unique strain of hopefulness from the very same terrain" ([23], p. 143). The plea itself, "Disburden me of Time" (*Enthebe mich der Zeit*) ([21], p. 89), gestures toward the experimental aim of this essay in placing Benjamin's desire to be released or disburdened from time as a kind of lens through which to read his discussions of messianic time in the *Begriff*, written in the early months of 1940 leading up to his own suicide. The suggested re-reading of Benjamin's desire to be "disburdened" from time—this is Skoggard's translation of the verb *entheben*—is near the desire for a messianic liberation from historical time (*Befreiung*) itself, or, as I wish to call it, the desire to be *divested* from historical time's accumulating powers and their effective temporal inequalities. This will be the notion of messianic time put forward in this essay.

2.2. "La situation" [...] and Its Ending

Benjamin begins his last major work, *Über den Begriff der Geschichte*, with the evocative story of a puppet, a dwarf, and a game of chess. The story is well known and has factored significantly in the

---

[7]   Here, see the important reflections of Peter Fenves ([11], pp. 21–24). Heinle also figured in important ways in Benjamin's
      later work on Colour—cf. ([11], pp. 67, 290, n. 2). On the poems themselves, see Beatrice Hanssen [17].
[8]   On stylized form and politics, see Jill S. Kuhnheim [19]. See, too, the interesting study of Susan Blood [20].

work of Žižek, Agamben and others ([24], esp. pp. 3–10; [25], p. 145). The story itself does not need to be recounted here, but the question we might pose to the "philosophical counterpart" (*ein Gegenstück in der Philosophie*; ([8], vol. 1, Thesis §1) to the chess-playing automaton has to do with the identity of the *Schachspieler* on the other side of the board. Against whom is the game being played and what are the stakes? We will return to this below, but here I want to suggest that the opponent is in fact *historical time*, that *empty, homogenous time* of capital, and what is at stake is the idea of *progress* and its production of a *vested self*—that form-of-life which historical time packages, values, speculates and leverages, and then collects on the accrued interest or dumps and moves as loss.

Leading up to his penning of *Über den Begriff der Geschichte* in 1940, Benjamin increasingly concerned himself with the dire and inescapable nature of the present political situation in Germany ([12], p. 658). Though Benjamin demonstrated little interest in publishing the *Begriff* in its current form owing to his fear it would be misunderstood ([26], vol. 1, pp. 286–87), its ideas were circulated among confidants. In varying correspondence, he stated that the work itself was motivated by the "experience of his generation in the years leading up to Hitler's war" ([12], p. 659). In particular, the operative polemic within the work was pointed against a particular understanding of "progress" (*Fortschritt*) which troubled Benjamin, cf. ([8], vol. 1, Theses §8–10, 12 and 13), and the many historians and politicians who were swept along and seduced by its promise owing to their failure to "grasp the order of the day" ([12], p. 662).

This notion of progress is an important backdrop for understanding what Benjamin will call the messianic task or vocation (*Aufgabe*) called for in each moment. Posing as "an historical norm" (*eine historische Norm*), fascism sold the German people on its rule by calling for a state of emergency (*Ausnahmezustand*) "in the name of progress" (*im Namen des Fortschritts*), ([8], vol. 1, Thesis §8).[9] Politicians and historians who opposed fascism eventually nullified their position of critique not by some capitulation with the political doctrines of the *Führer*, but by their tacit operation within the logic of a state of emergency owing to their "stubborn faith in progress" (*sturer Fortschrittsglaube*). In order to stand against fascism, then, one must disentangle oneself from the snares and entrapments of this logic—this history—entirely. To stand against fascism, one must stand outside fascism's enclosure and posturing as an historical norm. Historical materialism, for Benjamin, *is that politics* which introduces a conception of history against "accustomed thinking" (*gewohntes Denken*). It is a history of, and indeed, a history against, "every complicity" (*jede Komplizität*), and a politics away from "servile integration" (*servile Einordnung*), ([8], vol. 1, Thesis §10).

As Benjamin would write these reflections on history and time in the *Begriff*, he would elsewhere write to Theodor Adorno of the utter uncertainty of what time remained for him personally ([32], p. 339). In an attempt to escape the reach of the Nazis, Benjamin fled to France. He held an entry visa for the USA, a transit visa for both Portugal and Spain, but lacked the necessary exit visa from France. At the time, half of France was occupied by the Nazis along with the collaborationist Vichy regime [33]. And against all hope for an alternative, at some point on the evening of 26 September 1940, Benjamin composed a note for Henry Gurland to send to Adorno.

> In a situation presenting no way out, I have no other choice but to make an end of it. It is in a small village in the Pyrenees, where no one knows me, that my life will come to a close. I ask you to transmit my thoughts to my friend Adorno and to explain to him the situation in which I find myself. There is not enough time remaining for me to write all the letters I would like to write ([34], p. 946).

> *Dans une situation sans issue, je n'ai d'autre choix que d'en finir. C'est dans un petit village dans les Pyrénées où personne ne me connaît que ma vie va s'achever. Je vous prie de transmettre mes*

---

[9] On this complex notion of *Ausnahmezustands*, cf., e.g., [27–31].

pensées à mon ami Adorno et de lui expliquer la situation où je me suis vu placé. Il ne me reste pas assez de temps pour écrire toutes ces lettres que j'eusse voulu écrire ([26], vol. 6, p. 483).

The cruel turn of fate was that those in Benjamin's company were allowed to cross the borders into Spain the following day while the corpse of their companion remained behind.

How should we interpret Benjamin's suicide? His suicide, as he argued with respect to Heinle's death, was an acting out against *la situation* and the totalizing threats of conscription and internment. But what more can be said? In addition to his *Sonnette* and reflections on Heinle's death, Benjamin's understanding of Baudelaire's writings on suicide provide potential insight [35].

In "On the Heroism of Modern Life," Baudelaire makes a distinction between modern and ancient suicides and the peculiarities of representation within each epoch. In Baudelaire's text, Benjamin sees an early theorization of modernist aesthetics. Baudelaire, argues Benjamin, saw within classical artistic representations of suicide, particularly those of Hercules, Cato, and Cleopatra, a preservation and perpetuation of their image. Suicide, as it was classically represented, "affirms the validity of an idealized image" while modern representations, mark "a radical transformation" ([36], p. 501). Suicide within modernity resists this idealized timelessness and instead appears as disruption. As opposed to classical representations of suicide, the modern does not act in order to confirm or establish continuity with or in one's person. Rather, suicide within modernity is an act of disruption which opens to an unpredictable other—a metamorphosis ([36], p. 501).

Baudelaire spoke of "modernism" living within the break of the "grand tradition" of the past and the yet-to-be of the new ([35], p. 104). And Benjamin situated the *élan* of the individual acting within modernity as itself a resistance to the *life* produced within this break—within the productions and representations of modernity.

> The resistance that modernity offers to the natural productive *élan* of an individual is out of all proportion to [their] strength. It is understandable if a person becomes exhausted and takes refuge in death. *Modernity must stand under the sign of suicide*, an act which seals a heroic will that makes no concessions to a mentality inimical toward this will. Such a suicide is not resignation but heroic passion. It is *the* achievement of modernity in the realm of the passions. In this form, as the *passion particulière de la vie moderne*, suicide appears in the classical passage devoted to [Baudelaire's] theory of the modern ([35], p. 104).

Modernity (die Moderne) here, I suggest, is near *la situation* mentioned in his final letter left for Gurland to pass along to Adorno, cf. ([36], p. 505, n. 5). Modernity is marked by its assimilation of life into forms of enclosure, and thus alienates life from life itself.[10] In this respect, suicide is symptomatic of the enclosure even as it is a reaction to it. Jared Stark is worth quoting at length here:

> [Suicide] becomes a symptom, a cry for help to which the only appropriate response is to seek to prevent suicide (politically, medically, etc.). Understood as a symptom, however, suicide appears fundamentally as a mistake, in that it cannot achieve its own aims, such that the effort to prevent suicide itself becomes complicit with modernity's victory over individual agency. Modernity is thus imagined as a totalizing force that leaves no space for resistance ([36], p. 501).

---

10 Simmel's is an important voice on alienation, and more needs to be done on this topic in relation to Benjamin. Two passages are worth quoting from Simmel's *Philosophy of Money*: "[...] the various elements of our existence are [...] placed in an all-embracing teleological nexus in which no element is either the first or the last. Furthermore, since money measures all objects with merciless objectivity, and since its standard of value so measured determines their relationship, a web of objective and personal aspects of life emerges which is similar to the natural cosmos with its continuous cohesion and strict causality. The web is held together by the all-pervasive money-value, just as nature is held together by energy that gives life to everything" ([37], p. 453). And: "Whenever our energies do not produce something whole as a reflection of the total personality, then the proper relationship between subject and object is missing" ([37], p. 454; cf. [38,39]).

No space (or time) for resistance, that is, within *la situation* or *die Moderne* and their mappings of space, time, and being. However, suicide carries with it the political potential to tear, disrupt, and act outside conscription.[11] The desire to be disburdened and divested from time is thus the messianic longing of dying to the totalizing force of historical time and its logic of "progress"—of dying to the enclosure's power of packaging the *self*.

2.3. Dying to Time

Evgeny Pavlov, in his comparative study on Benjamin and Osip Mandel'shtam, suggests that "the question of time" dominated the aesthetics and poetics of modernism ([41], p. 445). In particular, he reads Benjamin's complex assemblage of time and history through the lens of his Moscow diary [42], placing it into conversation with Stalinist metaphysics of history. The diary itself has been treated elsewhere and need not concern us [43–47]. Of relevance here, however, is Pavlov's discussion of the "frenetic rhythms of the Revolution" which attempted to work an end, or victory over time in a collective effort to *kill time* ([41], p. 449). Though writing of the French Revolution, Benjamin himself speaks of a revolutionary attack on time as well. What distinguishes the revolutionary classes "at the moment of their action" (*im Augenblick ihrer Aktion*), according to Benjamin, is a "consciousness" (*Bewußtsein*) of exploding the continuum of time, of history ([8], vol. 1, Thesis §15). But what is this *Aktion*? It cannot be redemption as such. Redemption (*Erlösung*) and its image of possibility are set by time and the experience of existence within time ([8], vol. 1, Thesis §2). Ideas of redemption can themselves be indexed.[12] Revolutionary action is instead the disruption of history's representation of time as continuum or a chain of events and the enclosing of selves into its actualizing force.

Benjamin explicates this attack upon historical time by turning to the French Revolution, which, he states in Thesis §14 of the *Begriff*, was an idealist revolution in that it blew apart (*heraussprengte*) a history which presented itself as a ([8], vol. 1). Recalling Thesis §9, history is not "a chain of events" (*eine Kette von Begebenheiten*) ([8], vol. 1). The turn to history becomes revolutionary at the point it is informed by the now-time (*Jetztzeit*) of the oppressed.[13] The *Jetzteit* is the activation of the past into new possibilities to tear through and open the norm of sovereignty's history [23] (p. 144). The signal of the Revolution's disruption of the continuum of history was its ability to "introduced a new calendar" (*führte einen neuen Kalender ein*) ([8], vol. 1, Thesis §14). For Benjamin, the beginning of a new calendar functions as a kind of "historical time-lapse camera" (*ein historischer Zeitraffer*) ([8], vol. 1, Thesis §14). The purpose of a time-lapse camera, according to Benjamin, is to reveal action within real time which is difficult to perceive during real time. Experiences of time within the calendar keep recurring (*wiederkehren*) as days of remembrance of that first day made holy or special ([8], vol. 1, Thesis §14). Benjamin makes the distinction between the calendar and the clock in their ability to "measure" or account for the (*zählen*) time. Calendars are "monuments of an historical consciousness" (*Monumente eines Geschichtsbewußtseins*) ([8], vol. 1, Thesis §14). In addition, the clock measures, standardizes, disciplines, and enforces this historical consciousness. To live within historical time is thus to live within an historical consciousness and measurement of that time.

Benjamin saw an enactment of this revolutionary consciousness in an incident that occurred on the first evening of the Revolution. Allegedly, simultaneously and independently throughout several places in Paris, the clocks in the high towers of the city were fired upon. This literal assault on time enacts for Benjamin an awakening of consciousness to the historical consciousness of the time. It is also a disruption and destruction of that time—*arrêter le jour* (stopping the day),[14] as Benjamin takes

---

[11] This, of course, is quite delicate. Worth considering is the argument made by Ghassan Hage [40].

[12] Here there are important comparisons to be made with Derrida and the indestructible nature of justice; see [48–50].

[13] This turn to history is always at risk in that it takes place "in an arena" (*in einer Arena*) of sovereignty. This is the paradox which is also perilous: even the revolutionary step toward the tradition of the oppressed takes place within the enclosure of sovereignty and at its commands, ([8], vol. 1, Thesis §9).

[14] On the ground-clearing efforts of "destructive character," see ([22], p. 332).

from the French revolutionary rhyme—even as it is a commemoration of that disruption with new calendars of the Revolution itself (cf. ([8], vol. 1, Thesis §15).[15] On 5 October 1793, e.g., the demands of revolutionaries like Maréchal, Gorsas, and Manuel, came to fruition in the adoption of the new republican calendar. The calendar was composed by Danton's secretary, Fabre d'Églantine, and the mathematician, Romme ([55], pp. 496,686; [56], pp. 405–9, 430; [57], pp. 19–22). Benjamin is not entirely explicit on what is intended in this recourse to the calendar of the Revolution. Jonathan Israel, for example, reads the republican calendar as an instance—perhaps even a coordination—of wider "de-Christianizing initiatives" affecting daily life ([55], p. 496). Charles Taylor has himself provided an account of modern life lived in what he calls a "purely secular time," and what he perceives to be "the felt inadequacies of modern anthropocentrism, and the need to recover contact with greater force" ([58], pp. 322–51, esp. 329, 342). To place Benjamin within this conversation—viz., the formation of the secular and its time, cf. [59–61]—is to stress that *la situation* and *die Moderne* fashion a particular form-of-life in which Benjamin himself felt trapped and limited. This form-of-life is an historical consciousness enclosed and enforced within a particular calendar-ized time. The promise of the Revolution, then, is less on the formation of a new calendar as it was on its undoing of the sovereign measurements of the *Ancien Régime* and the tear it opened within its temporal organizations.

As with Benjamin's interpretation of Heinle's suicide, then, his own cannot be reduced to the desperate actions of one who had lost all hope. The step outside of this form-of-life, this vested self, *through the destruction of life* was a political act, a disburdening of oneself from sovereignty's totalizing enclosure of consciousness through its measurements and standardizing of time. It was an embodied expression of *killing time*—that final departure from the time of capital's accumulating powers and logic of progress.

3. Time Is Money and Vice Versa

On 28 December 1926, Benjamin mentions in his *Moscow Diary* a conversation he had with the playwright Bernhard Reich (1894–1972), where Vladimir Lenin was quoted to the effect that "time is money" ([62], p. 47). The quote itself appears in a wider context about watchmakers and Benjamin's contention that Russians are not particularly worried about time. The entry, sadly, does not delve into any reflection on the relationship between time and money—or the sovereign disciplining of the clock. But what if he had cf. [63]? Here I suggest is a moment for a new legibility of Benjamin—and, in turn, a point of critical intervention into our spiraling political-economic situation of global-finance capitalism. The purpose of this section is to appropriate Benjamin's notion of messianic time into a broad picture of monetary value within so-called "late-capitalism." The relationship between time and money, of course, touches upon fundamental relationships in life regarding value, sovereignty, gender, race, age, class, and access.[16] In this section, the compounding nature of inequalities effected within these fundamental relationships will be situated through a reading of Benjamin's fragment, *Kapitalismus als Religion* (1921) ([8], vol. 6, pp. 100–3). In addition, at the end, we will turn to a consideration of the messianic disburdening or divestment from the rule of historical time. Capitalism structures time because, in the end, time is money.

3.1. Time, Value, and Money

Georg Simmel suggested that money transformed the modern world into one big arithmetical problem, cf. [65]. Life becomes "absorbed" and packaged by these processes of "evaluating, weighing, calculating and reducing the qualitative nature of values to quantitative ones." This absorption and packaging leads to what Simmel terms "a much greater precision in the comparison of various contents

---

[15] On the radical vision of the French Revolution's attempt to remake time itself, see [51–54].
[16] Money here is intended both in its specificity, and, as Viviana Zelizer has brilliantly demonstrated, in its diverse and informal range, cf. [64].

of life" ([37], p. 444). My argument here, in addition to Simmel's important claim, is that the social effects of these complex processes of valuation lead not only to precisely rendered comparisons of various *contents* of life, but their varying *forms* as well. In other words, Simmel's narrative of modernity's increased precision in measuring the contents of life reflects a sordid tale of asymmetric valuations of and access between *forms*-of-life.[17]

As Simmel states:

> The mathematical character of money imbues the relationship of the elements of life with a precision, a reliability in the determination of parity and disparity, an unambiguousness in and arrangements in the same way as the general use of pocket watches has brought about a similar effect in daily life. Like the determination of abstract value by money, the determination of abstract time by clocks provides a system for the most detailed and definite arrangements and measurements that imparts an otherwise unattainable transparency and calculability to the contents of life, at least as regards their practical management. The calculating intellectuality embodied in these forms may in its turn derive from them some of the energy through which intellectuality controls modern life ([37], pp. 445–46).

Simmel's comparison between money and the clock is significant. The clock, for Simmel, made possible the determination of an abstraction of time which could then be fashioned into a technology of practical management. In Max Weber's history of *The Protestant Ethic and the Spirit of Capitalism* (1930), time measurements factored within a divine economy so as to condemn wasted time as "the first and in principle the deadliest of sins," because, in such an economy, idleness equates to time's labors lost for the greater glory of God ([66], p. 104). The determinations of profitability may have themselves shifted from imaginaries of divine economy, but their measurements remain similar ([58], p. 542). Within modernity, the *practical management* of time reduced the laborer's *form*-of-life into contents and movable parts through schemes of factory organization and scientific management, cf. [67,68]. This economizing of time into efficient movements and measurements of labor split labor-time from time itself [69]. As evident in Simmel's critique of labor theories of value, e.g.,—where he argued that labor itself cannot be the common measure of value owing to the theory's faulty presupposition of unconditional interchangeability between varying forms of labor—we see in the comparison between money and the clock unequal access to both ([70], p. 344, cf. 342–46; [71], pp. 70–72, 128–32; [72]; [73], pp. 125–26).

Though not entirely new,[18] our current moment within capitalism has compounded longstanding inequalities into basic spatio-temporal orientations cf. [64,74–77]. The abstraction of time into the objective measures of the clock highlight these dynamic inequalities. Such inequalities manifest themselves, e.g., in growing disparities in the life expectancies among contemporary Americans. Recent studies have demonstrated that the top "one per cent" of American men live 14.6 years longer than the poorest one percent [78,79]. The mounting and compounding inequalities within our current experiences of capitalism capitulate time and money into access to longer life. The complex processes of this history is an important one to tell, but, to return to the clock, the focus of this section is on the more immediate manifestations of the inequalities of time.

In *Discretionary Time* [80], Robert Goodin and his research team propose "time" as an appropriate "currency of egalitarian justice" within current political theory ([80], p. 3). Time is an appropriate comparable currency, they suggest, owing to time being both inherently egalitarian (everyone lives within a twenty-four-hour day) and inherently scarce (no one has access to *more* than twenty-four hours per day) ([80], pp. 3–4). And yet, somehow, some appear to have more time than others. By "more

---

[17] Zelizer's project, among other things, is in many ways an attempt to "capture the rich new social hues" which emerge in a money economy missed by Simmel's otherwise brilliant analysis of money ([64], p. 201).

[18] That is to say, the long history of inequality contains many rhyming verses. There are, however, important distinctions to be made between on the differences between "modern" and "postmodern" conceptions of capitalism. On which, see the many important works of Celia Lury, Wendy Brown, David Graeber, Luc Boltanski, Ève Chiapello, and Jim Conley.

time" they mean fewer constraints and greater choice over the use of their time. What they term "temporal autonomy" is a matter of access to greater time efficiency and autonomy ([80], p. 4). In other words, access to and control over time is shaped by social inequalities ([81], p. 3). The temporal rendering of life into a schedule is "connected to the schedules of others, especially our employers, our coworkers, and our family members" ([81], p. 3). This is what Dan Clawson and Naomi Gerstel term in their important study, *Unequal Time*, the "web of time." One's access to the twenty-four hours of the day depends upon where one lives within the hierarchies of their social web of time ([81], pp. 14–15).

In order to demonstrate such inequalities within the "web of time," Clawson and Gerstel propose the following scenario: It is 5:00 a.m. and your child is severely ill. It also happens to be the morning of an important day at work. What is to be done? Or, more to the point, what *can* be done? What possibilities exist? The options available at that moment depend upon where one resides within the web of time. Clawson and Gerstel examined the healthcare industry, interviewing a male surgeon (earning $360K per year), a female nurse ($70K), a male firefighter/EMT ($47K), and a female certified nursing assistant ($16K). A child's illness could happen (and has happened) to any of these workers. This is what Clawson and Gerstel refer to as "normal unpredictability." They discovered, however, that the level of "control over unpredictability" was markedly different, "with class and gender organizing those difference" ([81], p. 3). This important study complements others which demonstrate the many steep divides operative within workweeks cf. [82]. For example, "the more-educated work more hours, and the less-educated are unable to get enough hours" ([81], p. 5). The workweek is differentiated by gender, too, cf. [83]: on average, men are working forty hours per week and women thirty-five, cf. ([84], p. 35; [85,86]).

It may be that twenty-four hours are equally available to individuals throughout the day in some theoretical sense, but the profitability of those hours, and their rates of efficiency and return, vary drastically depending upon where one lives within the web of time. For those on the margins of this temporal web, time is expensive, inefficient, and unproductive. For those at the center, time produces higher rates of return. The inequality of labor hours amongst race, gender, and class reflects nothing about levels of effort or energy or laziness—or whatever. They reflect compensation and return inequalities. It is not that highly-educated white males work *longer hours* as such, but that those hours *count* as *labor hours*, and are compensated higher. Their access to time is more efficient and productive.

This inequality of access to the profitability of time crumbles a long-standing motivational cliché: everyone does *not* have the same twenty-four hours in a day. Access to time is relative to where one resides within the social web of time. "The control of time is one of the most pervasive—and most unrecognized—issues in our society" ([81], p. 268; [87]). And *time is money*. However, not everyone's time is valued or compensated the same. In addition, not everyone has equal access to the time of the day. Racialized, gendered, and classed time reproduce monetary inequalities. Unequal time equals unequal money. Inequalities experienced within the web of time are thus compounded by the inverse of this truism as well: viz., *money is time* ([72], p. 269). With greater access to the profitability of time in terms of monetary value, such value produces an excess of time—which, in turn, produces excess capital. Goodin's important study is thus slightly misleading in its fundamental presuppositions on the scarcity and egalitarian nature of time. Not everyone has access to the exact same twenty-four hours per day. Depending upon where one resides within the web of time, some have access to *more* than twenty-four hours per day—and, of course, some have access to *less*.[19]

3.2. Trapped in an Elevator

In order to illustrate the inequalities of time the previous section has attempted to articulate, consider the following scenario. An elevator has broken down at Central Bank with two people

---

[19] There are other ways, of course, to understand time. The focus here, however, is on an economized conceptuality of time. I am grateful to Seline Reinhardt for pointing this out.

inside: a single mother and a high-ranking banking executive. The single mother is putting herself through night school on student loans that the Bank has issued—and which the high-ranking banking executive's team manages. The woman has had to take time off from her hourly job to come into the bank to show identification and sign paperwork that needs to be processed in order to apply for an additional loan. Her children need to be picked up from daycare within the hour or she has to pay late penalties. The banker is returning to his office after a strategic meeting with his investment team which handles student loans. In this theoretical stoppage of time, time-value is experienced quite differently between the man and the woman. The woman's loans are accruing interest, she is punched out from work so is not garnering a wage at her day job, she will be late to pick up her kids from daycare and will have to pay penalty fees. The banking executive, however, as a salaried employee, is not losing his salary while trapped in the elevator. His investment team is executing his strategic plan, his hired *au pair* is looking after the needs of his children, and, as more time passes, the interest on the principle of the woman's loan grows.

There are far more complexities in this scenario than can be examined here. In this theoretical stoppage of time, for example, the banking executive may himself be losing profits. Being trapped in an elevator prevents him from maximizing the profitability of his time. Any loss of profit, however, occurs from a position of excess. The woman, however, is experiencing a compounded sense of loss from a position of scarcity. In both cases, time is money. Though certainly not optimally, the banking executive's time is making money even while trapped in the elevator. For the woman, time in the elevator is costing money. This theoretical stoppage of time thus reveals fundamental inequalities in the experience of time, access to time, and the monetary returns from time.[20]

The time value of money produces a monetary value of time. In addition, the growing inequalities of capital compound social disparities of time. Though not without controversy, Thomas Piketty's important analysis of *Capital in the Twenty-First Century* thus acquires added significance. In capitalist countries, argues Piketty, the return of wealth (r) tends to exceed the rate of growth (g) of the economy. His equation r > g reflects how the share of national income workers receive as their compensation decreases while the share of income going to owners of wealth continues to rise [88]. This is the vicious wheel of compounded inequality with which we are faced in our current cultural moment within global finance capitalism: the rich are getting richer, yes, but the wealthy are also getting more (or greater access to) profitable time.

3.3. Messianic Divestments

The final text to consider in my rereading of Benjamin and time is his *Kapitalismus als Religion* (1921)—what Eiland and Jennings refer to as Benjamin's text of "romantic anticapitalism" ([12], p. 149; cf. pp. 291–92, 513). The timeliness of Benjamin's thought for our current moment within global finance capitalism—or its sudden legibility—is in his diverse explorations of what Peter Fenves, in his important study on Benjamin and the shape of time, phrases, "the tension between the nondirectionality of time and the unidirectionality of history" ([11], p. 3). The experience of the former *as directional* is owing to the construction of sovereignty's promise of progress—viz., history. Fenves suggests Benjamin's interventions divined time as "plastic" ([11], p. 4). In addition, the messianic vocation of the historical materialist is to work an awakening to history's production of consciousness—to reveal the permanent contestability of all historiography ([23], p. 155).

Before turning to *Kapitalismus als Religion*, Thesis §6 in his *Über den Begriff der Geschichte* is an important moment in the interpretation being put forward in this essay ([8], vol. 1). If history, or the measurements and standardizations of time, is viewed as vesting interest for those in power, the articulation of the past occurs through a "moment of danger" (*Augenblick einer Gefahr*) ([8], vol. 1,

---

[20] This, of course, is the point Benjamin himself stresses when he states that only through time's momentary suspensions can one begin to see its vacillating structure, see ([41], pp. 450, 457).

Thesis §6). That moment is the persistent threat of becoming instrumentalized, made a "tool" (*Werkzeug*), for power's invested past; that is to say, for the value of one's existence to accrue worth for the gain of the "ruling class" (*herrschenden Klasse*) ([8], vol. 1, Thesis §6). Each "epoch" (*Epoche*) must "attempt," or "wrest" (*versuchen*), the "tradition" or "transmission" (*die Überlieferung*) of the past from this vesting ([8], vol. 1, Thesis §6). It is at this point where Benjamin introduces his notion of the messiah. The messiah is not merely a "redeemer" (*Erlöser*), but "the subduer of the antichrist" (*der Überwinder des Antichrist*) ([8], vol. 1, Thesis §6). Benjamin shifts the language from the Luther Bible of 1912, but the imagery of the one who "restrains" (*aufhalten*) from 2 Thessalonians 2:6–7 is present. The antichrist is the accumulator of worth from the existence of others as it precisely renders space, time, and being for others. The messianic need is long past the restraint of the antichrist. The antichrist is here and victorious. What is needed is a subduing of and disburdening (a divesting!) from this enemy (*Feind*). Remember from Thesis §3, "only a redeemed humanity receives the fullness of its past" ([8], vol. 1). And in Thesis §2, each *Geschlecht* is endowed with a weak messianic power. The historian is thus placed within a messianic economy of "fanning the spark of hope in the past" (*im Vergangenen den Funken der Hoffnung anzufachen*) away from its citable moments by, and the accrued interest of, the antichrist ([8], vol. 1).

In *Kapitalismus als Religion*, cf. [89], Benjamin suggests four features of the "religious structure" (*religiöse Struktur*) operative within capitalism that elicit these themes ([8], vol. 6, p. 100).[21] The first is that capitalism effects an enclosure, or sphere ([91], pp. 91–113; [92], pp. 128–41), in which all things find their meaning (*Bedeutung*) only in relation to the sphere. There is no meaning outside the cult. The cult of capitalism therefore produces standardized forms of meaning, value and relationality in its precise rendering of *space*. Secondly, Benjamin speaks of the permanence of the cult through its sacralizing of time. "There is no day that is not a feast day" (*keinen Tag, der nicht Festtag*) within the cult. Time is charged with the meaning-making of the enclosure, and, as such, all must rush to keep pace. The cult of capitalism thus produces standardized forms of meaning, value and relationality in its precise rendering of time. Third, Benjamin sees in the cult of capitalism a universalizing of *Verschulden/Schuld*. In this context, *Schuld* can signify "guilt" or "debt." According to Benjamin, the cult stands alone in its production of *Schuld* as opposed to the atonement schemes of other cults.[22] *Schuld* and not *Entsühnen* (absolving or atonement) becomes the operative dynamic within the cult. As such, the cult produces a rhythm, which hammers *Schuld* into an individual's consciousness (*dem Bewußtsein sie einzuhämmern*) ([8], vol. 6, p. 100).[23] It is through *Schuld*, then, that "identity" is minted, as the dynamics of personhood are assumed by—and then themselves assume—the logic of *Schuld*. The cult of capitalism thus produces standardized forms of meaning, value and relationality in its precise rendering of being. The fourth and final feature is in the cult's eclipse of "god." The hiding of god by the cult is not the death of the divine, but is its functional displacement or merging of the former into the latter. In the end, *debt becomes divinity*—*Schuld* becomes Sovereign. As Fredric Jameson phrases it, "we have come to think of capitalism [and no longer the divine!] as natural and eternal" ([94], p. 7). The precisely rendered valuations of space, time, and being by the divine have merged into and been acquired by the cult of capitalism. Its eternality and enclosing order have eclipsed what was formerly God's. Within this logic of *Schuld* and the totalizing enclosure of the cult—where standardized forms of meaning, value, and relationality are shaped through precise renderings of space, time, and being—there can be no working for reform in Benjamin's estimation. There can be only a "smashing"

---

[21] This religious structure is more fundamental for Benjamin than Weber's explication of the formation of capitalism as *conditioned by religion*. For Benjamin, *it is essentially religious*, cf. ([90], pp. 288–91).

[22] For a contemporary application of Benjamin's views on guilt and debt in relation to the Panama Paper's controversy, see Devin Singh [93].

[23] Benjamin continues that this universalizing and internalizing of "guilt" has even absorbed "God in the system of guilt," thereby rousing within the divine "an interest in the processes of atonement" ([8], vol. 6, p. 101). On rhythms and noises in Benjamin, see ([41], p. 453).

or "fragmentation" (*Zertrümmerung*), cf. ([11], pp. 125–51). The time for restraint is over. The antichrist is here.

At this juncture in the overall argument, it would help to consider Agamben's appropriation of the important work of Gustave Guillaume and his articulation of time and its representations. As Agamben summarizes Guillaume, "the human mind experiences time, but it does not possess the representation of it, and must, in representing it, take recourse to constructions of a spatial order." This latter construction is conceived of as *operational time*: the time the mind makes to realize a given time-image ([25], p. 65). In any stylized representation of time, however, time outside of these representations remains ([25], p. 67). Operational time, then, is the time needed to disburden oneself from and bring to a halt all representations of time. The *now time* (*ho nyn kairos*) of the messiah can therefore never fully live within the enclosure of a given historical or chronological moment ([25], p. 70). Messianic time is the tear and opening through which the sheer ungraspability of the *now* seizes time, and makes its end ([25], p. 100). What I want to call *the vested self*—capitalism's precise rendering of time, space and being—is given further valence in Benjamin's notion in Thesis §2 where he states that our "image of happiness" (*das Bild von Glück*) is affected by time and our experience of existence within time ([8], vol. 1). Time, for Benjamin, thus sets not only any understanding of happiness (*Vorstellung des Glücks*) but also where time is going—of redemption (*Erlösung*) ([8], vol. 1, Thesis §2). Benjamin's next move in Thesis §2 is complex. The past, he states, "carries with it a *temporal* [hidden] *index* by which it is referred to in redemption" (*Die Vergangenheit führt einen heimlichen Index mit, durch den sie auf die Erlösung verwiesen wird*) ([8], vol. 1). What exactly is *indexed*? If our conception of happiness is set by time, and happiness and redemption are linked, is not the very conception of redemption affected by time as well? How can one be redeemed if one's conception of redemption is assigned or given within the enclosure's representation of time? It is here where Benjamin inserts what he calls "a weak messianic power" (*eine schwache messianische Kraft*) which refers to past generations' expectation of *our coming* ([8], vol. 1, Thesis §2). And yet how should we think of this "expectation" (*Dann sind wir auf der Erde erwartet worden*) ([8], vol. 1, Thesis §2)? Would not even the conception of *expectation* itself be affected by time as well?

It is here, I suggest, that the expectation and longing for messianic time is for *divested existence*. Benjamin's weak messianic power is that longed-for experience of space, time and being (viz., *the vested self*) outside of completed philosophies of history and logics of "progress," cf. ([8], vol. 1, Thesis §4). The messianic rupture of time is thus its call for a divestment from the enclosure's historical citations and accumulation of, and trading on the space, time and being of others. As Benjamin elaborates in Thesis §5, the "past" (*Vergangenheit*) is not something to cite but to be seized by a present—the messianic now—which recognizes its concerns in an image of the past ([8], vol. 1).[24] And yet, he continues, the "true picture of the past *flits by*" (*Das wahre Bild der Vergangenheit huscht vorbei*) ([8], vol. 1, Thesis §5). True images are uncitable. The imagery of the past "flitting by" which Benjamin emphasizes in his text communicates a secretive escaping from one's creditors or obligations. The enclosure's citations of the past are always already invested. In addition, the historical materialist along with her messianic vocation works against this grain of universal history (*Universalgeschichte*) and citation, cf. ([8], vol. 1, Thesis §17) in order to awaken existence outside the logic of *Schuld* and progress, cf. [95]. Benjamin counters this approach with historical materialism's "constructive principle" (*konstruktives Prinzip*) of arresting thought, stopping it, and presenting it as "a constellation pregnant with tensions" (*in einer von Spannungen gesättigten Konstellation*; ([8], vol. 1, Thesis §17)).

The construction of such constellations introduces a "shock" (*Schock*). In addition, this shock "crystalizes" (*kristallisiert*) into a "monad" (*Monade*). Leibniz's *La Monadologie* (1714) is in view here [96]. For Leibniz, the monad was an *irreducible force* which makes possible the characteristics of the inertia

---

[24]   Cf. ([8], vol. 1, Thesis §5): "Nur als Bild, das auf Nimmerwiedersehen im Augenblick seiner Erkennbarkeit eben aufblitzt, ist die Vergangenheit festzuhalten. [...] Denn es ist ein unwiederbringliches Bild der Vergangenheit, das mit jeder Gegenwart zu verschwinden droht, die sich nicht als in ihm gemeint erkannte."

and impenetrability of bodies, and yet contains within itself the source of all its actions. They are the first principles of every *composed* thing. The historical materialist approaches each "historical subject" (*geschichtlichen Gegenstand*) *as a monad*. That is, each subject is viewed as a composed thing and yet within that composed thing contains the source of all its actions. It is within the structure of the monad, that one recognizes "the sign of a messianic cessation of happening,"—or, as Benjamin rephrases it, "a revolutionary chance in the fight for the oppressed past."[25] The structure of the monad is the result of a stoppage of time. In addition, this stoppage becomes a sign of the messianic which is a cessation and restraining of happenings. The messianic therefore brings about a stoppage of time wherein a chance arises for the oppressed past to emerge. Such a stoppage of time thus releases a revolutionary whisper for an existence outside of sovereignty's measurements and enclosures of historical time. The revolutionary gesture is that "tiger's leap into the past," which disinters "repressed emancipatory hopes and experiences from their tombs beneath the putative march of progress" ([23], p. 157).

4. The Pain of Becoming

In this essay I have proposed a reading of Benjamin's complex notion of *messianic time* as the revolutionary disburdening or divestment from historical time. By *divestment*, I mean a strategic reorientation away from capitalism's standardized meaning, value, and relationality and its precise rendering of space, time and being. It is the longing for divested existence—a life lived outside the *vested self*. In lieu of a conclusion, it is this reading I would like to lend toward the increased attention of messianism in recent years, which, I think, bears witness to its sudden legibility in providing vibrant suspensions to historical time's plasticity ([97], pp. 87–91, 155–61, 173–79, xvi). Moreover, the increased appearances of St. Paul, one of messianism's most active theorists, has become an interlocutor for contemporary thought with whom new ideas are finding expression and new forms of cultural contest mobilizing, cf. [98].

It is this Benjaminian rereading of the messianic as a longing for divested existence, I suggest, that might bring a new legibility to the apostle himself, and, by extension, fix a site for critical thought within our muddled moment of the sprawling enclosures of global finance capitalism. Agamben famously defined the messianic vocation as the *revocation of every vocation* ([25], p. 23), and wondered what it might mean to live *in the Messiah* ([25], p. 18). Agamben sees the "most rigorous definition of messianic life" explicated in the apostle's first letter to the Corinthians (esp. 1 Cor 7:29–32). In this text, the exchange between the *as not* and the *as if* produce the undoing of historical time and its citations through the formation of new communities of messianic longing ([25], pp. 35–39). But how can such formations and collectives emerge in our moment when even economic and environmental apocalyptic realities cannot shake the hold of capitalism's sprawl? Perhaps the fault of our moment rests in some measure with ourselves as critics. Are we, too, swept along by the logic of progress which troubled Benjamin in his own day? Can any critique get to the heart of capitalism's standardized forms of meaning, value and relationality that does not first question its purported state of emergency in the name of economic progress and prosperity? The need of the day is surely for monetary and temporal equality. But do our critiques themselves assume the logic of the forms-of-life produced by the enclosure of global finance capitalism?

Irving Wohlfarth surmises that if "Benjamin's generation was forced to recognize that 'capitalism will not die a natural death,' ours has had to learn the further lesson that capitalism is not, for the foreseeable future, going to die at all," quoted in ([23], p. 138). Within the traumatic temporalities fixed within late-capitalism, the end is no longer here nor is it arriving. The end itself has ended. In his elegant reading of Brecht's aesthetic and political vision, Fredric Jameson claims that what is needed in our moment is a Brechtian "embrace the pain of [...] Becoming, [of] passing away, in order

---

25 Cf. ([8], vol. 1, Thesis §17): "In dieser Struktur erkennt er das Zeichen einer messianischen Stillstellung des Geschehens, anders gesagt, einer revolutionären Chance im Kampfe für die unterdrückte Vergangenheit."

to reach our more satisfying human possibilities" ([94], p. 7). What Jameson sees in Brecht, we might well see in a post-Benjaminian reading of St. Paul, cf. [99]. "To live is Messiah; and to die to the [vested] self is gain" (Phil 1:21). Or elsewhere, "It is no longer "I"—the vested self, produced by capitalism's precise renderings of space, time, and being—who lives, but Messiah in me" (Gal 2:20). It is this messianic passing away, this killing of time, this disburdening from historical time's plasticity, which divests the self from historical time's accumulations and citations. The possibility for more satisfying alternatives rests outside the logic and promise of "progress," and packagings of the *vested self*. The pain of becoming therefore also includes the messianic pain of an *unbecoming*; a strategic reorientation of existence outside the sprawling enclosure ([23], p. 172).

Acknowledgments: I am grateful to Devin Singh, Nishant Pandey, Stanislava Vrabcheva, Ramina Sotoudeh, George Gonzalez, and Hind Lakhdar. Each provided timely readings and conversations at crucial moments in the life of this sprawling paper. I am also deeply grateful to the two anonymous reviewers.

Conflicts of Interest: The author declares no conflict of interest.

References

1. Milky Chance. "Stolen Dance." *Sadnecessary*. Lichtdicht Records, 2013. MP3.
2. Benjamin, Walter. *Briefwechsel 1933–1940: Walter Benjamin, Gershom Scholem*. Edited by Gershom Scholem. Frankfurt a.M.: Suhrkamp, 1985.
3. Lewis, Michael. *Flashboys: A Wall Street Revolt*. New York: W. W. Norton, 2014.
4. Patterson, Scott. *Dark PoolsHigh-Speed Traders, AI Bandits, and the Threat to the Global Financial System*. New York: Crown Business, 2012.
5. Arnuk, Sal, and Joseph Saluzzi. *Broken Markets: How High Frequency Trading and Predatory Practices on Wall Street are Destroying Investor Confidence and Your Portfolio*. Upper Saddle River: FT Press, 2012.
6. Fisher, Melissa S., and Greg Downey, eds. *Frontiers of Capital: Ethnographic Reflections on the New Economy*. Durham: Duke University Press, 2006.
7. Kwinter, Sanford. *Architectures of Time: Toward a Theory of the Event in Modernist Culture*. Cambridge: MIT Press, 2002.
8. Benjamin, Walter. *Walter Benjamin: Gesammelte Schriften*. Edited by Rolf Tiedemann and Hermann Schweppenhäuser. 7 vols. Frankfurt a.M.: Suhrkampf, 1974–91.
9. Decker, Carolin, and Thomas Mellewigt. "The Drivers and Implications of Business Divestiture—An Application and Extension of Prior Findings." Available online: http://edoc.hu-berlin.de/series/sfb-649-papers/2007-54/PDF/54.pdf (accessed on 23 August 2016).
10. Dranikoff, L. T. Koller, and A. Schneider. "Divestiture: Strategy's Missing Link." *Harvard Business Review* 80 (2002): 75–83.
11. Fenves, Peter. *The Messianic Reduction: Walter Benjamin and the Shape of Time*. Stanford: Stanford University Press, 2011.
12. Eiland, Howard, and Michael W. Jennings. *Walter Benjamin: A Critical Life*. Cambridge: Harvard University Press, 2014.
13. Benjamin, Walter. *Select Writings*. Edited by Michael W. Jennings. Cambridge: Harvard University Press, 1997–2003.
14. Nägele, Rainer. "Trembling Contours: Kierkegaard—Benjamin—Brecht." In *Walter Benjamin and History*. Edited by Andrew Benjamin. London: Continuum, 2005, pp. 102–17.
15. Benjamin, Walter. *One-Way Street*. Translated by Edmund Jephcott. Cambridge: Harvard University Press, 2016.
16. Benjamin, Walter. *Berlin Childhood around 1900*. Translated by Howard Eiland. Cambridge: Harvard University Press, 2006.
17. Hölderlin, Friedrich, Walter Benjamin, and Beatrice Hanssen. "'Dichtermut' and 'Blödigkeit': Two Poems by Hölderlin Interpreted by Walter Benjamin." *MLN* 112 (1997): 786–816.
18. Kraft, Werner. *Spiegelung der Jugend: Autobiographie*. Frankfurt a.M.: Suhrkampf, 1973.
19. Kuhnheim, Jill S. "The Politics of Form: Three Twentieth-Century Spanish American Poets and the Sonnet." *Hispanic Review* 76 (2008): 387–411. [CrossRef]

20. Blood, Susan. "The Sonnet as Snapshot: Seizing the Instant in Baudelaire's 'A une passante." *Nineteenth-Century French Studies* 36 (2008): 259–69. [CrossRef]
21. Benjamin, Walter. *Sonnets*. Translated by and with Commentary by Carl Skoggard. Portland: Publication Studio, 2014.
22. Jay, Martin. *Songs of Experience: Modern American and European Variations on a Universal Theme*. Berkeley: University of California Press, 2005.
23. Brown, Wendy. *Politics out of History*. Princeton: Princeton University Press, 2001.
24. Žižek, Slavoj. *The Puppet and the Dwarf: The Perverse Core of Christianity*. Cambridge: MIT Press, 2003.
25. Agamben, Giorgio. *The Time that Remains*. Translated by Patricia Dailey. Stanford: Stanford University Press, 2005.
26. Benjamin, Walter. *Gesammelte Briefe*. Edited by Christoph Gödde and Henri Lonitz. Frankfurt a.M.: Suhrkamp, 1995–2000.
27. Fossaluzza, Cristina, and Paolo Panizzo, eds. *Literatur des Ausnahmezustands (1914–1945)*. Würzburg: Königshausen & Neumann, 2015.
28. Voigt, Rüdiger, ed. *Ausnahmezustand: Carl Schmitts Lehre von der kommissarischen Diktatur*. Baden-Baden: Nomos, 2013.
29. Kermani, Navid. *Ausnahmezustand: Reisen in eine beunruhigte Welt*. München: C.H. Beck, 2015.
30. Wohlgemuth, Michael. "Die politische ökonomie des ausnahmezustands." *Wirtschaftsdienst* 89 (2009): 219–23.
31. Kaabi-Linke, Timo. "Technik im Ausnahmezustand: Wenn Dinge widerspenstig warden." *Zeitschrift fur Erziehungswissenschaft* 16 (2013): 267–85. [CrossRef]
32. Benjamin, Walter. *Briefwechsel 1938–1940: Theodor W. Adorno, Walter Benjamin*. Edited by Gershom Sholem. Frankfurt a.M.: Suhrkampf, 1994.
33. Payne, John. "'An Expensive Death': Walter Benjamin at Portbou." *European Judaism: A Journal for the New Europe* 40 (2007): 102–5. [CrossRef]
34. Benjamin, Walter. *The Arcades Project*. Translated by Howard Eiland, and Kevin McLaughlin. Cambridge: Harvard University Press, 1999.
35. Benjamin, Walter. *The Writer of Modern Life: Essays on Charles Baudelaire*. Translated by Michael Jennings. Cambridge: Harvard University Press, 2006.
36. Stark, Jared. "The Price of Authenticity: Modernism and Suicide in Baudelaire's 'La Corde'." *Modernism/modernity* 14 (2007): 499–506. [CrossRef]
37. Georg, Simmel. (1900) 1978. *The Philosophy of Money*. Translated by Tom Bottomore, and David Frisby. London: Routledge.
38. Capetillo-Ponce, Jorge. "Contrasting Simmel's and Marx's Ideas on Alienation." *Human Architecture: The Journal of the Sociology of Self-Knowledge* 3 (2004/2005): 117–21.
39. Beilharz, Peter. "Negation and Ambivalence: Marx, Simmel and Bolshevism on Money." *Thesis Eleven* 47 (1996): 21–32. [CrossRef]
40. Hage, Ghassan. "'Comes a Time We Are All Enthusiasm': Understanding Palestinian Suicide Bombers in Times of Exighophobia." *Public Culture* 15 (2003): 65–89. [CrossRef]
41. Pavlov, Evgeny. "Killing Time: Walter Benjamin, Osip Mandel'shtam and the Stalinist Metaphysics of History." *Russian Literature* LXIII (2008): 443–60. [CrossRef]
42. Benjamin, Walter. *Moscow Diary*. Edited by Gary Smith. Translated by Richard Sieburth. Cambridge: Harvard University Press, 1986.
43. Richter, Gerhard. "The Monstrosity of the Body in Walter Benjamin's 'Moscow Diary'." *Modern Language Studies* 25 (1995): 85–126. [CrossRef]
44. Vialon, Martin. "Zur Geschichte einer Freundschaft. Warum Walter Benjamins Moskau-Pläne scheiterten. Ein Epilog zum 100. Geburtstag von Asja Lacis und Walter Benjamin." *Zeitschrift für Germanistik* 3 (1993): 391–402.
45. Boym, Svetlana. "The Obscenity of Theory: Roland Bathes' 'Soirees de Paris' and Walter Benjamin's Moscow Diary." *Yale Journal of Criticism* 4 (1991): 105–28.
46. Djordjevic, Mira. "A German and a Croatian in Moscow: Walter Benjamin and Miroslav Krleza." *Literatur und Kritik* 305 (1996): 69–79.
47. Polsky, Stephanie. *Walter Benjamin's Transit: A Destructive Tour of Modernity*. Palo Alto: Academica Press, 2010.

48. Derrida, Jacques. "Force of Law: the 'Mystical Foundation of Authority'." *Cardozo Law Review* 11 (1989–90): 920–1045.

49. Derrida, Jacques. *Given Time: 1. Counterfeit Money*. Translated by Peggy Kamuf. Chicago: The University of Chicago Press, 1992.

50. Derrida, Jacques. *Specters of Marx: The State of the Debt, the Work of Mourning, and the New International*. Translated by Peggy Kamuf. New York: Routledge, 1994.

51. Shaw, Mathew. *Time and the French Revolution: The Republican Calendar, 1789–Year XIV*. Royal Historical Society. Woodbridge: The Boydell Press, 2011.

52. Perovic, Sanja. *The Calendar in Revolutionary France: Perceptions of Time in Literature, Culture, Politics*. Cambridge: Cambridge University Press, 2012.

53. Perovic, Sanja. "The French Republican Calendar: Time, History and the Revolutionary Event." *Journal for Eighteenth-Century Studies* 35 (2012): 1–16. [CrossRef]

54. Ciavatta, David. "The Event of Absolute Freedom: Hegel on the French Revolution and Its Calendar." *Philosophy & Social Criticism* 40 (2014): 577–605. [CrossRef]

55. Israel, Jonathan. *Revolutionary Ideas: An Intellectual History of the French Revolution from the Rights of Man to Robespierre*. Princeton: Princeton University Press, 2014.

56. Galante Garrone, Alessandro. *Gilbert Romme, storia di un rivoluzionario*. Torino: Einaudi, 1959.

57. Gross, Jean-Pierre. *Fair Shares for All: Jacobin Egalitarianism in Practice*. Cambridge: Cambridge University Press, 1997.

58. Taylor, Charles. *A Secular Age*. Cambridge: Harvard University Press, 2007.

59. Rosiek, Jan. "Apocalyptic and Secular Allegory: Or, How to Avoid Getting Excited—Walter Benjamin and Paul de Man." *Orbis Litterarum: International Review of Literary Studies* 48 (1993): 145–60. [CrossRef]

60. Nieraad, Jürgen. "Walter Benjamins Glück im Untergang: Zum Verhältnis von Messianischem und Profanem." *The German Quarterly* 63 (1990): 222–32. [CrossRef]

61. Newman, Jane O. "Enchantment in Times of War: Aby Warburg, Walter Benjamin, and the Secularization Thesis." *Representations* 105 (2009): 133–67. [CrossRef]

62. Benjamin, Walter. "Moscow Diary." *October* 35 (1985): 9–135. [CrossRef]

63. Kelman, David. "Introduction: Walter Benjamin in Latin America." *Discourse* 32 (2010): 3–15.

64. Zelizer, Vivian A. *The Social Meaning of Money*. New York: Basic Books, 1994.

65. Singh, Devin. "Speculating the Subject of Money: Georg Simmel on Human Value." *Religions* 7 (2016): article 80. Available online: http://www.mdpi.com/2077-1444/7/7/80 (accessed on 23 August 2016). [CrossRef]

66. Weber, Max. (1930) 2001. *The Protestant Ethic and the Spirit of Capitalism*. Translated by Talcott Parsons. London: Routledge.

67. Grachev, Mikhail. "Historic Horizons of Frederick Taylor's Scientific Management." *Journal of Management History* 19 (2013): 512–27. [CrossRef]

68. Lukács, Georg. "Reification and the Consciousness of the Proletariat." In *History and Class Consciousness: Studies in Marxist Dialectics*. Translated by Rodney Livingstone. Cambridge: MIT Press, 1971, pp. 83–222.

69. Löwy, Michael. "Capitalism as Religion: Walter Benjamin and Max Weber." *Historical Materialism* 17 (2009): 60–73. [CrossRef]

70. Dodd, Nigel. *The Social Life of Money*. Princeton: Princeton University Press, 2014.

71. Yuran, Noam. *What Money Wants: An Economy of Desire*. Stanford: Stanford University Press, 2014.

72. Kristjanson-Gural, David. "Money Is Time: The Monetary Expression of Value in Marx's Theory of Value." *Rethinking Marxism* 20 (2008): 257–72. [CrossRef]

73. Singh, Devin. "Irrational Exuberance: Hope, Expectation, and the Cool Market Logic." *Political Theology* 17 (2016): 120–36. [CrossRef]

74. Zelizer, Vivian A. *Economic Lives: How Culture Shapes the Economy*. Princeton: Princeton University Press, 2011.

75. Von Hagen, Jürgen, and Michael Welker, eds. *Money as God? The Monetization of the Market and its Impact on Religion, Politics, Law, and Ethics*. Cambridge: Cambridge University Press, 2014.

76. Amato, Massimo, Luigi Doria, and Luca Fantacci, eds. *Money and Calculation: Economic and Social Perspectives*. London: Palgrave MacMillan, 2010.

77. Patnaik, Prabhat. *The Value of Money*. New York: Columbia University Press, 2009.

78. Chetty, Raj, Michael Stepner, Sarah Abraham, Shelby Lin, Benjamin Scuderi, Nicholas Turner, Augustin Bergeron, and David Cutler. "The Association between Income and Life Expectancy in the United States, 2001–2014." *The Journal of American Medical Association* 315 (2016): 1750–66. Available online: http://jama.jamanetwork.com/article.aspx?articleid=2513561 (accessed on 23 August 2016). [CrossRef] [PubMed]

79. Specter, Michael. "Life-Expectancy Inequality Grows in America." *The New Yorker*, 16 April 2016. Available online: http://www.newyorker.com/news/daily-comment/life-expectancy-inequality-grows-in-america (accessed on 23 August 2016).

80. Goodin, Robert E., James Mahmud Rice, Antti Parpo, and Lina Eriksson. *Discretionary Time: A New Measure of Freedom*. Cambridge: Cambridge University Press, 2008.

81. Clawson, Dan, and Naomi Gerstel. *Unequal Time: Gender, Class, and Family in Employment Schedules*. New York: Russell Sage Foundation, 2014.

82. Weil, David. *The Fissured Workplace: Why Work Became So Bad for So Many People and What Can Be Done to Improve It*. Cambridge: Harvard University Press, 2014.

83. Folbre, Nancy. "Inequality and Time Use in the Household." In *The Oxford Handbook of Economic Inequality*. Edited by Brian Nolan, Wiemer Salverda and Timothy M. Smeed. Oxford: Oxford University Press, 2011, pp. 342–63.

84. Jacobs, Jerry A., and Kathleen Gerson. *The Time Divide: Work, Family, and Gender Inequality*. Cambridge: Harvard University Press, 2004.

85. Jacobs, Jerrry A., and Kathleen Gerson. "Who are the Overworked Americans? " *Review of Social Economy* 56 (1998): 443–60. [CrossRef]

86. Mishel, Lawrence. "Vast Majority of Wage Earners Are Working Harder, and for Not Much More: Trends in U.S. Work Hours and Wages over 1979–2007." Issue Brief 348. Washington: Economic Policy Institute, 2013.

87. Edgerton, David. "Time, Money, and History." *ISIS* 103 (2012): 316–27. [CrossRef] [PubMed]

88. Piketty, Thomas. *Capital in the Twenty-First Century*. Cambridge: Harvard University Press, 2014.

89. Hamacher, Werner, and Kirk Wetters. "Guilt History: Benjamin's Sketch 'Capitalism as Religion'." *Diacritics* 32 (2002): 81–106. [CrossRef]

90. Benjamin, Walter. (1921) 1996. *Selected Writings*. Translated by Rodney Livingstone. Cambridge: Harvard University Press.

91. Jacobs, Carol. *In the Language of Walter Benjamin*. Baltimore: Johns Hopkins University Press, 1999.

92. Jacobs, Carol. *Telling Time: Lévi-Strauss, Ford, Lessing, Benjamin, de Man, Wordsworth, Rilke*. Baltimore: Johns Hopkins University Press, 1993.

93. Singh, Devin. "Who Absolves the Priests? The Panama Papers, Transparency, and Confession." *Huffington Post*, 6 May 2016.

94. Jameson, Fredric. *Brecht and Method*. New York: Verso, 1999.

95. Benjamin, Andrew, ed. *Walter Benjamin and History*. London: Continuum, 2005.

96. Strickland, Lloyd. *Leibniz's Monadology: A New Translation and Guide*. Edinburgh: Edinburgh University Press, 2014.

97. Blanton, Ward. *A Materialism for the Masses: Saint Paul and the Philosophy of Undying Life*. New York: Columbia University Press, 2014.

98. Blanton, Ward. "Paul and the Philosophers: Return to a New Archive." In *Paul and the Philosophers*. Edited by Ward Blanton and Hent de Vries. New York: Fordham Press, 2013, pp. 1–40.

99. Welborn, Larry L. *Paul's Summons to Messianic Life: Political Theology and the Coming Awakening*. New York: Columbia University Press, 2015.

![religions logo] **religions**

Article

Speculating the Subject of Money: Georg Simmel on Human Value

Devin Singh

Department of Religion, Dartmouth College, Hanover, NH 03755, USA; devin.p.singh@dartmouth.edu;
Tel.: +1-603-646-3738

Academic Editors: Douglas James Davies and Michael J. Thate
Received: 17 April 2016; Accepted: 14 June 2016; Published: 23 June 2016

Abstract: This article initiates an inquiry into the sources and frameworks of value used to denote human subjects in modernity. In particular, I consider the conflation of monetary, legal, and theological registers employed to demarcate human worth. Drawing on Simmel's speculative genealogy of the money equivalent of human values, I consider the spectrum of ascriptions from specifically quantified to infinite human value. I suggest that predications of infinite human value require and imply quantified—and specifically monetary-economic—human value. Cost and worth, economically and legally defined, provide a foundation for subsequent eternal projections in a theological imaginary. This calls into question the interventionist potential of claims to infinite or unquantifiable human value as resistance to the contemporary financialization of human life and society.

Keywords: Simmel; Dodd; Foucault; money; value; financialization; secularization; theology

1. Introduction

The question of human value—its sources and justifications—and the practice of pricing human life remain a challenge to moral and theoretical discourse in the West. They also persist as sources of cognitive dissonance for social practice. Voices from across the political spectrum decry the bald or naked economization of human value. Even most defenders of free-market logic and rational choice shy away from full-throated claims for a straightforward pricing of human life. If anything, such must be done with utmost qualification and casuistry. Yet, such practices form the bedrock of economic policy and planning, actuarial and insurance practices, not to mention the wage system itself and its direct, monetary valuation of human labor. There is a widespread unease at quantifying human value, and recognition that it is implicated in practices like human slavery and trafficking, coupled with the awareness that our modern political and economic institutions would cease to function without it.

Inquiries into the broad swath of human history and civilization present a different picture, however, one wherein there appears a widespread practice of societies placing a monetary value on human life. One might even venture to say this is the norm. The question then becomes why, for a certain period in human history, this practice became construed as problematic, impossible, and even morally offensive. The deviation from the norm appears to be a conception of abstract, infinite, or otherwise *non-quantifiable* human value, a notion of worth conceived of often in *explicit resistance* to economic categories. This ideal is often the implicit substrate that is depicted as under "erosion" by the infiltration of money, pricing, and accounting measures into all areas of life. Even as this perspective continues to be marshaled in contemporary debates, greater understanding of its sources is necessary. In assessments of the "financialization of life", what tacit paradigms are operative, and what traces remain, serving as norms motivating critique [1–3]?

In the study of human societies, therefore, a central thread one needs to trace is the practice of determining human value in some relation to—whether conformity with or in contradistinction to—monetary economic categories. Seismic shifts of cultural proportion have apparently taken place in the broad transitions from archaic, to classical/medieval, to modern postures mediating money and human value. Such an evolution is not unlike the one Charles Taylor attempts to document in his massive *A Secular Age*. Taylor asks how the West transitioned from a cultural paradigm in which belief in God was presumed and taken for granted to a condition where belief is optional [4]. Similarly, I hope to identify some of the operative factors in the transition from an episteme wherein monetized human value was standard practice to one where infinite, abstract, and/or nonmonetary human worth is taken as an ethical and conceptual norm.

This comparison to Taylor is not arbitrary: the question of monetization and economic erosion of traditional social and "sacred" ties is bound up with debates about the nature of secularization. As we shall see, religious discourse, and theological and philosophical argumentation in particular, was centrally operative in the emergence of the new paradigm of abstract or infinite worth. Arguments marshaled against the financialization of life in early modernity are but the culmination of centuries of a new mode of thinking that eschewed the longstanding practice of evaluating human lives and bodies monetarily. The ongoing resistance to quantification in our contemporary moment is noteworthy because it continues to serve as an implicit ethical center amidst debates about the commodification of human life in modernity, even as many of its apparently theological supports have disappeared. To what extent do such "secular" paradigms of protest remain theologically informed or even derived?

One starting point for this inquiry is a progression explored by Georg Simmel in his study of money's effects on human society, culture, and self-understanding. He notes the transition from the widespread valuing of human life via money to the idea that such was anathema, some sort of affront to human dignity and worth. Following his gestural intuitions, I sketch three perspectival moments around the nature of human value in relation to money and economic categories more broadly: the archaic approach of directly quantifying human value through money, the transition to a phase of positing infinite human worth resistant to such calculations, and the move to our modern moment containing vestiges of claims to infinite worth with increasingly prominent practices of direct quantification.[1]

Genealogically, I am interested in how and in what ways each shift is not constituted as a clean break or radically new eruption of thought and practice, but contains traces and reconfigurations of previous frameworks.[2] In what ways do theologically and philosophically informed accounts of infinite, non-quantifiable human worth make use of an earlier monetized imaginary? How are monetary categories translated and sublated into philosophical claims about value? More troublingly, perhaps, have such normative invocations of infinite worth relied upon and perhaps conveyed the very economic categories against which they protest? Furthermore, in the shift to modernity, are we witnessing a "return of the repressed" monetary categories or—if we depart from "subtraction theories" of secularization—the emergence of a new synthesis and development? How does the secularization of theological notions of human worth (rightly contested as this narrative is) contribute to a new ensemble of values and techniques involved in current practices of the financialization of life?

This helps situate debates about the contemporary monetary valuation of human life amidst the mercurial sense that the "cash nexus" continues to transform relationships, desires, and loves. What notions of the self and subjective value undergird characterizations and critiques of such practices? Is it simply that such practices never "went away" despite a modern philosophical and theological overlay resistant to the idea of esteeming human worth through money? Can we speak of a return of archaic practices of the monetized value of human life? Or is what we now confront

---

[1] Obviously, such a typology itself needs massive qualification, since we cannot speak of an "archaic," "classical," or "modern" approach" in any thoroughgoing, monolithic, or enclosed sense. It functions for the time being as a heuristic.

[2] I take genealogy not as an attempt to trace linear lines of influence or discern pure "bloodlines" of conceptual relation, but to mark the shifts and permutations that contain echoes and redeployments of earlier categories in new contexts and toward new ends. On genealogy in this sense see [5,6].

something radically new? How have theological and philosophical discourses (those purportedly central to the formation of the self in the West) drawn upon and interacted with monetary economic concepts and practices?

In what follows, I review Simmel's basic presentation, hone in on specific elements in his genealogy, and set out several sites of investigation. My claim is that employing a monetary lens allows us to perceive one crucial link in the chain of permutations of human value in Western thought. Money—both as material technology and attendant conceptual category—offers a determinative scaffolding that is thoroughly engrained in our notions of value and worth. In reaction to, incorporation of, and efforts at distance from monetary economy and the power of price, practices of human valuation have transmuted this monetized scaffolding in various guises. Unearthing it is requisite for reckoning with its presence. What follows, then, are a set of speculative reflections as I move through several "stations" of potential inquiry. In limning such sites, I hope to chart a course for future investigation as part of the important emerging conversation around the confluence of religious and philosophical discourse with monetary economy.

2. Simmel's Genealogy

Georg Simmel's *The Philosophy of Money* is a multifaceted and sprawling work, covering matters of culture, psychology, religion, and philosophy in an attempt to provide a sociological account of money's effects on society and human consciousness [7].[3] Simmel's chapter, "The Money Equivalent of Personal Values," explores money's role in establishing benchmark valuations of human life. He sets out a broad trajectory of change from more bare and forthright monetary estimations of life and worth in archaic societies, to departures or even subversions of such economic logic brought about by developments in philosophical, theological, and ethical modes of thought.[4]

Simmel begins by observing that, in ancient societies, it was a commonplace to establish fixed valuations of human life based on monetary compensation for murder or accidental deaths. Simmel's sources are vague, but he appears to have in mind here various practices in the Ancient Near East, ancient Greek societies, and among Germanic tribes, grouped loosely under the category of *Wergild*.[5] This term denotes practices of quantifying insults and injuries and establishing terms of compensation. Its fundamental logic can be seen in the talionic reciprocity of Hammurabi's code, in the Solonic reforms and emergent legal traditions of Athens, as well as in the Torah. The term also encompasses prices for ransom of captives and reparations for loss of life. *Wergild* thus provides one conceptual starting point for thinking about estimations of human value. It was conceived of as a social good, as an intervention and stabilizing force used in part to avoid spiraling intra- or inter-communal violence in blood feuds.

Simmel begins with *Wergild* as a fundamental and widespread attribute of ancient societies, one that is "obviously purely utilitarian," but he does not explore factors in its emergence ([7], p. 359). The genesis of this concept is partly related to new conceptions in private property and possession, a transition from early subsistence to agrarian economies in the archaic period that marks a departure from modes of primitive accumulation. It also appears to index developments in abstract cognition, where a mediating third category is brought in to negotiate incommensurate goods or values. Whereas Hammurabi's code reflects identical, reciprocal exchange ("an eye for an eye"), employing a talionic principle that appears readily comprehensible, the notion of providing payment in money or in kind for an offense or injury is of a different order. In other words, arguably, it is an additional step

---

[3] The work did not receive significant attention initially, partly due to its resistance to disciplinary categorization. In Simmel's own telling words: "I know that I shall die without intellectual heirs, and that is as it should be. My legacy will be *like cash*, distributed to many heirs, each transforming his part into use according to his nature—a use which will no longer reveal its indebtedness to this heritage." Quoted in [8].

[4] Relevant studies of Simmel here include [9–11].

[5] See, e.g., [12,13]. Alternatively spelled *Wergeld*. Ingham notes the philological connection between "money (German *Geld*), indemnity or sacrifice (Old English *Geild*), tax (Gothic *Gild*) and, of course, guilt" ([13], p. 90).

in social and/or conceptual development to posit repayment or compensation for a wrong through the giving of an item not immediately related to the offense. What concepts and practices have to be in place to assert that, e.g., in cutting off your arm, I have removed something that *belongs* to you, and am now in your *debt*, and that, what is more, by *paying* you with these three bags of barley, which do not appear to have much to do with your lost arm, I *compensate* you for this loss?

Such forms of exchange might emerge in parallel with barter, itself coincident with new notions of private property, where non-identical goods are exchanged on the basis of some negotiated sense of qualitative and quantitative equivalence. And yet, as economic historians and anthropologist have persuasively argued, there is little evidence for the emergence of barter outside of a monetized imaginary [14,15]. In this case money represents that capacity for and token of the abstract "third" category that mediates these incommensurate goods. The implication, then, is that the cultural emergence of communal practices mediating non-identical compensation for injury or death is bound up with the invention of money and its uses in society.

Two key sites of inquiry for Simmel are slavery and bride price, both of which appear to establish monetary value for a whole human life. The slave's price, Simmel surmises, is linked to forecasted labor power. For female slaves, the price is modulated by labor power and "aesthetic" categories such as the slave's appearance. In the case of wives, price is fixed by tribal custom. Both cases represent an important advance from a presumably more primitive stage of acquiring slaves and wives via conquest and robbery. Not unrelated to *Wergild* type mediations to stave off violent retribution, monetary categories enter in to allow the transmission of humans among individuals and communities in a way that signifies some consensus (a type of agreement that, of course, significantly excludes those bought and sold).[6]

Beginning with this widespread practice of bald quantifications of the value of human life, limbs, organs, and status/honor (hence payments for insults), Simmel traces its transmutations into realms of law and justice, as well as in the emergence of an apparently novel idea of abstract and infinite human value. The primary archive we have of these practices of categorizing life through money appears in legal codes. *Wergild* is at once an economic and moral conception: as diverse communal proportions become standardized under some authority structure, codes of legalized recompense emerge. This moment of standardization marks an important juncture, where localized and individualized estimations of worth of a life, injury, or insult are detached from particular contexts and extended across a unified territory. This may be considered one step in the progression toward abstract value attributed to a human life.

These initial, generalized abstractions are radicalized, according to Simmel, in religion and in Christianity, in particular. From Christianity derives a notion of absolute human value: "Over and above all the details, relativities, particular forces and expressions of his empirical being stands 'man', as something unified and indivisible whose value cannot possibly be measured by any quantitative standard and cannot be compensated for merely by more or less of another value" ([7], p. 362). It remains unclear in Simmel's account whether Christianity (and preceding Judaic and Greco-Roman ethical codes upon which it draws) is a distinct paradigm operating in opposition to the monetary-economic, or whether it builds upon it. His description includes language of radical novelty and of synthesis and cultural development, from "lower" to "higher" and "more civilized"

---

[6] This opens up lines of inquiry into particularities of race, class, and gender in the fashioning of selfhood monetarily. While often missed by sweeping narratives of the self's development in Western thought, such factors are central to notions of identity in the West, so often oppositionally construed. Indeed, in what ways might the persistent monetization of slaves in modernity's colonial project be necessary for the types of universal (European) subjectivities being postulated ostensibly apart from economic categories? Such themes are explored variously in, e.g., [16,17]. Furthermore, how might bride price open onto questions of the exclusion of women in emerging theories of social contract, as explored in, e.g., [18]. In both cases monetization provides the double and a suppressed alterity that allows the fashioning of ideal subjects unencumbered by monetary-economic categories.

cultural forms, for which Christianity is a key symbol and driving force.[7] He certainly does not provide details of the mechanisms of this transition, but mentions in passing the role of ecclesial and legal authority, penance, language of grace and the infinite worth of the soul, as well as the construction of internal conscience and practices of self-policing. These elements require exploration for the ways monetary economy may or may not be operative. The next section explores several of these sites in relation to the question of law and equivalence.

3. Money, Law, Justice

One starting point for understanding the monetary evaluation of human life are legal codes and invocations of justice. Compensatory schemes appear foundational to correcting infractions of communal equilibrium, where balance must be restored.[8] Identical, reciprocal exchange is the fundamental logic. As noted, while the principle of reciprocity may still be operative, it is subject to additional layers of abstraction when incommensurate goods or monetary payments are brought in to correct imbalances or extinguish debts.

A critical stabilizing factor here, facilitating generalized abstraction of value, is sovereignty. The state (or other authority structure with the means of enforcement) establishes a fixed set of proportions, an authoritative accounting system that provides guidelines for compensation and in so doing enforces certain forms of valuation and terms of exchange. Simmel mentions this dynamic in passing, but I believe it is crucially important. Sovereignty is a central category for understanding the function of money, and by extension, is significant for grasping money's influence on subject formation and human valuation. The abstracting power of money, which Simmel recognizes and puts great stock in as a change agent in society, is neither a spontaneous nor intrinsic aspect of money. Or, better, it may be an intrinsic aspect of money, but only when money is properly understood in its function within legally and institutionally legitimated networks of exchange.

In other words, to invoke money is to invoke the state or other centralized, regulating, and enforcing authority that makes its circulation possible [13,22]. This is why money and law are co-implicated.[9] Not only does money lend its quantitative logic to legal categories of injury, compensation, and punishment, but legal frameworks legislate what may circulate as money, and what money's proportional relations are to other goods used as accounting bases. In considering the subject that is formed through the discipline of legal codes, we must also attend to the subject formed through monetary quantification.[10]

Punishment soon becomes conflated with legal codes that stipulate material compensation. To the utilitarian aims of providing quantitative restitution is added an institutionalized aim of inflicting pain on the transgressor. Simmel sees this conflation as partly owing to the intervention by sovereign authority:

> As long as or in so far as the consequences of an act of damage for the perpetrator are carried out by the victim himself, it will—apart from impulses of vengeance—be restricted to compensation of the victim. The victim is not interested in the personal situation of the criminal; his action is determined by utility and not by consideration for the person. This situation changes as soon as an objective power, such as the State or the Church, takes over the responsibility for the expiation of the crime. Because the damage to the victim is now no longer a personal event but rather a disturbance of public order or a violation of an ethical religious law, the condition of the criminal becomes the final purpose of the

---

[7] Simmel treats Christianity rather monolithically, and so genealogical work should ask *which* Christianities, if any, are operative in this transition. For Simmel on religion see [19]. For a treatment of the category of "religion" in general and the question of civilizational development, which notes in passing the significance of money for Axial Age religious paradigms, see [20].

[8] A classic study of the role of legal codes in maintaining social solidarity and equilibrium is [21].

[9] As Georg Friedrich Knapp, in his classic study of money, notes, "money is a creature of law." See [23].

[10] The Western "canon" often looks to the Greeks as one key site for the emergence of the Subject, where the human as such is taken as the measure of all things. This development should not be evaluated without attention to the revolutionary impact of money on Greek society and thought as explored in, e.g., [24,25].

action taken, whereas formerly his situation was only an indifferent accident for the person who sought compensation. Only here can we talk about punishment in the full sense of the word ... Money fines thus take on a totally different meaning from the former monetary compensation for wounding and killing. They are not supposed to compensate for the damage done, but to inflict pain upon the culprit ([7], p. 366).

This account troubles the dominant tale told about the origins and necessities of sovereignty. The fable posits the importance of an enforcing authority to regulate retaliation and prevent escalating communal violence. Sovereign power claims to prevent the "war of all against all" (Hobbes). In the case of money and law, the authority claims to provide a stabilizing standard (both in both monetary weights and measures and in legal codes) that prevents idiosyncratic reprisals or personalized reckoning systems of compensation. Yet, it is the distantiation and anonymity provided by sovereign mediation that transform compensatory schemes into punishments for offenses to sovereign authority itself. What was previously a utilitarian aim of compensating for loss now becomes construed as an offense to the honor of the governing power, and so must be punished accordingly. Sovereign power thus makes pain central, institutionalizing it.[11] Rather than simply making fines about economic repayment, sovereign power, with its "monopoly" on the means of violence, makes violence the means and ends of the punitive monetary circuit.[12]

Simmel explains, furthermore, why it is advantageous for sovereign power to reduce relations to monetary ones: this is the best way to extract obedience and manifest true obligation. The endless search for internal dispositions of subservience and postures of fealty can be mitigated, and successful service is rendered through extraction of monetary value:

The State cannot actually compel anybody to serve his military service, or to respect the life and property of others, or to testify, as long as the person is ready to accept the punishment for breaking the law. What the State can do in such circumstances is only to ensure that the guilty person accepts the punishment. Only with respect to one single category of the law is the enforcement of positive compliance possible, namely liability to taxation. The discharge of this duty can be enforced in the strict sense of the term—as can monetary private legal obligations—by removing the appropriate value from the liable person by force. Certainly it is true that this compulsion refers only to money payments and not even to economic services of any other kind. If someone is obliged to give a definite contribution in kind, he can never really be coerced into delivering it if he does not wish, under any circumstances, to produce it. However, something else that he owns can be taken away from him and transferred into money ([7], p. 401). [13]

---

[11] This is a central concern and object of criticism in [26]. Innes has been influential in credit and state theories of money, which maintain the centrality of the state in money's function. In this study he traces the gradual displacement of compensatory schemes by punitive ones as a result of state mediation of reparations. Both Simmel's and Innes's reflections should be brought into conversation with Foucault's study of modern disciplinary mechanisms and prisons. Relevant as well are Harcourt's reflections on the centrality of punishment to neoliberal forms of governance, explored in [27]. It may also be important to bring these dynamics into conversation with ideas of "the body in pain" as well as the place of "the flesh" in Western notions of the self. See, respectively, [28,29].

[12] Readers familiar with William Cavanaugh's revisionist genealogy of the modern nation state vis-à-vis religious violence may note the resonances here. Cavanaugh claims that the image of the state as stabilizing peacemaker in answer to the wars of religion is ideological. In what mays might this trade on a more longstanding dynamic of sovereignty invoked to bring the stability of monetary and economic equivalences through the veiled institutionalization of violence? See [30].

[13] This of course assumes that the one punished has resources to be converted into money. If not, obedience does not appear attainable in the way Simmel supposes. Such a person could be transferred to a debtor's prison or work program to provide the equivalent of value in labor to the state. But, following Simmel's logic, such a person could refuse to work, and would then simply need to be punished by the authority. This may be another insight into why the poor are deemed superfluous in society—not only failing to produce for the engines of capitalist industry, but being ultimately ungovernable by lacking monetary resources to extract. In actuality, it seems that the economy of pain and the offering of suffering are the most assured type of obligation that the state can extract.

Extracting money via compulsory taxation or fines is the one way in which sovereign power can enforce obedience. What is significant is that this authority structure encourages and facilitates a relationship mediated by money. Quantification allows for a better means of management and regulation, and the authority can garner better "returns" in obedience when couched in monetary obligation.[14]

Simmel's observation that money is a "claim upon society" here gains traction with implementation by the state.[15] The promise and deferral among the community that money facilitates are regulated and enforced in this case by sovereign authority. In this sense, then, while money has taken on various forms throughout history, and can be described in a variety of ways, a fundamental feature of monetary economy is regulation by some sovereign authority structure—be it chief, council, emperor, king, or state, for instance. This highlights the link between money and legal codes, whether formal or informal, as well as practices of recompense enforced by communal authority structures [13].

This characteristic of monetized sovereign power extends itself into the community. In extreme cases of tyranny, claims Simmel, a purely monetary relationship with the controlling center contributes to the breakdown of other communal bonds of solidarity:

> For the shrewd despot will always choose a form for his demands that grants to his subjects the greatest possible freedom in their purely individual relationships. The terrible tyrannies of the Italian Renaissance are, at the same time, the ideal breeding ground for the most unrestricted growth of the individual with his ideal and private interests ... [P]olitical despotism has been found to be accompanied by a licentious private libertinism. For its own benefit, despotism will restrict its demands to what is essential for it and will make its measure and kind endurable by granting the greatest possible freedom for everything else. The demand for money payments unites the two viewpoints in the most practical way possible ([7], p. 401).

The purely monetary relationship between the regulating authority and its subjects is dispersed among the community and comes to shape subjects themselves. In essence, subjects become mini-tyrants, free to exert their will and whim with minimal legal restriction. The moral liberty and proverbial licentiousness of the tyrant are reduplicated among the governed.[16] What is noteworthy here is the way in which sovereign power plays a role in the extension of monetary relations within a community. The supposedly "corrosive" power of money needs to be thought together with political power of this kind.[17] Furthermore, the ways in which subjects are formed through the discourses of law and under disciplinary mechanisms of governance has everything to do with money. Money, law, and subject formation appear co-implicated. Thinking about human value in terms of categories of justice, at least archaically, is therefore not so distant from monetary conceptions.

4. Abstract or Infinite Worth

As we have seen, abstract value is approached in part through the intervention of sovereignty, when value markers for human life are stabilized and standardized, divorcing them from individualized and localized forms of calculation. Yet, these standards are subject to the whims of sovereignty and are not yet transcendentally stabilized. Certainly, they do not yet rupture the calculative logic itself. Furthermore, while the notion of the great and exalted individual was present in antiquity, along with emerging notions of the status and dignity of humankind, there was no ancient conception of the

---

[14] The propensity toward more immanent and internalized forms of monetized governance is explored in [31].
[15] See Nigel Dodd's explanation of Simmel's view here in [32].
[16] On the links between excessive wealth and moral laxity in ancient reflection on tyranny, see, e.g., [33–35].
[17] It remains contested whether money actually corrodes cultural and relational ties or merely reconfigures them and in some cases creates tighter bonds of intimacy. Against the classic dirges by Nietzsche, Simmel, and Weber lamenting money's deleterious effects, Viviana Zelizer claims such readings are simplistic and that money simultaneous breaks and makes bonds and intimacies. See [36].

human being as such conceived of as infinitely valuable, claims Simmel. Christianity accomplishes this by bringing humanity into relation with God as the ground of worth:

> In that Christianity proclaimed the human soul to be the vehicle of God's grace, it became incommensurable with all worldly measures and has remained so. No matter how remote and alien this interpretation really is for actual human beings, its repercussions cannot be avoided where the whole person is at stake. His individual fate may be of no concern, but the absolute sum total cannot remain so ([7], p. 364).

For Simmel, Christianity implants in Western culture an idea of human worth exceeding any quantifiable categories. Simultaneously, money's increasing ubiquity serves to degrade its own prestige. The two notions of value move in opposite directions, with monetary calculation becoming more profane and estimations of human worth growing. This dynamic becomes visible in practices of penance. Simmel posits that Christianity contributes to an internalization of punishments through its particular mediation of an internal morality. Penance manifests as a type of self-punishment to atone for moral infractions. He also notes that money operates for a time as a satisfactory replacement for pain—one can either do penance or pay. This duplicates the parallel we saw between compensation through payment or through suffering seen in legal codes. Here it is mediated not by the sovereign state but by ecclesial authorities.

Yet, as money becomes more abundant and widespread it loses its sacral character and is no longer a satisfactory form of penance or payment for moral-spiritual infraction:

> That such payment was later considered to be totally insufficient and inappropriate penance testifies not against but in favour of the growing importance of money. It is precisely because money represents the value of incommensurable things and has become more colourless and indifferent that it cannot be used as an equivalent in very special and uncommon conditions where the innermost and most basic aspects of the person are concerned. This is not in spite of the fact that one can obtain almost anything for money, rather, it is precisely for this reason that money was no longer used to settle the moral-religious demands upon which religious penance rested [7].

Money's neutrality and ubiquity contrasted with the micro-level differentiations in the formation of conscience through penance and other disciplinary practices like confession. Each individual human was unique and infinitely valuable in a way that appeared to conflict with monetary evaluation. Recall that money is a critical means by which sovereignty extracts obligation, since it is unable, Simmel claims, ultimately to police internal postures and conscience. Yet, in ecclesial practice this internal posture is the *very site* of policing. Following Simmel's logic, this is also why monetary governance becomes less central in this spiritual economy. Diverse and unique logics of interiority diverge from the monolithic and generalized logic of money.

> The increasing valuation of the human soul with its uniqueness and individuality meets with the opposite trend in the development of money and in so doing accelerates and secures the abolition of penance as a fine. Money first attains the quality of cool indifference and complete abstractness in relation to all specific values to the extent that it becomes the equivalent of increasingly diverse objects. As long as the objects that may be acquired by money are limited in number, and as long as an essential part of economic values is excluded from being purchasable (as was the case, for example, with landed property over very long periods), money itself retains a more specific character and is not yet indifferent to either side. Under primitive circumstances, money may even possess the exact opposite quality of its real nature, namely sacred dignity, the quality of an exceptional value [7].

There are, no doubt, various reasons why Christianity facilitated a challenge to monetary notions of worth. Here we observe the convergence of monetary categories with a central technique of formation of the self. As the interiority of conscience is forged through disciplinary religious exercises, money is implicitly present as a category of thought and practice, lending itself to new structures of internal value judgment even as it is excluded from them. Money's increasing profanity provides a hedge around sacred practices of penance, helping to define their limits and purposes. [18]

At the same time, however, the soul's construal as infinitely valuable, because derived from the infinitely valuable creator, relies upon the quantification afforded by money, for it must distinguish itself from this widespread and accepted practice. We might even ask what meaning an infinitely valuable being has in a society that lacks the contrastive conceptual position of a quantifiable and hence finite conception of human worth. The quantifying power of money, as index of value, provides the implicit basis upon which ideas of infinite or non-quantifiable human worth can be constructed. Without opposition to the reductive ubiquity of money, these latter notions have little significance.

The problematic co-location of money and penitential practice also calls for a broader examination of the reconfigurations of law and ideas of the legal code itself within Christian discourse. The valuations of the law are precisely one site of contention: language of gospel and grace is counterposed to foregoing, culturally accepted, and economically-informed categories of judgment and justice. Yet, the language brought to bear against the law is certainly not non-economic. Identities are reconfigured ("neither Jew nor Greek", etc.) as the result of cosmic transactions and ascriptions of value ("you were bought with a price"). Grace has been "credited" to humanity's "account". Economy appears central in the Christian challenge to and reworking of the law within the language of salvation—or redemption. As humankind is given divine, infinite value, what becomes of the quantitative judgments of the law, since law has not been abolished but fulfilled? Since debt is an operative category of law (recompense and/or suffering is required because one "owes"), what does the Christian rhetorical play on debt language contribute to notions of the self, either as perpetually indebted or as one whose debts have been cancelled?[19]

Penance and related spiritual practices like indulgences certainly bring these economic and quantitative logics to light. I also suggest that there is much more of a link between so-called atonement theories than often granted, particularly when the monetary-economic dimension is considered.[20] Early ransom theories make economy most explicit, with talk of a payment made for the sake of captive humanity, which is often construed as in debt bondage to death or the devil. But Anselmian satisfaction theory works in quantitative categories as well, with language of amounts of honor, sacrifice, and obedience needed to placate the sovereign and compensate for offenses committed. Later penal and juridical theories associated with the Reformers, working with explicit frameworks of guilt, punishment, and exoneration, carry this archaic monetary logic forward.

Rather than three distinct theories of salvation, genealogical links might be uncovered that display an undergirding economic logic in Christian soteriology. When the relation of money and law is considered in light of the centrality of sovereign power, it becomes easy to see how God as redeemer/king/judge in these schemas operates as the one to whom compensation is due (and/or from whom payment comes). Whether or not it is humanity or God (in Christ) who fulfills such demands,

---

[18] It would be worthwhile to evaluate Luther's critique of indulgences in light of this phenomenon. Not merely a critique of works righteousness as conceptual problem, the challenge to indulgences may also be read as proclaiming the failure of money to compensate for and share equivalence with a spiritual economy. This would coincide with the more radical interiority projected by Luther's stress on individual faith and conversion, driving a sharper distinction between the economy of the soul and that of money. Suffering and penance are radicalized through the stress on anxiety, fear, and doubt that precede conversion.

[19] One would need to consider Nietzsche's genealogy of debt and guilt, as well as legal studies of the resonances between moral, legal, and economic debt, such as [37]. Relevant here too is how this legacy becomes translated into contemporary economies of debt and what this contributes to ideas of the human subject, as considered in, e.g., [15,38].

[20] Consider, e.g., Gustaf Aulén's classic study of soteriology and the various classifications and oppositional relationships he creates between theories. He hopes in part to undo the economic reciprocity he believes at work in Anselmian and Reformed soteriologies by retrieving the divine subject commandeering the salvation process as emphasized in some early ransom accounts. If anything, however, his study helps reveal the economic logic that ties all these theories together. See [39].

this does not disrupt the monetary economic logic at play. God may be portrayed as loving and gracious—attributes that many claim disrupt economic logic—but God's actions—as divine creditor and guarantor, for instance—are what appear determinative and foster a particular institutional and conceptual legacy.[21] Put differently, it is verbs not adjectives that make history.

Given the ongoing mutual influence and mirroring between church and state in Western development, what are we to make of money's role in the two economies of ecclesially-based conscience formation and policing, on one hand, and state-based techniques of body and population management, on the other? For it is in a modern biopolitical regime of governmental rationality that the two coincide, raising questions about the deployment of a money economy in regulating these practices in society.[22] Money appears to provide at least one crucial element in the axis that differentiates internal, sacred postures of soul and conscience from external management of bodies in the profane public sphere. It may be that the polarity facilitated by money, dividing internal and external ascriptions of value, is precisely why economy becomes the site of convergence in modernity of these two loci of governance.

5. The Self and Its Exchanges

In light of conscience formation as central to the interiority that we have come to take for granted in ideas of selfhood in the West, identity appears implicated in the monetization of human value. Many theories of identity claim that self-construction occurs partly (or fully) through relationships and via one's sense of commonality with and distinction from other subjects (who themselves are co-emerging). In a sense, various exchanges take place between oneself and another, even as these I-Thou poles are in formation [43,44]. To what degree can we see the impact of monetization on these relational exchanges, both in mirroring and transforming them? What theological dimensions are relevant for consideration here? Much work remains to be done to unearth these links. Simmel's intuitions provide one provocative route forward.

For Simmel, one path toward abstract and infinite value is made possible through ideas of humanity's relation to an infinite subject—God. The soul can then become "the vehicle of God's grace ... incommensurable with all worldly measures." Implied here is a notion of exchange in which the value of the divine subject is transferred to that of the human-in-relation. As Simmel puts it:

> For the first time in Western history, a real ultimate purpose for life was offered to the masses, an absolute value of existence, quite independent of all the details, fragments and contradictions of the empirical world: salvation of the soul and the kingdom of God. Now there was room in God's house for every soul, and every single one, the meanest and the lowest as well as the soul of the hero and the sage, because each was infinitely valuable by being the representative of its eternal salvation. Through their relationship to the one God, all significance, absoluteness and transcendency was reflected back upon them. The tremendous authoritative dictum that preached an eternal destiny and infinite significance of the soul suspended with one stroke all that was merely relative, all merely quantitative differences in worthiness ([7], p. 363).

The description here is ambiguous. While Simmel appears to conceive of the sources as "quite independent" of quantitative measures, there is a sense that this notion of absolute value depends upon such fragments if only to subsume and sublimate them. The result is a conception of value that either extrapolates from and exceeds or breaks with quantification. If it exceeds it, it can be said to make use of a more fundamental understanding of quantitative categories, generalizing them infinitely. If it

---

[21] The theological history of this economic logic is explored, idiosyncratically, in [40].
[22] Of course, in addition to Foucauldian reflections on biopolitics and governmentality (societal and administrative levels), it will be important to consider how ideas of the care and government of the self (micro-level practices) interact with monetary economic conceptions. See, respectively, [41,42].

breaks with quantification, the seeds of quantification remain in this oppositional construal, requiring the negation for the construction of quantification's other.

Augustine is one key figure to whom the search for theological sources of selfhood often turns. For Charles Taylor, Augustine posits God as the stable Subject and ground for a symbolic order, providing the scaffolding for interiority ([43], pp. 127–42). A fixed, absolute structure to reality is assured by God, and the self is called forth in part through striving to perceive and relate to this ground of ultimate reality. The fixity and stability of number (drawing on Pythagorean and Neoplatonic sentiments) provide evidence of consistent ordering in a rational universe that enables continuity for this emerging subject. An overarching, external, and independent framework is thus perceptible and provides a sense of foundation. The power of the number and of mathematical certainty index a Logos who makes extensions of one's identity across time (and, ultimately, into eternity) possible.

Such a fixed table of values in the universe, into which the soul is transposed and over which God is supreme, invites speculation as to its conceptual sources. In such a schema, God may either be conceived of on a continuum with such values, as their pinnacle and fruition, or be kept radically transcendent to and distinct from such a hierarchy. In either case, it appears that a notion of quantifiable value that can be categorized and ranked is required, whether to be superseded by an ultimate value, or oppositionally depicted against a transcendent value. In what ways are culturally fundamental, economically inflected categories of worth subtly at work?

Worthwhile to consider here as well is not only how Augustine construes human relationality to God but how he posits human relationships with one another in light of this overall framework. Within the hierarchy of values and concomitant loves/desires is the well-known distinction between *usus* and *fructus* [45]. All things are to be *used* in the pursuit of finding true *enjoyment* in God. Earthly loves cannot be the ultimate resting place of desire's gaze. The position of the neighbor here and the degree to which Augustine posits or indirectly contributes to a type of means-ends calculus is the subject of debate. Is (proto-)utilitarian logic at work? Is there a sense of mobilizing certain goods for the sake of profit, for the accumulation of greater, eternal goods? To what extent does such a framework—marshaled for the glory of God and good of humans, who will be most fulfilled when rightly oriented to this God—indirectly foster a legacy of instrumentalizing human life for the sake of an abstract goal or gain?

In light of Simmel's reflections, the legal subject, valued in part through quantifiable means, may be seen as reconfigured through Augustinian and broader Christian frameworks. In what sense is a more primary assumption of the monetary worth of human life assumed and subsumed into more abstract schemas? If monetary categories define relations among persons under situations regulated by sovereignty, this may provide a backdrop to an understanding of humanity as standing before its divine king and creditor. Release from the law through economy reinscribes both, seen now at once cosmically and in the space of radical interiority.

6. "Return" of the Pricing of Life

Simmel's speculative recounting here is, of course, completely up for contention. It serves as one provocative starting point for thinking about money, human value, and subject formation. Theorizing the shift from an early, culturally unproblematic (or, at least, uncontested) utilitarian calculus used to measure human value and administer justice to cosmic construals of infinite human value exploding all attempts at quantification might shed light on the points of contention today around these very issues. It may also provide a framework for constructive proposals to mediate these conflicting impulses.

For Simmel, money could serve as a regulative ideal useful in constructing an ideal template for social relations. This stemmed in part from the correlation between money, human value, and relationality that we have explored. As Nigel Dodd explains, Simmel proffered an idea of "perfect money" as a horizon of possibility that coordinated potential arrangements for humans in society ([46], cf. [47,48]). Simmel's concept of perfect money is a regulative, "Kantian" ideal that establishes perfect equilibrium of exchanges in society. Perfect money is not a reality, given the ebbs and flows in trust as well as knowledge that cause prices to fluctuate and introduce a distance between money as sign of value and the value of the commodity it represents. Dodd makes the link with Simmel's exploration of socialism, which signals a removal of the money sign from society, now unnecessary due to a more perfectly calibrated relation between goods and needs. Such a reality is most likely not achievable, but serves as a guide by which to orient social relations.

Noteworthy here is the tension Dodd identifies between what Simmel sees as money's abstracting and equalizing power coupled with the qualitative differences enjoined by socialism's emphasis on complimentarity:

> In PM [*Philosophy of Money*], Simmel associates ethical perfection with a form of *absolute* equality whereby individuals are treated as *identical*. Besides absolute equality, he also refers to *complete* equality, and *communistic* equality. The form of equality he associates with conceptual perfection in *Soziologie*, on the other hand, is *relative*, based on individual *difference*: "Society is a construct of unlike parts." ([46], p. 153; cf. [49]).

Here we see questions of price, abstract worth, and relationality come to a head in contrasting visions of society around competing bases of evaluation. The abstract equivalence afforded by money does have an egalitarian function, reducing all individuals to a sameness and flatness. And yet, the equality promoted by a socialist vision, at least in Simmel's estimation, emphasizes the unique contribution of each part to the whole, thriving on difference and diversity. Simmel's critique of Soviet forms of state socialism was precisely their failure to realize this vision by instead instituting a bureaucratized and reductive quantification that obliterated difference.

Almost paradoxically, achieving ideal socialist qualitative relations requires the perfection of money, where money so purely and precisely coordinates the value of commodities in exchange that it drops out of the equation. In other words, a social arrangement without money is one that allows valuation based on differing standards of worth. Such is achieved, however, not without money but through money and its radicalization and perfection. Simmel acknowledged that such was ultimately impracticable but served as a guiding principle. This vision of socialism is not entirely unlike a Marxist prognosis of the need to proceed *through* capitalism and its radicalization in order to facilitate the transition to communism. Whereas, in the case of Marx, such progress was made through changes in relations of production, in this angle of Simmel's vision, the possibility is captured in alterations in money's efficiency and function.[23]

For Simmel, then, money's reductive equivalence and leveling effects were to be resisted precisely—and paradoxically—through intensification of money's consequences. This was for him one way to negotiate its increasing and apparently inevitable ubiquity, reconciling it to a vision that retained qualitative distinction and evaluative measures disassociated from money. This attempt also continues to negotiate the paradox of money's effects as in part conveyed through Christianity: the abstract, infinite, or non-quantifiable aspect of the soul moves dialectically with money's abstracting power, so that each reinforces the other. Rather than simply an outpost of resistance to money's quantification, the abstract human value championed by (some streams of) Christian theological discourse may *amplify* money's abstracting capacities in human society as the West has developed.

Here we see that some of the internal contradictions and tensions in Western economy and society are in part the inheritance of Christianity's own ambiguities and tensions. *Each* individual soul is loved intensely by and brought into relation with God, highlighting qualitative distinction, as well as individual identity and worth. Yet *every* soul is valued in this way, and in relation to the *infinite* God, providing an equalizing and flattening function. The paradoxes traced by money—at once providing a

---

23 Such a hope is what continues to undergird alternative monetary schemes, with digital currencies like Bitcoin taking center stage as utopian possibilities of radical abstraction that might somehow promote free and egalitarian societies.

concrete pricing function to certain lives or facilitating an abstract and unquantifiable worth of life in general—mirror the paradoxical effects on the soul of relation to God.[24]

If the idea of non-quantifiable human value is part of a Christian legacy in the West, how should we interact with, mobilize, or—if we deem such necessary—dismantle it? Is it a good that merits defense and rehabilitation? Or might it actually amplify monetarily quantified evaluations? Simmel's provocative reflections and preliminary genealogy raise both possibilities. The contemporary battle against the quantifying power of money is not as straightforward as it might initially appear. The matter is not as simple as finding non-monetary sources of value or eschewing the price mechanism and reductive power of the number. For money's various capacities, forms, and effects appear deeply tied to the legacy of theology and philosophy as they have developed in the West (cf. [50]). The major tools of analysis and resistance appear to have emerged, troublingly, from the same concepts and practices that have led to our current predicament. How we value human life is one central site of contestation, one that requires teasing out and mapping these relations more clearly, as we determine where we are, what we value, and who we want to be.

Acknowledgments: This article is a revised version of a paper presented at the Yale Religious Studies symposium, "Love in a Time of Capital: Relationality and Commodification as Subjects of Religion," in May 2014. Thanks in particular to Vincent Lloyd for critical response and to all symposium participants for feedback and interaction around these ideas. Thanks as well to Nigel Dodd, Frederick Wherry, and Viviana Zelizer for broader conversation around these themes.

Conflicts of Interest: The author declares no conflict of interest.

References

1. Martin, Randy. *Financialization of Daily Life*. Philadelphia: Temple University Press, 2002.
2. Epstein, Gerald A. *Financialization and the World Economy*. Cheltenham: Edward Elgar Publishing, 2005.
3. Arrighi, Giovanni. *The Long Twentieth Century: Money, Power, and the Origins of Our Times*. London and New York: Verso, 1994.
4. Taylor, Charles. *A Secular Age*. Cambridge: Belknap Press of Harvard University Press, 2007.
5. Agamben, Giorgio. *The Signature of All Things: On Method*. Cambridge: Zone Books, MIT Press, 2009.
6. Foucault, Michel. "Nietzsche, genealogy, history." In *The Foucault Reader*. Edited by Paul Rabinow. New York: Pantheon, 1984, pp. 76–100.
7. Simmel, Georg. *The Philosophy of Money*. London and Boston: Routledge & Kegan Paul, 1978.
8. Levine, Donald. *Georg Simmel on Individuality and Social Forms*. Chicago: University of Chicago Press, 1971, p. xii, emphasis added.
9. Cantó-Milà, Nathàlia. *A Sociological Theory of Value: Georg Simmel's Sociological Relationism*. Bielefeld: Transcript Verlag, 2005.
10. Frisby, David. *Georg Simmel*. London: Routledge, 2002.
11. Frisby, David. *Simmel and Since*. London: Routledge, 1992.
12. Grierson, Philip. *The Origins of Money*. London: Athlone Press, 1977.
13. Ingham, Geoffrey K. *The Nature of Money*. Cambridge: Polity, 2004.
14. Hudson, Michael. "The archaeology of money: Debt versus barter theories of money's origins." In *Credit and State Theories of Money: The Contributions of A. Mitchell Innes*. Edited by L. Randall Wray. Cheltenham: Edward Elgar Publishing, 2004, pp. 99–127.
15. Graeber, David. *Debt: The First 5,000 Years*. Brooklyn: Melville House, 2010.
16. Gilroy, Paul. *The Black Atlantic: Modernity and Double Consciousness*. Cambridge: Harvard University Press, 1993.

---

[24] This paradox is traced by Foucault in regard to pastoral power and the role of the shepherd, who at once prizes each individual sheep and yet may sacrifice one for the sake of the whole. This prefigures modern biopolitical focus on populations through the management and expendability (because abstract) of individual bodies. Again, economy is the site of convergence of these impulses. See [41].

17. Mignolo, Walter. *The Darker Side of the Renaissance: Literacy, Territoriality, and Colonization*. Ann Arbor: University of Michigan Press, 1995.
18. Pateman, Carole. *The Sexual Contract*. Stanford: Stanford University Press, 1988.
19. Krech, Volkhard. *Georg Simmels Religionstheorie*. Tübingen: Mohr Siebeck, 1998.
20. Bellah, Robert N. *Religion in Human Evolution: From the Paleolithic to the Axial Age*. Cambridge: Belknap Press of Harvard University Press, 2011.
21. Durkheim, Emile. *The Division of Labor In Society*. New York: The Free Press, 1964.
22. Wray, L. Randall. *Credit and State Theories of Money: The Contributions of A. Mitchell Innes*. Cheltenham: Edward Elgar Publishing, 2004.
23. Knapp, Georg F. *The State Theory of Money*, Abridged ed. London: Macmillan, 1924.
24. Seaford, Richard. *Money and the Early Greek Mind: Homer, Philosophy, Tragedy*. Cambridge: Cambridge University Press, 2004.
25. Schaps , David M. *The Invention of Coinage and the Monetization of Ancient Greece*. Ann Arbor: University of Michigan Press, 2004.
26. Innes, Alfred Mitchell. *Martyrdom in Our Times: Two Essays on Prisons and Punishment*. London: Williams & Norgate, Ltd., 1932.
27. Harcourt, Bernard E. *The Illusion of Free Markets: Punishment and the Myth of Natural Order*. Cambridge: Harvard University Press, 2011.
28. Scarry, Elaine. *The Body in Pain: The Making and Unmaking of the World*. New York: Oxford University Press, 1985.
29. Santner, Eric L. *The Royal Remains: The People's Two Bodies and the Endgames of Sovereignty*. Chicago: University of Chicago Press, 2011.
30. Cavanaugh, William T. *The Myth of Religious Violence: Secular Ideology and the Roots of Modern Conflict*. Oxford and New York: Oxford University Press, 2009.
31. Auvinen, Tero. "At the intersection of sovereignty and biopolitics: The di-polaric spatializations of money." *Foucault Studies* 9 (2010): 5–34.
32. Dodd, Nigel. *The Social Life of Money*. Princeton: Princeton University Press, 2014.
33. Morgan, Kathryn A. *Popular Tyranny: Sovereignty and Its Discontents in Ancient Greece*. Austin: University of Texas Press, 2003.
34. Steiner, Deborah. *The Tyrant's Writ: Myths and Images of Writing in Ancient Greece*. Princeton: Princeton University Press, 1994.
35. Seaford, Richard. "Tragic money." *Journal of Hellenic Studies* 118 (1998): 119–39. [CrossRef]
36. Zelizer, Viviana A. *The Purchase of Intimacy*. Princeton: Princeton University Press, 2005.
37. Schmitt, Carl. *Über Schuld und Schuldarten. Eine Terminologische Untersuchung*. Breslau: Schletter, 1910.
38. Lazzarato, Maurizio. *The Making of the Indebted Man: An Essay on the Neoliberal Condition*. Los Angeles: Semiotext(e), 2012.
39. Aulén, Gustaf. *Christus Victor: An Historical Study of the Three Main Types of the Idea of the Atonement*. London: S.P.C.K., 1965.
40. Agamben, Giorgio. *The Kingdom and the Glory: For a Theological Genealogy of Economy and Government*. Stanford: Stanford University Press, 2011.
41. Foucault, Michel. *Security, Territory, Population: Lectures at the Collège de France, 1977–1978*. New York: Palgrave Macmillan, 2007.
42. Foucault, Michel. *The Government of Self and Others: Lectures at the College de France, 1982–1983*. New York: Palgrave Macmillan, 2010.
43. Taylor, Charles. *Sources of the Self: The Making of the Modern Identity*. Cambridge: Harvard University Press, 1989.
44. Ricœur, Paul. *Oneself as Another*. Chicago: University of Chicago Press, 1992.
45. Augustine. *Teaching Christianity (de Doctrina Christiana)*. Brooklyn: New City Press, 1990.
46. Dodd, Nigel. "Simmel's perfect money: Fiction, socialism and utopia in *The Philosophy of Money*." *Theory, Culture and Society* 29 (2012): 146–76. [CrossRef]
47. Dodd, Nigel. "On simmel's pure concept of money: A response to ingham." *Archives Européennes de Sociologie* 48 (2007): 273–94. [CrossRef]

48. Dodd, Nigel. "Redeeming Simmel's money." *Hau: Journal of Ethnographic Theory* 5 (2015): 435–41. [CrossRef]
49. Simmel, Georg. *Sociology: Inquiries into the Construction of Social Forms.* Leiden: Brill, 2009.
50. Singh, Devin. "Monetized philosophy and theological money: Uneasy linkages and the future of a discourse." In *The Future of Continental Philosophy of Religion.* Edited by Clayton Crockett, B. Keith Putt and Jeffrey W. Robbins. Bloomington: Indiana University Press, 2014, pp. 140–53.

MDPI AG

St. Alban-Anlage 66

4052 Basel, Switzerland

Tel. +41 61 683 77 34

Fax +41 61 302 89 18

http://www.mdpi.com

Religions Editorial Office

E-mail: religions@mdpi.com

http://www.mdpi.com/journal/religions

www.ingramcontent.com/pod-product-compliance
Lightning Source LLC
Chambersburg PA
CBHW051314020426
42333CB00028B/3335